The New Synthese Historical Library
Texts and Studies in the History of Philosophy

VOLUME 45

The titles published in this series are listed at the end of this volume.

THE MOMENT OF CHANGE

A Systematic History in the Philosophy of Space and Time

by

NICO STROBACH

*Westfälische Wilhelms-Universität,
Münster, Germany*

KLUWER ACADEMIC PUBLISHERS
DORDRECHT / BOSTON / LONDON

A C.I.P. Catalogue record for this book is available from the Library of Congress.

ISBN 0-7923-5120-7

Published by Kluwer Academic Publishers,
P.O. Box 17, 3300 AA Dordrecht, The Netherlands.

Sold and distributed in North, Central, and South America
by Kluwer Academic Publishers,
101 Philip Drive, Norwell, MA 02061, U.S.A.

In all other countries, sold and distributed
by Kluwer Academic Publishers,
P.O. Box 322, 3300 AH Dordrecht, The Netherlands.

Printed on acid-free paper

Printed in the Netherlands.

MOTTO
(three versions of one thought)

Ἐν ἄλλῳ ἄρα χρόνῳ μετέχει καὶ ἐν ἄλλῳ οὐ μετέχει·
οὕτω γὰρ ἂν μόνως τοῦ αὐτοῦ μετέχοι τε καὶ οὐ μετέχοι; - Ὀρθῶς.
(So [the One] partakes [in being] in one chronos and does not partake [in it] in another?
Only in this way could it both partake and not partake in the same? - Correct.)

Plato

Time, one could say metaphorically, is man's escape from contradiction.

Georg Henrik v. Wright

Marschallin: Philosophier' Er nicht, Herr Schatz !
                 Und komm' Er her ...!
                 Jetzt wird gefrühstückt.
                 Jedes Ding hat *seine* Zeit.
                 (Won't He be philosophic now, Mylove!
                  And come to me...!
                  Now let's have breakfast,
                  Each thing has its proper time)

Hugo von Hofmannsthal/Richard Strauss, Der Rosenkavalier

TABLE OF CONTENTS

PART I: THE MOMENT OF CHANGE
FROM ANTIQUITY TO THE 19th CENTURY

PART III: A SYSTEMATIC SUGGESTION

PREFACE

This book is a systematic history of one of the oldest problems in the philosophy of space and time: How is the change from one state to its opposite to be described? To my knowledge it is the first comprehensive book providing information about and analysis of texts on this topic throughout the ages.

The target audience I envisaged are advanced students and scholars of analytic philosophy and the history of philosophy who are interested in the philosophy of space and time. Authors treated in this book range from Plato, Aristotle, the logicians of the late Middle Ages, Kant, Brentano and Russell to contemporary authors such as Chisholm, Hamblin, Sorabji or Graham Priest, taking into account such theories as interval semantics or paraconsistent logic.

For the first time, two main questions about the moment of change are explicitly kept apart: Which (if any) of the opposite states does the moment of change belong to? And does it contain an instantaneous event? The texts are discussed within a clear framework of the main systematic options for describing the moment of change, sometimes using predicate logic extended by newly introduced logical prefixes.

The last part contains a new suggestion of how to solve the problem of the moment of change. It is centred around a theory of instantaneous states which provides a new solution to Zeno's Flying Arrow Paradox.

I have aimed at making each chapter self-contained together with the introduction because many readers may just want to learn about a particular author's view. A list at the end of the book informs the reader at a glance which authors and texts are treated in detail. A quick survey of the book is given in section 1.4 of the introduction.

The three versions of the motto are from Plato's 'Parmenides' (155e10/11), from v. Wright's 'Time, Change and Contradiction' (p.125) and from Act I of the 'Rosenkavalier' (rehearsal mark 47, piano score).

The original German version of this book was accepted as a PhD thesis by the Faculty of Arts (Philosophische Fakultät) of Westfälische Wilhelms-Universität Münster, Germany, in 1995. I am grateful to the Dean of the Faculty for the kind permission of publishing the thesis in translation.

I am grateful to *Fernando Inciarte* who supervised the thesis in Münster and is responsible for its Aristotelian flavour. It has profited from very valuable comments made by *Eva Maria Krause, Ludger Jansen, Wolfgang Büchner, Michael Esfeld, Burkhard Hafemann, Michael-Thomas Liske, William Charlton, Stephen Priest, Richard Sorabji, Simo Knuuttila* and an anonymous referee. Thanks also go to *Gordon Howie* without whose Greek lessons I could not have written part I, and to the Kluwer publishing team: *Maja S.M. de Keijzer, Annie Kuipers* and *Evelien Bakker*.

I am grateful to my mother, *Elfi Rautmann*, and to *Joseph Boasson* for the very good times I spent working at home in Braunschweig and for their never-tiring interest in what I was doing. My father, *Berndt Strobach*, provided invaluable help with translating the text and with proof-reading. *Melissa Maguire* checked the whole translation and made the text a good deal more readable (of course I am solely responsible for any remaining mistakes). The house of *Hanna* and *Hans-Otto Wilmer* in Lengerich was always a good place to work in. It is due to *Mechthild Wilmer* that the time I spent writing was not only an interesting, but also a very happy time. I am especially grateful to *Bertram Kienzle* of Heidelberg University who made me start writing it and who, as an external supervisor, never stopped encourageing my work on it.

Niko Strobach, Münster 1998

INTRODUCTION

1. CONTENTS

1.1. General introduction

"Three, two, one, zero..." the countdown ends. "Ready, steady..." - we are waiting attentively for the "go!". We wait for a certain position of the hands of the clock or for an announcement on the radio, until, sure of having passed a certain boundary in time to which we have attached some meaning, we wish each other a happy new year. We conjure up time by conjuring up the moment of change. Doing so is a way of becoming aware of time. This can be felt especially when we notice that our becoming conscious of the beginning of the new year is always a little late with respect to the beginning itself. So, suddenly, we are facing questions of metaphysics. What is time? What is the relation between time and present? How can a boundary in time be conceived and experienced?

Of these question, it is not the big one concerning the nature of time which I want to tackle in this book. Rather, I want to deal with the question concerning the structure of a temporal boundary. This question too is 'thorny'[1], philosophers say. Trying to answer it is supposed to lead into an 'aporia'[2], a 'puzzle'[3] or even a 'paradoxon'.[4] Nevertheless, philosophical texts on the moment of change are not very numerous. So I was able to examine the main texts in parts I and II of the present book within a comprehensive systematic framework without having to limit myself to a single epoch. Interestingly, almost every systematically conceivable answer concerning the moment of change has been argued for in the past. For that reason I was able to call the book a systematic history. The main aim in parts I and II is information and analysis, but I will also give my own evaluations of the texts throughout. They prepare for my own suggestion of how to treat the moment of change which is presented on the comparatively few pages of part III.

1.2. Terminology

Some terminology is required in order to be able to state the problem:

I use the word 'change' in a sense which is a little more narrow than usual, excluding *processes* from being *changes* as I use the word. For the more general sense I use the word 'alteration'. This corresponds to a distinction naturally made in German between 'Veränderung' (general meaning) and 'Wechsel' (narrow meaning) which I would like to preserve. Every change in the more limited sense takes place between two opposite states. Their obtaining simultaneously would be a contradiction.

1

A change is, thus, a certain type of alteration. There are two kinds of change to be distinguished, which I call 'successions', or s-changes, and Cambridge-, or C-changes. Both differ from the other remaining kind of alteration, process, in two ways: (1) In contrast to processes, they have no duration. (2) In contrast to processes, they do not take place by realizing a continuum of intermediate states between the state they begin with and the state they end with.

An *s-change* always takes place between two positive states, e.g. between rest and motion, on and off, alive and dead, green and red or c sharp and a flat (these states following immediately upon one another). The most prominent example for an s-change has always been the change between rest and motion (followed by the change between alive and dead).[5]

C-changes do not take place between positive states. Instead, they consist in the beginning or ending of one positive state which is reflected by the fact that we might answer the question "Is this red?" by saying "yes" at one time and by saying "no" at another, while acting vice versa when confronted with the question: "Is it false that this is red?".[6]

Every s-change consists of two C-changes: the ending of the old and the beginning of the new state. The s-change between rest and motion, e.g., consists of a C-change between rest and non-rest and the C-change between non-motion and motion. Nevertheless, it would be a mistake to forget about s-changes after this point is clear because it is not yet clear exactly how the two C-changes which make up an s-change "coincide", and whether they do so in the same way in every case.

So, according to the terminology of this book, *a change is an alteration which, though not being a process, takes place between two states which are opposed in such a way that their obtaining simultaneously would be a contradiction.* And there are *two kinds of change:*

  a) Successions, or: s-changes
  b) Cambridge-, or: C-changes.

A succesion takes place between two 'positive' states such as motion and rest or being away from a particular place and having reached this place. A C-change, on the other hand, takes place between 'contradictories', e.g. moving and not moving.

1.3. The main questions
What exactly is the problem? It is to find a satisfactory conceptual treatment of what we observe; for what is happening is obvious. Nothing prevents us from looking at it in as much detail as we are interested in. Let us, for example, look at a car which is first still, and then moves. Of course we know what it looks like when a car is simply standing there; and we know

what it looks like when it is moving. So we also know what it looks like when it is first simply standing there, and then moving. What we do not know is until exactly when the car is standing there and from exactly what time on it is moving. It is not vagueness which makes us feel uncomfortable. It is rather the feeling that we could be very precise about this and thus should be - but that, on the other hand, when trying to be we seem to come into conflict with the most fundamental laws of traditional logic:

"The train leaves at noon", says the announcer. But can it? If so, when is the last instant of rest, and when the first instant of motion? If these are the same instant, or if the first instant of motion precedes the last instant of rest, the train seems to be both in motion and at rest at the same time, and is this not a contradiction? On the other hand, if the last instant of rest precedes the first instant of motion, the train seems to be in neither state during the intervening period, and how can this be? Finally, to say there is a last instant of rest, but not a first instant of motion, or vice-versa, appears arbitrary. What are we to do?[7]

In order to put these (and some more) problems into a kind of systematic order, I will distinguish between two main questions concerning the moment of change. I have called them the question how to *describe* it, and the question how to *classify* it. The question about the correct *description* of the moment of change is:

> Which (if any) state obtains at the limit between the old state and the new state?

The question about the correct *classification* of the the moment of change is:

> When (if at all) does an *event* of changing take place?

The two main questions regarding the moment of change should be clearly kept apart. They can be answered fairly independently. So far, no author has distinguished the two questions explicitly. This should, however, be done because otherwise an answer to one of the questions might easily be taken to be an answer to the other question - which it is not.

1.3.1. The options for describing the moment of change
§1 A look at fig. 1 will make clear the options available to answer the question of how to describe the moment of change. In fig. 1 we have a representation of a process. It could be the representation of a journey of an object *a* through space. It could in fact have been produced by a sort of measurement: If *a* were, say, a toy locomotive able to move along a perfectly straight toy railway; and if a pencil were fixed to *a* reaching down to a sheet of paper underneath the railway which is pulled down slowly and regularly at a right angle to the direction of *a*'s movement - then we would obtain fig. 1 as a physical trace of *a* being at rest, then accelerating, moving at a constant

speed, slowing down, and being at rest again. This trace obviously consists of three different sections: the two straight lines parallel to the time axis represent periods of rest and the middle section represents a period of motion.

 Fig. 1

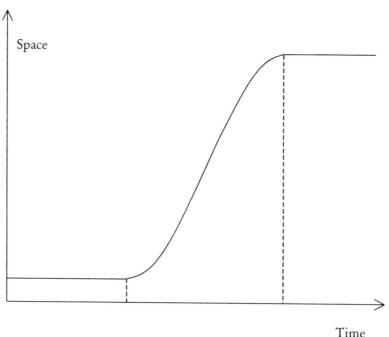

§2 There are two striking regions in fig. 1: the region where the first and the second section meet, and the region where the second and the third section do. I know of no text about the moment of change whose author denies that the two regions' being striking may be explained in terms of there being two extraordinary *instants*.[8]

Doubtless, these instants are the boundaries between a period during which *a* is at rest (and during which the first and the third part of the trace have come about) and a period, during which *a* is in motion. This is why they will be called *limiting instants* in what follows.

Also fig. 2 contains a limiting instant; it is especially easy to recognize. Fig. 2 is not a picture of a process between an initial and a 'target' state, but it delineates a *discontinuous change* between two incompatible states. It might be the repesentation of a part of the on/off-function of a lightbulb or the corresponding trace of a measurement[9].

Fig.2

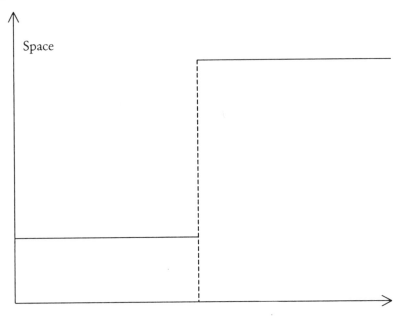

§3 Unfortunately, both pictures, fig. 1 and fig. 2, are characteristically useless for a description of the moment of change. We may look at them in every detail and still do not see what is the case at the limiting instant. We only know: something is the case here up to the limiting instant and is not the case any more from the limiting instant on (let us call this the 'old state'). In addition to that, something else is the case from the limiting instant on which had not been the case up to it (let us call this the 'new state'). A description of the moment of change permits the following four options:

(1) The 'Either/or-option': exactly one of the two states obtains at the limiting instant; either the old state or the new state.
(2) The 'Neither/nor-option: Neither the old nor the new state obtains at the limiting instant.
(3) The 'Both-states-option': Both the old and the new state obtain at the limiting instant.

(4) The 'Either-way-option': In a certain respect, the old state still obtains at the limiting instant, in another respect it does not. Moreover, in a certain way the new state already obtains at the limiting instant, but in another way it does not.

All four options have been advocated. However, a thorough look at them (which is taken in parts I and II) shows that, when applied, they are not all equally successful. In fact, the both-states-option and the either-way-option turn out to be very implausible candidates.

I will attempt to show that working with the neither/nor-option suits one sort of change very well (namely s-changes between rest and motion), but is unsuitable for another sort (namely C-changes). The either/or-option is just opposite: it fits C-changes, but it is inappropriate for s-changes between rest and motion. Thus, a study of the texts on the moment of change suggests a mixed description choosing the either/or-option for one sort of case and the neither/nor-option for the other.

1.3.2. The classification of the moment of change

§1 The description of the moment of change on the one hand and its classification (as characterized above) on the other exhibit an amazingly strong, though not total, independence of one another. As long as an author holds the view that there *is* an event of changing related to the moment of change, the most interesting question is what he thinks of the thesis I will call 'Plato's premiss'. It is first to be found in the 'Parmenides' (156c) and can be expressed like this:

> An event of changing cannot take place while the old state still obtains;
> but when the new state already obtains it cannot take place either.

As might immediately be suspected, there is a peculiar tension between the use of the either/or-option in the description of the moment of change and Plato's premiss in the classification. One of the most interesting questions concerning the moment of change will prove to be how authors try to resolve this tension.

§2 There is one important 'caveat' I have to state with regard to the classification of the moment of change: I was not able to base the assessment of an author in this respect on an abstract definition of what an *event* is. Instead of asking whether a change, according to a certain conception, satisfies the abstract definition of an event I can only appeal to our intuitive knowledge how the word 'event' is properly used. This appeal is legitimate since we have this knowledge as competent speakers of English. The other way was not open for two reasons: (1) I would have to take sides in the debate about the ontological status of events. This debate is centred around a controversy between Kim and Davidson an evaluation of which would be another book.[10] (2) I would have to render in abstract terms the temporal structure of an event in general. This has appeared to be an exceptionally difficult task: Lombard, for example, identifies, with a certain plausibility, events with alterations ('changes' in a broader sense than the one in which I use the term).[11] But stating whether a change is an alteration as Lombard sees it, is just as difficult as telling if it is an event. It has to be admitted that so far the most precise characterization of the general structure of events seems to be Galton's claim: "Events involve change".[12] That is not much. I admit that I could not find anything better either.[13] I hope there will soon be a precise structural characterization of events in general. But as things are, there remains the appeal to linguistic intuition.

1.4. Survey
1.4.1. Parts I and II
In parts I and II of the present book I take a close look at historical and contemporary texts on the moment of change within the framework of the terminology and the main questions which have been introduced in the preceding sections:

Part I deals with texts on the moment of change from antiquity to the 19th century: texts by Plato (ch. I,1), by Aristotle (ch. I,2), texts in late medieval logic books (ch. I,3) and a controversy between Kant and Mendelssohn (ch. I,4).

(1) Plato
The earliest text on the moment of change is the digression on 'the sudden' in the second part of Plato's late dialogue 'Parmenides' (155e/157b). Using the change between rest and motion as an example and, of course, assuming Plato's premiss, Plato argues that a change cannot take place in a χρόνος, but takes place at an ἐξαίφνης ('the sudden') at which neither the old state nor the new state obtains.

Plato's text allows three different reconstructions of the *logical* status of the 'sudden' one of which leads to a contradiction and another to statements of indeterminate truth-value. A third reconstruction assumes that Plato had already developed the Aristotelian concept of *privation* at least to such an extent that, by employing it, he could describe the moment of change without a contradiction but also with just two truth-values.

Furthermore, two ways of interpreting the digression *ontologically* can be distinguished:

Plato-1: A χρόνος is an instant while an ἐξαίφνης is something which, although it can be asked about in a 'when'-question, is somehow beyond time.

Plato-2: A χρόνος is a special sort of period (a phase of a state or a part of such a phase) while an ἐξαίφνης is a limiting instant between two χρόνοι.

According to Plato-1, Plato uses the *either/or-option* for the *description* of the moment of change. As to the question of *classification*, he *banishes the event of changing* (whose existence he clearly assumes) *from time*. According to Plato-2, Plato uses the *neither/nor-option* and allows an event of changing to take place at the limiting instant. Several ancient texts on the moment of change (by Sextus Empiricus, Aulus Gellius and St. Augustine) can be shown to support my view that Plato-2 should be favoured.

(2) Aristotle

In chapter I,2 I attempt to provide an interpretation of Aristotle's statements on the moment of change in Physics VI and VIII as a controversy between him and Plato. I agree with Richard Sorabji that Aristotle uses *two different descriptions* of the moment of change:

a) He uses the *neither/nor-option* for the s-change between rest and motion, because he holds both motion and rest to be impossible at instants. The reason for this is that Aristotle holds both motion and rest to be *comparative properties*, i.e. properties which are assigned to an object by comparing its states at different instants with a certain period of time in between.

b) For *non-comparative properties* (such as being white) which an object *can* have at an instant, Aristotle assigns the limiting instant at the end of a process to the state which is reached as a result of the process. One of the reasons for doing so is that, if instants are densely ordered, there is no last instant of not yet having reached the terminal state. Thus, in the case of non-comparative properties, Aristotle uses the *either/or option*.

In chapter I,2 I furthermore clarify what Aristotle means by the term 'the first [time] in which something has changed' (τὸ ἐν ᾧ πρώτῳ μεταβέβληκεν). I elaborate a suggestion by Hans Wagner that 'first' is often not meant temporally in the relevant passages, but rather with respect to a *hierarchic order*, and that the text is, thus, not primarily concerned with a succession of instants but with overlapping periods.

Furthermore, Aristotle's statements can be interpreted in connection with his distinction between κίνησις and ἐνέργεια in such a way that a text on the moment of change by Plotinus can be understood as a (however unconvincing) criticism of Aristotle's approach.

Aristotle is shown to have held an exceptional attitude towards the *classification* of the moment of change: He denies that changes are events. In a postscript to chapter I,2 I attempt to sketch, from Aristotle's imaginary perspective, a plausible story how Aristotle's treatment of the moment of change might have developed out of Plato's.[14]

(3) The Middle Ages

Chapter I,3 deals with the elaboration and further development of Aristotle's ideas in the '*incipit et desinit*' chapters of late medieval logic books. It is based on original texts as far as they are available and otherwise on the excellent studies of these texts by Curtis Wilson and Norman Kretzmann. First, the texts' *contents* are examined and evaluated, and then the amazingly dense and precise *form* in which they are presented.

a) With few exceptions, medieval logicians use the *either/or-option* when describing the moment of change. However, they restrict themselves to C-changes and do not treat s-changes explicitly. It can be shown that for s-changes they implicitly reach the same result as Aristotle (i.e. the neither/nor-option), although they have a somewhat different view from Aristotle's on motion or rest at instants.

Concerning the question whether there are first or last instants of something, most logic books distinguish between '*res permanentes*' (which exist wholly at one time) and '*res successivae*' (the different parts of which exist at different times). A translation of this distinction into a distinction between permanent and successive *properties* shows that this approach is indeed rather plausible.

b) The *form* of the medieval analyses of incipit- and desinit statements is so reminiscent of modern *tense logic* that it can be rendered by introducing notational signs which are analogous to Prior's tense operators. On the other hand, employing these prefixes alone does not solve a particular problem for the description of the moment of change, which was already thoroughly discussed in the Middle Ages (especially by William of Ockham): the problem of oscillation, i.e. the multiple beginning and ending of a state between two instants. In later medieval texts this problem is solved by using the word 'immediate' (immediately) in a very precisely defined sense.

(4) Kant, Mendelssohn, Schopenhauer

Chapter I,4 is concerned with some of the few texts on the moment of change from the 18th and early 19th century which form a kind of interlude between the sophisticated treatment of the moment of change in the late middle ages and then again in the 20th century. A debate between Kant and Moses Mendelssohn (which can be traced in Mendelssohn's 'Phädon' and in a part of the paralogism-chapter of Kant's first Critique) is discussed as well as a paragraph from Schopenhauer's dissertation. As a result, it has to be said that, regardless of the fame of their authors, the level of argument of these texts is disappointing.

Part II concentrates on texts on the moment of change dating from the 20th century. Here, the authors are grouped according to the option they use for the description of the moment of change.

(1) The either/or-option
The discussion of texts by Richard Sorabji and by Frank Jackson and Robert Pargetter shows the main problem of using the either/or-option for the description of the *s-change between rest and motion*: if one does not want to assign the limiting instant to one of the states in question arbitrarily, but rather with good reason, one has to rely on the concept of *instantaneous velocity*. But there are problems to both associating an instant of zero instantaneous velocity with an instant of rest and to the very concept of instantaneous velocity.

Among the advocates of the either/or-option, Antony Galton is prominent in suggesting an especially radical answer to the question of classification: Galton's argument, restricted to *C-changes*, is reminiscent of the *banishing of change from time* according to 'Plato-1':

> At every instant a certain state obtains or it does not obtain. Whenever an event of changing between two states (whose existence is postulated by Galton's event logic) takes place, neither the old state nor the new state may obtain (due to Plato's premiss). Therefore, C-changes do not take place at any time.

This solution is formally possible, but, as a criticism by Bertram Kienzle makes clear, it is counter-intuitive. Thus, a *dilemma* with regard to C-changes becomes apparent if, as is plausible, they are described by using the either/or-option: *Either Plato's premiss must be abandoned, or C-changes must be banished from time.*

(2) The either-way-option
Roderick Chisholm and Brian Medlin are to be viewed as advocates of the two-ways-option. It can be shown that in order to use the two-ways-option for the description of the *s-change between rest and motion* they have to work with definitions of rest and motion at an instant which are counter-intuitively weak (according to these definitions, something is at rest at an instant t even if t is bounded by a period of rest on only one 'side' - the same applies for motion). The application of the two-ways-option to *C-changes* turns out to be quite unintelligible. Both Chisholm and Medlin experiment

with *different kinds of negation* in order to escape this consequence. Their attempts fail.

(3) The both-states-option
Of course, an application of the both-states-option to C-changes leads to *contradictions*. However, this is the very reason why Graham Priest, the inventor of Hegelian 'paraconsistent logic', applies it. Chapter II,3 makes clear that there is no real motivation for doing so apart from some kind of emotional affinity towards contradictions which I do not share.

(4) The neither/nor-option
Chapter II,4 traces an application of the neither/nor-option in Hamblin's articles on interval semantics. Hamblin's approach is reconstructed as a distinction between *object-language* (his 'interval semantics') and *meta-language* (natural language) in such a way that concepts like 'starting' and 'stopping' are analysed away in object-language statements.

However, in order to prevent violating the law of excluded middle, Hamblin has to deny that anything can be the case at an instant. Thus, a statement like

"The car is standing in front of the house at 8 o' clock"

would be nonsense in just the same way the statement

"Cesar is a prime number"

might be nonsense. However, denying that anything can be the case at an instant is counter-intuitive. Doing so implies, for example, denying that the clockhands of a correct clock at noon point exactly upwards. So the only thing Hamblin can succeed in making us doubt is that instants are empirically accessible - but not that something is the case at instants.

(5) The Neutral Instant Analysis
The position called 'Neutral Instant Analysis'[15] describes the limiting instant between rest and motion as neutral, i.e. as an instant of neither rest nor motion. Thus, it implies using the neither/nor-option when describing the s-change between rest and motion. However, by doing so it presupposes the description of C-changes according to the either/or-option: the neutral instant at the end of a period of rest e.g. is both the first instant at which something is not at rest and the last instant at which it is not in motion while first or last instants of rest or motion do not exist.

In Chapter II,5 I trace the Neutral Instant Analysis in texts by David Bostock and Norman Kretzmann, and I argue that it can also be found to be implicitly contained in Bertrand Russell's famous definition of rest and motion in §442 of his 'Principles of Mathematics'.

The Neutral Instant Analysis is *more successful than the other approaches* in describing the moment of change, because it is a mixed description using *different options for different cases*, thus being able to stay within the framework of *traditional two-valued logic*. It is reminiscent of Aristotle's and, even more strongly, of the medieval descriptions of the moment of change.

The Neutral Instant Analysis leaves the question of classification of the moment of change open. The greatest problem of the Neutral Instant Analysis is that it induces a certain *phenomenological unease* when it comes, e.g., to the question: What does anything *look like* when it is neither in rest nor in motion?

1.4.2. A look ahead to part III

Part III contains my systematic suggestion how to describe and classify the moment of change. As far as results are concerned, I propose a version of the Neutral Instant Analysis and, thus, a description of the moment of change which preserves the fundamental laws of logic, the law of non-contradiction and the law of excluded middle.

My description of the moment of change is more strongly based on epistemological arguments than has been usual hitherto. It should therefore remove the phenomenological unease. The starting point is the idea that instants are empirically inaccessible and that, therefore, instantaneous states are nothing we observe but something we construe. A method of construing them is established which tranfers the concept of 'limes' from mathematics to epistemology. As side-effects, this method provides an explanation why the principle "natura non facit saltus" is attractive, a solution to Zeno's flying arrow paradox and a refutation of Russell's reductionist theory of motion.

Concerning the *classification* of the moment of change, I propose to regard changes as *instantaneous events*. Since I think that *all* changes are events (also those which should be described by using the either/or-option), I propose to *abandon Plato's premiss* (I will show that it is not as plausible as it looks). Only by doing this can all changes both be regarded as *events* and be kept *datable* in time within two-valued logic. I suggest that changes can be *witnessed* but that they cannot be *observed* because they do not take any time; and I suggest that we experience *aspects* of them, but that we cannot experience them to be happen*ing*. The banishment of change from time is avoided.

2. LOGICAL PRELIMINARIES

2.1. Basics of the notation used

Talking about a moment which contains a single all-important limiting instant requires a degree of precision in expressing one's thoughts which cannot be achieved entirely informally. On the other hand, talking about a number of different positions held by different authors with different historical, terminological and metaphysical backgrounds requires some flexibility and ontological generosity; this makes the use of a newly defined formal language in the strict sense unattractive. Defining several full-fledged formal languages (one for each chapter) would have made reading the text very difficult. Therefore, I chose the compromise of writing chains of formal signs which will easily be recognized as expressions of a sort of predicate logic, but which are strictly speaking not expressions of a predicate *calculus*.

Rather, even typical signs of the predicate calculus such as the general quantifier ($\forall$) or the existential quantifier ($\exists$) are to be viewed as mere abbreviations of 'For all...' or 'There is a...'. The same applies for $\wedge$ ('and'), $\neg$ ('it is not the case that'), $\vee$ (inclusive 'or') and $\rightarrow$ (material 'if...then') and for signs known from set theory.

Although I will not use a formal language in the strict sense, I have tried to achieve an unambiguous, unified terminology for the comparison of different philosophical positions by using a notation and, consequently, a reconstruction of thoughts which agrees with the basic intuitions underlying the use of the predicate calculus. The two most important ideas behind this notation are:

(1) A classical proposition, the non-lingual bearer of a truth-value, can be analysed in a way which is reflected in the formulas of predicate logic. It can be analysed as expressing the fact that one or several objects satisfy one or several predicates. This analysis may be done in different ways. For example, the proposition that on the 21st of January, 1996, the city lake in Münster is frozen but not yet safe for ice-skating, can be analysed like this: the city lake in Münster satisfies the predicate "...is frozen on the 21st of January, 1996, but not safe for ice-skating". It can also be analysed like this: the city lake in Münster satisfies the predicate "...is frozen on the 21st of January, 1996" but does not satisfy the predicate "...is safe for ice-skating on the 21st of January, 1996". But it can also be analysed as: the 21st of January 1996 satisfies the predicate "...is a time when the city lake in Münster is frozen" but does not satisfy the predicate "...is a time when the city lake in Münster is safe for ice-skating".

Predicates which take a *time* in at least one of their argument-places, I call *temporal predicates*. I will call one-place temporal predicates as in the last two examples *temporal statements*: logically, they take times; but it is natural to render their meaning by a sentence in natural language which is syntactically complete, such as "The city lake in Münster is frozen" or "The city lake in Münster is safe for ice-skating". What such a sentence is referring to is usually called a 'tensed proposition' or 'chronologically indefinite proposition'.[16] Depending on the context, I will often write temporal statements as syntactically complete sentences or as sentences with a gap for a time-reference to be filled in. So I will often claim that phrases such as "Object *a* is moving" or "Object *a* is moving at..." are *satisfied* by a certain time.[17] Since sentences like "Object *a* is moving" are syntactically complete, there is no reason why they should not be put behind a 'that'. That they are predicates nevertheless, and not classical propositions, I will express by abbreviating them by capital letters like 'P'.

(2) A predicate-name and a logical *prefix* attached to it is a new, complex predicate-name, naming another predicate. As the use of a prefix follows certain strict rules, a prefix acquires a sort of 'meaning' (details in 2.3.). The two parts of a complex predicate-name will be hyphenated.

In part III, prefixes for functions will be introduced which basically work in the same way as prefixes for predicates: the combination of the name of a function with a prefix is the name of a new function.

2.2. Ontology

Predicates can, according to their meaning, be satisfied by objects of rather different kinds (I will use lower case letters for them):

- Instants (t, t_1, t_2...)
- Periods (c, c_1, c_2...)
- 'Then-Objects' (d, d_1, d_2...).
- physical objects (a, b, c...)
- points in space (s, s_1, s_2...)
- qualitative 'spans' (e, e_1, e_2...)

Some kinds of *sets* will also play an important role, too: *intervals* (peculiar sets of instants), *divisions* of periods (peculiar sets of periods) and *two-place determinable functions*. Details are given where they are introduced.

2.2.1. Then-Objects

Then-objects appear in the chapter on Plato (ch.I,1) only. Not all then-objects are times according to every possible interpretation of the digression in the 'Parmenides'. Thus according to Plato's terminology a 'sudden' is something about which you can ask a question starting with 'When...?' and by reference to which such a question can be answered; but it is not necessarily a time. 'Then-objects' satisfy statements like "*a* is red at..." or "*a* is changing at...". But it is not indisputable whether Plato regarded "*a* is changing at..." as a *temporal* statement.

2.2.2. Instants and periods

The time-ontology I chose requires explanation: it is based on the idea that there are not only instants but also periods. Talk of periods cannot be reduced to talk of sets of instants (intervals), whereas talk of intervals can be reduced to talk of instants and periods.

t is to be the set of all *instants*. It will usually be assumed that instants are densely ordered, i.e. that between any two instants there is another instant. It will also be assumed that time is infinite (although this does not matter very much for our topic). There does not seem to me to be a fundamental problem in adapting arguments which work within dense time-order to a continuous time-order. In addition to such strange times as 'a third of a second after 12:00' there will simply be even stranger times such as '$\sqrt{2}$ seconds after 12:00'. Instants have no duration, i.e., no temporal extension whatsoever.[18] They are limits in time, mere boundaries of periods.

C is to be the set of all *periods*. The fundamental and peculiar property of periods is that they have a certain duration[19]. Time-atomists know periods of minimal duration. In contrast to them, I will assume that periods are infinitely divisible into subperiods, unless indicated otherwise. A period is not the same as a duration ('60 minutes' refers to a duration, but not to a period). The union of C and t I call T, the set of all times.

2.2.2.1. Relations between periods

There have been attempts to work with periods as entities in their own right, which have become known by the somewhat misleading name 'interval semantics'. The name is misleading because an interval is usually defined as a set of instants which fulfils certain requirements. The 'intervals' of interval semantics, on the other hand, are no sets of instants, but periods.[20]

The first attempt to construe interval semantics, in C. Hamblin's article on the moment of change 'Starting and Stopping', has remained the most famous one.[21] However, not only does Hamblin's idea as put forward in this article provoke some criticism on intuitive grounds (cf. ch.II,4); his attempt is also formally unsatisfactory: the set of axioms Hamblin provides there is incomplete, as he himself admits in a later article.[22] Moreover, in 'Starting and Stopping', Hamblin exaggerates his overall strategy by abolishing instants altogether, not even allowing them to be construed as 'secondary' entities dependent on periods. In the later article ('Instants and Intervals'[23]) Hamblin offers different axioms and revises his intuition.

Hamblin's system is a first order predicate logic with identity.[24] I will follow Hamblin in some of his definitions. This is independent of questions of axiomatization. They are of no concern here because all I need to discuss the moment of change is a notation, not a tool for formal deductions.

Hamblin starts with the primitive relation '$<$' between periods which is interpreted as 'wholly precedes'. Using this relation, he defines other relations between periods, e.g. abutment (on the 'left' or 'past' hand side)[25]:
Definition 'Abutment' (A): cAc_1 iff $c < c_1 \wedge \neg \exists c_2 [c < c_2 \wedge c_2 < c_1]$.

Apart from abutment, a very important relation between periods is containment. It can simply be defined in the following manner:
Definition 'Containment' (C):

$$c_1 C c_2 \text{ iff } \forall c_3 [c_3 < c_2 \rightarrow c_3 < c_1] \wedge \forall c_4 [c_2 < c_4 \rightarrow c_1 < c_4].^{26}$$

According to this definition, c_1 is contained in c_2 iff all periods preceding c_2 precede c_1 as well, and all periods which are preceded by c_2 are also preceded by c_1. According to this definition, every period is contained in itself. It will often be useful to exclude this. So the following definition should be added, defining 'proper containment' introducing the sign '$^\circ$': $c^\circ c_1$ iff $cCc_1 \wedge \neg c_1 Cc$.

2.2.2.2. The division of a period

The division of a period c will, in what follows, be understood as a set of abutting periods, the first and the last element of which are bounded by the same instants by which c is also bounded. To be precise:

Let c be a period, let $n \geq 1$. A set $\mathbf{A}_c := \{c_i \mid i=1,...,n\}$ of periods is a division of c iff
(i) $c_i A c_{i+1}$ for $i=1,...,n-1$.
(ii) For all c' with c'Ac holds: $c'Ac_1$.
(iii) For all c' with cAc' holds: $c_n Ac'$.

2.2.2.3. Instants as boundaries of periods

In his later article 'Instants and Intervals', Hamblin overcomes interval semantics in its extreme form and allows the introduction of instants as ordered pairs of periods.[27] Unlike Hamblin, I assume that instants are there anyway. An instant is the boundary between a period and another period. I believe that an instant may be uniquely identified by a pair of periods, but it *is* not a pair of periods, it is a boundary.[28] Taking this disparity between our views into account, I nevertheless mainly follow his definitions for '$=$' and '$<$' between instants.[29] They become:

Let (c,c_1) be a pair of periods identifying the instant t, and let (c_2,c_3) be a pair of periods identifying the instant t_1,
then: (1) $t=t_1$ iff cAc_3
         (2) $t<t_1$ iff $c < c_3 \wedge \neg cAc_3$.
('$t<t_1$' is therefore to be read as "t is earlier than t_1".)

2.2.2.4. Relations between periods and instants

In addition to Hamblin's relations between periods, I will often use the relations '...goes from ... to...' (notated: '...:[...,...]'), 'falls-within' and 'bounds' which are defined as relations between instants and periods as follows:

> Definition '...goes from... to...': Let (c_1,c) be a pair of periods identifying the instant t and let (c,c_2) be a pair of periods identifying the instant t_1, then: $c:[t,t_1]$ iff $c_1Ac \wedge cAc_2$.
>
> Definition 'falls within': t falls within c iff $\exists\, t_1,t_2\ [c:[t_1,t_2] \wedge t_1 < t < t_2]$.
>
> Definition 'bounds': t bounds c iff $\exists t_1\ [\ c:[t,t_1] \vee c:[t_1,t]\ ]$.

The open interval $I =]t_1,t_2[$ can thus be explained as the set of all instants which fall within c iff $c:[t_1,t_2]$. The closed interval $I = [t_1,t_2]$ is just the set of all instants which fall within or bound c iff $c:[t_1,t_2]$.

2.3. Prefixes

A predicate may have a complex name consisting partly of the name of another predicate and partly of a prefix. A 'naming rule' for making a new predicate name out of a given predicate name and a prefix determines in which way a prefix is informative: a prefix does not have a meaning of its own, but the meaning of a predicate with a complex name stands, via the naming rule of the prefix, in a certain systematic relation to the meaning of the predicate whose name is contained in the new, complex predicate-name. Prefixes may, but need not necessarily, be viewed as second order operators on extensions of predicates. Every naming rule for a prefix consists (i) of a 'combination rule' which determines the kind of predicates the prefix may be attached to and (ii) of a semantical rule which gives truth conditions for expressions which include the complex predicate name containing the prefix. In some cases, it is possible to translate the role of a prefix roughly into the role of an expression of natural language (usually an *adverb*) which may then, *cum grano salis*, be called the meaning of this prefix.

   In order to show how prefixes work, one example will here suffice. More prefixes will be introduced in the same way where they are needed.

2.3.1. 'Throughout' as an example

Let us take as an example the naming rule which gives the sign '*' roughly the 'meaning' of the adverb 'throughout'. Before considering this rule, let us establish the following principle:

> Unless indicated otherwise, a period already satisfies a temporal statement even if that which the statement is referring to is only the case 'somewhere' during the period.[30]

If, for example, a is in motion for just an hour of a certain day, then this day satisfies the statement "a is in motion" just as well as the hour throughout which a is in motion satisfies the statement. Nevertheless, it is useful to be able to express the idea that something is the case throughout a period. It is for this purpose that we introduce the sign '*' as the 'throughout'-prefix by the following naming rule:

NR1) (1) combination rule: '*' may be combined with the name of a temporal statement P in order to yield the name of a new statement.
(2) Semantical rule: (a) *-P(t) iff P(t)
(b) *-P(c) iff $\forall c_1 [c_1 Cc \rightarrow P(c_1)]$.

Some expressions containing the negation sign or the '*'-prefix interestingly exhibit relations corresponding to the classical square of logic. For if 'P(c)' is to be read as " 'Somewhere' in c it is the case that P", then '¬P(c)' must be read as " 'Nowhere' in c is it the case that P", *-P(c) as "It is the case that P throughout c" and ¬*-P(c) as " 'Somewhere' in c it is not the case that P" (cf. fig. 3).

Moreover, it seems to be characteristic of statements referring to *temporally extended events* that *-P(c) is never true with respect to them because they are heterogeneously structured.[31] For if c is an hour in which M+N get from Münster to Osnabrück and P is the predicate "...is a period in which M+N get from Münster to Osnabrück", the following is true: $\neg \exists c_1 [c_1{}^\circ c \land P(c_1)]$.[32] For a *state* with a certain duration, *-P(c) would, however, be characteristically true.

Fig.3

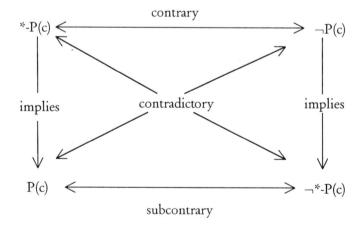

*-P(c) <————— contrary —————> ¬P(c)

implies   contradictory   implies

P(c) <————— subcontrary —————> ¬*-P(c)

2.4. s-changes, C-changes and the limiting instant

The notation introduced up to now already allows the precise characterization of s- and C-changes. It is also possible to state precisely in which way every s-change consists of two C-changes. However, doing this requires more formal notation than any reader will want to digest at this point. It is therefore done in a separate text, appendix A at the end of the present book. The characterization of s-changes and C-changes provided there leaves open the question of which (if any) state obtains at the limiting instant. The attempts which have been made to answer this question are central in what follows, because this question·is exactly the question of how to *describe* the moment of change. The formal characterization also leaves open the question whether there is any event which corresponds to the noun 'change' and which is therefore denoted by this noun. This question is the question of how to *classify* the moment of change. The systematic history of the answers which have been proposed concerning these questions will be told in parts I and II of this book, before a new suggestion for answering them is made in part III.

CHAPTER 1

PLATO

1.1. THE DIGRESSION ON THE SUDDEN IN PLATO'S 'PARMENIDES'

1.1.1. Introduction

Plato makes such a concentrated start to thinking about the moment of change that, once more, Whitehead's proverbial characterization of the history of Western Philosophy as just a footnote to Plato is confirmed.[1] The issue is treated in the so-called digression or 'section 2a' (155e/157b) of the second part of his late dialogue 'Parmenides'. The passage has been of interest to commentators ever since antiquity. To give an adequate impression, the most important sentences of this digression deserve to be quoted at some length before they undergo analysis:

"...can [the] one, when it partakes of being, not partake of it, or partake of it when it does not partake of it?" "No, it cannot." "Then it partakes at one < chronos > and does not partake at another; for that is the only way in which it can partake and not partake of the same thing." "True." "And is there not also a < chronos > when it assumes being and when it gives it up? [...But] when being in motion it comes to rest, and when being at rest it changes to motion, it must itself be in no < chronos > at all." "How is that?" "It is impossible for it to be previously at rest and afterwards in motion, or previously in motion and afterwards at rest, without changing." "Of course." "And there is no < chronos > in which anything can be at once neither in motion nor at rest." No, there is none." [...] "Then when does it change? For it does not change when it is at rest or when it is in motion or when it is in < a chronos >." "No, it does not." "Does this strange thing, then, exist, in which it would be < ... > when it changes?" "What sort of thing is that?" "The < sudden >. [...For] there is this strange < nature of the sudden squatting > between motion and rest..."[2]

Plato's solution to the problem of the moment of change is a terminological invention, be it a *terminus technicus* or rather a *terminus mysticus*: the sudden, τὸ ἐξαίφνης.[3] This passage on the sudden has been more influential in metaphysics than I will be able to show in this analytic study. Often enough, the sudden was considered to be some kind of gate through which the extratemporal forms could somehow enter time[4]. Other passages where Plato uses the word ἐξαίφνης[5] make it very probable that he intended at least to allude to the theory of forms. But the aim of this allusion is not quite clear here. I will therefore consciously neglect this allusion and all the reactions it has triggered off.[6]

Apart from metaphysical interpretations there exist several thorough analytical studies of the passage. They disagree on what is meant by the term 'sudden'. As this affects what is meant by the term 'chronos', they disagree on what a chronos is, too. G.E.L. Owen states:

It is generally held that Plato's purpose was to show that there can be no period of time during which a thing can be neither A nor not-A, and consequently that the change from one to the other must occur at a point of time.[7]

And Colin Strang writes:

The 'sudden' [...] is *clearly* what we mean by a durationless instant. It is contrasted with chronos, which is *equally clearly* time qua duration.[8]

On the other hand, David Bostock says:

...a time (a χρόνος) in this context is *surely* intended as a moment or instant of time (a νῦν). ...it would be *quite wrong* to interpret Plato as here introducing the idea of a temporal point or instant [by introducing the 'sudden'] *as if it were what was needed for the solution of his problem.*[9]

I want to add another interpretation of the passage to the already existing analytic ones. Of course, I would not do so if I were fully content with any of them. There are two reasons for my discontentment:

(1) All the interpretations I have seen fail to keep apart two different tasks; it is, however, useful to do so. One of these tasks is to look at the *logical status of the sudden* in Plato's argument. The other task is to determine what the sudden is actually meant to be here, i.e. to look at the *ontological status of the sudden*.[10]

(2) I think that the existing interpretations, when concerned with the ontological status of the sudden, are either wrong in interpreting certain key words of the passage or that they burden a plausible interpretation with implausible additional assumptions.

Thus, David Bostock misinterprets Plato by assuming that by χρόνος he must have meant 'instant' and, consequently, by ἐξαίφνης ('the sudden') some mysterious extratemporal item. Colin Strang, on the other hand, does the right thing when taking a chronos to be a stretch of time or period, while regarding Plato's 'sudden' as an instant but seems to think that this interpretation is only possible if Plato was a time-atomist. This assumption, though not implausible, is not necessary and draws the attention away from the really interesting points of Plato's argument.

In order to arrive at a different interpretation from Bostock's and Strang's, I will procede in three steps:

i) analyse the text (1.1.2.)
ii) look at the logical status of the sudden as opposed to its ontological status
(1.2.). This will result in three different versions (A, B and C) of reading the
passage, of which I think version C is the most plausible.
iii) look at the ontological status of the sudden (1.3.). This will provide two
possible coherent interpretations, Plato-1 and Plato-2, of which I prefer the
second (χρόνος = period; ἐξαίφνης = instant).

My interpretation of Plato's text, then, consists in a combination of the
results from (ii) and (iii) which seem most plausible to me. In chapter I,4. I
will draw attention to several ancient sources (Aulus Gellius, Sextus
Empiricus, St.Augustine), which, in my view, support Plato-2.

1.1.2. Survey of the text
In order to make the structure of the passage transparent, it can be divided
up into five sections:
    (a) the very general claim (reminiscent of the law of non-contradiction)
that the obtaining of a state and the 'not-obtaining' of it may follow one
another but may not overlap (155e8/156a1).
    (b) an enumeration of pairs of opposite states such as being/becoming or
being similar/dissimilar (in which the details are not very clear) (156a1/b8).
    (c) the main argument, with a negative result, taking rest and motion as
an example of opposite states (156a1/b8).
    (d) a positive formulation of the same result, using and characterizing the
term 'the sudden' (156d1/e2).
    (e) the application of the result from (c) and (d) to the other examples
from section (b) (156e2/157b5).
    The claim of (a) provides the logical framework for the argument,
concerning in a very abstract manner 'partaking in being' and 'not partaking
in being'. The object concerned throughout the passage is the somewhat
mysterious 'One', τὸ ἕν, the general topic of the second part of the
'Parmenides'. Fortunately, the One is here hidden in the personal endings of
the Greek verbs and is totally unimportant for the content of the argument.
One may presuppose that anything that applies to the 'One' "applies
indifferently to anything capable of change" (as Colin Strang puts it).[11]

155e8 Ἆρ' οὖν, ὅτε μετέχει, οἷόν τε ἔσται τότε μὴ μετέχειν,
ἢ ὅτε μὴ μετέχει, μετέχειν; Οὐχ οἷόν τε.

"...can [the] one, when it partakes of being, not partake of it, or partake of it when it
does not partake of it?" "No, it cannot."

Just as one may assume that what applies to the 'One' applies to other
objects as well, one may also assume that what is said about 'partaking in

being' applies to any other property as well.[12] From 155e8 a conclusion is drawn about two χρόνοι (whatever a χρόνος may be):

155e10/11 Ἐν ἄλλῳ ἄρα χρόνῳ μετέχει καὶ ἐν ἄλλῳ οὐ μετέχει·
οὕτω γὰρ ἂν μόνως τοῦ αὐτοῦ μετέχοι τε καὶ οὐ μετέχοι - Ὀρθῶς.

"Then it partakes at one <chronos> and does not partake at another; for that is the only way in which it can partake and not partake of the same thing." "True."

On this basis, Parmenides tries to persuade his interlocutor in step (b) that there must be a 'chronos' when the One seizes being (μεταλαμβάνει τοῦ εἶναι) and another one when it gives up being again (ἀπαλλάττεται αὐτοῦ 156a1-4). 'Seizing being' is identified with 'becoming' (γίγνεσθαι), giving it up with perishing (ἀπόλλυσθαι 156a4/b1). The couple 'dissolving'/'contracting' (διακρίνεσθαι/συγκρίνεσθαι 156b5) is included in the same collection as well as 'growing'/'diminishing' (αὐξάνεσθαι/φθίνειν 156b8). It is clear that Plato here means processes which take time. This is a little less clear with the other examples he gives ('becoming one and thereby ceasing to be many'/'becoming many and thereby ceasing to be one' (156b1-4) and 'becoming similar'/'becoming dissimilar' (ὁμοιοῦσθαι/ἀνομοιοῦσθαι 156b6/7), but I do not think that they are very important.

The main argument (step c) and d)) is formulated in terms of a concrete example: the beginning and ending of a κίνησις; its starting from or its transition into a στάσις[13]. As in Aristotle's Physics, κίνησις may mean more than just local motion here: 'becoming' in general is later called a κίνησις and 'being' a στάσις[14]. As he does in (b), Plato is dealing with a *pair* of examples here:[15] a transition from motion to rest (parallel to growing etc.) and another one from rest to motion (parallel to diminishing etc.).

After introducing the pair of examples to state his main point, Plato all of a sudden (!) puts forward his main thesis, for which he gives reasons only afterwards:

156c1/3 "Ὅταν δὲ κινούμενόν τε ἵστηται καὶ ὅταν ἑστὸς ἐπὶ τὸ κινεῖσθαι μεταβάλλῃ, δεῖ δήπου αὐτό γε μηδ᾽ ἐν ἑνὶ χρόνῳ εἶναι.

"...when being in motion it comes to rest, and when being at rest it changes to motion, it must itself be in no <chronos> at all."

In formulating this thesis, Plato uses the verb μεταβάλλειν. This verb can be used for describing a process which takes time (we will see in ch. I,2. that Aristotle uses it this way). But here it rather refers to a 'switch' (Strang)[16]. So everyday usage obviously did not commit the speaker of ancient Greek to a decision as to whether he wanted to talk about a sudden change or about a process when using this word. The same applies to the corresponding noun μεταβολή.

In order to make his claim plausible, Plato has to bar two escape routes:

(1) that there might be a 'chronos' at which something is neither at rest nor in motion:

156c6/7 Χρόνος δέ γε οὐδεὶς ἔστιν, ἐν ᾧ τι οἷόν τε ἅμα
μήτε κινεῖσθαι μήτε ἑστάναι.

"...there is no < chronos > in which anything can be at once neither in motion nor at rest."

(2) that the switch might still/already take place during rest or motion:

156c9/d1 οὔτε γὰρ ἑστὸς ὂν οὔτε κινούμενον μεταβάλλει,
οὔτε ἐν χρόνῳ ὄν.

"...it does not change when it is at rest or when it is in motion or when it is in < a chronos >."

This is, formulated as a concrete example, what in the introduction I called 'Plato's premiss'.

As the escape routes are barred, Plato can have his Parmenides put forward the question with full force:

156c8 Πότ' οὖν μεταβάλλει;
"Then when does it change?"

The answer to this in a negative formulation is 156c1/3: the main thesis. But Plato also gives a positive answer 'in which' (ἐν ᾧ) a thing is when switching from one state to another:

156d1-3 Ἆρ' οὖν ἔστι τὸ ἄτοπον τοῦτο, ἐν ᾧ τότ' ἂν εἴη, ὅτε μεταβάλλει;
- Τὸ ποῖον δή; - Τὸ ἐξαίφνης.

"Does this strange thing, then, exist, in which it would be < ... > when it changes?" "What sort of thing is that?" "The < sudden >."

The 'sudden' is thus characterized by Parmenides' rhetorical question as ἄτοπον. Literally this means 'out of place'. One may interpret this as meaning 'absurd' (and this is the usual meaning, for example when used by the Sceptics[17]), but one might also interpret it as meaning 'beyond our reach'. Strang finds the fitting solution of calling the sudden 'a weird sort of thing'[18]. The sudden is said to be squatting in the middle between motion and rest, being in no 'chronos whatsoever'.[19] Apart from that, the sudden is said to be 'that into which and out of which the switching occurs'[20].

Plato once more applies the result of sections c) and d) explicitly to 'the One'.[21] This supports the idea that up to that point he wanted to make a very general claim. He again states, clearly referring to 156c1/2 and 6/7, that at the sudden something is neither at rest nor in motion:

156e5/7 μεταβάλλον δ' ἐξαίφνης μεταβάλλει, καὶ ὅτε μεταβάλλει, ἐν οὐδενὶ
χρόνῳ ἂν εἴη, οὐδὲ κινοῖτ' ἂν τότε, οὐδ' ἂν σταίη.

"But in changing, it changes <suddenly>, and when it changes it can be in no
chronos, and <...> will then be neither in motion nor at rest."

At the end of the passage (section e): 156e2/157b2) the result is applied to
the other pairs of processes mentioned in section b): it deals, for example,
with the change from being (which is here called a στάσις) to the process
(κίνησις) of perishing, and the change from non-being to the process of
becoming[22].

The most interesting feature of section e) is that Plato goes so far as to say
that at the sudden something is in neither of two so strictly opposed states as
'being similar' and 'being dissimilar'. And, although the sentence is not
absolutely clear, he says that at the sudden something neither is nor is not
(in a certain state) (οὔτε ἔστι τότε οὔτε οὐκ ἔστι).

The application to the other examples is very short and not very
convincing. Plato takes the idea that something neither contracts nor
dissolves or that it neither grows nor shrinks to be just as amazing as the idea
that something should be neither in motion nor at rest. But this is not
astonishing at all. In analogy to section c)/d) one would expect that
something at the sudden is neither contracting nor contracted or neither
growing nor grown.

So the clearest sections are: a)155e8/156a1, c)156c1/d1; the main
argument using the example of rest and motion with a negative result, and
d)156d1/e2; the positive formulation of the result using the word ἐξαίφνης.
These are the sections I will concentrate on when examining the possible
interpretations.

1.2. THE LOGICAL STATUS OF THE SUDDEN

§1 In interpreting the digression on the sudden one is faced with the same
problem as when trying to interpret the second part of the 'Parmenides' as a
whole: Perhaps Plato simply tried to show the consequences of problems by
formulating them as paradoxes. He might have been motivated by an insight,
gained in his old age, that reality is fundamentally contradictory. But
conceivably Plato just wanted to show how important it is to solve certain
problems by stating them in paradoxical terms.[23] Possibly the paradoxes are
not real; there is a consistent idea behind them which is only camouflaged
by the paradoxical formulation and which has to be uncovered.[24] It is
impossible to say which way the 'Parmenides' *must* be read. One can only
say which way one wants to read it.

I want to point out three ways of reconstructing our passage with respect to the logical status of the sudden. Version A contains the denial of both the law of non-contradiction (LNC) and the law of excluded middle (LEM) in connection with the sudden. Version B denies the LEM for the sudden, but not the LNC. Version C presupposes that Plato camouflaged the real structure of the argument. According to version C both the LEM and the LNC are untouched by the peculiarities of the sudden.

§2 For all three versions I presuppose:

(1) Both a 'chronos' and an 'exaiphnes' are such that they can be mentioned in answer to a question starting with "When...?". We should, however, not rashly conclude that whatever can be mentioned in this way is a time. So let us simply call objects which can be mentioned in an answer to a "When...?"-question 'then-objects'.[25] One subset of the set of then-objects is obviously the set of 'chronoi', the other one the set of 'exaiphnes'.

(2) Plato's argument is quite general and not restricted to 'the One'. So let us reconstruct it with just some physical object called 'a'.

(3) Not all then-objects are *relevant* in every case: in a case concerning a only such then-objects are relevant at which a exists. This restriction is important, since, for example, it is not at all strange that at times when a does not exist it is neither true that a is at rest nor is it true that it is in motion. For one of the possible ontological interpretations of 'exaiphnes', a further restriction will be necessary as to which then-objects are relevant in a particular case.

§3 All the three versions agree on the following basic structure of the passage:

Section (a) is about two relevant then-objects, d_1 and d_2, and a property F. The following is true:

There are no two relevant then-objects d_1 and d_2 such that a is F at d_1 and a is not F at d_2 or a is not F at d_1 and a is F at d_2, and yet d_1 and d_2 are identical. (155e8)

From this, the inference to the next sentence in the text is correct, if (as presupposed) the set of relevant 'chronoi' is a subset of the set of relevant then-objects. It is, in this case, simply a specialization from then-objects to 'chronoi' and may be rendered as:

For any two then-objects d_1 and d_2 from the set of relevant chronoi:
If a is F at d_1 and is not F at d_2, then d_1 is not identical with d_2. (155e10/11)

Section c) turns out to have a syllogistic structure:

Premiss 1 ('Plato's premiss' - 156c9/d1):
For any relevant then-object d: If a is switching from rest to motion (or vice versa) at d, then it is not true that a is at rest at d, nor is it true that a is in motion at d.

Premiss 2 ('LEM for chronoi' - 156c6/7)
There is no then-object d from the set of relevant chronoi so that it is neither true that a is at rest at d; nor is it true that a is in motion at d.

Conclusion ('negative thesis' - 156c1/3)
There is no then-object d from the set of relevant chronoi so that a is switching from rest to motion (or vice versa) at d.

In section d) it becomes clear why the set of relevant chronoi is only a subset of the set of relevant then-objects. There is another set of relevant then-objects: the set of 'exaiphnes'. An 'exaiphnes' is definitely a then-object: it is "that in which something is just then (τότε) when it is switching"; and by saying "ἐν τῷ ἐξαίφνης" one may answer the question: "When (πότε) is something changing?" (156d1/3). We shall assume that the union of these two subsets is the set of all relevant then-objects, i.e. that they are exhaustive. If that is the case, we are are justified in inferring from the negative thesis in section c) the positive thesis in section d):

If there are to be then-objects at which a is switching, but all then-objects from the set of chronoi are excluded, then only then-objects from the set of 'exaiphnes' remain as candidates for the then-object at which a is switching.

That there are indeed then-objects at which a is switching is an existence claim which can, of course, not be inferred here. But if we postulate that there are such objects, then it is fair to infer the 'weird thesis' of 156e5/7:

There is a relevant then-object d which belongs to the set of 'exaiphnes', and it is neither true that a is at rest at d nor that a is in motion at d.

§4 Section (b) - 156a1/b8 - indicates that Plato assumes rest and motion to be opposed to one another in just the same way that being similar and being dissimilar are. And section (a) indicates that they are opposed in the same way as having and not having any property whatsoever (what is true of partaking in being may well be assumed to be true of any property): so to be at rest for a when a exists, to Plato, is simply not to be in motion. In section (e), Plato even explicitly states as a result of his argument that at the 'exaiphnes' something neither is nor is not in a certain state. As ch. I,2. will show, Aristotle thought motion and rest to be opposed in a slightly different way. For Plato, however, what is said about rest and motion may as well be presented in terms of an arbitrarily chosen property F. The argument will be so presented in versions A, B and C.

§5 M_a (from μεταβάλλει) is to be a statement which takes then-objects. It is to be read as "a changes at...". F_a is another statement, arbitrarily chosen but about a, which takes then-objects.[26] **D** is the set of relevant then-objects, **X** the set of relevant 'chronoi', and **E** the set of relevant 'exaiphnes'.

1.2.1. Version A

Two negations cancel each other. Thus if there is any place where the LEM does not hold, there is trouble with the LNC, too. For if a is neither F at the sudden nor not F at it, we may conclude that it both is and is not F then. This is especially tricky, since in section (a) Plato explicitly asserts that nothing ever both does and does not have the same property simultaneously. But surely Plato recognized this when he deliberately wrote a phrase like οὔτε ἔστι τότε οὔτε οὐκ ἔστι. This means that he wanted to construe the argument in such a manner that the result is just the opposite of the starting point.[27] According to version A, the logical structure of the passage comes out thus:

(a) $\neg\exists d_1 d_2 \in D[((F_a(d_1) \wedge \neg F_a(d_2) \vee \neg F_a(d_1) \wedge F_a(d_2)) \wedge d_1 = d_2]$ 'LNC'

  $\forall d_1 d_2 \in X [F_a(d_1) \wedge \neg F_a(d_2) \rightarrow d_1 \neq d_2]$ 'specialized LNC for chronoi'

(c) $\forall d \in D [M_a(d) \rightarrow \neg F_a(d) \wedge \neg\neg F_a(d)]$ 'Plato's premiss'

  $\neg\exists d \in X [\neg F_a(d) \wedge \neg\neg F_a(d)]$ 'LEM for chronoi'

  ———————————————————————

  $\neg\exists d \in X [M_a(d)]$.   'negative thesis'

(d) $\forall d \in D [M_a(d) \rightarrow d \in E]$.   'positive thesis'

  $\exists d \in D[M_a(d)]$.   'existence claim for exaiphnes'

  $\exists d \in E[\neg F_a(d) \wedge \neg\neg F_a(d)]$.   'weird thesis'

Now this rendering of the passage is certainly weird enough: it denies both the LEM and the LNC and is, thus, on the edge of logical anarchy.

1.2.2. Version B

Obviously, Plato is trying to keep the sudden separate from the opposite states between which the switching occurs. But according to version A this very attempt leads to the accumulation of such states to produce a contradiction. In view of this result it seems attractive to reconstruct Plato's argument differently by denying the LEM but holding the LNC.

Interestingly, the first sentence in section (a) only forbids a violation of the LNC for all then-objects; the LEM may be violated for some then-objects if it can be denied independently of the LNC. In the second sentence, the LEM is only stated for chronoi - the exaiphnes might be exempt from it. As a result the LEM and the LNC could be denied independently if there were no rule of double negation. If two negations did not cancel each other, there would be no contradiction involved in saying that *a* neither is F nor is not F at the sudden.

The situation recalls modern intuitionistic propositional logic[28], since it is characteristic for this kind of logic that two negations do not necessarily cancel each other. Is it possible to apply this idea to the moment of change? Well, it could be claimed that only if d is a chronos either $F_a(d)$ or $\neg F_a(d)$ have to be true, but not if d is an 'exaiphnes'. There might be an epistemological justification for this: while a chronos is in time in such a way that it is empirically accessible (so that one can tell by experience whether or not something is the case at it), this may not be possible for the 'sudden'. 'Empirical verifiability' would play the same role for the physical statements involved here as provability plays for mathematical statements in intuitionism. However, this idea soon encounters a problem: $\neg p \land \neg\neg p$ is not valid in intuitionistic logic. For if one simply substitutes q for $\neg p$, one obtains a contradiction ($q \land \neg q$), but the LNC holds in intuitionistic logic, too.

Thus, if there is a special Platonic logic for the sudden it must be rather different from intuitionistic logic. And it can be sketched: it would have to be a three-valued logic which has, apart from the statement-values true and false, a third statement-value 'neither-nor' (only true and false shall be called *truth*-values here). In this way a conflict with the LNC can be avoided. It must be assumed that a proposition can only bear exactly one statement-value.[29] In this way, one excludes the proposition that *a* is F at the 'sudden' is both 'neither-nor' and true, let alone both true and false.

Step (a) in Plato's argument now emerges as the statement that a proposition never bears more than one truth value. This follows, of course, from the principle that no proposition can bear more than one statement-value, since all truth-values are statement-values. But in this way, a proposition may not have any truth-value at all but the statement-value 'neither-nor'. The LEM does not hold in this case: at the most the principle holds that every proposition must at least have one statement-value.[30] In this interpretation, the LEM is stated additionally in step c), but for chronoi only, without holding for exaiphnes as well.

The reconstruction of the passage, according to version B, takes place on a meta-level, compared to the reconstruction in version A: it does not deal with the propositions themselves but is about statement-values of propositions. This can be rendered by introducing three meta-signs W, F and Ø which are to be read as "has the statement value 'true' / 'false'/ 'neither-nor' ":

(a) d_1, d_2 cannot be elements of **D** if it is true that
    $WF_a(d_1)$ and $FF_a(d_2)$, or: $FF_a(d_1)$ and $WF_a(d_2)$ and also: $W(d_1 = d_2)$.   'LNC'

(b) If d_1, d_2 are elements of **X**, then it is true that
    If $WF_a(d_1)$ and $FF_a(d_2)$, then $W(d_1 \neq d_2)$.   'specialized LNC for chronoi'

(c) If d is an element of **D** then it is true that
    If $WM_a(d)$, then: $\emptyset F_a(d)$.   'Plato's premiss'
    d cannot be an element of **X**, if $\emptyset F_a(d)$.   'LEM for chronoi'
    _____
    d cannot be an element of **X** if $WM_a(d)$.   'negative thesis'

(d) If d is an element of **D**, then it is true that
    If $WM_a(d)$, then d is an element of **E**.   'positive thesis'

    There are elements of **D**, such that,
    if d is such an element, then $WM_a(d)$.   'existence claim'

    There are elements of **E**, such that,
    if d is such an element, then $\emptyset F_a(d)$.   'weird thesis'

What makes the sudden 'weird' according to version B is, first of all, the denial of the LEM with respect to it. There is a price to be paid for this: it must be regarded as a statement of fact that *a* neither is nor is not F, since a statement value 'neither-nor' is introduced. This is a problematic step. One could object that it is impossible to state that *a*-neither-is-nor-is-not-F; that one can only neither state that *a*-is-F nor that *a*-is-not-F (which in effect means: to remain silent). The denial of the LEM could then only be interpreted as a renounciation of making a statement. Thus however, the behaviour of someone who denies the LEM does not differ from that of a plant (as Aristotle drily remarks in a similar case).[31]

1.2.3. Version C
Our passage can, perhaps surprisingly, also be reconstructed in such a way that both the LNC and the LEM hold, within the framework of a classical two-valued logic. In this case the statement that something neither is nor is not (so-and-so) at the sudden must be interpreted as containing different senses of 'not': One has to distinguish between the usual propositional negation on the one hand and a sort of negative predicate on the other.

    One might intuitively justify version C by assuming that there is a decisive difference between such then-objects at which *a* could not even possibly be F and such then-objects at which it *could* be F but is not. In this terminology, 'non-F' would be exactly the property which *a* has whenever it could be F but is not. Furthermore, chronoi would be then-objects at which *a* could be F at least in principle, while at an exaiphnes *a* could not even in principle be F.

In order to render this in a heplful notation it is useful to introduce a new sign, the prefix 'non'.

BR2) (1) Combination rule: 'non' may be combined with the name of a one-place predicate P, which can be satisfied by an object o (of whatever kind); the resulting combination is the name of a new predicate.
(2) Sémantic rule: non-P(o) iff
(i) $\neg$P(o).
(ii) o could satisfy P.[32]

§3 *a* could not even possibly be F at the sudden. From this it follows that non-Fa(d) cannot be true if d is a sudden. Moreover, at the sudden the following is true:

$$\neg F_a(d) \wedge \neg non\text{-}F_a(d).$$

This is because although non-F_a(d) implies, $\neg F_a$(d), the reverse does not hold. With this in mind we can reconstruct our passage while leaving both the LEM and the LNC untouched:

(a) $\neg\exists\ d_1,d_2 \in D\ [(F_a(d_1) \wedge \neg F_a(d_2) \vee \neg F_a(d_1) \wedge F_a(d_2)) \wedge d_1 = d_2].$ 'LNC'
    $\forall d_1,d_2 \in X\ [F_a(d_1) \wedge \neg F_a(d_2) \rightarrow d_1 \neq d_2]$ 'specialized LNC for chronoi'

(c) $\forall d \in D\ [M_a(d) \rightarrow\ \neg F_a(d) \wedge \neg non\text{-}F_a(d)]$ 'Plato's premiss'
    $\neg\exists d \in X\ [\ \neg F_a(d) \wedge \neg non\text{-}F_a(d)]$ 'LEM for chronoi'

    $\overline{\neg\exists d \in X\ [M_a(d)]}$ 'negative thesis'

(d) $\forall d \in D\ [M_a(d) \rightarrow d \in E]$ 'positive thesis'
    $\exists d \in D[M_a(d)]$ 'existence claim'
    $\exists d \in E[\neg F_a(d) \wedge \neg non\text{-}F_a(d)]$ 'weird thesis'

One needs to be aware of the fact that Plato's premiss appears somewhat restricted in this version: according to this reconstruction, Plato's argument does not extend to C-changes from *a* being F to *a* not being F but is restricted to changes from F to non-F. As version A tells us, applying Plato's premiss to C-changes too, within two-valued logic, leads to a contradiction. So according to version C, Plato's term μεταβολή does not mean the same as 'Cambridge-change' means in modern terminology. It only appears to. This has an important consequence for the classification of the moment of change: If Plato's premiss is to hold generally and, thus, be extended to C-changes (according to version C, Plato does not say anything about this), then a change either takes place at a time for which the LEM does not hold, or it must be banished from time.

Version C is especially interesting for a historical reason too: it is based on an extremely Aristotelian concept: the non-prefix exactly expresses the Aristotelian notion of privation, as will be seen in ch. I,2.1.(c). Thus, if version C is a plausible interpretation, this demonstrates that the Aristotelian concept of steresis was already preconceived in Plato's 'Parmenides', at least to such an extent that it is useful for the interpretation of the passage on the sudden.

§4 There may, however, still be the following objection to version C:

> This version gives a hint towards a satisfactory solution but does not go far enough. One should say instead: the attempt to satisfy the argument-place of a predicate like "*a* is in motion at..." by filling in an exaiphnes results in utter nonsense. The set of exaiphnes does not even belong to the domain of such a predicate. Thus "*a* is in motion at the sudden" is just as nonsensical as "Cesar is a Prime number". This sentence does not even state a proposition and is, therefore, neither true nor false. But by saying that it is neither true nor false we do not violate the LEM in our object-language. We just state on the level of meta-language: "The sentence 'Cesar is a prime number' is neither true nor false, since it does not express any proposition". The same applies to the sudden: Plato does not claim that at the sudden the world is such that neither of the opposite states obtains; he only claims on the level of meta-language: "The sentence '*a* is in motion at the sudden' is neither true nor false but simply nonsense".

It is definitely worth considering the solution to the problem of the moment of change which is recommended by this objection. But it is much nearer to Hamblin than to Plato and will therefore only be discussed in ch. II,4. The reason is that it presupposes a distinction between object- and meta-language. That Plato draws such a distinction while asserting such statements "at the sudden something is neither nor is it not" (in a certain state), is very improbable.

1.3 THE ONTOLOGICAL STATUS OF THE SUDDEN

§1 Thus far we have only dealt with logical relations between two sorts of then-objects, without contemplating what these 'Then-objects' might actually be. This is what is to be done now. As a result, we shall obtain two different interpretations, 'Plato-1' and 'Plato-2'. I favour 'Plato-2'. I also think that Plato-2 is corroborated by several ancient sources. Nevertheless,

'Plato-1' is also a possible interpretation in the strict sense of the word: a kind of object is assigned to each key word in Plato's text.

§2 Let us remember that we called the set of all instants t, the set of all periods C and their union, the set of all times, T. Let us say that t_a, C_a and T_a are subsets of t, C and T respectively, namely the sets of all periods throughout which and of all instants at which a exists. The question of how to interpret Plato's text on the sudden can now be posed in the strict sense of 'interpretation' as: Is X, the set of relevant chronoi, on the one hand, and is E, the set of relevant exaiphnes, on the other hand, to be identified with one of the sets t_a, or C_a or with some specific subset of one of them?

§3 Being in motion and being at rest are somehow 'opposites' in a different way than 'being white' and 'being black'. For we would not object to saying that, for example, a car may be, throughout some period of its existence, neither black nor white. But we will not admit that there may be a period of the car's existence throughout which it is neither at rest nor in motion. Similarly, we will not admit that something is neither F nor fails to be F throughout any period of its existence. Let us state this by saying that being at rest and being in motion or being F and not being F are, taken together, 'periodically exhaustive'.[33]

Plato certainly claims that at the sudden of two periodically exhaustive states neither the one nor the other obtains. Thus we can exclude from the start the idea that the sudden might be a period (however short): Plato's μεταβολή, unlike Aristotle's, is not a process.

§ 4 After this is excluded, possible positions are:

(1) Being in motion and being at rest as well, as being F and failing to be F, are not only periodically exhaustive; there is also not even an *instant* of time at which a is neither in rest nor in motion; nor is there one at which a is neither F nor fails to be F such that rest and motion, or being F/failing to be F, would even be *instantaneously exhaustive* pairs of properties.

(2) Being in motion/being at rest as well as being F/failing to be F are periodically exhaustive but not instantaneously exhaustive.

(3) Being in motion/being at rest is a periodically but not an instantaneously exhaustive pair of properties while being F/ failing to be F is both periodically and instantaneuosly exhaustive.

Position (3) is Aristotle's position (cf.ch.I,2.) but certainly not Plato's since Plato treats both pairs of opposites on a par. So we have to ask ourselves: should we rather ascribe (1) or (2) to Plato?

Position (1) is to be identified with Plato's position if one assumes the chronoi in his text to be instants. This leads to banishing the sudden and, with it, change, from time. Thus, a sudden would be something extratemporal. Position (2) emerges as Plato's position if one takes the chronoi to be a special sort of period. Therefore the sudden is regarded as an instant.

1.3.1 'Plato-1': χρόνος = instant

§1 Interpretation Plato-1 which takes the chronos to be an instant is mainly a reconstruction of Bostock's interpretation. This is certainly what first comes to mind for a modern reader (who is used to instants) on reading Plato's passage on the sudden. It is, expressed in the terminology of my summary of the text above:

> Section (a): There is no instant of a's existence at which something is both F and is not F. Thus, if a is F at an instant t_1 and is not F at an instant t_2, then t_1 and t_2 cannot be identical.
> Section (c): a is not switching, with respect to being F, at any instant. For in order to do so, this instant would have to be one at which a is neither F nor is not. But there is no instant of a's existence such that a neither is nor is not F at it.
> Section (d) The then-object at which a is switching is, accordingly, a little strange (though it exists): the LEM does not hold for it and, apart from that, it is beyond time.

In this way D, the set of the then-objects of a's existence, is seen as the union of t_a (the set of instants of a's existence) and E (the set of suddens at which a is switching). Consequently, not all then-objects are times: a sudden is a then-object, but no time. t_a is a subset of T_a, but E is not. Our predicate M_a is thus not really a *temporal* statement (taking times as arguments); it only looks as if it were.

Such banishing of the change between states from time does have an advantage: the LEM holds for everything in time. The sudden is something 'weird'; but since it is not in time, time remains sane. (However, we should remember that, according to logical version C, the aim to hold the LEM for everything in time can also be achieved without taking this extreme measure).

Banishing the change from time is rather a counter-intuitive procedure, though. In the text we have lexically, a time-reference: the temporal τότε ... ὅτε (then, when). And yet, paradoxically, it does not refer to a time. Is it possible, within the framework of this suggestion, to distinguish between the starting of a car from a place on Monday morning and the starting of the same car from the same place on Tuesday morning if the car's starting does not take place at any time? It is possible to argue that one can at least approximate each starting of the car arbitrarily exactly in time. If one does so one will notice that one is approximating a different sudden for the starting of the car on Monday than for that on Tuesday. This idea of approximation might even be a plausible explanation for Plato's expression of the sudden as 'squatting in the middle between rest and motion'.

But even so it remains an enormous problem to imagine some event happening if it is not happening at any time. Is saying that it happens at no time not the same as saying that it never happens? Mills and Owen believe that only Aristotle has seen this fatal consequence of Plato-1, for:

...to take the argument as proving this is to take it as proving that there is never such an occurence as being at the sudden.[34]

And they do not think that Plato would have wanted this.

§2 One might attempt a distinction between a radical and a less radical reading of Plato-1 in order to make it a little more intuitive:

radical version: There are no changes since they are logically impossible.
moderate version: We all observe daily that changes do take place. But logical analysis shows that we cannot assign to a change any time to which we would refer by a normal time-reference (such as 'at t').

Everything speaks against the idea of Plato being so Parmenidian as to have held the radical position. But as an adherent of the moderate position he would still face the question, "What do you mean by saying that changes 'take place' beyond time? Either an event takes place in time or it never takes place at all". He could only answer with something like, "It does not fail to happen but it does fail to happen in time. I wouldn't say that it never happens, but that somehow some extratemporal realm occasionally interferes with time..." It is easy to see how problematic such a 'never-say-never'-reply is. Unfortunately, the only other possible reaction then is to assume the radical position, which seems rather mad.

1.3.2. 'Plato-2'
(a) Is the interpretation χρόνος = period possible? - three objections
§1 The absurdities of Plato-1 can be avoided by interpreting the keywords 'chronos' and 'exaiphnes' differently. 'Chronos' need not necessarily mean 'instant'. Why should it not mean 'stretch of time' or 'period' (as it always does in Aristotle)? If it did, 'exaiphnes' could mean 'instant' instead, thus allowing change to be put back into a place in time. But is it possible to identify Plato's chronoi with periods? There are some serious objections to this. Owen protests:

[According to the law of the excluded middle] there can be no period of time during which a thing can be neither A nor not-A, and consequently [in Plato's view] the change from one to the other must occur at a point of time. [...But] by the same law of excluded middle not only is there no period but there is no point of time at which a thing can be neither A nor not-A.[35]

However, this does not really rule out the interpretation 'exaiphnes' = 'instant'. Perhaps Plato did not mind the LEM not holding for instants since they were not to be taken seriously as objects but were merely boundaries (and perhaps considered to be something very unusual anyway). Possibly he did not even intend to, and in fact did not, violate the LEM at all because he had something similar to our logical version C in mind. Nonetheless, there are two more important objections by Bostock:

[1] A temporal point or instant obviously *is* 'in time'...[36]

...but has the sudden not just been declared as not being in time (ἐν ἑνὶ χρόνῳ)? Conceivably it is a mistake to translate 'ἐν ἑνὶ χρόνῳ' with the abstract phrase 'in time'. Perhaps one should rather render it as 'throughout any period'. The phrase οὐδ' ἐν ἑνὶ χρόνῳ would then simply indicate that a change does not take time which is very compatible indeed with its taking place instantaneously.

§2 But the simple equation 'χρόνος = period' will not do. Bostock's second objection (which he thinks compels us to identify 'chronoi' and instants) shows this clearly:

[2] If it [the χρόνος] were not [an instant, but a period], then we could reply that there is no difficulty in finding a stretch of time such that the thing is in motion for part of the stretch and at rest for the remainder, and this could then count as a time (a χρόνος) such that the thing was not in motion 'in' it either. And then we could go on to say that the change itself occurs 'in' this time without upsetting any of Plato's premisses.[37]

It is clear that Bostock goes too far at this point: one of the premisses is in any case upset by proceeding in this way. For if one interprets chronos as 'period', then in section c) of Plato's argument the specialized LEM for chronoi says that there is no period such that *a* is neither at rest nor in motion during it; Plato's premiss states that *a* is neither in motion nor at rest when it is switching. It is possible to read the statement "*a* is neither at rest nor in motion at d" differently when considering periods. A strong reading would be: "*a* is neither at rest nor in motion throughout d". A weak reading would be: "*a* is neither at rest throughout d nor in motion throughout d". According to the weak reading the then-object at which *a* is switching could indeed be a period. So far Bostock is right. But he fails to notice two things: (1) the weak reading is not compulsory. (2) If we adopt the weak reading the specialized LEM for chronoi is simply false (and so since it acts as a premiss, no conclusion follows): there *is* a period in which *a* is neither at rest throughout nor in motion throughout. Only by adopting the strong reading can we keep the specialized LEM for chronoi correct (I therefore favour it). However, if Plato's premiss is correct, there will be no more periods among the candidates for the then-objects at which *a* is switching: a period throughout which *a* is neither at rest nor in motion, although it exists, obviously does not exist.

Nevertheless, Bostock's objection raises the problem of what to do with any period in which *a* is partly at rest and partly in motion. In addition to that, section (a) of Plato's argument already makes clear that not all periods can count as chronoi. For Plato says there that only in different 'chronoi' can something first be at rest and then in motion. So what Plato means by 'chronos' cannot be simply a period of *a*'s existence: X is not to be identified with C_a. But this does not rule out identifying X with a *sub*set of C_a. Thus Bostock's objection shows: an interpretation that takes a 'chronos' to be extended must add the restriction that a 'chronos' may not be 'state-transcendent'.

(b) Preparing for 'Plato-2': Strang's interpretation and its criticism by Mills
§1 One way of avoiding Bostock's objection is to regard the 'chronoi' as time-atoms of temporal extension, but without parts (for if a 'chronos' has no parts *a* cannot be partly in motion and partly at rest in it such that it is neither at rest throughout nor in motion throughout it). Colin Strang does exactly this[38], and so in fact arrives at a possible interpretation of our passage: the chronoi are time-atoms and the suddens are their boundaries:

...whether or not the thing moves in the course of, say, a hundred atomic durations depends on whether or not it is at rest (or non-moving) in the same place for each of them: if [it is] at different places for each of them, then [it] certainly [is] in motion over the composite duration. So when, and how (comes the insistent question) does the moving get done? But [...] there is an answer: not in any time, but between the atomic nows.[39]

Thus an object is said to be in motion at a time-atom z with respect to the preceding and subsequent time-atoms. If it is at z-1 and also at z+1 in a different place from the place it occupies at z, then it is said to move at z. However, it gets from one place to another without taking any time, jerking through space between the time-atoms:

What the thing enjoys at the now is an absence of both motion and rest. [...] What he [Plato] is denying is not that a thing can move but that it can move onward at the now. [...] Plato, if I am right, shows that the process (genesis) takes place, gets done, between the (atomic) nows or, more strictly, between the now and the after.[40]

§2 Strang takes Plato's 'now' to be a 'chronos'. For this he refers to Parm. 152b3/4 where there is indeed some mention of a νῦν χρόνος (which is rather difficult to interpret). Thus anyone wanting to interpret a 'chronos' as something temporally extended seems to be committed to attributing to Plato some idea of an extended present. But why not? Even Aristotle, whose enormous influence made the idea of an instantaneous present as the extensionless boundary between past and future so prominent, differentiates between a logical present instant (πρῶτον νῦν) and an extended phenomenal νῦν.[41] So talk of a νῦν χρόνος in Plato does not exclude that a 'chronos' may be temporally extended.[42]

§4 Assuming Plato to be a time-atomist, Strang starts looking for a

temporal item between the now and the after, [...which] should be in contact with both and [...] the thing should, when in this intermediate position but not elsewhere, be in process.[43]

This 'temporal item' is to be the ἐξαίφνης from 156c. It is a 'durationless instant', while a 'chronos', a time-atom, does have temporal extension. Strang's interpretation of Plato's statement that something is in no 'chronos' when it is changing is:

...to say that the sudden is not in any time is to say that it is no part of any duration.[44]

Strang describes exactly what the graphic representation of an object's 'local function' must look like, according to his interpretation, i.e. like stairs linked by risers:

Mark the riser with an arrow pointing upwards, indicating direction of motion. Then the posture of the arrowed riser will fully satisfy the description Plato gives (1) of an object at the temporal item [..] between the now and the after and (2) of the sudden. For (1) the object in question is [...] in contact with both the now and the after [...]. And (2) if we take the first tread to be the last atomic duration of a period of rest, and the second tread to be the first of a period of motion, then the riser between them does indeed squat between motion and rest and [...] the resting thing does indeed switch to motion from it and to it.[45]

Fig.4 gives an impression of what he means, L_1, L_2 and L_3 being space-atoms, A_1, A_2, A_3 and A_4 time-atoms and D_1, D_2 and D_3 Strangian 'risers'.

§4 Strang's interpretation shows one way of interpreting the 'chronos' as temporally extended. But it is not unquestionable whether Plato really was a time-atomist. What is even more problematic is K.W. Mills'demonstration that Strang interprets Plato as holding a very bad theory[46]. If one follows the principle of interpreting an author *ad meliorem partem*, then this speaks against Strang's interpretation, if a better one can be found. Mills' criticism depends entirely on Strang's making Plato a time-atomist, not on the decision to regard 'chronoi' as periods. To start with, Mills does not think that Strang's interpretation solves any problems:

What Plato claims here [according to Strang] is that the now does not have enough temporal room in it to accomodate motion. [...] But is there, in the durationless instant, more temporal room than in the now? [47]

Fig.4

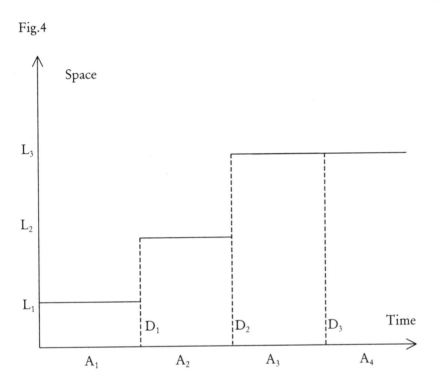

His decisive criticism takes the shape of the following example[48], which is represented in fig.4: L_1, L_2 and L_3 are positions of a.[49] A_1 - A_4 are time-atoms and D_1 - D_3 are the suddens between them. Now a switches from motion to rest at D_2, for it is in different places at A_1 and at A_2, and therefore, according to Strang's definitions, it is in motion during the interval $A_1 + A_2$; at A_3 and A_4, a is in the same place, and, therefore, at rest during $A_3 + A_4$. The first problem is: when does a get from L_2 to L_3? According to Strang, at the sudden between A_2 and A_3. But then it is moving at D_2, and at a sudden nothing is moving according to Plato's premiss. Should one therefore postpone the switch for one time-atom? One cannot: D_3 separates A_3 from A_4 at which a is in the same place and therefore at rest. One may also add to

Mills' criticism that, strictly speaking, according to Strang's definitions, a is
neither in motion nor at rest during the time-atom of A_3.

(c) χρόνος = 'phase'

I shall now attempt to reconstruct Plato's argument χρόνος as a sort of
period and ἐξαίφνης as an instant without assuming the χρόνοι to be time-
atoms. I want to leave open the question of whether Plato thought a period
of uninterrupted rest or motion to be infinitely divisible into subperiods (as
Aristotle did); and (which is closely connected with this question) whether
he also admitted instants where nothing actually changes but where one
might divide a period in thought, or whether the suddens are the only
instants he knows.

What Plato, I think, is doing in the passage on the sudden is so intuitive,
but unspectacular, that one hardly notices it at first sight: when talking of a
with respect to a property F, Plato divides up the existence of a into
subperiods of two kinds:[50] such subperiods throughout which a is F and
such throughou which a is not F. It is these periods he calls chronoi. Thus,
no *absolute* division of a's existence takes place, but one *relative* to F.

To state this more precisely, let us define c as an F-period of a iff a is F
throughout c and c as a no-F-period iff a is not F throughout c.
Furthermore, c is to be called an F-phase of a iff c is an F-period of a but is
not contained in any other F-period of a, and c is to be called a no-F-phase of
a iff c is a no-F-period of a but is not contained in any other no-F-period of
a. Thus, phases are maximal periods of a state.

Let **M** be the set of all F-periods of a and of all no-F-periods of a. And let
M' be the set of all F-phases of a and of all no-F-phases of a (**M'** is a subset of
M which is, of course, a subset of C_a). It is easy to see that the set of all
motion-phases of a is, according to this terminology, coextensional with the
set of all no-rest-phases of a. This is exactly what we meant by calling rest
and motion periodically exhaustive.

Thus the set of chronoi in Plato's argument, **X**, reveals itself to be
identical with (1) either **M** or (2) **M'** (I think, (2) is somehow more probable
but (1) works too). Accordingly **E**, the set of suddens in the argument, is
either (1) t_a or (2) a subset of it, which we may call t_a'. In this case t_a' is the
set of those instants t such that t belongs to t_a and t bounds a period
belonging to **M'**.

The set of chronoi with respect to a's being or not being F would thus be
either (1) the set of all periods during which a exists and either is F
throughout or exists and is not F throughout; or (2) it is the set of all phases
qualified like this. The set of exaiphnes with respect to a's being or not being
F, **E**, would then be either (1) t_a, the set of all instants that fall within a's

existence (in this case, there might be more 'suddens' than actual changes; this does not contradict the text which contains only the implication that whatever is switching is doing so at a sudden, but not the converse that there is no sudden at which no switching takes place). Or **E** would be $t_a{}'$, the set of all instants at which a exists and at which an F-phase and a no-F-phase of a abut (in this case there are just as many 'suddens' relevant for the case considered, i.e. F, as there are changes with respect to F).

This interpretation satisfies section (a) of the argument: no element of **M** is at the same time an F-period and a no-F-period of a (this holds *a fortiori* for phases). And no element of t_a (or $t_a{}'$ resp.) is an instant at which a is both F and not F. Moreover, the specialized LEM for chronoi in section (c) holds, for there is no element of **M** (or **M'**) which is neither an F-period nor a no-F-period of a.

The decisive difference between Plato-2 and Plato-1 is that Plato-2 is only concerned with times: Plato-2 knows of no extratemporal sudden. The banishment of change from time is avoided. It accepts that there are times, i.e. the instants which qualify as suddens, for which the LEM might not hold. However, logical version C has shown that there is a way of reading the argument such that the LEM holds in any case. This makes a combination of the logical version C and the ontological interpretation Plato-2 most attractive.

Plato-2 is well compatible with the idea that Plato invented absolutely extensionless instants and christened them ἐξαίφνης. In this sense, Strang's opinion that the digression in the 'Parmenides' is the 'birth of the instant'[51] has some plausibility. However, a chronos need not have a standard length and need not be indivisible, as Strang thinks.

1.4.HISTORICAL DIGRESSION

§1 In my view, several ancient sources support Plato-2. Sextus Empiricus, when dealing with the problem of the moment of change, most clearly uses a division of two phases (i.e. a dead-phase and a not-dead-phase of Socrates). Aulus Gellius comments directly on our passage. In his interpretation the sudden is nothing extratemporal, but a 'somehow new time at the boundary'. St. Augustine points towards the dangers of banishing change from time by using phase divisions again.

§2 As a philosophical puzzle, the digression in the 'Parmenides' seems to have been well-known throughout antiquity. The Roman author Aulus Gellius (died c. 130 AD)[52] mentions the digression in an anecdote about the philosopher Taurus in his book 'Noctes Atticae' (L VI,13) and literally quotes Plato's text. ἐξαίφνης was, thus, a philosophical *terminus technicus* known to an educated citizen of the Roman Empire half a millenium after Plato. Gellius does not introduce his puzzle by talking about Plato's mysterious 'One', but illustrates it with an example whose fascination seems unsurpassable, so often is it encountered in texts on the moment of change:

Quaesitum est, quando moriens moreretur; cum iam in morte esset, an tum etiam, cum in vita foret.

The question was asked when someone who is dying actually dies, when he is already dead or when he is still alive.

Without any hesitation we get a division into phases here. Periods longer than a phase do not appear. Anyone who decides on one of the two alternatives, Gellius thinks, would make a fool of himself.[53] He therefore rules out the either/or-option. But the both-states-option and the neither/nor-option do not seem to be any good either:

multoque absurdius esse videbitur, si aut utrumque esse dicas aut neutrum.

It would be even more absurd if you said either 'both' or 'neither'.

Anyone who makes an either/or-decision here can assign the 'fieri' either to the phase of 'est' or into the phase of 'non est':

qui artem disceret, quando artifex *fieret*; cum iam *esset*, an tum, cum etiam *non esset* ?

Someone who studies art, when does he become an artist? When he is one, or when he is not yet?

Gellius tells us none of these alternatives was historically successful.[54] The real solution, with which he credits 'our Plato', is, strangely enough after what has been said before, 'neither/nor':

Sed Plato, inquit, noster neque vitae id tempus neque morti dedit. [...] peperit ipse expressitque aliud quoddam novum in confinio tempus, quod verbis propriis atque integris 'την ἐξαιφνῆς φύσιν' appellavit.

But our Plato gave this time neither to death nor to life. He himself invented and gave a name to a somehow new time at the boundary which he called in his own and appropriate words 'the nature of sudden'.

No mention is made of the idea that the word ἐξαίφνης might refer to anything extratemporal. A "Quando...?"-question is to be answered by referrring to a time ('tempus' here corresponds to ἐν ᾧ). Therefore, according to Gellius, since Plato, two kinds of times have had to be distinguished: (1) the good old 'tempora' and (2) the 'quoddam novum in confinio tempus'.

One should not overrate Gellius, since 'Noctes Atticae' is anything but a philosophical work. As a hint towards Plato-2 one should, however, not underrate this passage either.

§3 The way in which Sextus Empiricus introduces the problem of the moment of change[55] resembles Gellius in so far as two different states are as a matter of course once again assigned to two different χρόνοι. Thus, we again have a division into phases:

...ὁ Σωκράτης ἤτοι ὢν θνῆσκαι ἢ μὴ ὤν. δύο γὰρ οὗτοι χρόνοι, εἷς μὲν ὁ καθ' ὃν ἔστι καί ζῇ, ἕτερος δὲ καθ' ὃν οὐκ ἔστιν ἀλλ' ἔφθαρται. διόπερ ἐξ ἀνάγκης ὀφείλει κατὰ τὸν ἕτερον τούτων θνῆσκειν. ὅτε μὲν οὖν ἔστι καί ζῇ, οὐ θνῆσκει. ζῇ γὰρ δήπουθεν. θανὼν δὲ πάλιν οὐ θνῆσκει, ἐπεὶ δίς ἔσται θνῆσκων, ὅπερ ἄτοπον. Οὐ τοίνυν θνῆσκει Σωκράτης.

Socrates dies either when existing or when not existing. For these are two < chronoi > - the one that in which he exists and is alive, the other that in which he exists not but has perished; wherefore he must necessarily die in one or other of these periods. Now he does not die when he exists and is alive; for, to be sure, he is alive; nor, again, does he die when he has died, since then he will be dying twice over, which is absurd. So then, Socrates does not die.[56]

Of course, this 'proof' is only adequate for Sextus Empiricus. Obviously Socrates did die. In this way, the sceptic arrives, as usual, at 'isosthenia' (the game of arguing for and against an opinion ending in a draw).

§4 Knuuttila believes St. Augustine to have favoured the idea (similar to Plato-2) that a change takes place at an instant at which the LEM does not hold.[57] In my view, St. Augustine is not particularly clear on this matter, especially concerning the LEM. But it is his very uncertainty which makes the text interesting. It shows how close a solution with instants appears to the banishment of change from time for someone who is not as used to instants as we are, who have grown up with Newtonian physics:

Quaerendum est, quando [homo] erit moriens. Etenim antequam mors veniat, non est moriens sed vivens; cum vero mors venerit, mortuus erit, non moriens. Illud ergo est adhuc *ante* mortem, hoc iam *post* mortem. Quando ergo *in* morte? Tunc enim est moriens...[58]

It is questionable when [a man] is dying. For before death comes, he is not dying but alive. When death has come, then he is dead, not dying. So this is still before death, that is already after death. Now when is he in death? Well, when he is just dying...

The justification for this is based on the assumption that there must be three different states corresponding to the three 'time' references 'ante mortem', 'in morte' and 'post mortem': 'vivens', 'moriens' and 'mortuus'[59]. However, St. Augustine maintains that it is very difficult to tell (difficillime definitur) when someone is 'in death', which is the middle one of the three states. The state of being alive and the state of being dead can be grasped, since they are temporally extended. But:

Perit [homo] igitur inter utrumque, quo moriens vel in morte sit; quoniam si adhuc vivit, ante mortem est; si vivere destitit, iam post mortem est. Numquam ergo moriens, id est in morte, esse conprehenditur.

[A man], thus, perishes between the two [phases], where he would be dying or in death; when he is still alive, he is before death; when he has ceased to be alive, he ist already past death. So never can dying, i.e. [being] in death, be grasped.

Clearly, St.Augustine argues with a phase division, just as Gellius and Sextus Empiricus do. Equally clearly, he is hesitating to admit the extensionless boundary between the phases as a full-fledged time. The reason St. Augustine gives for his hesitation is quite interesting. He is afraid of the consequences of Plato-1, the banishment of change from time:

Nonne ergo videndum est, ne ista ratione mors corporis nulla esse dicatur? *Si* enim est, *quando* est, quae in ullo et in qua ullus esse non potest?

Do we have to watch out now, whether for this reason the death of the body is claimed to be something which is not there at all? *If* it is there, *when* is it there, that which can be in no one and in which no one can be?

This is not very convincing, since an instant may well be both extensionless and the required time for a change. St. Augustine himself at once counterbalances his worries by the following reasoning:

Sed rursus si nulla mors est ante quid vel post, quid est quod dicitur ante mortem sive post mortem? Nam et hoc inaniter dicitur, si mors nulla est.

If, again, death does not exist before or after which [something is the case], what is it that we refer to by saying 'before death' or 'after death'? For this would be foolish to say if there were no death.

So the result is just one argument against another (rather resembling 'isosthenia'). St. Augustine's conclusion is that, as so often, here is something which cannot be explained by means of language (nec ulla explicari locutione possit), but which, all the same, we cannot not help believing (nec ulla ratione vitari). He does not seem to mind this deficiency too much, since he maintains that the best thing is to go on talking as usual (again, an almost sceptical consequence[60]):

Loquamur ergo secundum consuetudinem (non enim aliter debemus) et dicamus 'ante mortem', priusquam mors accidat [...]. Dicamus etiam cum acciderit: Post mortem illius vel illius factum est illud aut illud.

So let us talk as usual (we cannot do otherwise anyway) and let us say 'before death' before death occurs... let us also say, once it has occurred, [things like]: "After the death of so-and-so such-and-such happened."

Even if St. Augustine does not really present a solution to the problem of the moment of change, his text is interesting insofar as it makes clear that dividing time into phases relative to properties is a habit that still came natural in late antiquity.

§5 Apart from the sources I have quoted, a further argument seems to me to exist for Plato-1 rather than Plato-2. It is the very unusual use of the word χρόνος which Plato-1 assumes: (1) a dense order of instants would have to be so usual to Plato that he allows motion and rest at instants. (2) Plato would have to have called an instant χρόνος; this never happens in Aristotle (who knows instants and describes instants very clearly), and I would be very amazed to see a passage of any Greek philosopher where this clearly happens.

1.5. DESCRIPTION AND CLASSIFICATION OF THE MOMENT OF CHANGE ACCORDING TO PLATO-1 AND PLATO-2

1.5.1. The description of the moment of change
1.5.1.1. The neither/nor-option in Plato-2
According to what has been said, Plato-2 is obviously using the neither/nor-option to describe the moment of change. According to the logical reconstruction C, he might even have found a way of avoiding a violation of the LEM while doing so.

1.5.1.2. The either/or-option in Plato-1
It is not quite so obvious how Plato-1 is to be classified in one of the options for describing the moment of change. However, I think that upon a little reflection it becomes clear that, according to Plato-1, Plato is using the either/or-option:

According to Plato-1, the sudden is no time. Since Plato-1 works with densely ordered instants, the limiting instant (whose existence may be assumed) must be either the first or the last instant at which one of the states in question obtains. Plato-1's reason for banishing change from time is that all instants are exhausted for either the one or the other state, so that there is no time left for the 'switching' between the states.

Plato does not state any preference for assigning the limiting instant to the one rather then to the other state. One can only say that, according to Plato-1, either rest or motion must obtain there, a must either be F or not be F. An adherent of Plato-1 might say that only Aristotle made an attempt at the systematization of this point by looking at the peculiar structure of processes.

1.5.2. The classification of the moment of change
Both interpretations, Plato-1 and Plato-2, agree on Plato's classification of the moment of change as an event which takes place at the sudden and nowhere

else. They disagree on what the sudden is, however: According to Plato-1, the sudden is beyond time. So anyone who favours Plato-1 must be able to make sense of an extratemporal event. Plato-2, on the other hand, dates the event of switching to the limiting instant between a phase of the old and a phase of the new state, so that no extratemporal event is necessary.

The fact that Plato postulates an event of changing emerges from the following indications: (1) reservation of the word μεταβολή for changes which take no time, (2) the metaphor of 'seizing being and letting it go' and (3) Plato's insistence on the idea that "nothing changes without a change taking place" (οὐδὲ μὴν μεταβάλλει ἄνευ τοῦ μεταβάλλειν - 156c7). The event at the sudden has no temporal extension whatsoever. Nevertheless it is there, taking place: an object does not simply arrive in the target position, but virtually switches from motion to rest. An object is not just not F any more, but virtually switches from being F to not being F.[61]

To Bostock there seems to be danger of regress involved in postulating changes as events in this way:

> [Plato] raises a question not only about the instantaneous change from being F to being not-F, but also about the equally instantaneous change from being F to changing from being F to being not-F, and clearly there is a potential here for an infinite regress.[62]

However, this danger is, I think, avoided, if one allows an event of changing only between such states which are themselves temporally extended but not between an extended state and an instantaneous event.

One does not have to look far for a motivation of Plato's classification of the moment of change. It is the high rating of Plato's premiss. One might object that this rating is a result of thinking about changes as if they were processes, which seems unjustified (during a process, clearly neither the initial state nor the target state obtains). However, there need not necessarily be any analogy with processes involved in the idea that a can neither have the change between opposite states in front of it nor be behind it when it is instantaneously changing. In our text, Plato clearly keeps processes and instantaneous changes apart.

1.5.3. Evaluation

I am inclined to think that Plato-2 in connection with logical version C best represents Plato's view. Instants were still something very unusual for Plato. Plato's talk of the sudden as a 'weird sort of thing' might then be interpreted as an expression of his inabilty to imagine instantaneous properties and of his amazement about this. The question poses itself as to whether historical development has meanwhile enabled us to imagine such things, or whether we perhaps merely just imagine that we can imagine them.

CHAPTER 2

ARISTOTLE

There is no other place where opinions of such complexity concerning the moment of change can be found as appear in Aristotle's Physics. In this chapter, I shall try to put them into some systematic order. I shall often refer back to the digression in Plato's 'Parmenides', as in many places Aristotle's opinion can be interpreted as a (probably very consciously formulated) opposition to Plato. When interpreting other passages, I will show how Aristotle's treatment of the moment of change is integrated into the overall frame of his philosophy through the use of the technical vocabulary peculiar to Aristotelian metaphysics.

I will start (in 2.1.) by summing up those parts of the Aristotelian doctrine of space, time and the continuum which are relevant for his discussion of the moment of change in Physics VI and VIII, always pointing to the great differences between Aristotle's and Plato's terminology. Chapters 2.2. and 2.3. deal with the two different descriptions of the moment of change Aristotle proposes: the description with respect to 'comparative properties' such as rest and motion (2.2.) and the description with respect to 'non-comparative' properties such as being white (2.3.). In chapter 2.4. I want to clarify what exactly Aristotle's peculiar characterization of the limiting instant as the ἐν ᾧ πρώτῳ μεταβέβληκεν means. In this respect it will be important to distinguish between the use of the word πρῶτον with regard to a temporal order (2.4.1.) and the use of this word with regard to a hierarchic order (2.4.2.) (the latter being a use which is usually neglected in connection with the 'Physics'). Chapter 2.5. links Aristotle's description of the moment of change with his well-known distinction between κίνησις and ἐνέργεια; this chapter will also be concerned with Plotinus' objections to Aristotle's description of the moment of change, because they are based on this very distinction. Chapter 2.6. is concerned with Aristotle's denial of the existence of instantaneous events. This denial places him in a very peculiar position with respect to the question of how to classify the moment of change. A summary (2.7.) is followed by a postscript (2.8.) in which I try to tell, from Aristotle's imaginary point of view, the highly speculative story of how Aristotle's opinion might have developed out of Plato's position and as a reaction to it.

2.1. ARISTOTLE: PHYSICS VI AND VIII - BASICS

§1 Historically, the philosophical treatment of the moment of change begins with a battle of giants: it is difficult to imagine two texts more closely related to one another with respect to the issue treated and to the words and examples used than the digression in Plato's 'Parmenides' and Aristotle's Physics VI: the texts have all the key words in common: κίνησις, μεταβολή, χρόνος; in both of them the phrase ἐν ᾧ ((temporal) 'in which') appears as an abstract, technical term; according to both texts different kinds of objects may be an ἐν ᾧ, but they may all be referred to by the word 'then' (τότε). However, the texts differ strikingly in the way the key words are related to one another:

> There is no μεταβολή taking place in a χρόνος. κίνησις excludes μεταβολή. The ἐν ᾧ of μεταβολή is the weird sudden, ἐξαίφνης, squatting in the middle between κίνησις and στάσις. This is, roughly speaking, Plato's view.

> μεταβολή does take place in a χρόνος. κίνησις implies μεταβολή. The ἐν ᾧ of μεταβολή is unproblematic; the difficulty is the ἐν ᾧ πρώτῳ. In a certain sense, there is a ἐν ᾧ πρώτῳ of completed μεταβολή; but it is in the middle only according to *number* and *concept* - according to *fact* it is (at the end of a process) to be assigned to the later state. This is what Aristotle says.

Although the Greek expressions can be interpreted differently (as we have seen in the chapter on Plato), the overlap of Aristotle's and Plato's terminologies is obvious; so there should be no doubt that we here encounter the traces of a specialists' debate.[1]

§2 The time ontology of Physics VI is much less problematic than the time ontology of the digression in Plato's 'Parmenides' with its mysterious εξαίφνης. Aristotle knows two sorts of times: χρόνος and νῦν. χρόνοι are periods, νῦν are instants. There is no trace of any possibly extratemporal 'then'-object in Aristotle, such as Plato's ἐξαίφνης. Rather, there is a trace of Aristotle's disapproval of his teacher's poetic creativity in dealing with this very word. To Aristotle, ἐξαίφνης is clearly a term of psychology, not a term appropriate for the metaphysics of the moment of change, for with ἐξαίφνης he associates[2] a period which may well contain a process but which is just too short for its contents to be observed:[3]

222b14/15[4] τὸ δ᾽ ἐξαίφνης τὸ ἐν ἀναισθητῳ χρόνῳ διὰ μικρότητα ἐκστάν
[That happens] 'suddenly' [which] occurs in a period unobservable because of [its] smallness.[5]

Aristotle's use of the words χρόνος and νῦν clearly differs from Plato's, too. This is true irrespective of which interpretation of Plato's text is favoured (of course, according to the interpretation someone chooses, there will be different differences):

A χρόνος in Physics VI and VIII is always a period of a certain duration. It can be divided into parts, and into as many parts as one pleases.[6] These parts are periods again. It would be wrong to say, though, that a period *consists* of subperiods or that the subperiods constitute the period. That would be the view of a time-atomist who, in the end, hopes to reach irreducible elementary particles of periods: time atoms. Aristotle is clearly no time atomist, and he would clearly take the view that subperiods come about only through an act of dividing up a period. As we have seen, this is not as clear in Plato.

An Aristotelian χρόνος may be state-transcendent, in contrast to a χρόνος in Plato (which might be an instant, or, more plausibly, a phase): in a passage (which requires some further comment later on) in Phys. 236b19/22, Aristotle explicitly calls a year the χρόνος of a state which obtains only for one day of that year and not for the remaining 364 days.

§3 According to Aristotle, one can go on dividing up a period as long as one wishes, without arriving at any instants. Nevertheless, instants *belong to* a χρόνος; they are its boundaries (boundary = πέρας)[7], or they fall within the χρόνος as the boundary between two of its subperiods. Instants are not only found where two phases abut (as they seem in Plato): One will get an instant whenever one divides a period; and one can divide a period wherever one likes. Consequently, instants are densely ordered.
Aristotle calls 'belonging to' a period either as a boundary or as an 'internal' instant (falling within a period) 'being in' (εἶναι ἐν)[8].

The assumption that a period is characteristically a continuum reaching from one instant to another is put in a nutshell by Aristotle when he simply states:

237a6/7 τὸ μεταξὺ τῶν νῦν χρόνος

< A period > is that which is intermediate between nows[9]

§4 In Physics VI, Aristotle calls instants 'nows' (νῦν). The word νῦν is not used exclusively for instants though; it may be applied to short periods too: Aristotle acknowledges the existence of an extended present, and he does not deny that it might be the present relevant for *psychology*. But what is relevant in *metaphysics* is the non-extended, indivisible boundary between past and future as introduced in the essay on time (Physics IV, 10 - 14) and described again in VI,3. This metaphysical present is prior to the psychological present: if a period may be called νῦν at all, then this is only because it contains a relevant present instant; it is νῦν only dependently, with regard to something other than itself (καθ' ἕτερον), namely the present instant, which is called the 'independent' or 'first now' (καθ' αὐτὸ, πρῶτον). This differentiation is, for example, found in 233b33/34 which reads:

Ἀνάγκη δὲ καὶ τὸ νῦν
τὸ μὴ καθ' ἕτερον ἀλλὰ καθ' αὐτὸ καὶ πρῶτον λεγόμενον
ἀδιαίρετον εἶναι.

Necessarily, too, the now - the now so-called not derivatively but in its own right and primarily - is indivisible.

The 'dependent now', as one may conclude reversely, *is* divisible. Instead of νῦν, Aristotle also uses the word σημεῖον (literally: 'limiting mark') in a digression in Physics VIII which is important for his treatment of the moment of change (263b9/264a6).

Those instants which bound a χρόνος or fall within a χρόνος Aristotle regards as belonging very closely to this χρόνος. This becomes clear when he talks about something being the case 'everywhere' in a period (ἐν ὁτῳοῦν), for by 'everywhere' he clearly means all possible subperiods of the period as well as all instants belonging to the period[10]. However, this is relevant only if what is in question can be the case at instants at all (in Aristotle's view). It is important to note that in some passages about the moment of change, dealing with rest and motion and containing the phrase ἐν ὁτῳοῦν this is not the case, since in Aristotle's view there can be no rest or motion at instants; there the phrase refers to all possible subperiods of a period only.[11]

2.2. THE MOMENT OF CHANGE BETWEEN COMPARATIVE PROPERTIES SUCH AS REST AND MOTION

2.2.1. Rest and motion in Aristotle
(a) κίνησις and μεταβολή in Physics VI

The expressions κίνησις and στάσις refer to something more general than local motion and rest in a place. They apply to any sort of continuous process (such as alteration of shape, colour, size, temperature), or the absence of such a process. Nevertheless, since the issue is clear enough, I will often simply use 'motion' and 'rest' as translations *pars pro toto*.

A clear distinction between the words κίνησις and μεταβολή is difficult to find anywhere in the Physics. μεταβολή seems to be the more general term which covers not only processes in which already existing objects are involved, but also processes of the coming-to-be and the perishing of objects. A κίνησις is always also a μεταβολή, although not every μεταβολή might be a κίνησις. Sometimes both words are used interchangeably: in 236b19/25, Aristotle claims something to be true of a 'changing thing' which 'is changing' (τὸ μεταβάλλον, μεταβάλλει) and he formulates the proof of this claim immediately afterwards by talking about 'the moving thing' which 'is moving' (τὸ κινούμενον, κινεῖται).[12] Thus, in Aristotle, the two words are not opposed in the way they are in Plato, where, as we saw, μεταβολή excludes κίνησις.[13]

(b) No κίνησις, στάσις, μεταβολή at instants
It is quite generally assumed that Aristotle does not allow any κίνησις or στάσις at instants. The reason for this is that to Aristotle nothing is able to go through a process such as getting from here to there at a durationless instant.[14] Aristotle bases his refutation of Zeno at the end of Physics VI on this intuition (in whichever way this refutation is exactly meant and whether or not it is convincing). Although I cannot go into detail here (I will to some extent in part III), I think the refutation as well as the (correct) intuition behind it would still be unharmed if Aristotle had allowed what we find quite natural today: to say that *a* is in motion at t if t falls within a period throughout which *a* is in motion. He does not allow this,[15] however, and has thus had to face the reproach of having hampered the development of modern physics.[16] Possibly Aristotle's extreme view should be seen as an over-reaction to Zeno. We will have to take this view into account, in any case.

The word μεταβάλλειν in Physics VI refers to a continuous process, since κίνησις implies μεταβολή. Thus the latter word in Aristotle always means an alteration which takes time, never an instantaneous event or 'switching' as in Plato.[17]

(c) Rest as the στέρησις of motion: periods as ἐν ᾧ of κίνησις and στάσις
For Aristotle, the fact that there is no rest at an instant is implied by the fact that there is no motion at an instant.[18] This is so because rest is the στέρησις, the absense of motion (264a27/28). The way in which Aristotle describes the relationship between rest and motion actually gives us a very clear definition of στέρησις:[19]

239a10/14 ἐν ἀμερεῖ μὲν γὰρ οὐκ ἠρέμεσεν
διὰ τὸ μὴ εἶναι κίνησιν ἐν ἀτόμῳ
ἐν ᾧ δὲ τὸ ἠρεμεῖν, καὶ τὸ κινεῖσθαι
τότε γὰρ ἔφαμεν ἠρεμεῖν, ὅτε καὶ ἐν ᾧ πεφυκός κινεῖσθαι μὴ κινεῖται τὸ πεφυκός.

[A thing] cannot have been resting in that which has no parts, because there cannot be motion in that which is indivisible, and that in which rest takes place is the same as that in which motion takes place (for we said that rest occurs if a thing which naturally moves is not moving when and at a time in which motion would be natural to it).

According to this, a property F is the steresis of a property G iff an object is G whenever it is not F but could be F.

The expression ἐν ᾧ in this passage is meant temporally, as it is in almost all passages relevant to the moment of change in Physics VI:[20] it is the general term for χρόνος and νῦν, for period and instant, the two different sorts of times Aristotle knows. In what follows, ἐν ᾧ can thus simply be translated by 'time'. Plato, in the digression of the 'Parmenides', uses the same expression for a then-object when he is not ready to commit himself to calling it either an ἐξαίφνης or a χρόνος. Plato's very choice of words when he calls the ἐξαίφνης 'that in which' (ἐν ᾧ) something is changing is a another indication of how closely related the two texts are.

(d) Comparative and non-comparative properties
Aristotle implicitly distinguishes two sorts of properties when writing about the moment of change (in contrast to Plato who does not differentiate in this respect). An example of the first sort of properties is 'being in motion' or 'remaining white', an example of the second sort is 'being in a certain place' or 'being white'. This distinction has been termed a distinction between 'relational' and 'non-relational' predicates (in a contemporary systematic article).[21] I will rather call it the distinction between 'comparative' and 'non-comparative' properties.[22] *Comparative properties* are properties which are assigned to an object by comparing its states at different instants between which there is always a certain period of time.[23] Non-comparative properties are properties which do not have this structure. A comparative property might be 'defined' in a certain context by referring to non-comparative properties. Russell has drawn attention to this by defining motion as "being at different places at different times".[24] In part III it will be important to notice a radical difference between Aristotle and Russell on this issue. For the moment, it is rather more interesting to see the striking similarity between Russell's definition and the definition of rest and motion in Aristotle which shows that both philosophers regard rest and motion as comparative properties:

239a14/17
ἔτι δὲ καὶ τότε λέγομεν ἠρεμεῖν, ὅταν ὁμοίως ἔχῃ νῦν καὶ πρότερον
ὡς οὐχ ἑνί τινι κρίνοντες ἀλλὰ δυοῖν τοῖν ἐλαχίστοιν
ὥστ᾽ οὐκ ἔσται ἐν ᾧ ἠρεμεῖ ἀμερές.

...we say that a thing rests when it is now in the same state as it was in earlier, judging rest not by any one point but by at least two: consequently that in which a thing is at rest cannot be without parts.

239a27/ 29

οὕτως γὰρ λέγομεν ἠρεμεῖν, ὅταν ἐν ἄλλῳ καὶ ἄλλῳ τῶν νῦν ἀλεθὲς ᾖ εἰπεῖν ἐν τῷ αὐτῷ

We say that [something is] at rest whenever in one and yet another of the nows it is true that [something] is in the same [state, e.g. place].[25]

The times at which the states which are compared obtain are instants at which something is a certain shape or colour, is in a certain place etc. Between them there is a period of process or of remaining as before. So we may insert 'place', 'shape', 'colour' etc. after the words 'the same' (τῷ αὐτῷ). This is important because it shows another difference from Plato: Aristotle clearly allows that something is of a certain shape, colour or in a certain place at an instant;[26] at least according to one interpretation of Plato's text (i.e. Plato-2), nothing similar exists in Plato.[27] Just as κίνησις means process in general, ἠρεμία means 'remaining as before' in general and is not restricted to rest in a place.

(e) opinions differing from (b)

There are two exceptions from the general opinion that there is no motion or rest at an instant according to Aristotle. They are to be found in articles by Norman Kretzmann and Richard Sorabji. Kretzmann tries to connect his 'Neutral Instant Analysis' for the moment of change between rest and motion with Aristotle.[28] Sorabji, in the first version of his article 'Aristotle on the Instant of Change',[29] argues the view that Aristotle allows motion and rest at instants in some places.

Kretzmann's interpretation has a serious handicap: according to his own characterization of the 'Neutral Instant Analysis' (which I will examine in detail in ch.II,5), someone who favours this view is committed to holding that 'neutrality' is a very peculiar and exceptional property of the limiting instant between rest and motion, whereas at other instants motion or rest frequently occur. Sorabji is thus right in using the fact that Aristotle explicitly denies motion and rest at any instant as an objection to Kretzmann.[30] Nonetheless, Sorabji himself, in the first version of his article, tries to obtain the blessing of the *philosophus* for a systematic suggestion of his own (discussed in ch.II,1) by dividing up the relevant passages of Physics VI and VIII into two different historical 'layers'. According to this idea, in the passages belonging to the first layer, Aristotle denies rest and motion at instants, whereas he allows both in the passages belonging to the second, more progressive layer. Sorabji has revised his opinion, as can be seen in the second and, even more clearly, in the third version of his paper.[31]

A difficulty lies in the fact that Sorabji could indeed, for the view he expresses in the first version of his article, refer to a rather strange passage in

236a15/27. Unfortunately, the proof this passage consists of is of crucial importance to Aristotle's treatment of the moment of change.[32] Since his second version, Sorabji has read this passage as a *reductio ad absurdum*, during which single Greek letters exceptionally refer to time-atoms. This is one way of dealing with the problem. It should also be noted that the proof in 236a15/27 not only remains intact if one omits the problematic lines; it even fits a certain proof-scheme, which is characteristic of Aristotle's treatment of the moment of change in at least three other passages of Physics VI (236b25/32, 235b34/236a5 and 238b31/36), much better. So perhaps there is something wrong with the text.[33] Wagner and Cornford/Wicksteed take the passage as somewhat loosely formulated. Cornford/Wicksteed consequently translate ἠρεμεῖ as 'is unchanged'. This is another way of dealing with the problem, for Aristotle can allow something to '*be* unchanged' at an instant; incompatibility with the rest of the 'Physics' would only occur if he said that something can *remain* unchanged at an instant.[34]

2.2.2. The moment of change between rest and motion
Twice, Aristotle describes the problem of the moment of change not as a problem with the principle of excluded third but with the principle of non-contradiction. One of the passages[35] deals with the s-change between rest and motion:

234a34/b5
ἔτι δ' εἰ τὸ αὐτὸ μὲν ἔστι τὸ νῦν ἐν ἀμφοῖν τοῖν χρόνοιν,
ἐνδέχεται δὲ τὸν μὲν κινεῖσθαι τὸν δ' ἠρεμεῖν ὅλον,
τὸ δ' ὅλον κινούμενον τὸν χρόνον ἐν ὁτῳοῦν κινηθήσεται
τῶν τούτου καθ' ὃ πέφυκε κινεῖσθαι,
καὶ τὸ ἠρεμοῦν ὡσαύτως ἠρεμήσει,
συμβήσεται τὸ αὐτὸ ἅμα ἠρεμεῖν καὶ κινεῖσθαι.
τὸ γὰρ αὐτὸ ἔσχατον τῶν χρόνων ἀμφοτέρων, τὸ νῦν.

...inasmuch as it is the same now that belongs to both the times,
and it is possible for a thing to be in motion throughout one time and to be at rest throughout the other,
and that which is in motion or at at rest for the whole of a time will be in motion or at rest
in any part of it in which it is <able> to be in motion or at rest:
It will follow that the same thing can at the same time be at rest and in motion;
for both times have the same extremity, viz. the now.

Yet can this be a problem with which Aristotle himself is faced? I do not think so. I rather think that from what has already been said in general about rest and motion in Aristotle, it is clear that (indicative mode yes or no) Aristotle is here describing a problem *he* does not have. Instants falling within a period or bounding it may be included when something is said about 'any part' or 'the whole' of a period. But, according to Aristotle, nothing is able (πεφυκός) to move or to be at rest at instants. So at the limiting instant between a phase of motion and a phase of rest, nothing can be any more in motion or at rest than at any other instant. Thus for the problem of the moment of change between motion and rest (which causes so much trouble in Plato's 'Parmenides') Aristotle has a trivial solution which follows from motion and rest being comparative properties. A simple *a fortiori* argument ("No motion or rest at any instant, let alone at any limiting instant") leaves him no choice but to use the neither/nor-option in this case.[36]

2.3. THE MOMENT OF CHANGE BETWEEN NON-COMPARATIVE PROPERTIES

2.3.1. *The limiting instant at the end of a process as an instant of the target state*
It is possible to consider the same situation with respect to comparative properties such as being in motion or being at rest or with respect to non-comparative properties such as being in a target position or being white. Aristotle's description of the moment of change with respect to non-comparative properties is different from the one he gives for comparative properties (this differentiation is, as Richard Sorabji rightly remarks, indeed no small achievement). What Aristotle does with non-comparative properties becomes clear in the second passage where Aristotle notes the danger of contradiction in connection with the moment of change. It is the following digression in Physics VIII, 263b9-15:

δῆλον δὲ καὶ
ὅτι ἐὰν μή τις ποιῇ τοῦ χρόνου τὸ διαιροῦν σημεῖον τὸ πρότερον καί ὕστερον ἀεὶ τοῦ ὑστέρου τῷ πράγματι
ἔσται ἅμα τὸ αὐτὸ ὄν καὶ οὐκ ὄν καὶ ὅτε γέγονεν οὐκ ὄν.
τὸ σημεῖον μὲν οὖν ἀμφοῖν κοινόν, καὶ τοῦ προτέρου καὶ τοῦ ὑστέρου,
καὶ ταὐτόν καὶ ἓν ἀριθμῷ,
λόγῳ δ᾽ οὐ ταὐτόν (τοῦ μὲν γὰρ τελευτή, τοῦ δ᾽ ἀρχή).
τῷ δὲ πράγματι ἀεὶ τοῦ ὑστέρου πάθους ἐστίν.

It is also plain
that unless we hold that the point of time that divides earlier from later always belongs only to the later as far as the thing is concerned,
we shall be involved in the consequence that the same thing at the same moment is and is not, and that a thing is not at the moment when it has become.
It is true that the point is common to both times, the earlier as well as the later, and that, while *numerically* one and the same,
it is not so *in definition*, being the end of the one and the beginning of the other;
but *so far as the thing is concerned* it always belongs to the later affection.

Aristotle's distinction of different roles (ἀριθμῷ, λόγῳ, τῷ πράγματι) for the limiting instant has had historical consequences: Brentano's theory of the 'plerosis' of a boundary seems to be anticipated here[37] as well as a distinction between 'instans temporis' and 'instans natur[a]e' made by some philosphers in the late Middle Ages[38] (probably they as well as Brentano were directly influenced by this passage).

Yet what could be the reason for assigning the limiting instant to the later state here? This becomes clear if one takes a look at the 'proof' for his claim, which Aristotle gives after 263b15. The first part of the proof, at least, works with the example of an object, D, which is first white and then gradually darkening in a process.[39] The text reads:

263b15/24

χρόνος ἐφ' ᾧ ΑΓΒ, πρᾶγμα ἐφ' ᾧ Δ.
τοῦτο ἐν μὲν τῷ Α χρόνῳ λευκόν, ἐν δὲ τῷ Β οὐ λευκόν.
ἐν τῷ ἄρα Γ λευκὸν καὶ οὐ λευκόν.
ἐν ὁτῳοῦν γὰρ τοῦ Α λευκὸν ἀληθὲς εἰπεῖν,
εἰ πάντα τόν χρόνον τοῦτον ἦν λευκόν, καί ἐν τῷ Β οὐ λευκόν.
τὸ δὲ Γ ἐν ἀμφοῖν.
οὐκ ἄρα δοτέον ἐν παντί, ἀλλὰ πλὴν τοῦ τελευταίου νῦν ἐφ' οὗ τὸ Γ.
τοῦτο δ' ἤδη τοῦ ὑστέρου.
καὶ εἰ ἐγίγνετο οὐ λευκὸν καὶ ἐφθείρετο τὸ λευκὸν ἐν τῷ Α παντί,
γέγονεν ἢ ἔφθαρται ἐν τῷ Γ.
ὥστε λευκὸν ἢ μὴ λευκον ἐν ἐκείνῳ πρῶτον ἀληθὲς εἰπεῖν...

Let us suppose a time ACB and a thing D,
D being white in the time A and not white in the time B.
Then D is at C white and not white;
for if we were right in saying that it is white during the whole time A,
it is true to call it white at any moment of A, and not white in B,
and C is both in A and B.
We must not allow, therefore, that it is white in the whole of A, but must say that it is so in all of it except the last now C.
C already belongs to the later period,
and if in the whole of A not white was becoming,
at C it had become or perished.
And so [...] that is the the first moment at which it is true to call the thing not white...

A and B are subperiods of the period considered; C is the boundary instant between A and B. What happens to D at the end of the proof is difficult to see.[40] But whatever that may be, so much can be said with safety: what Aristotle assigns to the later state is the limiting instant *at the end of a process*. So the end of a process is what he envisaged when making his seemingly rather general statement in 263b9ff.

If we take this into account, Aristotle's assignment makes a lot of sense in the context of his treatment of continuity in Physics VI. If we imagine D being painted black it follows from the continuity of space that there is *no* last instant at which D's surface would contain one last irreducibly small, indivisible white spot: such a thing does not exist if space is continuous. If we imagine D as darkening all over at once, like a white wall in fading light, then there is a continuum of shades from white to black, and thus *no* last shade before black which would contain a minimum amount of white. This means that there is no last instant at which D has not quite reached the 'target state'. This already presents us with quite a good reason for regarding the problematic limiting instant as an instant when the target state has in fact been reached with the limiting instant assigned to the later state (being black): if instants are densely orderd and there is a limiting instant (which it is reasonable to assume) and at every instant something has either to be the case or not, and if there is no last instant at which something is not the case, then there is a first instant at which this *is* the case.

Hence Aristotle's solution does not just consist of the simple instruction: "Any problematic instant should be assigned to the later state!". There would be no motivation for doing this.[41] In 263b10, Aristotle assigns the limiting instant to the later state because he is in this passage occupied with the end of a process and not with its beginning. Analogously, at the *beginning* of a process, the limiting instant would have to be assigned to the initial state (there is no first intermediate state reached, and thus no first instant of having left the initial state).[42] The word ἀεί in 263b12 refers only to *ends* of processes. There is no difficulty in applying the solution concerning being white to being at the target place of a motion. Aristotle's position may then be summed up as follows:

There are, in such changes no first position a mobile could occupy after the *terminus a quo* and no last position it could occupy before the *terminus ad quem*. [..T]he actuality of the condition in which an object rests has intrinsic limits[43].

Thus, the option Aristotle uses for describing the moment of change when, at the beginning and at the end of a continuous process, non-comparative properties are involved, is the either/or option.

2.3.2. Discontinuous changes and substantial change
2.3.2.1. Discontinuous change
Discontinuous changes are not genuine changes according to Aristotle[44] (which may, of course be regarded as a shortcoming of his theory, if such changes exist). Sorabji has shown that Aristotle seems to construe them as dependent on processes,[45] so that, in that case, there would always be an indirect answer, too, about what is true with respect to the limiting instant.

For example, the sudden 'being-covered-with-ice' of a pond[46] (in fact Aristotle's example) happens to be the result of a continuous process of cooling down. So the limiting instant is an instant of the pond being covered with ice, the non-genuine change from not being covered with ice to being covered with ice being dependent on the process of cooling down.

2.3.2.2. Substantial change

Aristotle does not give a detailed account of substantial changes (becoming and perishing) comparable to the elaborate treatment in Phys. VI and VIII of changes in objects. Rather, what he has to say about substantial change has to be inferred from passages in different parts of the 'Physics' and 'De Generatione et Corruptione'. The inference of what Aristotle's view on substantial change is has traditionally proved to be difficult, since Aristotle's terminology is not quite consistent on this point.[47]

Knuuttila stresses that Aristotle differentiates between substantial change and other kinds of change in Physics V1, where Aristotle reserves the term κίνησις for changes in existing objects (e.g. qualitative change and local motion).[48] Both γένεσις (coming-to-be) and φθορά (perishing) are clearly said to be no κίνησις. Every κίνησις is said to be a μεταβολή, however not every μεταβολή is a κίνησις, since only change in an object (μεταβολή ἐξ ὑποκειμένου εἰς ὑποκείμενον) is a κίνησις. Aristotle's reason for this is that coming-to-be and perishing (unlike changes in an object) are between contradictory terms (καθ' ἀντίφασιν), i.e. being and non-being: there are no degrees of substance.[49]

Consequently Aristotle in Physics V1 denies that a substantial change is a κίνησις. From this, Knuuttila infers that according to Phys. V1, "generation and corruption of substances [is] the standard type of the instantaneous non-kinetic change between contradictory terms."[50]

According to this interpretation Physics V1 conflicts with numerous other passages where generation and corruption are treated as processes. For example in Physics III 1-2 building a house is an example of κίνησις[51]. In Physics I7, generation and corruption are clearly described as processes (though the word κίνησις is not used there), and in Phys. IV 222b31/32 both μεταβολή and kinetic change are said to take time. Apart from that, coming-to-be and perishing are said to take place quickly or slowly.[52]

Knuuttila seems to think that it is wrong to treat generation and corruption as processes. I suppose his reason is that there are no intermediate states between existence and non-existence, but that they would have to exist if a process were to take place, because a process consists in passing through intermediate states. So Knuuttila takes Physics V1 as a "metaphysically revised classification of changes" which is later than the other passages.[53]

For the most part, I agree with this interpretation. However, I do not think that one should place Physics V1 above the other passages because there *is* a plausible way of talking about coming-to-be and perishing as processes. In my opinion the differences between Physics V1 and the other passages are mostly terminological. It seems to me that according to the terminology of Physics V1 γένεσις and φθορά are exactly analogous to discontinuous changes in objects as described in 2.3.2.1. The only difference is that they are the discontinuous changes from non-existence to existence or vice-versa. Let us call this use γένεσις[1] and φθορά[1]. I think that in the other passages Aristotle uses the key terms as referring to the processes on which γένεσις[1] and φθορά[1] depend. So in the terminology of the other passages the γένεσις of an object is a process which takes place before the object exists. At any instant which falls within this process the object does not exist yet. The limiting instant at the end of the process is the first instant of its existence. Perishing, φθορά, however, is a process in which the object decays while still existing. Only the limiting instant at the end of the process is the first instant of its non-existence. Thus, coming-to-be and perishing in this sense are processes but they are not processes *between* existence and non-existence. Rather, existence is the end-term of the process of coming-to-be, and non-existence is the end-term of the process of perishing. We might call this use γένεσις[2] and φθορά[2]. As a result, then, γένεσις[1] and φθορά[1] are special kinds of discontinuous change (namely between existence and non-existence), while γένεσις[2] and φθορά[2] are the processes on which γένεσις[1] and φθορά[1] depend.

According to this view, what was said about the limiting instants of κίνησις applies to γένεσις[2] and φθορά[2], simply because γένεσις[2] and φθορά[2] *are* kinds of κίνησις. So I suggest that there are two different uses of γένεσις and φθορά in Aristotle but that both the uses of γένεσις and φθορά have their definite place in Aristotle's treatment of the moment of change. Under this interpretation, objects would usually have a first instant of existence, but no last instant of existence (while there is a first instant of non-existence). As will be seen in ch. I,3, this is the typical view of the Middle Ages.

2.3.3. An attempt to reconstruct the proof in Phys.235b17/28
We are so familiar with dense time that we may hardly find it necessary to prove the statement that something is in the target state at the limiting instant at the end of a process. The statement is very plausible indeed, and I could rely on this plausibility when presenting Aristotle's position in the preceding paragraphs. For Aristotle it was not so easy. He was not facing time-atomists as merely theoretical opponents. So he needed a more abstract proof of his position than the one given above. We may, therefore, expect to

find such a proof somewhere in Physics VI. In my view, it is contained in
235b17/28.

2.3.3.1. The proof in Phys. 235b17/28
235b17/28 reads as follows:

(i) τὸ μεταβεβληκὸς ἔσται ἐν ᾧ μεταβέβληκεν [...]
(ii) ἐπεὶ γὰρ
(a) ἐξ οὗ μεταβέβληκεν ἀπολέλοιπεν
(b) ἀνάγκη δ'εἶναί που
(c) ἢ ἐν τούτῳ [=B] ἢ ἐν ἄλλῳ ἔσται
(iii) εἰ μὲν οὖν ἐν ἄλλῳ (οἷον ἐν τῷ Γ), τὸ εἰς τὸ Β μεταβεβληκὸς πάλιν ἐκ τοῦ Γ
μεταβάλλει εἰς τῷ Β
(iv) οὐ γὰρ ἦν ἐχόμενον τὸ Β, ἡ δὲ μεταβολὴ συνεχής.
(v) ὥστε τὸ μεταβεβληκός, ὅτε μεταβέβληκεν, μεταβάλλει εἰς ὃ μεταβέβληκεν.
(vi) τοῦτο δ' ἀδύνατον.
(vii) ἀνάγκη ἄρα τὸ μεταβεβληκὸς εἶναι ἐν τούτῳ εἰς ὃ μεταβέβληκεν.
(viii) φανερόν οὖν ὅτι καὶ τὸ γεγονός, ὅτε γέγονεν, ἔσται...

[i] ...that which has changed must be in that to which it has changed...
[ii] For,
[a] since it has left that from which it has changed
[b] and must be somewhere
[c] it must be either in that to which it has changed or in something else.
[iii] If, then, that which has changed to B is in something other than B, say C, it
must again be changing from C to B;
[iv] for B was not assumed to be contiguous, and change is continuous.
[v] Thus we have the result that the thing that has changed, at the moment when it
has changed, is changing to that to which it has changed,
[vi] which is impossible:
[vii] that which has changed, therefore, must be in that to which it has changed.
[viii] So it is evident likewise that that which has come to be, at the moment when it
has come to be, will *be*...

The logical structure of the passage is a disjunctive syllogism *modo tollendo
ponente* (either p or q is the case; p is not the case, therefore q).[54] In order to
show that p is not the case, Aristotle conducts an indirect proof. In (i) the
aim of the proof is stated. In (ii) it is shown that if (a) and (b) are assumed
then (c) all possibilities except the aim of the proof and a statement opposed
to it are excluded. In (iii) a statement contrary to the aim of the proof is
assumed, and from it a conclusion is drawn which in (v) emerges as self-
contradictory. (iii) is given a slightly obscure motivation in (iv). (vi) says that
(iii) cannot be true, since it has been shown to be self-contradictory in (v).
Therefore the statement which was to be proved must be true, which is
repeated once again as a 'QED' in (vii). (viii) adds a concrete example of this
rather abstract statement.

The content of the proof is not as transparent as its structure (as happens quite often in the 'Physics'). There is no certainty to be reached as to what is meant here. However, the following interpretation seems to be rather attractive:

(i) Aim of the proof: *a* is in the target state at the end of a process.
(ii) If, at the limiting instant at the end of a process, it is
(a) not in the initial state any more
(b) but has to be in some state of the process
(c) then it is either in the target state or in some intermediate state
(iii) If we assume that it is in one of the intermediate states
then there is a period (beginning at the limiting instant) during which it gets from the intermediate state into the target state.
(iv) Thus, there would be a period between *a*'s being in the intermediate state and *a*'s being in the target state (=B); but the target state immediately abuts the process.
(v) Therefore, that which has completed a process (=*a*), and is therefore in the target state, is not in the target state.
(vi) This is impossible.
(vii) Therefore, at the limiting instant at the end of a process, the target state has already been reached.

2.3.3.2. Attempt at a reconstruction

It is systematically rather interesting whether this proof can convince us. It seems to me that Aristotle's idea here is indeed rather elegant and convincing:

If we assume that, at the limiting instant, the target state has not yet been reached, then there is an environment abutting the limiting instant (towards the future) such that at any instant of this environment the target state has still not been reached (*natura non facit saltus*). But it is the very characteristic of the limiting instant at the end of a process that at least immediately *after* it the target state has been reached, so that there is no environment abutting the limiting instant (towards the future) such that at any instant of this environment the target state has still not been reached. Therefore it is self-contradictory to claim that at the limiting instant the target state has not been reached. If it is not the case that the target state has not been reached at the limiting instant, it must be the case that it has been reached (since at every instant, some state obtains). This is why the target state has been reached at the limiting instant at the end of the process.

It is, however, not quite clear yet exactly how density of time influences the result (it is clear, though, that this can only happen in (iii)). It is also not clear yet whether the argument survives formal reconstruction. In my view, a formal reconstruction of the argument is possible and the argument holds. However, the reconstruction is all but trivial. It is therefore rendered in a separate text, appendix B at the end of the book.

2.3.3.3. Comments on the proof and its reconstruction

Two more comments on the reconstruction of the proof 235b19/26 are necessary:

(1) Analogously to this proof it can be demonstrated that the initial state still obtains at the limiting instant at the beginning of a process:

If we assume that, at the limiting instant, the initial state has been left, then there is an environment abutting the limiting instant (towards the past) such that at any instant of this environment the initial state has already been left (*natura non facit saltus*). But it is the very characteristic of a limiting instant at the beginning of a process that at least immediately *before* it the initial state has not been left yet, so that there is no environment abutting the limiting instant (towards the past) such that at any instant of this environment the initial state has already been left. Therefore it is self-contradictory to claim that at the limiting instant the initial state has been left. If it is not the case that the initial state has been left at the limiting instant, it must be the case that it still obtains (since at every instant, some state obtains). This is why the initial state still obtains at the limiting instant at the beginning of the process.

Aristotle does not try to demonstrate this.[55] In fact, he rather neglects the limiting instant at the beginning of a process. However, it may be concluded indirectly that Aristotle would have accepted the result of this proof, because in 236a15 he denies the existence of a 'beginning of a process' (ἀρχή μεταβολῆς). It will be shown in the next section that this claim can make sense, exaggerated though it may seem.

(2) Aristotle is careful to state explicitly as an assumption in 235b20 that an object must be assigned a position in space at every instant of its existence (...εἴπερ ἀνάγκη τὸ μεταβεβληκὸς εἶναι που ἢ ἔν τινι).

This assumption of at least one indispensable instantaneous property of a physical object is all the more interesting because we cannot be sure if Plato would have made it as well.

2.4. πρῶτον AND ἐν ᾧ πρώτῳ

2.4.1. *The temporal meaning of* πρῶτον

If at the limiting instant between a period throughout which *a* is becoming white and a period throughout which *a* is white, *a* is white, then there can be no doubt that the limiting instant is the *earliest* instant at which *a* is white, the first instant according to temporal order within a certain environment. Thus Sorabji is right in saying about Aristotle's description of the moment of change at the end of a process:

...there is a first instant of being in the terminal state after a process of transition (and hence, presumably, no last instant of not being in that state)[56].

Aristotle himself says in 263a24 that at the limiting instant something is πρῶτον, *first*, in the target state. In 235b7 an instant is mentioned at which something "can first be said to be changed"[57] (ὅτε πρῶτον μεταβέβληκεν). In addition to that, there are no less than four elaborate demonstrations in Physics VI 4 and 5 in which some mention is made of an ἐν ᾧ πρώτῳ, of "the first time in which" something happens or has happened, namely of the first time in which something can be said to be changed, or in which it is in motion or stopping (236b19/32, 238b25/239a8, 235b32/236a5,236a7/27). Finally, πρῶτον may be regarded as the logical superlative of the comparative πρότερον. Frequently πρότερον simply means 'earlier', for example in the definition of time, the main result of the essay on time in Physics IV 10-14, which says that χρόνος[58] is the "number of motion with respect to earlier and later" (πρότερον καί ὕστερον).

One might therefore be tempted to assume the equation "ἐν ᾧ πρώτῳ = *earliest instant*" to be true. However there are two good reasons not to do so. The first reason to doubt this equation is that for most of the time Aristotle is not talking about instants at all when he uses the phrase ἐν ᾧ πρώτῳ. The second reason is that πρῶτον possibly does not mean 'earliest' in this phrase. At least the following three observations support the idea that Aristotle is generally not talking about instants when using the phrase ἐν ᾧ πρώτῳ (the idea that πρῶτον does not even mean 'earliest' will be discussed in detail in 2.4.2.):

(a) Two of the four demonstrations in Physics VI mentioned above show that the ἐν ᾧ πρώτῳ cannot always be meant to be an instant. They deal with (and search for) the first time in which something is in motion or is changing (236b19/32); and with the first time in which something is stopping, while 'stopping' is clearly the process of coming to a halt by slowing down (238b25/239a8). The result that no such 'first time' is found would be compatible with the idea that 'first time' always means 'earliest instant'. But in order to show this within the framework of his theory,

Aristotle would simply have to restate his view that there is in any case no instant at which something is in motion or in the process of coming to a halt; consequently, *a fortiori* there is no earliest instant at which something is in motion etc. However, this argument does not appear in the demonstrations at all. They are all about periods and of a very different structure.

(b) In several places, Aristotle's reason for saying that in a certain case there is no ἐν ᾧ πρώτῳ is that a period is infinitely divisible.[59] If the ἐν ᾧ πρώτῳ were by definition an instant, this would not make any sense.

(c) Aristotle insists on there being neither a 'firstote period' nor a 'first size', since everything continuous is divisible; and he links this with the statement that (in most cases) there is no ἐν ᾧ πρώτῳ:

237b21/22 πᾶν γὰρ μέγεθος καὶ πᾶς χρόνος ἀεὶ διαιρετά.
ὥστ᾽ ἐν ᾧ ἂν ᾖ, οὐκ ἂν εἴη ὡς πρώτῳ.

...all magnitudes and all periods of time are always divisible. Consequently, whatever a thing may be in, it is not in it < first > .

If the ἐν ᾧ πρώτῳ were by definition an instant, this would not make any sense.

All that has been said so far would be compatible with the idea that a 'first time' is meant here to be an earliest time, but not necessarily an instant but possibly also a period. Thus, the equation stated above might be modified to "ἐν ᾧ πρώτῳ = earliest time", a time being a period *or* an instant.

This equation already means some progress for the interpretation of the text, since it accounts for the fact that no period which is a first time is in fact to be found. This can be seen by reflecting upon what an 'earliest period' could be: an earliest period would have to be the irreducibly first period of a series of periods contained in a phase throughout which something is the case. But for such a thing to exist, there would have to be some reason to view a phase as being naturally divided into particular subperiods. Of course, someone might arbitrarily divide up the phase and call the first element of the resulting division 'No1', the one abutting it 'No2' etc. But he will meet with problems if his 'period No1' can be divided again, for in that case, he will have to do some relabelling, because he would really only be entitled to call the first half of the alleged 'No1' the 'real No1', the second half would be the 'real No2' etc. Unfortunately, the relief of having found the 'real No1' will not last for long, when it becomes apparent that it is itself divisible again. Only a time-atomist can hope to find the best possible resolution of the phase, which would have to be preferred to any other division.

There is no preferable *division*[60] of a period if, as Aristotle thinks, periods are infinitely divisible; so there is then no hope of finding the 'real No1' (of course, there is a first element relative to every division). The same would be true of a 'first distance' which would be the distance covered during the absolutely earliest section of a process; a thing which does not exist. This rather convincing argument seems indeed to be at the core of the long and elaborate passages in Phys. VI5, 236a27/b19 and VI6, 236b32-237b22. The conclusion is clear enough:

239a21/22 χρόνος δ' οὐκ ἔστι πρῶτος οὐδὲ μέγεθος οὐδ' ὅλως συνεχὲς οὐδέν. ἅπαν γὰρ εἰς ἄπειρα μεριστόν.

...there is no <first> time - nor magnitude nor in fact anything continuous; for everything continuous is divisible into an infinite number of parts.

Only a time-atom could be an 'earliest period' at which something is the case. Nevertheless, there are other passages in which by ἐν ᾧ πρώτῳ nothing 'earliest' seems to be meant.

2.4.2. The hierarchic meaning of πρῶτον

As we have seen, πρῶτον in Aristotle's Physics does sometimes mean 'earliest' or 'first with respect to temporal order'. But, as I want to show now, this is not the only use of this word and it is not the most important use of it in connection with the moment of change. πρῶτον has a second meaning which suggests a translation such as 'first with respect to hierarchic order', 'immediate', 'prime', 'primary' or even 'principal'. It is (extensionally) true that the time at which, according to Aristotle, a process has πρῶτον been completed (and which he also calls τὸ ἐν ᾧ πρώτῳ) is the earliest instant at which the process is over. But this is not what Aristotle is principally interested in when he describes the limiting instant at the end of a process in the relevant passages of Physics VI; rather, he is interested in basing the temporal meaning of πρῶτον, belonging in the realm of physics, on a hierarchic meaning of the word belonging in the realm of metaphysics.

This can be inferred from the fact that the structure common to the four decisive demonstrations has nothing to do with an 'earliest' time; in this context Aristotle explicitly defines πρῶτον as meaning something totally different (235b32). So far, this has been clearly remarked upon by Hans Wagner and by Ross[61] and has often been recognized correctly by Hardie and Gaye in their translation. The following paragraphs may be viewed as a systematic elaboration of what they saw, especially about what Wagner says in his commentary at the end of his translation of the 'Physics' into German.[62] It is difficult to tell exactly which conditions a time has to meet in order to be called ἐν ᾧ πρώτῳ in a certain respect when πρῶτον is used in its hierarchic meaning. Frequently, one has to reconstruct these conditions indirectly from the structure of the demonstrations in which the word ἐν ᾧ πρώτῳ occurs. However, the result is clear enough in order to show that Aristotle calls the limiting instant at the end of a process πρῶτον in the hierarchic sense, and why.

2.4.2.1. Why an hierarchic ordering of times might make sense
Putting times into an hierarchic order with respect to what is the case at them might look very strange at first sight: Why do we need a relation of 'being superior' when we already have a relation of being earlier/later? However, Aristotle has two good reasons for ordering times hierarchically:

(1) Terminologically, this enables him to link his analysis of processes with other parts of his metaphysics.

(2) It enables him to state a relation between periods where one period is contained in another, such that the terms 'earlier' and 'later' can, intuitively, not be applied.

2.4.2.2. The definition of πρῶτον in 235b33
The hierarchic definition of πρῶτον, which Aristotle gives (almost perfectly hidden in a demonstration) in 235b33, is much more general than the context of Physics VI requires:

λέγω δὲ πρῶτον ὃ μὴ τῷ ἕτερόν τι αὐτοῦ εἶναι τοιοῦτόν ἐστιν

...by 'primary' I mean a thing's being such-and-such not because < of something else's > being such and such.[63]

According to this, an object a is πρῶτον (prime) with respect to a property F (τοιοῦτόν εἶναι), iff there is no x different from a (ἕτερόν) which is F as well, such that a is F only because (τῷ) x is F.

For a full characterization of πρῶτον, the following explanatory features may be added:

(1) Iff there is such an x, then this x is πρότερον to a with respect to F, πρότερον meaning 'superior'. This is why in 236a4 Aristotle achieves a *reductio ad absurdum* by deducing from the assumption that something πρώτου πρότερον exists, i.e. an item superior to the highest item in an hierarchic order.

(2) If a is prime with respect to F, then a has the property F independently of whether there is an x which is F, too (such that it might be superior to a). Thus, with respect to being F, a is independent.

(3) If there is an x which is superior to a with respect to F, then a is dependent on this x with respect to being F.

(4) If a is prime with respect to F then there is no x which is superior to a with respect to F. But a does not have to be superior with respect to F to all other objects which are F (it usually *is* superior to some of them; but this is

not necessary). Thus, there can be several different objects which are prime with respect to F.

We can express this more precisely in terms of predicate logic: The extension of a predicate (let us call it P) may have prime elements. Those would be such elements of P for which there is no element of P which is superior to them (in the sense stated in (2)) with respect to P. Of course, it might happen that an extension of a predicate does not contain any prime element at all.

2.4.2.3. πρῶτον κινοῦν and οὐσία

§1 Aristotle applies his concept of the prime object with respect to a property in two very prominent places: (a) he says that an οὐσία is a πρώτως ὄν (Met. 1028a30). (b) He claims, in Met.XII, that a πρῶτον κινοῦν exists.[64] In both cases, his use of πρῶτον exactly corresponds to the definition in Phys. 235b33:

§2 A πρῶτον κινοῦν is a prime object with respect to the property of moving something: A πρῶτον κινοῦν does not move something because it is moved by something else; there is nothing else which would be superior to it with respect to this property. A πρῶτον κινοῦν moves something independently of whether anything else moves anything. As far as its moving something is concerned, it is independent. The set of objects which are superior to an object which moves something only 'mediately' always includes a πρῶτον κινοῦν. But this does not mean that there is only one πρῶτον κινοῦν: the strange passage in Met XII in which Aristotle calculates that there must be fifty-five prime movers[65] (although the main argument of this Met. XII seems to be in favour of monotheism) is compatible with the definition of πρῶτον in Phys. 235b33.[66]

§3 A πρώτως ὄν is a prime object with respect to the property of existence (for well-known reasons, this property is rather out of fashion today): it exists independently of something else. There is no other object which is superior to it with respect to this property. As far as its existence is concerned, it is independent. The οὐσία is superior to its accidentals with respect to existence; they are, on the other hand, dependent on it: they only exist as the properties of an οὐσία. They can only be there because there is the οὐσία on which they are 'based'. However, there must not necessarily be only one οὐσία: The characterization of it as πρώτως ὄν leaves the question open how many substances there are.

2.4.2.4. The temporal ἐν ᾧ πρώτῳ as part of a hierarchy

The ἐν ᾧ πρώτῳ, the 'prime time' for something being the case, can be regarded as the prime element of a temporal statement.[67] The interesting question about it now becomes: which are the conditions an element from the extension of a temporal statement has to meet in order to be a prime element of this extension?

Aristotle adds an indirect example to his abstract definition of πρῶτον with respect to times. For in 236b19/25 the prime, or immediate, time at which something is the case is contrasted with a time at which something is only the case with respect to something else (καθ' ἕτερον), or mediately:

236b19/25

Ἐπεὶ δὲ τὸ μεταβάλλον ἅπαν ἐν χρόνῳ μεταβάλλει,
λέγεται δ' ἐν χρόνῳ μεταβάλλειν
[1] καὶ ὡς ἐν πρώτῳ
[2] καὶ ὡς καθ' ἕτερον
(οἷον ἐν τῷ ἐνιαυτῷ ὅτι ἐν τῇ ἡμέρᾳ μεταβάλλει),
ἐν ᾧ πρώτῳ χρόνῳ μεταβάλλει τὸ μεταβάλλον,
ἐν ὁτῳοῦν ἀνάγκη τούτου μεταβάλλειν.

Since everything that changes changes in a period
and since we talk of 'changing in a period' both as
[1] [changing] 'in it first', and as
[2] [changing in it] 'with respect to something else'
(e.g. 'in a [certain] year', because it changes on a [certain] day [of the year]),
that which changes in a[n allegedly existent] first period,
must be changing in everything that belongs to it.[68]

It is important for Aristotle to state here that the the claim that something is the case during a period can be made with differing 'force'. It is possible to say that something might be the case although it is not the case throughout the period but only for part of it. Again, this is a differentiation not to be found in Plato. Moreover, it is the very differentiation we have already encountered under another name as the distinction between 'dependent' and 'independent now' (πρῶτον νῦν and νῦν καθ' ἕτερον).[69]

The example in 236b19/25 concerns an alteration which takes exactly one day of a year. Clearly, the alteration does take place during that year. The year is, thus, an element of the extension of the predicate "...is a time in which an alteration takes place". But the *day* during which the alteration 'really' takes place, and which is, of course, also contained in the extension of this predicate, is superior to the year. The year is therefore certainly not a prime element of this extension. It is not quite clear, though, whether one would be entitled to conclude reversely that the day is.

The example already shows that a period c can only be prime element of the extension of a temporal statement P, if it does not contain any 'redundant' subperiods. To be more precise, no division of c might exist such that (at least) one element of the division satisfies P but another one does not. For if the opposite were the case, then that subperiod of c which satisfies P would obviously be superior to c (be it or be it not itself an ἐν ᾧ πρώτῳ). Once one is used to the terminology, this is rather intuitive: it is indeed plausible to say that the year in the example is a year during which an alteration takes place *just because* it contains a day during which an alteration takes place. It is also plausible to say that the year is only mediately a time during which an alteration takes place, and is, in this respect, dependent on the special day it contains.

2.4.2.5. *The structure of the πρῶτον-demonstrations in Physics VI*

§1 We now know enough about Aristotle's hierarchic ordering of times to be able to look closely at the four 'πρῶτον'-demonstrations in Physics VI, where he applies this idea. Two of these demonstrations work with the statement μεταβέβληκεν ("*a* can be said to be changed") in two different senses, between which Aristotle clearly and explicitly differentiates in 236a7/15. The two other demonstrations are about the statements κινεῖται ("*a* is moving") and ἵσταται ("*a* is stopping"):

D1) 236b25/32 κινεῖται
D2) 238b31/36 ἵσταται
D3) 236a15/27 μεταβέβληκεν 1st case
D4) 235b32/236a4 μεταβέβληκεν 2nd case

As usual, we will regard statements as predicates. In doing so, it is possible to state precisely which conditions a time must meet in order to be prime time of the statement (i.e. prime element of the extension of this predicate).

§2 All four demonstrations are indirect proofs. The aim of the proof is in all four cases to show that the following, stated in our terminology, is true:

> If a period c is a prime element of the extension of P, then every subperiod of c must satisfy P as well; i.e. it must be true that *-P(c).

In order to show this, the two remaining possible cases are excluded first:

(a) No subperiod of c satisfies P. Consequently, Aristotle says, c cannot possibly satisfy P either. If c is no element of the extension of P, it is, of course, no prime element of it either.

(b) Not all subperiods of c satisfy P, only some do. Those subperiods of c which do not satisfy P are redundant (as we have seen in the example of the year and the day); therefore a subperiod of c which does satisfy P is superior to c with respect to P, such that c cannot be prime element of the extension of P.

From (a) we see that Aristotle's proof strategy has to be restricted to statements of peculiar content, if it is to make sense. For example, an hour may satisfy the predicate "...is a time during which M + N get from Münster to Osnabrück" and this might in fact take an hour; but the first and the second half of this hour do not satisfy the predicate. Thus, from the fact that no subperiod of a period satisfies a predicate it may not be concluded that the period itself does not satisfy it either.[70]

For a different context (Met.Θ6), Michael-Thomas Liske has pointed out that when the scope of an Aristotelian claim is concerned one has to be careful whether Aristotle is using a verb 'transitively' or 'intransitively'. The transitive use of 'to go' would, for example, be 'to go from A to B', while for the intransitive use starting and target position do not matter.[71] With this distinction in mind, it is easy to say how the scope of Aristotle's demonstrations D1) to D4) must be restricted: they only work for statements in which the verb is meant intransitively - and we may thus assume that this is the way the verbs are meant there.

§3 Each of the demonstrations proves no more than that a prime time must have the following conditional property: *if* it is divisible, the same which is true for the whole must be true for all its parts. However, in D2) and D3), Aristotle states immediately or almost immediately afterwards that for the case considered there is simply no prime time.[72] In D4) he states that there is no prime *period*.[73] Since only periods are divisible, but instants are not, the question arises as to why he does not examine instants separately from periods. In addition to that, there is the question, why, after proving the conditional statement, Aristotle immediately continues with the unconditional statement that there is no prime time at all for the case considered. So it is necessary to reconstruct the tacit assumptions which might justify this step.

It is clearly apparent why it is sufficient to examine periods for D1) within the framework of the 'Physics': instants cannot satisfy the statement "*a* is moving" anyway. That it is also sufficient to examine periods for D2) follows from the fact that it is sufficient to examine them for D1). Aristotle explicitly points out that according to his terminology something which is stopping (ἵσταται) is (while slowing down) still moving (once more, Aristotle's terminology is diametrically opposed to Plato's in the 'Parmenides'):[74]

238b24/28 τὸ ἱστάμενον, ὅτε ἵσταται, κινεῖσθαι [...] φανερὸν ὅτι καὶ ἐν χρόνῳ ἵστασθαι ἀνάγκη

that which is coming to a stand, when it is coming to a stand, must be in motion. [...] From this it evidently follows that coming to a stand must occupy a period of time.

If every case of stopping is a case of moving, but moving is not possible at instants, then neither is stopping. This is why instants do not matter for the examination of the statement ἵσταται.

§4 A demonstration such as D1) to D4) would be sufficient to show that there is no prime period in the case considered, if the following were true:

If all subperiods of c statisfy P (i.e. if *-P(c) is true), the only option left open, then c *clearly* cannot be a prime element of the extension of P.

This is because such a demonstration would be a *reductio ad absurdum*: the only case which remains possible according to it would be a case in which c *obviously* cannot be a prime element of the extension of P. This would be intuitively plausible, if *every subperiod of a period were superior to the period if what is true for the period is true for the subperiod*, too. For the following reasons, it is very probable that this is indeed what Aristotle thought:

(1) Aristotle says that there is no ἐν ᾧ πρώτῳ with respect to κινεῖται (238b36). He clearly means the intransitive use of the verb here, otherwise he could not say in D1) (vgl. 236b25/32):

εἰ μὲν οὖν ἐν μηδετέρῳ κινεῖται ἠρεμοίη ἄν ἐν τῷ παντί

...if it is motion in neither of the two parts, it will be at rest in the whole...

In every subperiod of a period throughout which *a* is moving, *a* is moving, too. Aristotle denies the existence of an ἐν ᾧ πρώτῳ in this case, and at the same time *-P(c) is true. This also answers the question of whether in the example of the day and the year the day is a prime time: it is not, although the day is superior to the year with respect to the statement μεταβάλλει. There is no prime time for this statement, for μεταβάλλει and κινεῖται are used interchangeably in 236b19/32.

(2) Aristotle gives the following reason for his claim that there is no ἐν ᾧ πρώτῳ of rest: there is no ἐν ᾧ πρώτῳ of motion, because motion and rest are only possible during periods.[75] Every subperiod of a period of *a*'s uninterrupted rest is a period of rest, too. Hence Aristotle again denies the existence of an ἐν ᾧ πρώτῳ for a case in which *-P(c) is true.

(3) Aristotle gives as a reason for there being no ἐν ᾧ πρώτῳ for the cases mentioned in (1) and (2) the explanation that every period is divisible.

All this makes sense only if a period c for which *-P(c) is true, *obviously* cannot be a prime time of the extension of P, since all its subperiods must be regarded as superior to c.

§5 The impression we have gained step by step of the conditions which a time must meet in order to be a prime time of the extension of a predicate should be that these conditions are rather unfair for periods:

> If a time z is to be prime time of the extension of P, at least the following must be true:
> (i) z satisfies P.
> (ii) There is no part of z which does not satisfy P (if there were, there would have to be another part of z which does satisfy P in order for z to satify P, but this other part of z would then be superior to z with respect to P).
> (iii) There is no part of z which satisfies P (if there were, the part would be superior to z with respect to P).

A period which can be divided up into parts will never be able to fulfil all of these requirements at once. For in the case of divisible periods (iii) is incompatible with *-P(c), but (ii) implies *-P(c). Aristotle conceives every period to be divisible into parts. So he cannot allow any extended ἐν ᾧ πρώτῳ: *no period can ever be a prime time*. For a time-atomist, things would look different, of course, since for a time atom, (ii) and (iii) are compatible: time atoms have no parts anyway. Thus, a time atom can fulfill (i) to (iii). Again, Aristotle puts it in a nutshell, while discussing his example ἴσταται:

239a8 ἐπεὶ οὖν χρόνος ἐστίν ἐν ᾧ πρώτῳ ἴσταται, καὶ οὐκ ἄτομον, ἅπας δὲ χρόνος εἰς ἄπειρα μεριστός, οὐκ ἔσται ἐν ᾧ πρώτῳ ἴσταται.

Since, then, that in which primarily a thing is coming to a stand must be [i.e. would have to be] a period of time and not something indivisible, and since all time is infinitely divisible, there < will not > be anything in which primarily it is coming to a stand.

Sometimes, a paradoxical formulation is the clearest expression of a thought possible.

2.4.2.6. *perfective statements:* μεταβέβληκεν[1] *and* μεταβέβληκεν[2]
§1 In 236a7-15 Aristotle twice applies his proof strategy to the (grammatically) perfective statement μεταβέβληκεν for which he clearly distinguishes two different senses:

λέγεται δὲ τὸ ἐν ᾧ πρώτῳ μεταβέβληκε διχῶς,
τὸ μὲν ἐν ᾧ πρώτῳ ἐπετελέσθη ἡ μεταβολή
(τότε γὰρ ἀληθὲς εἰπεῖν ὅτι μεταβέβληκεν),
τὸ δ᾽ ἐν ᾧ πρώτῳ ἤρξατο μεταβάλλειν.
τὸ μὲν οὖν κατὰ τὸ τέλος τῆς μεταβολῆς πρῶτον λεγόμενον
ὑπάρχει τε καὶ ἔστιν
(ἐνδέχεται γὰρ ἐπιτελεσθῆναι μεταβολὴν
καὶ ἔστι μεταβολῆς τέλος,
ὃ δὴ καὶ δέδεικται ἀδιαίρετον ὂν διὰ τὸ πέρας εἶναι)
τὸ δὲ κατὰ τὴν ἀρχὴν ὅλως οὐκ ἔστιν.
οὐ γὰρ ἔστιν ἀρχὴ μεταβολῆς,
οὐδ᾽ ἐν ᾧ πρώτῳ τοῦ χρόνου μετέβαλλεν.

There are two ways of using the phrase "the first [time] in which something can be said to be changed":
a) On the one hand [this phrase may denote] "the first [time] in which a change can be said to be accomplished" (for then [something] can truly be said to be changed);
b) on the other hand [this phrase may denote] "the first [time] in which something began to change".
Now that which we call 'first' with respect to the *end* of a process indeed exists.
(a process may end and then there is the end of a process,
of which it has been shown that it is indivisible because of being a [mere] boundary).
But with respect to the *beginning* of a process, such a thing does not exist at all.
For there is no beginning of a process,
no first [time] of a period in which something was changing.[76]

So μεταβέβληκεν is in one sense synonymous with ἤρξατο μεταβάλλειν; in another sense it is synonymous with ἐπετελέσθη ἡ μεταβολή. Both explanatory phrases contain verbs in the aorist. This is important in order to see which meaning of the perfective verb Aristotle stresses here: μεταβέβληκεν is not to be viewed as a past tense but rather as an expression of the perfective aspect (this is the reason for the somewhat complicated translation given above: anything more simple would have had to contain a past tense).[77] If we regard both kinds of μεταβέβληκεν as statement-predicates, their semantics can be roughly rendered so:

A time satisfies μεταβέβληκεν[1] iff it is a time in which a process has its beginning, since a subprocess starting from the initial state of the overall process is completed in it.

A time satisfies μεταβέβληκεν[2] iff it is a time in which a completion of the overall process takes place.

§2 μεταβέβληκεν[1] cannot be satisfied by an instant: it is not possible that a subprocess can *be* complet*ed* at an instant: at an instant it can only be in the state of having been completed. Thus, in this sense no process can have its beginning at an instant. The same applies to the limiting instant at the beginning of a process: it is the last instant at which the initial state still obtains and at which the process has not yet begun. Therefore, only a period can possibly be an ἐν ᾧ πρώτῳ for μεταβέβληκεν[1].[78] However, we already know that no period can ever be an ἐν ᾧ πρώτῳ. Aristotle demonstrates this by applying his (by now well-known) proof strategy in D3).[79] Since instants do not satisfy μεταβέβληκεν[1] this entitles him to claim that there is no prime time for μεταβέβληκεν[1] at all because there is no prime period for it.

§3 In connection with periods, the result for μεταβέβληκεν[2] is the same as for μεταβέβληκεν[1]. Aristotle confirms this reflection by applying his proof strategy again in D4) which is concerned with μεταβέβληκεν[2].[80] However, as regards μεταβέβληκεν[2], the search for an ἐν ᾧ πρώτῳ is not yet over after periods have been examined. This is because μεταβέβληκεν[2] can also be satisfied by instants. In fact, an instant satisfies μεταβέβληκεν[2] iff it is the limiting instant at the end of a process. Since an instant as a mere boundary without any extension has no parts, it can, without difficulty fulfil conditions (i) to (iii) of 2.4.2.5.§4, which a divisible period could not meet. We can now understand why Aristotle calls the limiting instant at the end of a process ἐν ᾧ πρώτῳ of μεταβέβληκεν[2]; and why it is a sufficient reason for this when he points out that, due to being a mere boundary, it is indivisible (ἀδιαίρετον διὰ τὸ πέρας εἶναι).

§4 The result of our examination is: it is true that the limiting instant at the end of a process is the first instant of the target state according to temporal order; this is exactly why the process comes to an end there: before it, the target state has not yet been reached and from this instant on, the target state has already been reached. But when Aristotle says that the limiting instant is an ἐν ᾧ πρώτῳ μεταβέβληκεν, then he says something totally different and much more complicated than that. The limiting instant is declared to be a prime time according to hierarchic ordering, an assertion which is very typical of his thinking. Wagner sees this clearly when commenting 235b32/236a7:

Section 235b32-236a7 presents us with an (indirect) proof concerning the completion of the process. The claim made here is an answer to the question: do we have to conceive the completion of the process as something extended in time or rather as an instant? The answer is: the immediate time of the completion of the process can only be an instant. [...] πρώτον means here: 'in the original, direct, immediate sense' [...]: a life may have come to an end on the 24th of January, 1900 at 10:15 sharp. Since the eleventh hour before noon of the 24th of January, 1900 is a part of the 24th of January, 1900, a part of January 1900, and January 1900 a part of the year 1900, one may also say that this life came to an end on the 24th of January, 1900 or in January 1900. But the latter times are not the immediate time. The non-immediate times of the completion of a process are periods (with duration and divisibility); the immediate time, however, is, according to the claim, necessarily an instant.[81]

2.4.2.7. *The hierarchic meaning of* πρῶτον - *a summary*

That Aristotle's opinion, which Wagner and Ross correctly recognize in the example, is based on a more general theory can be seen by summing up the conditions collected from Physics VI which a time must fulfil in order to be a prime time with respect to a statement P, and the conditions which a time must fulfil in order to be superior to another time with respect to P. The following two more details also have to be taken into account for this, in addition to that which we have already seen earlier:

(1) Intuitively, with respect to μεταβέβληκεν[2], the limiting instant at the end of a process is superior to all periods within which it falls.

(2) Not every instant at which something is the case is a prime time for P, but it obviously only is if it does not fall within a period throughout which something is the case (otherwise, every instant at which a is white, would be a prime time).

If we take this into account, we may sum up:

A time z is, according to Physics VI, a prime element of the extension of a statement P iff
(i) z satisfies P
(ii) There is no (proper) part of z which does not satisfy P.
(iii) There is no (proper) part of z which does satisfy P.
(iv) There is no period c for which holds: *-P(c) and z falls within c.

A time z is superior to a time z_1 with respect to P, iff
(i) z satisfies P and z_1 satisfies P.
(ii) (a) z is a period c and z_1 is a period c_1: $c°c_1$ or $c_1°c$.
  (b) z is a period c and z_1 is an instant t: *-P(c) and t falls within c.

To sum up, the way in which Aristotle places times into an hierarchic order can be seen not only to be comprehensible but also, in Physics VI, to have been worked out with impressive logical rigour.

2.5. κίνησις, ἐνέργεια AND ἐν ᾧ πρώτῳ

2.5.1 κίνησις *and* ἐνέργεια

Aristotle is more interested in processes than in discontinuous changes, and more interested in the limiting instant and the end of the process than in the limiting instant at the beginning of it. The reason for this may well be that the terminological and theoretical background of his treatment of the moment of change is his distinction of κίνησις and ἐνέργεια (roughly: 'process' and 'actualization').[82]

According to Met.Θ6, an ἐνέργεια is, in contrast to a κίνησις, something which can be present and completed at the same time. In that passage, Aristotle is thinking of cases which do not involve a target state: for example thinking about something or being happy. Aristotle's examples in Met.Θ6 are πρᾶξεις, examples of human action, which Aristotle divides into cases of κίνησις and ἐνέργεια. However, the distiction may be extended to any kind of 'happening'.[83]

An ἐνέργεια is a state to which a process leads. So the ἐνέργεια characteristically has an ἐν ᾧ πρώτῳ. The κίνησις leading to the ἐνέργεια has no ἐν ᾧ πρώτῳ, just as remaining within an ἐνέργεια, the ἠρεμία, has none.

Aristotle thus regards the limiting instant of the moment of change at the beginning or the end of a process as being the limit between two qualitatively different happenings, κίνησις and ἐνέργεια. This is another difference between Aristotle and Plato, who interprets the same instant as being the limit between two states which are not qualitatively differentiated but treated equally.

2.5.2 Plotinus' criticism of Aristotle
Aristotle's opinion on the moment of change, as he states it in Physics VI, naturally provokes criticism, since he not only says nothing about the limiting instant at the beginning of a process, but even makes the misleadingly formulated claim that "there is no beginning of a process" (οὐ γὰρ ἔστιν ἀρχὴ μεταβολῆς, 236a14). A reaction to this, which also refers to the distinction between κίνησις and ἐνέργεια, can be found in Plotinus' 'Enneads' (VI,1 §16).[84]

Plotinus distinguishes between walking (βάδισις) as an example of a κίνησις and walking a certain distance (namely a στάδιον). In his view, not walking 'in itself' is incomplete after half of the distance, but only walking *the whole distance* is, where the distance is the 'object' of the walking (τὸ πρᾶγμα οὗ ἐστοχάζετο):

τὸ ἐλλεῖπον οὐ τῆς βαδίσεως οὐδὲ τῆς κινήσεως ἦν, ἀλλὰ τῆς ποσῆς βαδίσεως.

...what was lacking would not belong to walking or movement, but to walking a certain distance.[85]

Plotinus is of the opinion that a κίνησις 'in itself' does not take any time (χρόνος). Only a motion up to a specific target place does. Just as an ἐνέργεια, a κίνησις 'in itself' (and not to a specific target place) may take place in a non-chronos (ἐν τῷ ἀχρόνῳ). An ἀχρόνος, as the context shows, can only be an instant. Covering a certain distance is a property which, according to Plotinus, the motion has only *per accidens* (κατὰ συμβεβηκὸς).

Plotinus sums up Aristotle's opinion as: (1) a motion is infinitely divisible, (2) there is no beginning of the period in which and from which the motion starts, and (3) there is no beginning of the motion itself. Plotinus says that all this is nonsense (namely an ἀλογία).[86]

While (1) is certainly something Aristotle holds, the claim that Aristotle holds (2) is unjustified. However, (2) is natural if one reads (3) in a way which is based on misinterpreting Phys. 236a14 as postulating everlasting motion. This is exactly what Plotinus does (I stated above what I think to be a correct interpretation of the passage):

ὥστε ἐξ ἀπείρου συμβαίνοι ἂν τοῦ χρόνου κεκινῆσθαι τὴν ἄρτι ἀρξαμένην καί αὐτὴν ἄπειρον εἰς τὸ ἀρξάμενον εἶναι

...it would result that the movement which has just begun has been in motion from infinite time, and that movement is infinite in respect of its beginning.

If, Plotinus continues, one assumes that there can be a motion 'in itself', it is perfectly possible to say that motion 'in itself' begins at an instant (...κίνησιν ἦρχθαι ἐν ἀχρόνῳ), while time only passes when it becomes a motion across a certain distance (ὁ δὲ χρόνος τῷ τοσηνδε γεγονέναι). In other passages, says Plotinus, even Aristotle allowed instantaneous change (Plotinus literally quotes Phys. 186a15/16, in order to support this view,[87] a passage which, though not too clear, does show some affinity to such an idea).

How is Plotinus' suggestion to be evaluated? Clearly, he is very conscious of the difference between using verbs transitively and intransitively:[88] what he does is simply to distinguish between a verb taking an object and a verb not taking an object. His view that a motion may begin at an instant is certainly not implausible, although (notwithstanding the Aristotelian terminology Plotinus uses) I think his intution is Platonic rather than Aristotelian here.[89] However the reason he gives for his view is unsatisfactory: the idea of a motion 'in itself' is rather strange; of course, some walking from one place to another has been completed halfway, but this has taken time, and it is an instance of walking from one place to another. In fact every instance of walking is walking from one place to another (this is essential to walking, not just accidental) and that is also why every instance of walking takes time.

Plotinus is right in saying that some walking from A to x has been completed before walking from A to B has been completed; indeed, already then nothing is missing from some walking having taken place, merely from walking the whole distance. Aristotle, however, would not deny this. And

Plotinus himself is wrong in concluding from this that walking from A to x
does not take any time. The getting from A to x does not take place at the
limiting instant. It rather takes place between the limiting instant and any
later instant (in a certain environment), and therefore, during a period of
time.

2.6. ARISTOTLE'S CLASSIFICATION OF THE MOMENT OF CHANGE

2.6.1. The reversal of Plato's terminology

§1 It seems as though Aristotle systematically reverses the terminology of the
digression in Plato's 'Parmenides':

(1) In contrast to Plato's use, in Physics VI the words μεταβολή and
κίνησις refer to the same object, i.e. a process. Thus, while Aristotle has no
fewer than two words for process, he cannot use μεταβολή for an
instantaneous event of switching between states any more.

(2) Stopping is, according to Aristotle, some event which takes place
towards the end of a period of motion. The statement ἵσταται therefore
describes, in contrast to Plato's use, no instantaneous event.

(3) Aristotle characterizes the limiting instant by using perfective
verbforms. This is another difference from Plato who uses the present tense
for this purpose. According to Plato, an object at the limit between κίνησις
and στάσις satisfies the presentic statement μεταβάλλει; at this limit, an
event of changing is present. Aristotle, however, describes the limiting
instant as an instant when a μεταβολή, a temporally extended process, has
just been completed; so what should *be happening* then? In Aristotle's
systematic terminology, this is no more than an analytic truth:

235b7/8 ...ἀνάγκη τὸ μεταβεβληκός ὅτε πρῶτον μεταβέβληκεν εἶναι ἐν ᾧ
μεταβέβληκεν

that which has changed must at the moment when it has first changed be in that to
which it has changed.[90]

That this claim is actually quite informative, can only be seen if one
remembers that Plato, instead of using the words πρῶτον μεταβέβληκεν,
would have said μετα-βάλλει; and that this, according to Aristotle's use of
the words, would be a contradiction.

2.6.2. Why the reversal makes sense: no instantaneous events

What sense, then, does Aristotle's reversal of Plato's terminology make? In
fact, I think this can be seen quite clearly from what has been said so far:
Aristotle's terminology in Physics VI[91] is designed to make the idea of an
instantaneous event at the limiting instant appear as a misuse of language.
The real μεταβολή takes place in a period; it is process, κίνησις, and not

something opposed to process. Trying to describe an instantaneous 'switching' taking place in a 'sudden' without duration with the use of the word μεταβολή must, thus, look very much like an unjustified idealization of everyday language.

This allows an inference as to what Aristotle's classification of the moment of change must have been: in the doctrine of processes he advocates in the 'Physics' there is no room for instantaneous events (and, consequently, no name; you do not have to name what does not exist). Aristotle's events are extended processes and nothing else. The limiting instants at the beginning or end of a process are nothing but boundaries of the process. Nothing happens at them: at the limiting instant at the beginning of the process nothing has happend yet, and at the limiting instant at the end of it nothing is happening any more.

Aristotle can thus simply neglect Plato's premiss that an event of changing at the limiting instant can only take place when neither the old nor the new state obtains: no event of changing takes place at the limiting instant. Therefore, it poses no problem for him that his description of the moment of change for non-comparative properties entails that at the limiting instant either the old or the new state obtains. He need not worry about when an event of changing takes place as all instants are taken by either the old or the new state since, to him, there is no such thing as an event of changing between the old and the new state of a change.

2.6.3. Problems in Aristotle's classification of the moment of change

Aristotle's position is consistent and thoroughly designed. But it is so radical, that one can hardly follow it without coming into conflict with intuition. An example of this is Kretzmann's interpretation of Aristotle's views about the moment of change. Kretzmann sees exactly where Aristotle's oppostion to Plato resides:

> What Aristotle seems concerned to avoid is the analysis of that transition as a change of rest to motion. [...] There is no change of rest to motion or of motion to rest. [...] The instant t_c is simply the [...] limit of the state of rest as well as the [...] limit of the state of motion.[92]

Nonetheless he formulates Aristotle's own position in a peculiar way by writing:

> The acquisition of any changed state takes place instantaneously.[93]

The 'taking place' of an 'acquisition' very strongly suggests an instantaneous event again, where Aristotle does not think there are any. It is obviously rather difficult to abandon the idea of instantaneous events as radically as

Aristotle does. This might indicate that Aristotle solution is too radical to be attractive.

It is also quite questionable to what extent Aristotle succeeds in making discontinuous change dependent on processes. It seems to be especially difficult not to regard discontinuous changes as instantaneous events. A pond is first not frozen and then frozen. It has changed when it *is* frozen. Can this be so, if no event has taken place? "Without an event of changing, nothing will change", Plato said. Aristotle makes it difficult if not impossible to formulate this objection in *his* terminology because of his reversal of Plato's language. But this does not mean that he can actually get rid of the objection.

2.7. SUMMARY

It is not easy to describe Aristotle's views on the moment of change according to the systematic framework of this thesis, if at the same time one wants to do justice to his originality, which often consists of the consequent use of his own very peculiar and highly systematic technical vocabulary comprising the concept of πρῶτον and the distinction between κίνησις and ἐνέργεια as well as the concept of στέρησις and consequently the assessment of rest and motion as comparative properties. This, at least, can however be said:

Aristotle offers a precisely motivated *description* of the moment of change; it is a mixed description, using different systematic options for different cases. We have seen that *for comparative properties he uses the neither/nor-option, while for non-comparative properties he uses the either/or-option*, i.e. a sort of either/or-option which assigns the limiting instant at the beginning of a process to the initial state and the limiting instant at the end of a process to the target state.

Aristotle's *classification* of the moment of change entails the denial of the existence of an instantaneous event at the limiting instant. This offers the chance to avoid a banishment of change from time, even though instants are densely ordered and exhaustively distributed to the obtaining or not obtaining of a non-comparative state: since there is no event of changing anyway, no event of changing needs to be banished from time. If there is no event of changing, then Plato's premiss that an event of changing can only take place when of two opposite states one does not obtain any more and the other does not obtain yet, is of no interest.

Although Aristotle denies an instantaneous event at the limiting instant, the limiting instant has nevertheless a very special role. Aristotle makes this clear for the limiting instant at the end of a process, by ascribing to it the complicated and interesting property of being an ἐν ᾧ πρώτῳ μεταβέβληκεν. He does, however, neglect the limiting instant at the beginning of a process and he does not provide a really thorough discussion of why there is no discontinuous change. This shortcoming is more than balanced by:

- the thoroughness of his reaction to Plato's view, whose terminology he reverses completely,
- his arguing against time atomism
- a treatment of the moment of change within the overall terminological and systematic framework of his philosophy (for example by the hierarchic use of the word πρῶτον and the involvement of the distinction between κίνησις and ἐνέργεια)
- a thorough understanding of the problems of continuity and dense time
- the invention of the distinction between comparative and non-comparative properties.

All this serves his amazingly well-balanced motivation, which, in all its technicality and precision, never loses touch with common sense.

2.8. POSTSCRIPT: PLATO AND ARISTOTLE

Since there are several possible interpretations of the digression in Plato's 'Parmenides', the only thing that can be said with certainty about the relationship between this text and Aristotle's Physics VI is that it is very close. In order to say more, one would have to decide first which interpretation of Plato's text one wants to declare as being Plato's real opinion. As ch. I,1. has shown, the decision is not easy. It would, however, be unsatisfactory to conclude the chapter on Aristotle's opinion on the moment of change without saying anything about its relation to Plato. I will therefore make a suggestion as to how to reconstruct Aristotle's view on Plato's opinion in the 'Parmenides' which is highly speculative and thus perhaps a little unscientific. The suggestion is that Aristotle might have interpreted the digression in the 'Parmenides' as follows:

> "Let's neglect for a moment the terminological differences between Plato and myself concerning the words μεταβολή and κίνησις. Let's also forget for a moment that Plato always worked with states while I am the first philosopher to analyze processes. Then I should say that Plato meant the same by χρόνος as I do: a period. I therefore assume that his strange 'sudden' is meant to be a boundary in time. This is just what I call a 'now': an instant. It's difficult to tell what he means by saying that an object *a* at the sudden neither is F nor is not F. I do not think that he

wanted to violate the law of excluded middle. He just wanted to say that, if t is a 'sudden', then the following is true:

$$\neg F_a(t) \land \neg \text{ non-}F_a(t).$$

This is no violation of the law of excluded middle. For "non-$F_a(t)$" means that a is not F at t but could be. But in fact a is neither F at t, nor could it be. At an instant, Plato thinks, a is neither F nor does have the steresis-property of F.

I agree with him on that as far as *comparative* properties are considered. Thus for his main example, the s-change between rest and motion, I obtain just the same result as he does: at the temporal boundary between a phase of motion and a phase of rest, a is neither in motion nor at rest, for at a temporal boundary nothing could possibly be in motion, but nothing could possibly be at rest either (since rest is the steresis of motion and can only obtain where there could possibly be motion as well).

Plato's solution is all right if, as he thought, no object could ever be in any state at an instant (an exception would have to be his strange instantaneous state of switching, but let's forget about that). But that is wrong. Probably, Plato simply could not imagine that there are good reasons for ascribing some properties to objects at instants, for example the property of being white. But it can be done. Contrary to what Plato thought, the result is that at every instant at which a is G, and G is a *non-comparative* property, a could at least be G. This is why for non-comparative properties, the times at which a is not G are exactly those times at which a has the steresis-property of G. Therefore, for non-comparative properties there is no t for which holds $\neg G_a(t) \land \neg$ non-$G_a(t)$; you only get this result for comparative properties. When non-comparative properties are concerned, Plato's solution is insufficient, since an object *can* have a non-comparative property at an instant."

The possibility of telling such a smooth story is, in my view further support for the opinion that the ontological interpretation Plato-2 together with the logical version C (no banishment of change from time, no violation of the LEM) should be favoured as an interpretation of the digression in the 'Parmenides'. Only this interpretation makes Aristotle's statements on the moment of change appear as constructive criticism, a further stage in a development that Plato had begun.

Combining any other interpretation of Plato's text with Aristotle's views must lead to assuming total discontinuity between the opinions of teacher and pupil on this matter. It could only amount to something like: "Plato allows instants at which a violation of the law of excluded middle takes place; only Aristotle shows how this can be avoided"; or even: "Plato banishes change from time; Aristotle brings it back to instants."

Of course, the possibilty of telling a plausible tale does not prove that the interpretation of Plato's text which I favour (Plato-2) is correct. Nevertheless I think that in this way Plato-2 and an attractive interpretation of Aristotle's remarks on the instant of change mutually support one another. No certainty can be reached as to the correctness of the interpretations. Plausibility is the most one can expect with these ancient and difficult texts. However I think they are worth the trouble.

CHAPTER 3

THE MOMENT OF CHANGE IN THE MIDDLE AGES

3.1. INTRODUCTION

Occupation with the moment of change in the Middle Ages starts out from Aristotle but progresses from there, as is typical of philosophy of the period. Not only does a lot of systematization take place in relation to the moment of change, but also considerable further development. The level of argumentation in the 13th and 14th century is not regained until the 20th century.

In descriptions of the moment of change, the either/or-option is strongly favoured, and the focus is on C-changes. Treatment of s-changes is not explicit. It has to be inferred, but this can be done fairly safely. The same is true of the classification of the moment of change. It is especially interesting that medieval authors usually implicitly deny Plato's premiss.

I shall begin this chapter with a short historical survey. In the main part of this chapter I shall then first discuss *what* most medieval authors wrote about the moment of change (ch. 3.2.) and only then *how* they did it. The reason for this is that they 'notated' what they had to say in a rather indirect way, which is rendered more clearly, the better one knows the contents.

3.1.1. Historical survey

The typical place in which a medieval logician would describe the moment of change is the logical analysis of statements containing the words 'incipit' (begins) and 'desinit' (ceases).

The texts occupied with this topic are very numerous. A thorough account of the historical development of such analyses would fill a book, not just a chapter. Since my aim is a systematic history of the moment of change from antiquity until today I will have to restrict myself to giving a broad outline which stresses what is systematically interesting and provides an overall idea. Very good expert work has been done for example by Wilson and Kretzmann. The following account is often based on the results of their research.[1] I will not discuss in detail, to what extent a 'logical strand' and a 'physical strand' can be distinguished in the medieval treatment.[2] Neither will I discuss other purely historical questions. A short summary will suffice here:

Kretzmann points out that the words 'incipit' and 'desinit' were already discussed at the end of the 12th century.[3] For the problem of the moment of change only texts from the 13th century onwards are interesting: the influence of the (now better known) 'Physics' becomes obvious. The commentators of the 'Physics' again have particular difficulties with what had already provoked Plotinus' criticism, and which asked for a creative solution: Aristotle's claim that there was no 'beginning of a process'. Averroes tries to tackle the limiting instant at the beginning of a process somewhat awkwardly by using the distinction between actus and potentia, obtaining the rather obscure result that the limiting instants exist only in potentia. However, in Averroes we also find the first application of the distinction between 'res permanens' and 'res successiva'; a distinction with a great career ahead of it.[4] Albert the Great seems to be in basic agreement with Averroes on the moment of change[5]. Aquinas assumes a 'first indivisible' (an instant?) of motion before which there has been no motion and at which something has still not moved yet.[6] He seems to have been well aware of Aristotle's motivation for assigning the limiting instant at the end of the process to the later state[7].

Towards the end of the 13th century, Aristotle's treatment of the moment of change in the 'Physics' is not only commented on but also shows its influence in the analyses of 'incipit'- and 'desinit'-statements, which are found in short separate chapters of logic books, in sophismata literature and even in separate treatises. William of Sherwood (who died between 1266 and 1271) and Petrus Hispanus (died 1277) occupy themselves with first and last instants. This subject even seems to become rather fashionable in the 14th century. Walter Burleigh (died 1343), in his elaborate treatise 'De primo et ultimo instanti', deals with the 'primus instans rei' and the 'ultimum instans non esse rei';[8] John of Holland published a 'Tractatus de primo et ultimo instanti' in 1369; William Heytesbury[9] and also William of Ockham[10] turn their attention to the subject of 'De incipit and desinit' as does Thomas Bradwardine,[11] just to mention the most interesting authors.

Finally, there is a lot of thorough analysis of more complicated sentences containing the words 'incipit' and 'desinit' in sophismata literature. The complication usually arises with iterations of these expressions ("Sortes desinit esse non desinendo esse") and with changes of subject with regard to definite descriptions ("Sortes desinit esse albissimus hominum").[12] Outstanding among this sort of text is an amazing collection of very complex sophisms containing the expressions 'incipit' and 'desinit' by Richard Kilvington.[13]

3.1.2. Characteristic features of the texts

The very titles of the texts mentioned already give a hint towards characteristic features of the texts. Those characteristic features become especially clear if contrasted with Aristotle's appoach:

(1) They are primarily about *instants* of a state. An 'instans' is the Aristotelian νῦν. Periods do not play an important role, while they do do so in the 'Physics'.

(2) Only the temporal order of instants is discussed. As I tried to show in the preceding chapter, in Aristotle's treatment of the moment of change hierarchic order is at least as important as temporal order. In this respect, the medieval authors appear more technical, matter-of-fact and modern. Most of them assume dense time order as Aristotle introduced it in the 'Physics'. But they dispense with other features of Aristotle's theory.[14]

(3) The beginning and the end of a state are always treated as equally important. In contrast, Aristotle's neglectful treatment of the limiting instant at the beginning of a process has proved to be problematic.

(4) The use of the words 'incipit' and 'desinit' corresponds far more closely to Plato's presentic μεταβάλλει than to Aristotle's perfective μεταβέβληκεν which aims at casting doubt on the existence of instantaneous events.

(5) Suggestions for describing the moment of change are usually formulated in terms of the analysis of language. Answers are not sought to such questions as "When does such and such a state begin?" but to questions like "If sentence p contains the word 'incipit', what is a sentence equivalent to p which does not contain this word any more?" However, inasmuch as late medieval logicians answer questions of the second sort, their answer always unambiguously implies an answer to the corresponding question of the first sort.[15]

3.2. THE CONTENT OF MEDIEVAL INCIPIT-/DESINIT-ANALYSES

3.2.1. res permanens and res successiva
3.2.1.1. Characterization of the distinction

In most cases the medieval authors mentioned above distinguish between 'res permanens' and 'res successiva' when analyzing 'incipit'- and 'desinit'-statements. Both expressions appear in Latin translations of certain passages from Aristotle, and they seem to have been taken from there. In these passages, which are in no way prominent, the distinction is no more than stated; it is not used to make a point about the moment of change. The application of this distinction to the moment of change is a genuinely

medieval invention.[16] It will turn out, however, that the intuition behind it
has Aristotelian roots. A 'res permanens' is something of which all the parts
can exist at the same time,[17] while a 'res successiva' is something of which
the parts can only exist one after another:[18]

Res permanentes[19] sunt, quarum esse est *simul secundum omnes earum partes* ut lapis,
lignum. Res successivae sunt, quarum esse non est simul secundum omnes earum
partes, sed *esse earum consistit in successione partium*, ita quod eis repugnat habere
omnes partes simul, cuiusmodi sunt tempus et motus.[20]

Such things are called 'res permanentes' whose being with respect to all their parts is
simultaneous, e.g. a stone or a piece of wood. Such things are called 'res successivae'
whose being is not simultaneous with respect to all their parts, since it would
contradict them to have all their parts simultaneously, as for example a [period of]
time and a motion.

'Stone', 'piece of wood' or 'man'[21] are examples that fit the definition of 'res
permanens' without difficulty: their parts lie beside, behind or on top of
each other. The fact that they have a history during which they may lose
parts and gain others does not touch the fact that they exist as a whole at
each instant of their history. By contrast, the parts of a movement or action,
i.e. their subperiods, exist one after another; and this is the reason why the
movement is not there as a whole at any one specific instant.

It should be noted that the distinction between 'res permanens' and 'res
successiva' is not identical with the one Aristotle made between κίνησις and
ἐνέργεια: quite definitely rest is no κίνησις. However, if we remain with
Aristotle's definition of rest,[22] rest is a 'res successiva', in that 'rest' according
to that definition is 'remaining in a place'; and that cannot happen at a single
instant. Socrates and pieces of wood as typical 'res permanentes' are counter-
examples to such an identification, too. These examples are not actions or
processes. Therefore they are certainly not Aristotelian ἐνέργειαι.
Nevertheless, there are obviously parallels as well: an Aristotelian ἐνέργεια
can exist and have existed at the same time for the very reason that it always
exists as a whole, i.e. completely. A κίνησις cannot exist and have existed at
the same time for the very reason that while it is present it is never present
as a whole. It is not yet complete while it is present but it is already past
when it has reached its target. 'Being white' is an ἐνέργεια, a movement
from A to B is a κίνησις. A 'res permanens' exists as a whole at every instant
of its existence; and 'whiteness' is an example of it. A 'res successiva' is never
there as a whole at any one instant; and 'movement' is an example of it.

3.2.1.2. What does 'res' mean?

§1 It is not at all easy to see what the word 'res' in this context meant to the
medieval logician. One would be puzzled by the question "Is there a first or
last instant of a man?" and everyone would be tempted to correct it to "Is

there a first or last instant of a man's existence?". On the other hand, the question "Is there a first instant of a motion?" sounds correct. Thus, the examples for 'res permanens' and the typical examples for 'res successiva' such as 'motion' and 'period of time' or 'running'[23] seem to belong to different categories.

Moreover, if one looks at more examples, one is faced with 'res permanentes' which are completely different to pieces of wood or stones. Typical examples referring to a 'res permanens' would be:

(RP1) Socrates begins to be white.[24]
(RP2) Socrates begins to be well.[25]

But, amazingly, Socrates occurs as the grammatical subject in examples for a 'res successiva' as well:

(RS1) Socrates begins to run/move.[26]
(RS2) A movement starts.[27]

That is to say, in RP1, RP2 and RS1 it is not Socrates at all, the grammatical subject of the sentence, who is to be an example of 'res permanens' or 'res successiva': he cannot very well be both 'res permanens' and 'res successiva'. Rather, the state of being white, the 'whiteness', is a 'res permanens'; just as 'running' or 'motion' is a 'res successiva'. Kretzmann takes that into account when (in some cases) translating 'res' as 'state'.[28] But this cannot be done in all of the cases, for one would hardly be able to say that a stone or a piece of wood is a state, which one would have to if always translating 'res' as 'state'. So, from *our* perspective, states as well as things seem to fall under the concept of 'res permanens'.

This distinction was apparently not made in the Middle Ages. On the contrary, medieval logicians seem to have conceived not only stones but states, too, as things. A movement or whiteness are 'res' which can only occur in something else, for example Socrates. The existence of the object 'movement' depends on the existence of the object called 'Socrates'. The one object exists only in dependence on and 'in' the other. The movement or whiteness are actually regarded as things that exist. This way of thinking is unusual. But once one is used to it, one can recognize the logical form which not only the first three but all four examples have in common, and to reformulate the examples accordingly. RS1 then emerges as identical with RS2 (apart from the fairly unimportant addition 'in Socrates'):

(RP1') Whiteness begins to exist (in Socrates).
(RP2') Being well begins to exist (in Socrates).
(RS1') A movement begins to exist (in Socrates).
(RS2') A movement begins to exist.

The occurence of whiteness or being well, stones and pieces of wood all belong to the same ontological category. Even Socrates does. For doubtlessly, RP3 would be admissable as an example of the same sort:

(RP3) Socrates begins to exist.[29]

Not only are we unused to this ontology; an unusual habit of thinking also corresponds to it with regard to which property is attributed to the res in an 'incipit'- or 'desinit'-statement: in a medieval logician's view the same property is ascribed to all the beginning or ending 'res' which are referred to in these statements: the property of existence.[30]

§2 My proposal for overcoming the heterogenity of the concepts of 'res permanens' and 'res successiva' consists in re-establishing the difference between 'permanent' and 'successive' on the level of properties. It is then not necessary to concern oneself with the kinds of 'things' a medieval logician might have assumed or what the word 'res' might have meant to him in cases when we have problems in translating it by 'thing'.[31] So let us introduce a classification of properties into p-properties and s-properties analogously to the classification of 'res' into 'res permanens' and 'res successiva': being white, being Socrates or being a piece of wood are p-properties; being in motion, getting well etc. are s-properties. In what follows I shall proceed from the assumption that it is intuitively clear in which way a p- or an s-property corresponds to a 'res': The 'res' corresponding to 'being white' is 'whiteness', the 'res' corresponding to 'being Socrates' is Socrates, the 'res' corresponding to 'being in motion' is a movement etc. Let us assume that 'being in motion' is always 'moving from somewhere to somewhere', in contrast to moving from a specific place A to a specific place B (analogously for all kinds of processes), even though, of course, a movement always goes from a specific starting point to a specific target position.[32]

§3 The next step is to lay down some 'translation rules' for a number of medieval expressions:

(1) An 'instant of the existence of a res permanens' is an instant at which something has a p-property. For example an instant of Socrates' existence is an instant at which something has the property of being Socrates.

(2) An 'instant of the existence of a res permanens in a' is an instant at which a has a p-property. For example an instant of the existence of whiteness in Socrates is an instant at which Socrates has the property of being white.

(3) An 'instant of the existence of a res successiva' is an instant at which something is in the course of having an s-property.

(4) An 'instant of the existence of a res successiva in *a*' is an instant at which *a* is in the course of having an s-property. Thus, for example an instant at which a running exists in Socrates is an instant at which Socrates is in the course of having the property of running, i.e. an instant at which Socrates is running.

We will not concern ourselves further with what 'existence' or 'whiteness' may mean in other contexts. However, we still need to state precisely what p-properties and s-properties are. And we have to state what exactly 'being in the course of' means.

3.2.1.3. p-properties and s-properties
It is plausible to identify p-properties with non-comparative properties and s-properties with comparative properties. In this way one would label 'rest' as a 'res successiva', as is perfectly plausible: both being at rest and being in motion were considered to be comparative properties, while being white etc. was not. This identification, however, has little to do with what the medieval logicians themselves thought to be characteristic of the difference between 'res permanens' and 'res successiva'. In order to account for what they thought, I think the following way of defining p- and s-properties is appropriate:

(B1) F is a p-property iff there is a predicate P such that
   (i) P refers to F.[33]
   (ii) $\forall \chi \, [P(c) \rightarrow \exists t[t \text{ falls-within } c \wedge P(t)]]$.[34]

(B1) F is a p-property iff there is a predicate P such that
   (i) P refers to F.
   (ii) $\forall \chi \, [P(c) \rightarrow \neg \exists t[t \text{ falls-within } c \wedge P(t)]]$.

Thus for example, being white is a p-property, because the following is true: for every period during which *a* is white (at least for a while) there is an instant which falls within this period at which *a* is white (for a period throughout which *a* is white it is even true that at every instant which falls within this period *a* is white). Running from x to y, on the other hand, is an s-property, because the following is true: whichever period one considers during which *a* runs from x to y, there is no instant which falls within this period during which *a* runs from x to y.

3.2.1.4. 'being in the course of'
The meaning of 'being in the course of' as used in 3.2.1.2.§3 still has to be clarified. In order to put this precisely, let us introduce the new prefix 'State', which, more or less, means 'being in the course of':

NR3) (1) Combination Rule: 'State' may be attached to the name of a p-predicate (i.e. a predicate which has periods as its domain) in order to obtain the name of an i-predicate (i.e. a predicate which has instants as its domain).

(2) Semantical Rule: State-P(t) iff ∃c [*-P(c) ∧ t falls-within c].

It should be noted that State-P(t) might be true although P(t) is false. This is the case if P stands for "*a* moves from x to y ...": even if Aristotle is right in saying that *a* cannot move from x to y at an instant, and thus no instant can satisfy P, *a* may nevertheless be *in the course of* moving from x to y at an instant t; and thus t may satisfy the predicate State-P.

3.2.1.5. Digression: instants of motion

For the interpretation of medieval texts it is indeed necessary, in the case of s-properties, to speak in the indicated way of something's 'being in the course' of having the property F. This requires more detailed explanation which turns our attention to a progressive deviation from Aristotle which occurs in the Middle Ages: the invention of instants of motion.

Aristotle denies that a thing can have a comparative property at an instant. He was in no way willing to talk of motion at an instant. Nevertheless, a medieval logician analyzing 'incipit'- and 'desinit'-statements has in mind the question: "Has the *res successiva* 'running' in *a* a first or a last instant?" which means: "Is there a first or last instant at which *a* is in the course of running?". Tension becomes apparent here between the Aristotelian tradition from which the distinction between 'res permanens' and 'res successiva' stems, and a deviation from this tradition, which consists in assuming a way in which it is possible to talk reasonably about, for example, 'being in the course of running'.

Aristotle's view was shown in ch. I,2 to be too extreme: his denial goes beyond the plausible view that something cannot get from one place to another at an instant. Consequently, one is free to hold this view and still to consider as an instant of motion of *a* an instant which falls into a phase of motion of *a*, and to say of such an instant that it is an instant at which *a* is in the course of moving. Interestingly, this is exactly what happens in the late Middle Ages, since some clear idea had developed in the 14th century of what 'being in the course of moving', i.e. 'motion at an instant' might be. This can be seen by considering the following thought experiment which is found in John of Holland:[35]

If, at t, two rain drops while falling down (and thus being in motion) merge into one, one may be tempted to think that t has to be a first instant of motion of the resulting drop; for never before t was the resulting drop in motion (it did not exist before t); at t, however, it is already in motion (thus, there would, unusually, be a first instant of the 'res permanens' 'motion of the resulting rain drop').

Thinking along such lines, though, John argues, one does not take into account what 'motion' would have to mean in this case. In order to be considered to be in motion at t, the resulting drop would not only have to be found in another place within an indefinitely short time after t, but also before t. But before t it did not exist at all.

The reasoning is un-Aristotelian enough. There is a definition here of what it means for an object to be in motion at an instant (to be in the course of moving); and John then demonstrates that the definition is not fulfilled in the case in question. He explicitly makes a step which is nowhere to be found in Aristotle: something is 'in motion' at an instant iff this instant falls within a period throughout which a is in motion; if this is the case, a is in the course of moving at that instant.[36]

This means that it makes sense to the medieval logician to ask whether there are first or last instants of motion, since there are instants of motion, whereas in Aristotle's view there could trivially be no first or last instants of motion as there are no instants of motion anyway.

3.2.2. The assignment of the limiting instants

There is evidently wide agreement in the medieval discussion of the moment of change on three essential points:[37]

(1) A number of crucial features of dense time are clearly conceived by most authors in the 13th and 14th century.[38] A very clear summary of them is found in Burleigh's 'De primo et ultimo instanti':[39]

Regule [...]
i) [...] in quibuscumque rebus est dare primum instans esse rei, in eisdem non est dare ultimum instans non esse rei.
ii) [...] in quibuscumque rebus est non dare primum instans esse rei, in eisdem est dare ultimum instans in quo res non esse.
iii) [...] in quibuscumque est dare ultimum instans in quo res habet esse, in eisdem non es dare primum instans in quo res habet non esse.
iv) [...] in quibuscumque non est dare ultimum instans in quo res habet esse, in eisdem est dare primum instans in quo res habet non esse.

Rules:
i) Of whatever things ('res') there is a first instant of existence, there is no last instant of non-existence.
ii) Of whatever things there is no first instant of existence, there is a last instant of non-existence.
iii) Of whatever things there is a last instant of existence, there is no first instant of non-existence.
iv) Of whatever things there is no last instant of existence, there is a first instant of non-existence.

(2) The existence of a 'typical' 'res permanens' such as Socrates is assigned a first instant. (Opinions on last instants of 'res permanentes' differ, sometimes in texts by the same author. For example, Walter Burleigh accepts last instants of 'res permanentes' in 'De primo et ultimo instanti',[40] but denies last instants of 'res permanentes' in 'De puritate artis logicae'.[41] The motivation for these decisions is not quite clear.[42])

(3) The existence of a 'res successiva' such as motion is neither assigned a first nor a last instant.

If time is assumed to be dense, point (3) can be taken to be motivated by (v) there being no last instant at which *a* is still in the initial position and not the least bit distanced from it, consequently (vi) there being no first instant at which *a* is at a certain distance from the initial position; (vii) there being a first instant at which the target position is reached; and that (viii) there being, therefore, no last instant at which *a* is the shortest possible distance away from the target position.[43] This view is partly found in Physics VIII, where Aristotle reasons that 'according to fact' the end of the process is to be assigned 'to the latter [state]', and that the earlier state can only be said to obtain 'except for the last now'. What goes beyond Aristotle, though, is the acceptance of instants of motion in general as described in section 3.2.1.5.

The above statements i) to iv) are not only highly plausible. If dense time is assumed, there is an elegant way of proving them. Take, for example, Walter Burleigh's proof for i):

[1] Si enim sit dare primum instans in quo res [i.e. Sortes] habet esse, sit illud instans B, probo quod non sit dare ultimum instans in quo Sorte[s] habet non esse.
[2] Quia si sic, sit illud A.
Ergo A est ultimum instans in quo Sorte[s] habet non esse.
et B est primum instans in quo Sortes habet esse [...]
[3] Certum est quod A est ante B. [...]
[4] Qu[a]ero tunc aut sunt mediata aut immediata.
[a] Non immediata, quia tunc esset instans immediatum instanti, cuius oppositum est probatum sexto Physicorum.
[b] Ergo sunt mediata.

[5] Ergo inter A et B cadit tempus medium
et in illo tempore medium nec potest dici quod Sortes est,
nec quod Sortes non est, si A sit ultimum instans non esse.
[6] Apparet hoc impossibile, scilicet,
quod aliquando nec sit, nec non sit,
[7] quia ubi est dare primum instans esse,
ibi non est dare ultimum instans non esse.[44]

1) If there is a first instant at which a thing [in what follows: Socrates] exists, call it B,
I prove that there is no last instant at which Socrates does not exist.
2) For, let us assume there were such [last instant], call it A.
Then A is the last instant at which Socrates does not exist,
and B is the first instant at which he exists
3) Clearly, A precedes B [since the beginning of Socrates' existence is concerned].
4) So I ask whether they follow one upon another immediately or not.
a) They do not follow one upon another immediately, because, if they did, there
would be an instant immediately following another one, which is contrary to what is
proved in [Aristotle's] Physics VI.
b) So they are apart.
5) Therefore, there is a time which falls between A and B
and in this time you can neither say that Socrates exists,
nor that he does not exist (if A is to be the *last* instant of his non-existence).
6) It is obviously impossible that something neither exists nor does not exist,
7) so that where there is a first instant of being, there is no last instant of non-being.

The proof is wholly satisfactory once we replace the reference to Aristotle's
authority by the assumption of dense time (the very characteristic of which
is that between any two instants there is another one). So are the proofs for
the other rules which are conducted in the same manner. Correspondent
proofs for i) to iv), using modern set-theoretical vocabulary, are given in
appendix C at the end of this book.[45]

3.2.3. Differentiation vs. economy: two strategies of reacting to problems within the field of 'res permanens'

Obviously a number of (as a rule, earlier) authors were convinced of having
at their disposal, by their distinction of 'res permanens' and 'res successiva',
a simple systematization of 'desinit' and 'incipit'-statements. Otherwise this
differentiation would hardly have found such wide acceptance. A number of
(as a rule, later) authors reacted to problems which this opinion faced by an
elaborate differentiation within the framework of the original distinction, as,
for example, can be seen in John of Holland. William of Ockham, on the
other hand, reacted by rejecting the distinction between 'res permanens' and
'res successiva' as useless for the systematization of 'incipit'- and 'desinit'-
statements.

3.2.3.1. Simple answers (William of Sherwood and Burleigh I)

William of Sherwood generally assigns a first but no last instant to the existence of a 'res permanens'; the author of 'Summulae Logicales', a treatise wrongly attributed to Peter of Spain, arrives at the same result.[46] The same opinion is found in Burleigh's 'De puritate artis logicae'.[47] John Le Page assigns both first and last instant to all 'res permanentes';[48] and so does Peter of Auvergne.[49] All authors mentioned assign neither first nor last instants to the existence of a 'res successiva', a trait typical of this period.[50] A treatise possibly written by Henry of Ghent agrees with William of Sherwood concerning 'res permanentes', but, very exceptionally, allows a last instant for 'res successivae'.[51]

3.2.3.2. Further differentiation: for example John of Holland and Burleigh II

The problems which lead to further differentiation are encountered within the category of 'res permanens'. This is as a result of there being 'res permanentes' that have so much to do with processes or motion that, intuitively, first and last instants should be denied to them just as they are to 'res successivae'.

(a) There are instantaneous and durable 'res permanentes'. There is a first instant as well as a last one of the existence of an instantaneous 'res permanens'. This instant, and nothing but it, is the time of existence of such a 'res', in the sense that it ceases to exist at the same instant at which it begins to exist.[52] An example is the position of an object at an instant of motion.[53]

(b) Some durable 'res permanentes' depend on 'res successivae', and some do not. There is no first or last instant of a 'res permanens' which depends on a 'res successiva', just as there is no first or last instant of the 'res successiva' on which it depends. A medieval example of such a dependent 'res permanens' would be the 'truth of the statement 'Socrates is running'', a surprising but by no means nonsensical example (note that the statement is wholly true at every instant of Socrates' jog).[54]

(c) Independent 'res permanentes' require differentiation too. So there is a first and a last instant of the existence of a certain shade of blue. But there is no last instance of the existence of a 'blue' which gradually fades; it does not depend on a process, but its fading constitutes a continuous process. And wherever a continuous process is concerned there are no first or last instants.[55]

Such an elaborate differentiation as is carried out by John of Holland and by Walter Burleigh in 'De primo et ultimo instanti'[56] may make the classification into 'res permanens' and 'res successiva' appear as secondary: 'res permanentes' have to be differentiated only because it turns out that the border between 'res permanens' and 'res successiva' does not coincide with the border between those things which have first and last instants and those which do not, as may originally have been hoped.

3.2.3.3. 'res permanens'/'res successiva': an irrelevant distinction? (William of Ockham)

One way of reacting to the lack of coincidence hoped for is therefore to make internal distinctions within the category of 'res permanens' to such a degree that in the end the original borderline appears to be unimportant. This is what happens (consciously or unconsciously) in John of Holland and Walter Burleigh. Another way of reacting to the lack of coincidence consists in declaring the differentiation into 'res permanens' and 'res successiva' to be irrelevant to the analysis of 'incipit'- and 'desinit'-statements. This path is chosen by William of Ockham:

> ...ab aliquibus diversimode assignantur exponentes respectu diversorum. Unde dicunt quod aliter exponuntur respectu successivorum et respectu permanentium. Sed quamvis sic posset esse ad voluntatem utentium, non tamen videtur multum rationabile. Ideo dico quod respectu cuiuslibet possunt habere easdem exponentes, sed aliter sunt ubi ponitur hoc verbum *incipit* et ubi ponitur hoc verbum *desinit*.

> By some [authors, incipit- and desinit-statements] are analysed differently with respect to different things. That is why they say that [such statements] are [to be] analysed differently with respect to res successivae and with respect to res permanentes. But although this may be what they want, this does not look very reasonable. Therefore I would say that [such statements] are [to be] analysed as consisting of the same components with respect to any thing whatsoever, but differently with respect to whether they contain the word 'incipit' or the word 'desinit'.[57]

Since here, for the sake of economy, something is dropped because it is thought to be of no use, it is hardly surprising that it is Ockham's reaction. However, in this case Ockham might be rather exaggerating economy. Since he declares the distinction between 'res permanens' and 'res successiva' to be irrelevant, he simply assigns both first and last instants to all 'objects'. I think that Sorabji is right in calling this treatment 'inferior' in comparison with, for example, Walter Burleigh's.[58]

3.2.4. An implicit 'Neutral Instant Analysis' of the change between rest and motion?

§1 There remains the question of how medieval authors treated the s-change between comparative properties such as rest and motion. No explicit treatment is found. I think, however, that an opinion can be inferred.

Rest as well as motion[59] should be regarded as a 'res successiva': rest is, as one could say following Aristotle, remaining in a place. In contrast to being in a place, remaining in a place does not obtain as a whole at an instant. One would, thus, be inclined to regard as an instant of rest, analogous to motion, such an instant as falls within a phase of rest, but not an instant which merely bounds such a phase. There would not, then, be any first and last instants of rest. This agrees with the existence of a 'res successiva' which does not have any first or last instants. The result is that neither rest nor motion would have any first and last instants. Consequently, the limiting instant between a phase of motion and a phase of rest would be 'neutral'. This amounts to a very early version of the 'Neutral Instant Analysis', which characteristically regards the limiting instant as an instant which is exceptional because *a* is neither at rest nor in motion at it.[60] In my view, it is plausible that such an analysis is indeed implicitly contained in the medieval approach.

§2 If this is the case, there is an interesting consequence for the characterization of rest and motion which is closely connected with the invention of instants of motion mentioned above. To Aristotle, rest is the στέρησις of motion,[61] an expression commonly translated as *privatio* (privation). So according to Aristotle, rest *is* non-motion. The privation obtains wherever the positivum does not obtain but *could* obtain. At the limiting instant, as well as at *any* instant, non-motion (rest) does not obtain, since non-motion can obtain only where motion could obtain and, in Aristotle's view, motion could in no way obtain at an instant.

In the late Middle Ages things look different: John of Holland applies the distinction between 'positivum' and 'privatio' to first and last instants in a quite un-Aristotelian way. As there is neither a first nor a last instant of motion (i.e. of a 'res successiva'), there is a first and a last instant of the complementary privation 'non-motion'. John does not make it explicit whether non-motion is to be identified with rest.[62] But it is very probable that he would have characterized instants of rest analogously to his characterization of instants of motion. Interestingly, according to this approach, non-motion could not be then identified with rest. Rest could not be the privation of motion, since the privation would have to occur *wherever* the 'positivum' does not obtain, but could. Unlike Aristotle, John thinks that at the limiting instant, as an instant, motion *could* obtain, but it does not. Thus, if rest does not obtain there, rest cannot be the 'privatio' of motion.

3.3. THE FORM OF MEDIEVAL INCIPIT-/DESINIT-ANALYSES

3.3.1. Medieval and modern tense logic

Medieval logicians had a very peculiar semi-formal way of expressing their description of the moment of change. I think this is best appreciated by paying attention to the remarkable similarities which their texts about 'incipit' and 'desinit' exhibit to the formal logic of tense which Arthur Prior developed in the 1960s. In fact, medieval and modern tense logic are so similar to one another that I suppose anyone with some knowledge of modern tense logic and faced with the task of summing up medieval texts on the moment of change will catch himself writing Priorian formulas. However, in certain passages he will realize that the tools of modern tense logic available to him are not adequate for the medieval analysis, i.e. that medieval tense logic was more precise than its modern counterpart.

For our notation based on the predicate calculus we will 'borrow' the typical signs of Priorian tense logic F, P, H and G. In Prior, they are operators on sentence variables; here we will use them as prefixes, with, however, practically the same semantics. They roughly render the following expressions of natural language:

> F:"It is true in the future of ... that ..."
> P: "It is true in the past of ... that ..."
> G: "It is true throughout the future of ... that ..."
> H: "It is true throughout the past of ... that ..."

The past of t is the set of all instants earlier than t, the future of t the set of all instants later than t. As well as the tense-prefixes we will have to introduce a negation prefix '~', because the usual operator of propositional negation cannot be part of a predicate-name. The tense-prefixes and the negation prefix are introduced by the following naming rules:

NR4) (1) Combination Rule: '~' can be attached to the name of a temporal statement in order to obtain the name of a new temporal statement.
> (2) Semantical Rule: $\sim$-P(z) iff ¬P(z).

NR5) (1) Combination Rule: F, P, G and H can be attached to the name of a temporal statement taking instants in order to obtain the name of a new temporal statement taking instants.
> (2) Semantical Rule:
> (a) P-P(t) iff $\exists t_1[t_1 < t \wedge P(t_1)]$.
> (b) F-P(t) iff $\exists t_1[t < t_1 \wedge P(t_1)]$.
> (c) H-P(t) iff $\forall t_1[t_1 < t \rightarrow P(t_1)]$.
> (d) G-P(t) iff $\forall t_1[t < t_1 \rightarrow P(t_1)]$.

If it is the case that p in the future of t and if one chooses t as one's point of view one will say that it *will be* the case that p; if it is the case that p in the past of t and if one chooses t as one's point of view one will say that it *was* the case that p.

3.3.2. The standard form of the analysis of incipit- and desinit-statements

Sometimes medieval authors explicitly mention first and last instants of states, or write about 'intrinsic' or 'extrinsic' boundaries of states.[63] But even without this, one can tell a medieval author's opinion on whether there are first or last instants and, if so, for which states, when looking at the way in which he analyses 'incipit'- and 'desinit'-statements: it unambiguously entails whether, in the case at hand, he assumes first or last instants of a state.

'incipit' and 'desinit' are phrases to be analysed: exponibilia. They must be expounded by paraphrase. This is done in a certain standard form from which only rare deviations are found. Wilson summarizes the analytical options open to a medieval logician according to this standard form (taking William of Sherwood as an example) and remarks that they represent the logicians' peculiar technical language on the subject of first and last instants:

> ...incipit may be expounded [depending on what case is being considered] either by a positing of existence in the present instant (per positionem praesentis) and denial of existence in the past, or by a denial of existence in the present instant with positing of existence in the future. Similarly, desinit may be expounded either by a positing of existence in the present instant and denial of existence in the future, or by a denial of existence in the present instant and positing of existence in the past. This is the logician's manner of stating that the boundaries of periods of duration may be either intrinsic or extrinsic.[64]

The small number of standard analytical options facilitates comparison between the differrent texts and allows a quick survey of the text itself. They allow the author a very concise presentation of his view on the moment of change. Their drawback is that through this form of presentation one rarely gets a hint about the motivation for a particular analysis (as has already become apparent). Another disadvantage is a certain indirectness.

As a result of what has been said so far, the options for analysing the sentence (1) "*a* begins to be white" seem to be:

(1a) *a* is white and was not white before.
(1b) *a* is not white and will later on be white.

The options for the analysis of (2) "*a* ceases to be white":

(2a) *a* is not white and was white before.
(2b) *a* is white and will later on not be white any more.

The options for analysing the sentence (3) "*a* begins to move" and (4) "*a* ceases to move" are, analogously:

> (3a) *a* is in motion and was not in motion before.
> (3b) *a* is not in motion and will be in motion.
> (4a) *a* is not in motion and was in motion.
> (4b) *a* is in motion and will not be in motion.

In William of Sherwood there are indeed analyses formulated like this, because, as a relatively early author, he lacks one crucial word to make things precise.[65] But even before formulating the options more precisely, it is worthwhile elaborating a little further on how these analyses are meant. I shall do so by concentrating on (1a) and (1b) as well as on (3a) and (3b). (1) in itself, like (1a) and (1b), is ambiguous. It is not clear how the present tense 'begins' is to be understood in (1) and how we are to understand 'before' in (1a) and 'later on' in (1b).

3.3.3. Temporal and atemporal present tense

It is generally possible to distinguish between two uses of the present tense which I propose to call 'temporal' and 'atemporal' present tense. The sentence "*a* begins to be white" may mean "At some time in the course of history *a* begins to be white". This would be the atemporal use of the present tense[66].

If medieval logicians had meant the atemporal sense of the present tense they would not have been interested in fixing a definite instant as the date of a change. It becomes apparent, however, that the change is to be dated, so that the present tense of 'incipit' ('begins') or 'desinit' ('ceases') is always temporal and not atemporal:

William of Ockham, for example, writes about the sentence "Sortes incipit esse albus" ("Socrates begins to be white") as being true "in aliquo instante" ("at a certain instant"). He also distinguishes between a precise and a less precise use of the words 'incipit' and 'desinit', depending on whether the use of these words involves the precise concept of an instantaneous present or the less precise concept of a temporally extended present.[67] Both these statements only make sense if the analysis aims to tell whether 'incipit' is true with respect to a certain present time, i.e., if the temporal use of the present tense is meant.[68]

Furthermore, one author, William Heytesbury, is criticized by other medieval authors for permitting both (1a) and (1b) as an analysis of (1) in the same case, because (1a) and (1b) contradict one another.[69] This criticism would be completely incomprehensible if the present tense in (1) were atemporal. For, by reading (1) with an atemporal present one my claim as an analysis of (1) that there is an instant for which (1a) is true; and that there is an instant for which (1b) is true. The two instants need not be identical, and as long as they are not, (1a) and (1b) do not at all contradict one another. Things look different, however, once we read 'begins' in this case as a temporal present tense. One cannot claim without contradiction that (1a) as well as (1b) are true for the same instant t, and then take this as the instant at which a begins to be white. The first conjunct of (1a) says that a is white at t while the first conjunct of (1b) says that it is not white at t.

This shows that the present tense of 'incipit' and 'desinit' is a temporal present tense, actually referring to a time present.

3.3.4. The motivation behind the standard form

If one reads (1) as a temporal present tense and assumes that (1a) and (1b) are the only options available, one has to decide on which is right, as they cannot both be true. William of Sherwood believes (1a) to be the correct analysis of (1). (1b) he considers to be false. His motivation is unambiguous: he is of the customary opinion that 'whiteness' is a 'res permanens' and has a first instant. Besides, he chooses (3b), against (3a). And he is of the usual opinion that a 'res successiva' has no first or last instant.[70]

The first instant of the existence of whiteness in a is the limiting instant between a phase of a's being not white and a phase of a's being white. Now if one wants to fix a definite instant for which it is true that a begins to be white, then it is this. In fact, a is white at this instant, as (1a) requires but (1b) denies. If one wants to fix one definite instant at which a begins to move, then this is the limiting instant between a phase in which a does not move and a phase in which it does. However, it is not true to say that a is in motion at it, as (3a) denies but (3b) requires.

This is sufficient motivation for starting the analysis of (1) with a 'positio praesentis' in the shape of the first conjunct of (1a). And it is also satisfactory motivation for starting the analysis of (3) with a 'remotio praesentis' in the shape of the first conjunct of (3b). Neither is there any objection to the 'remotio praesentis' being followed by a 'positio futuri' as the second conjunct of the analysis of (3). The great majority of authors obviously agree on that.

3.3.5. The deficiencies of William of Sherwood's approach and overcoming them by use of the word 'immediate' (the prefixes ImmF and ImmP)

However, the 'remotio praeteriti' in the analysis of (1) and the 'positio futuri' in the analysis of (3) are not generally expressed in the shape found in (1a) or (3b) but in a more precise formulation. The shape of the 'remotio praeteriti' in (1a) and likewise the one in (3b) is not only ambiguous but in addition both possible readings expose themselves to a criticism which makes them unacceptable. A clear example of some authors' awareness of these deficiencies is found in William of Ockham:

For the ambiguity first: The role of the words 'before' and 'later on' is not sufficiently clear: (1a) may be read to mean (1a') but may also be read to mean (1a''), while W stands for the statement "*a* is white":

(1a') $W(t) \wedge P\text{-}\sim\text{-}W(t)$.
(1a'') $W(t) \wedge \sim\text{-}P\text{-}W(t)$.

Both possible readings turn out to be unsatisfactory. According to the semantics of *P* and *H*, (1a'') may be transformed into:

$$W(t) \wedge H\text{-}\sim\text{-}W(t).$$

(3b) may mean (3b') or (3b''), while B stands for the statement "*a* is moving":

(3b') $\sim\text{-State-}B(t) \wedge F\text{-State-}B(t)$.
(3b'') $\sim\text{-State-}B(t) \wedge G\text{-State-}B(t)$.[71]

It is easy to see that (1a'') does not satisfy our expectations. (1a) was meant to indirectly express that there is a first instant at which *a* is white. But in which precise sense is t to be a first instant which satisfies W? Not, at any rate, in the following sense:

$$W(t) \wedge \neg\exists t_1 [t_1 < t \wedge W(t_1)].$$

For this would exclude there having been any other W-phase of *a* previously. But clearly, the expression 'first', when talking about 'first instants', must always be understood as 'first in a certain environment'. Ockham recognizes this clearly when criticizing an analysis of the statement "Sortes incipit esse albus" in the shape of (1a''):

Non enim exponens sua negativa de praeterito est talis 'Sortes non fuit albus', quia talis propositio in qua ponitur 'incipit' potest esse vera et illa negativa de praeterito falsa; sicut si Sortes sit primo albus et postea niger et tertio fiat albus, tunc in aliquo instanti est haec vera 'Sortes incipt esse albus' et tamen haec est falsa 'Sortes non fuit albus', quia positum est quod prius fuit albus. Sic etiam dicimus quod haec arbor incipit modo florere, et tamen floruit anno praecedenti.[72]

For its negative [component] in the past tense is not to be rendered as "Socrates was not white [at any time before]". For such a statement in which [the word] 'begins' occurs may be true and [, in spite of that,] this negated past tense [statement] false. Thus, if Socrates is first white, and then black and becomes white again, then, at a certain instant, the [statement] "Socrates begins to be white" is true while, nevertheless, the [statement] "Socrates was not white [at any time before]" is false, because we have assumed that Socrates has been white before. In the same way we also say that this tree begins to bloom, and yet it already bloomed last year.

(3b'') is similarly unsatisfactory. It assumes that, once having started to move, *a* never stops again.

But while (1a'') and (3b'') demand too much, the requirements of (1a') and (3a') are too weak to satisfy our intuition: according to (1a') every instant at which *a* is white after once not being white is one at which *a* begins to be white. And according to (3b') every instant at which *a* is not in motion is an instant at which *a* begins to move if it ever moves at some later time.

Ockham's opinion about (1a') is that (1a') can be justified in a certain sense if the instants permitted for substitution are limited to such instants as fall into a short period after the limiting instant between two phases. This makes sense if one wants to to render a certain imprecise use of 'incipit' and 'desinit' ("improprie et large"). This use, according to Ockham, is found in everyday language, where the concept of an extended present plays an important role, as encountered in the fourth book of the Philosopher's 'Physics':[73]

...tunc sic exponitur: 'sic est, et non diu ante fuit'. Sicut dicimus quod haec arbor incipit florere, quando nunc floret, et non multum ante, isto anno floruit et tamen heri floruit; sicut etiam dicimus vulgariter 'iste incipit missam', quamvis dixerit Introitum.[74]

...it is then analysed like this: "It is so-and-so, and has not been so for long". So we say that this tree begins to bloom when it is in bloom now but [has not been so] for long, if it was in bloom, but only yesterday. So we say colloquially: He is beginning the mass, although he has already sung the introit.

(1a') and (1a'') fail as analyses of (1), (3b') and (3b'') as analyses of (3). William of Ockham's proposal of how to analyse (1) better agrees with most of the prominent later texts[75] because it contains just one more word than William of Sherwood's earlier proposal (1a'):

...exponentes istius 'Sortes incipit esse albus' sunt istae 'Sortes est albus' et 'Sortes non fuit *immediate* ante albus'.[76]

The components of "Socrates begins to be white" are as follows: "Socrates is white" and "Socrates was not white *immediately* before".

This means that his suggestion for the analysis of (1) is:

(1a*) *a* is white and was not white immediately before.

For the moment the precise meaning of the crucial word 'immediately' may not be clear, although one feels that it removes the problems of (1a') and (1a''). Sentences containing the word 'immediate' are themselves among the phrases to be analysed, they are 'exponibilia'.[77] At least this much is clear: if the insertion of this word into (1a') brings about so much more precision, this cannot be rendered by Prior's conventional tense-logic. If (1a*) is a conceivable enhancement of precision, medieval tense logic must be admitted to be more precise in this point than modern tense logic: it is time to catch up with the 14th century.

Conscious analysis of the word 'immediate' is not found before a very late text, the 'Logica parva' of Paul of Venice.[78] However, it is found. And, in my view, it is a very early example of what mathematicians today call an 'environment':

'immediate ante a tu fuisti' sic exponitur: 'ante a tu fuisti et non fuit instans ante a quin inter id et a tu fuisti' [...] 'immediate post b tu eris' sic exponitur: 'post b tu eris et nullum erit instans post b quin inter id et b tu eris'[79].

"You were immediately before a" is analysed like this: You were before a and there was no instant before a except that you were between it and a". [...] "You were immediately after b" is analysed like this: "You will be after b, and there will be no instant after b except that you were between it and b".

At first sight, this seems to amount to returning to analyses such as (1a'') or (3b''), which have proved to be unsatisfactory for the very reason that they cannot cope with the 'oscillation'[80] between states, because they only 'react' to the existence of the absolutely first instant of a state. Does this passage not seem to read: "Before t_a P applies to instants, and there is no instant before t_a for which it does not apply; i.e. P applies to all instants before t_a."? It seems to read like this, but it does not. Such a paraphrase would overlook the crucial word 'between' because it is hard to relate. What does the 'id' in 'inter id' refer to?[81]

Paul's definition makes no sense until one realizes that "ante a tu fuisti" already contains a quantification which claims the existence of an instant. It is this very 'hidden' instant that 'id' refers to:

$P\text{-}P(t_a)$ is equivalent to $\exists t\,[t<t_a \wedge P(t)]$. We may therefore render Paul's first example as:

$$\exists t\,[t<t_a \wedge P(t)] \wedge \neg\exists t_1\,[t<t_1<t_a \wedge \neg P(t_1)]$$
or $\quad \exists t\,[t<t_a \wedge P(t)] \wedge \forall t_1\,[t<t_1<t_a \wedge P(t_1)].$

That there is an instant before t_a which satisfies P is secured a fortiori by the fact that there is an instant before t_a such that all instants between it and t_a satisfy P. We may therefore simplify:

$\quad$ (A) $\quad \exists t\,\forall t_1\,[t<t_1<t_a \rightarrow P(t_1)].$

According to this, P would apply immediately before t_a if there were an (however short) interval before t_a such that all instants of this interval satisfy P. This definition agrees with intuition. So does an analogous one for what it means that P applies immediately after t_a, which can be derived in the same manner from Paul's second example:

(B) $\exists t \,\forall t_1 \,[t > t_1 > t_a \rightarrow P(t)]$.

From what has been said, and in order to be able to render the higher degree of precision of (1a*) over (1a) the introduction of two new prefixes, 'Imm$F$' and 'Imm$P$', suggests itself. They correspond to the expressions 'immediately after' and 'immediately before'. They acquire their 'meaning' by the following naming rule:

NR6) (1) Combination Rule: see NR5)
        (2) Semantics: (a) Imm$P$-P(t) iff $\exists t_1 \forall t_2 \,[t_1 < t_2 < t \rightarrow P(t_2)]$.
                         (b) Imm$F$-P(t) iff $\exists t_1 \forall t_2 \,[t < t_2 < t_1 \rightarrow P(t_2)]$.[82]

We can now render (1a*), as an analysis of (1) ("a begins to be white") in a formula very similar to (1a'):

(1a**) $W(t) \wedge \text{Imm}P\text{-}\sim\text{-}W(t)$.

Analogously, we can analyse (3b) (= "a begins to move") as (3b*) (= "a is not in motion but will be in motion immediately hereafter") and render it as:

(3b**) $\sim$-State-B(t) $\wedge$ Imm$F$-State-B(t).

A small step more demonstrates just how far the medieval 'logician's manner' which we have reconstructed indeed renders opinions concerning first and last instants of states unambiguously. We only have to consider what makes an instant the first or last instant of a P-interval: obviously, t is the first instant of a P-interval iff it satisfies t, but there is an interval, however short (open or half-closed), 'up to t' such that no instant of this interval satisfies P. It is the last instant of a P-interval iff there is such an interval 'from t on'.
An instant t is, thus, the first instant of a P-interval (closed or half-closed) iff
    (a) $P(t) \wedge \exists t_1 \,\forall t_2 [t_1 < t_2 < t \rightarrow \neg P(t_2)]$.
Analogously, t is the last instant of a P-interval iff
    (b) $P(t) \wedge \exists t_1 \,\forall t_2 [t_1 > t_2 > t \rightarrow \neg P(t_2)]$.
If a P-interval has no first instant, and is therefore an interval which is (at least) open towards the past, then the following is true of t if t is its (extrinsic) boundary towards the past:
    (c) $\neg P(t) \wedge \exists t_1 \,\forall t_2 [t_1 < t_2 < t \rightarrow P(t_2)]$.
And if it has no last instant, then the following is true of t as its (extrinsic) boundary towards the future:
    (d) $\neg P(t) \wedge \exists t_1 \,\forall t_2 [t_1 > t_2 > t \rightarrow P(t_2)]$.
Now the second conjunct of (a) kann be rewritten as "Imm$P$-$\sim$-P(t)"; the second conjunct of (b) can be rewritten as "Imm$F$-$\sim$-P(t)"; the second conjunct of (c) as "Imm$P$-P(t)"; and the second conjunct of (d) as "Imm$F$-

P(t)". What we obtain are precisely the typical medieval analyses of 'incipit'-
and 'desinit'-statements:

(a') P(t) ∧ Imm$P$-˜-P(t)
(b') P(t) ∧ Imm$F$-˜-P(t)
(c') ˜-P(t) ∧ Imm$P$-P(t)
(d') ˜-P(t) ∧ Imm$F$-P(t).

A final example can now be given to demonstrate the efficiency of the
standard logician's manner of describing the moment of change in late
medieval texts: the 'incipit'/'desinit' analysis given by Walter Burleigh in 'De
puritate artis logicae'.[83] The existence of the 'res permanens' 'whiteness' has,
such is the usual opinion, a first instant. At this instant it is true that *a*
begins to be white. If we notate the predicate "*a* begins to be white at..." as
'Inc-W', this can be elegantly expressed by analysing Inc-W(t) as (1a**):

Inc-W(t) iff   W(t) ∧ Imm$P$-˜-W(t).

In a different language:

'Sortes incipit esse albus' hoc est: 'Sortes est albus et sine medio non fuit albus'.
"Socrates begins to be white" means: "Socrates is white and was not white
immediately before".

An opinion which is not very clearly motivated but often found is that a 'res
permanens' has no last instant and ceases to be at the first instant which is
not an instant of its existence any more. If we notate "*a* ceases to be white
at..." as 'Desin-W', we can express this as:

Desin-W(t) iff   ˜-W(t) ∧ Imm$P$-W(t).

The same is true for the ceasing to be of a 'res permanens' such as 'motion':

...'desinit' tam in successivis quam in permanentibus exponitur eodem modo, scilicet
per negationem praesentis et positionem praeteriti.
'ceases' is analyzed in the same way for 'res successivae' and for 'res permanentes',
i.e. by a denial of the present and an assertion of the past.

Instantaneous 'res permanentes' are exceptional insofar as they cease to be at
the same instant at which the come to be. The analysis of a 'desinit'-
statement about an instantaneous 'res permanens' must therefore be in the
manner of (b'):

...in his, quae solum habent esse per instans, exponitur 'desinit' per positionem
praesentis.
...for [objects] which have their being at one instant only, 'desinit' is analysed by an
assertion of the present.

Since a 'res successiva' not only has no last instant but also no first instant, its 'incipit' must be analyzed in the manner of (3b**). Take, for example, the statement "Socrates starts running at..." ('Inc-R') and "Socrates is running at..." ('R'):

   Inc-R iff   ˜-State-R(t) ∧ Imm$F$-State-R(t).

Again, in a different language:

...in successivis debet exponi per negationem praesentis et positionem futuri, ut: 'Sortes incipit [currere]' hoc est: 'Sortes nunc non currit et sine medio curret'.

For 'res successivae' one should analyse ['begins'] by a denial of the present and an assertion of the future, for example "Socrates begins to run" as "Socrates is not running but will be running immediately afterwards".

Burleigh has only to justify this with a hint at some typical features of dense time[84] in order to complete his description:

...huius ratio est, quia in permanentibus est accipere primum instans esse termini, sed non in successivis; ubi non est accipere primum esse, ibi est accipere ultimum non esse, ideo in successivis est accipere ultimum non esse.

The reason for this is that for 'res permanentes' a first instant of being of the term is to be accepted, but not for 'res successivae'. Where no first [instant] of being is to be accepted, a last [instant] of non-being is to be accepted. Therefore a last [instant] of non-being is to be accepted for 'res successivae'.

It is easily seen that 'Inc' and 'Desin' are nothing other than two new prefixes which, combined with the name of an i-predicate, yields the name of a new i-predicate. Which instants satisfy a complex predicate so named depends on whether the i-predicate to whose name the prefix is attached refers to a 'res permanens' or to a 'res successiva'. A naming rule with which Burleigh could agree would be:

   NR7) (1) Combination Rule: 'Inc' and 'Desin' may be combined with the name of a temporal statement taking instants in order to obtain the name of a new temporal statement taking instants.
   (2) Semantical rule: (i) If P is a p-predicate:
                   (a)   Inc-P(t) iff P(t) ∧ Imm$P$-˜-P(t)
                   (b)   Desin-P(t) iff ˜-P(t) ∧ Imm$P$-P(t)
               (ii) If P is an s-predicate:
                   (c)   Inc-P(t) iff ˜-State-P(t) ∧ Imm$F$-State-P(t)
                   (d)   Desin-P(t) iff ˜-State-P(t) ∧ Imm$P$-State-P(t).

(P is a p-predicate iff P refers to a property F, and F is a p-property; P is an s-predicate iff P refers to a property F', and F' is an s-property.)

   Other medieval logicians would perhaps have disagreed with condition (b). If, for example, one wanted to assign a last instant to a 'res permanens',

the semantics for the 'desinit' of a 'res permanens' would have to be:
Desin-P(t) iff P(t) $\wedge$ Imm$F$-˜-P(t).

It is no exaggeration to state in a summary that a description of the moment of change with respect to C-changes cannot be expressed any more briefly and more precisely than in the medieval 'logician's manner'.

3.4. DESCRIPTION AND CLASSIFICATION OF THE MOMENT OF CHANGE IN THE MIDDLE AGES

3.4.1. Description

Considering the result, the mainstream method of describing the instant of change in the Middle Ages displays great conformity with Aristotle: for the description of C-changes, the either/or-option is used; and this is justified by the peculiar structure of the beginnings and endings of processes in a time-model according to which periods are infinitely divisible and, thus, instants are densely ordered. Opinion about s-changes (e.g. between rest and motion) can, as in Aristotle, only be perceived indirectly. But what can be reconstructed is again a result also found in Aristotle: the application of the neither/nor-option.

However, there are deviations from Aristotle as well. In Aristotle, some uncertainty about discontinuous changes could be seen. In the Middle Ages the distinction between 'res permanens' and 'res successiva' can help to clarify this: even if a person's coming to be is regarded as a discontinuous change, the medieval mainstream description allows a first instant of his/her existence, since a person is a typical 'res permanens'.

The application of the either/or-option to motion (and analogously to rest) when describing the change between motion and non-motion as a C-change is also new compared to Aristotle. This application presupposes a concept of motion at instants which is not found in Aristotle but *is* found in the late Middle Ages.

The motivation for describing the s-change between rest and motion (as far as it can be reconstructed) is influenced by the invention of talk about rest and motion at instants: the application of the neither/nor-option is no longer trivial, as it was in Aristotle. It rather results from the fact that both rest and motion are considered as 'res successivae' and that there are good reasons for denying first and last instants to a 'res successiva'.

The distinction of 'res permanens' and 'res successiva', and in the same way the further differentiation in the field of 'res permanens' (however awkward, sometimes, in detail) is never art for art's sake, but shows an amazing intuitive awareness of the problem of when one should assign first or last instants to a state and when one should not. I presume that the distinction between 'res permanens' and 'res successiva' corresponds to the distinction between comparative and non-comparative properties; and if so, the distinction seems by no means unreasonable.

3.4.2. The classification of the moment of change

Only indirectly can one tell what classification of the moment of change a medieval logician may have undertaken. However, I think that there is rather a clear indication that, if asked, he would have conceived the beginning or ending of a state as an instantaneous event: He accepts one single instant at which it is true that a state begins or ends. At the end of a process, the process *comes* to an end ('desinit'); it is not the case that it *has* just been complet*ed* as Aristotle's μεταβέβληκεν suggests. The present tense of 'incipit' and 'desinit', in contrast to the perfect tense Aristotle uses, should not be underrated. In my view, it exhibits a strong tendency towards considering C-changes as instantaneous events. This, once again, is a completely un-Aristotelian tendency.

A description of a change using the either/or-option and a classification of it as an instantaneous event in time are incompatible, assuming one holds Plato's premiss: if one holds the view that an event of changing at the limiting instant can only take place if neither the old state nor the new state obtains, then clearly, one cannot at the same time hold the view that such an event takes place at the limiting instant and assign the limiting instant to the old or to the new state. However, the instant of, for example, 'incipit' of a state is either an instant at which this state already obtains ('res permanens') or is an instant at which it does not yet obtain ('res successiva'). The first conjuncts of medieval analyses of 'incipit'- and 'desinit'-statements leave us in no doubt that the medieval logicians were well aware of this. This means that, in the classification of the moment of change, they pay a price for their analysis: they must reject Plato's premiss, although it seems rather plausible. According to the medieval mainstream view, the instant at which a person begins to exist is an instant at which he/she already exists. And at an instant when he/she begins to move he/she is not yet in motion.[85]

On the other hand, it becomes clear that keeping Plato's premiss while at the same time considering C-changes as datable events in a dense time involves an even higher price: using the neither/nor-option for contradictory changes and, therefore, abandoning the law of excluded middle.

3.4.3. A counter-current to the medieval mainstream

If deviations from the described mainstream view exist at all one might expect them to consist in one or another logician rating Plato's premiss highly enough to consistently use the neither/nor-option, even in the description of C-changes. The opposite is true: there is, actually, a current among the logicians of the 14th century which deviates from the mainstream, yet, this minority of logicians, most important among them John Baconthorpe and Landulf Carracioli, use the both-states-option for the description of the moment of change.[86]

They distinguish between an 'instans temporis' and an 'instans natur[a]e'.[87] This is a distinction reminiscent of the distinction of roles of the limiting instant made by Aristotle (Phys.263b9) according to which this instant is "one according to number but not according to concept". However, while Aristotle unambiguously assigns the limiting instant to one state only, logicians of the medieval counter-current seem to be of the opinion that two 'instantia nature' can coincide in one 'instans temporis' in such a way that this 'instans temporis' materially belongs to two contradictory states. While at an 'instans nature' no two contradictory states can obtain, this *is* in fact the case at an 'instans temporis', at which two 'instantia nature' of contradictory states exist. (John Baconthorpe, incidentally, believed the *philosophus* to be on his side owing to his use of a translation of Aristotle which was wrong in an important passage.[88])

The supposed motivation of the representatives of the counter-current for occupying themselves with the moment of change at all, may appear strange to us.[89] In order that Jesus Christ might be free of original sin from the first instant of his existence, Mary had to be cleansed of it before the conception of Jesus Christ: the earlier the better. 'As early as possible' means 'at the first instant of her own existence'. However, in order to be cleansed she had to have original sin. As she did not exist before, so that she could not have had it previously, she had to have it at the first instant of her existence and at the same time to be cleansed of it.

Philosophical questions come and go, but logic remains the same whatever it is applied to. So the question which poses itself in evaluating the medieval counter-current is whether applying the both-states-option is of any use. That does not depend on the issue in question but on whether one regards objective contradictions[90] as a desirable component of one's theory. This is a question to be dealt with in more detail in ch. II,3. in which a close look will be taken at a contemporary advocate of objective contradictions.

CHAPTER 4

KANT, MENDELSSOHN, SCHOPENHAUER

4.1. HISTORICAL PRELIMINARIES

The moment of change has had its peak seasons as a philosophical problem. It was discussed during the classical period of Attic philosophy, in the late Middle Ages and, in great variety, in the 20th century. By contrast, there appears to be a wide gap in the examination of the moment of change which coincides with the peak season of modern subject philosophy. The reason for this might be that *this* period was, in a sense, the dark ages of analysis of language and logical inquiries, rather than the Middle Ages. This evaluation is borne out in some passages from 18th and early 19th century texts, where, nonetheless, statements about the moment of change *are* found. Although not attaining the argumentative level of the 13th and 14th centuries, as a historical interlude between the Middle Ages and the 20th century they are worth close examination, not least because of the fame of the protagonists: Moses Mendelssohn and Immanuel Kant on the one hand, and Arthur Schopenhauer on the other. To prevent confusion when discussing Kant's and especially Mendelssohn's text it may be helpful to recapitulate some results which were 'state-of-the-art' during the late Middle Ages:

(1) We experience daily that certain things come into being and cease to exist, regardless of the question of whether perhaps their matter may ultimately be indestructible. It may not be so easy to give a good description of how this happens, but difficulties in this matter should hardly lead to a denial of our everyday experience. Medieval logicians have discussed, in this context, the old example of the change between life and death. However, sensibly enough they have had no doubt that Socrates in fact ceased to exist. The question of *whether* his soul continued to exist was of no importance to their analyses of 'incipit'- and 'desinit'-statements; they did not attempt to find logical obstacles to Socrates' death in the nature of time.

(2) Something either exists in time, or does not exist. Between an instant of an object's existence and an instant of non-existence, a process through any intermediate stages can no more be imagined than between an instant of having a property and an instant of not having it. This is nothing to do with the peculiar philosophical problems of existence, but simply with the word 'not'. If we abide by the fundamental laws of logic and assume time to be dense we cannot claim that there is a last instant of existence as well as a first

111

instant of non-existence. This does not, however, call into question the occurrence of changes between existence and non-existence. A change between existence and non-existence (like any change) takes place in such a way that a phase of the old state abuts a phase of the new state without any time gap in between.

(3) The statements of (1) and (2) are independent of the idea that any coming into being or ceasing to exist might have to happen in a process (that may be or may not be so). Even if that is so, no process takes place between existence and non-existence or vice versa, but at best from existence *in full size or vigour* to non-existence or vice versa. During such a process existence at half of the normal force or at a quarter of full size is, of course, still existence and in no way an intermediate state between existence and non-existence.

4.2. KANT VS. MENDELSSOHN

4.2.1. Moses Mendelssohn's 'Phädon'

Impressed by reading Plato's dialogues, Moses Mendelssohn undertook some kind of adaptation of Plato's 'Phaedo'.[1] The result is a piece of elegant German 18th century prose, thoroughly enjoyable for its style, and at the same time a piece of appallingly bad argument. In contrast to Plato's 'Phaedo', Mendelssohn's 'Phädon' contains an attempt to prove the immortality of the soul for which the moment of change is of prime importance. An alteration (Veränderung) is defined by Mendelssohn's Socrates as "the changing of opposite properties which a thing can possibly have" ("die Abwechselung der entgegengesetzten Bestimmungen, die an einem Dinge möglich sind").[2] According to this definition, an alteration could be (1) a process from an initial state to a target state, for example the changing between the properties of being in Hamburg and being in Munich; (2) but also an s-change between two states which, taken together, are at least duratively, possibly even instantaneously indispensable, for example being at rest and being in motion, or on/off. Surprisingly, Mendelssohn denies the possibility of (2). As 'opposite' ('entgegengesetzt') only such states are permitted as are the extreme points of a continuum of states:

Cebes [meint..:] Ich sollte nicht glauben, daß schnurstracks entgegengesetzte Zustände unmittelbar auf einander folgen könnten. - Richtig ! versetzte Sokrates. Wir sehen auch, daß die Natur in allen ihren Veränderungen einen Mittelzustand zu finden weiß, der ihr gleichsam zum Uebergange dient, von einem Zustande auf den entgegengesetzten zu kommen. Die Nacht folgt z.B. auf den Tag, vermittelst der Abenddemmerung, so wie der Tag auf die Nacht vermittelst der Morgendemmerung.[3]

Cebes [said]: I should not believe that altogether opposite states could follow one another immediately. - Right! replied Socrates. We also see that Nature in all her alterations knows how to find a middle state which allows her a transition from one state to its opposite. Night, e.g., follows day by way of dusk, just as morning follows night by way of dawn.

Mendelssohn tries to justify this opinion by pointing towards permanently effective forces ('Kräfte') which prepare the alteration while the initial state prevails.[4] This is, however, insufficient justification: against the background of the very indistinct notion of 'forces', instananeous change is in no way excluded (preparation through 'effective forces' is happening while the old state still prevails, so that the new state could very well follow without any further process when the time were ripe). Mendelssohn does not recognise this. He goes on to reason that, as instants are densely ordered,[5] there must always be a process between the old and the new state[6] such that at any instant which falls within the phase of the process, the object in question must be in one of infinitely many intermediate states. Again, there is no reason why density of time should entail this.

Mendelssohn emphasizes continuities from birth via death as far as decomposition.[7] It does not become clear, however, if he uses these words to refer to final instants of processes or to processes themselves. On the one hand, birth, death and decomposition are called alterations ("Veränderungen") which, he says, are "links in an uninterrupted chain" ("Glieder einer ununterbrochenen Kette"), "gradual wrappings and unwrappings of the selfsame thing which dresses and undresses in an infinite number of different shapes" ("allmählige Auswickelungen und Einwickelungen desselben Dinges, das sich in unzählige Gestalten einhüllet und entkleidet").[8] This points towards subprocesses of one large process, which is subdivided by the perceiving subject. In this sense Mendelssohn regards death and life as "parts of a continuous sequence of alterations which are linked to one another by gradual transitions in the most distinct manner" ("Glieder einer stetigen Reihe von Veränderungen, die durch stufenweise Uebergänge aufs Genaueste miteinander verbunden sind")[9], and from this draws the (questionable) conclusion that there is no "moment, when in all strictness it could be said: now the animal dies" ("Augenblick, da man, nach aller Strenge, sagen könnte: Itzt stirbt das Thier").[10] On the other hand, Mendelssohn characterizes death as:

[d]en [...] Zeitpunkt, da, wo sich die thierischen oder pflanzligten Bewegungen unseren Sinnen entziehen..[11]

the ...moment when the animal and vegetable movements remove themselves from our senses...

In this sense the words 'birth', 'death' and (ultimate) 'decomposition' can be regarded as referring to the *boundaries* of phases, 'epochs'[12], into which we subdivide a large process because it has visibly reached a new stage. The following distinction could clarify things: consider 'dying' as a process which still belongs to life; consider 'death' as a state which does not overlap with life; and consider the 'occurrence of death' as the end of the process of dying. Mendelssohn does not make any such distinction.

The process of aging whose last phase is dying, according to Mendelssohn, ultimately consists in small physical particles separating from one another, which, in composition, constitute the body.[13] Yet, the (atomic) particles continue to exist when the compound dissolves.[14] Mendelssohn's reason for this is the amazing core of his 'argument':

...giebt es wohl ein Mittel zwischen Seyn und Nichtseyn? - Keinesweges. - Seyn und Nichtseyn wären also zween Zustände, die unmittelbar aufeinander folgen, die sich einander die nächsten seyn müßten: wir haben aber gesehen, daß die Natur keine solchen Veränderungen, die plötzlich und ohne Übergang geschehen, hervorbringen kann. [...] Also kann die Natur weder ein Daseyn noch eine Zernichtung hervorbringen [.][15]

Now, is there a middle between being and non-being? - In no way. - Being and non-being would be two immediately consecutive states which would have to be next to each other: but we have seen that Nature cannot produce any such alterations which happen suddenly and without any transition. [...] Therefore Nature can neither bring forth being nor destruction.

There is no saying whether this is a matter of biological or logical impossibility. Mendelssohn argues with reference to the logical properties of dense time, but thinks that he is stating a biological impossibility. This becomes clear when he applies his idea to the soul. The soul can only cease to exist 'gradually' ('allmählig'), i.e. in the course of a process, or suddenly.[16] In this context Mendelssohn does not regard sudden destruction as logically impossible (no matter if time is dense):

Vielleicht vergehet die Seele plötzlich, verschwindet im Nu. An und für sich ist diese Todesart möglich. Kann sie aber von der Natur hervorgebracht werden? Keinesweges. [...] Zwischen Seyn und Nichtseyn ist eine entsetztliche Kluft, die von der allmählig wirkenden Natur der Dinge nicht übersprungen werden kann.[17]

Maybe the soul perishes suddenly, diappears all of a sudden. Actually, this manner of dying is possible. But can it be brought forth by Nature? In no way. [...] Between being and non-being, there is a terrifying gap which cannot be leapt across by the gradually effective nature of things.

God however, says Mendelssohn, can accomplish such a destruction ('Zernichtung'), although we may rely on His benevolence not to do so.[18]

To be on the safe side, Mendelssohn attempts to give a second proof that the soul cannot perish suddenly ('plötzlich').[19] As far as can be made out, it takes the following shape: we cannot tell exactly when the soul perishes; therefore it does not perish. This conclusion is just as dubious as Mendelssohn's reasoning for it: if there were an instant at which the soul perishes, this would have to be the instant of the body's death; but such an instant does not exist, because one cannot tell at which instant a body dies as there are continuous processes involved all the while. (At this point, of course, explanation would be necessary as to why the immortality of the body could not be proved in exactly the same way.)

The need for discussion remains concerning the possibility that the soul might not perish suddenly, but rather in the course of a process. This can, with some effort, be found in the very muddled final section of the argument:[20] if the soul were to perish in the course of a process, it would have to "diminish in force and inner effectiveness" ("an Kraft und innerer Wirksamkeit abnehmen"[21]); an occurrence which Mendelssohn does not only think possible, but even describes in detail.[22] The soul merely has to retain *some* activity, as it would otherwise perish.[23] However, it cannot perish in a natural way, as (Mendelssohn thinks) has already been proved, for this would be an impossible "leap from being to nothing" ("Sprung vom Daseyn zum Nichts").[24]

4.2.2. Kant's criticism of Mendelssohn

In no more than three sentences of the paralogism chapter of his first Critique (KrV B 413-415), Kant criticizes the passage of the 'Phädon' summed up in section 4.2.1. The criticism does not depend on Kant's transcendental philosophy of the Critiques. In particular, the main tenet of the paralogism chapter, that the soul is no object of experience, does not matter here. There is no intimate connection between Kant's statements on the moment of change discussed here and his transcendental philosophy. The passage in the paralogism chapter is, however, interesting as an attempt to reconstruct Mendelssohn's argument and as an attempt to react to its problems. What Kant reports of Mendelssohn is a surprisingly well-structured argument, if one compares it to the original source:

Dieser scharfsinnige Philosoph bemerkte bald in dem gewöhnlichen Argument, dadurch bewiesen werden soll, daß die Seele (wenn man einräumt, sie sei ein einfaches Wesen) nicht durch *Zerteilung* zu sein aufhören könne, einen Mangel der Zulänglichkeit zu der Absicht, ihr die notwendige Fortdauer zu sichern, indem man noch ein Aufhören ihres Daseins durch *Verschwinden* annehmen könnte.[25]

This acute philosopher soon noticed that the usual argument by which it is sought to prove that the soul - if it be admitted to be a simple being - cannot cease to be through *dissolution*, is insufficient for its purpose, that of proving the necessary continuance of the soul, since it may be supposed to pass out of existence through simply *vanishing*.[26]

Kant depicts Mendelssohn as having considered the soul as atomic (Mendelssohn does not explicitly say so in our passage, neither does he exploit this as an implicit assumption). Kant furthermore renders Mendelssohn as arguing that something could cease to exist if it (1) disintegrates into its parts (2) disappears ('verschwindet'). Now if (1) is not possible if the soul is atomic, (2) is not excluded yet. Kant goes on to say:

In seinem Phädon suchte er nun, diese Vergänglichkeit, welche eine wahre Vernichtung sein würde, von ihr dadurch abzuhalten, daß er sich zu beweisen getraute, ein einfaches Wesen könne gar nicht aufhören zu sein, weil, da es gar nicht vermindert werden und also nach und nach etwas an seinem Dasein verlieren und so allmählich in nichts verwandelt werden könne, (indem es keine Teile, also auch keine Vielheit in sich habe,) zwischen einem Augenblicke, darin es ist, und dem anderen, darin es nicht mehr ist, gar keine Zeit angetroffen würde, welches unmöglich ist.[27]

In his *Phaedo* he endeavoured to prove that the soul cannot be subject to such a process of vanishing, which would be a true annihilation, by showing that a simple being cannot cease to exist. His argument is that since the soul cannot be diminished, and so gradually lose something of its existence, being by degrees changed into nothing (for since it has no parts, it has no multiplicity in itself), there would be no time between a moment in which it is and another in which it is not - which is impossible.

Thus, Kant turns Mendelssohn's obscure argument into an unmistakably logical (and not biological) argument and eschews all talk of continuities in nature, forces and of the supposed impossibility of determining an instant of death. Kant's actual criticism is:

Allein, er [Mendelssohn] bedachte nicht, daß, wenn wir gleich der Seele diese einfache Natur einräumen, [und] sie [deshalb] keine extensive Größe enthält, man ihr doch, [nicht] intensive Größe, d.i. einen Grad der Realität [...], ableugnen könne, welcher durch alle unendlich vielen kleineren Grade abnehmen, und so die vorgebliche Substanz [...] obgleich nicht durch Zerteilung, doch durch allmähliche Nachlassung (remissio) ihrer Kräfte, (mithin durch Elangueszenz, wenn es mir erlaubt ist, mich dieses Ausdrucks zu bedienen,) in nichts verwandelt werden könne.[28]

He [Mendelssohn] failed, however, to observe that even if we admit the simple nature of the soul, [...] and therefore no extensive quantity, we yet cannot deny to it, [...], intensive quantity, that is, a degree of reality [...] and that this degree of reality may diminish through all the infinitely smaller degrees. In this manner the supposed substance [...] may be changed into nothing, not indeed by dissolution, but by gradual loss (*remissio*) of its powers, and so, if I may be permitted the use of the term, by elanguescence.

This criticism is strange in two respects:

(1) It is exaggerated. As we noted above, Mendelssohn points out explicitly that the soul, should it perish in the course of a process, "diminishes in force and effectiveness" ("Kraft und innerer Wirksamkeit abnehmen müsse").[29] He elaborates upon its experiencing a diminuition of activity towards the end of life.[30] Moreover he even discusses the possibility that the activity of the soul has, at last, come to a complete halt (everything "in it" should be "waste" ("öde")[31]), which would indeed, in Mendelssohn's opinion be its destruction ("Zernichtung").[32] Only, he reasons, this option is never realized, as it would be an impossible "leap from being to nothing".[33] Thus what Kant could rightly have criticized in Mendelssohn would not be his inability to recognize the option of the soul's 'elanguescence'. He can only object that Mendelssohn did not consider it seriously enough.

(2) One might expect Kant in what follows to deny that there must be both a last instant of existence and a first instant of non-existence of something (be it atomic or not). Only if both instants were to exist of necessity would one get the indicated impossibility. As we know from the last chapter, the typical answer given by a medieval logician would have been that no impossibility is involved here, since only one of these instants exists (an answer which is still quite up to date). Surprisingly, Kant does not dispute this extremely weak point of his reconstruction of Mendelssohn's argument. Franz Brentano already remarked that Kant takes a rather odd starting point for his criticism:

Kant [...] erkennt nicht dessen wahre Schwächen. Mendelssohn hielt es für einen Widerspruch, daß etwas Einfaches aufhöre, weil nach dem letzten Moment des Seins kein erster Moment des Nichtseins kommen kann. Er bemerkt nicht, daß man ebensogut sagen könnte, etwas *Zusammengesetztes* könne nicht aufgelöst werden, weil es nach dem letzten Moment der Verbindung keinen ersten Moment der Trennung geben kann.[34]

Kant misses the true weakness [of this proof]. According to Mendelssohn, it is contradictory to suppose that a simple substance ceases to be, since after the last moment of its existence there can be no first moment of its nonexistence. Mendelssohn does not note that one could prove the impossibility of breaking up a composite substance in a similar way: after that last moment at which its parts are together there can be no first moment at which they are separated.[35]

4.2.3. Evaluation of the controversy

§1 Kant indeed neglects Mendelssohn's main mistake: Mendelssohn does not keep apart the kind of states between which changes take place and the kind of states which bound a process. Existence and non-existence are states between which a *change* takes place. It is impossible to construe a *process* between them, because there are no intermediate states between them. However it does not follow from this that changes do not take place. A look at the following statements demonstrates clearly what goes wrong in Mendelssohn:

(P) Between the obtaining of the initial state and the target state of a process at least one intermediate state obtains.

(P+) Between the obtaining of the old state and the new state in any alteration (thus in a change, too) at least one intermediate state obtains.

(W) There is no intermediate state between existence and non-existence.

§2 Let us consider (P) first: (P) is plausible (although why is not clearly apparent). It is not enough to mention that time is dense. To argue that between any instant at which the initial state obtains and and any instant at which the target state obtains there is still another instant at which some state must obtain, prompts the response: "Of course. Either the initial state or the target state. What do we need an intermediate state for?". "Natura non facit saltus" as a counter-reply would be unsatisfactory, because it is merely a paraphase of (P) again. One would have to make two additional presuppositions:

(1) There is both a last instant of the initial state and a first instant of the target state.

(2) One can conceive of intermediate states between the initial state and the target state.

If these assumptions are added, one may indeed conclude that between the last instant of the initial state and the first instant of the target state, at least one of the intermediate states must obtain. Interestingly, this seems to be what Kant is doing in another passage in the first Critique (B 253), where he clearly presupposes (1) and (2):

Es frägt sich also, wie ein Ding aus einem Zustande =a in einen anderen =b übergehe. Zwischen zwei Augenblicken ist immer eine Zeit, und zwischen zwei Zuständen in denselben immer ein Unterschied, welcher eine Größe hat [...]. Also geschieht jeder Übergang aus einem Zustande in den anderen in einer Zeit, die zwischen zwei Augenblicken enthalten ist, deren der erste den Zustand bestimmt, aus welchem das Ding herausgeht, der zweite den, in welchen es gelangt. Beide also sind Grenzen der Zeit einer Veränderung, mithin des Zwischenzustandes zwischen beiden Zuständen, und gehören als solche mit zu der ganzen Veränderung.[36]

The question therefore arises how a thing passes from one state =a to another =b. Between two instants there is always a time, and between any two states in the two instants there is always a difference which has magnitude. [...] All transition from one state to another therefore occurs in a time which is contained between two instants, of which the first determines the state from which the thing arises, and the second that into which it passes. Both instants, then, are limits of the time of a change, and so of the intermediate state between the two states, and therefore as such form part of the total alteration.

Presupposition (2), however, limits the set of states for which the argument works to those states between which a process can take place at all.

§3 How about (P+) and (W)? (P+) is not just implausible; it is simply false. It is false because between those states between which changes take place one cannot conceive of a continuum of intermediate states. (W), however, is true for just the same reason for which (P+) is false.

The assumption of (P) and (W) is compatible with the assumption that there are changes between existence and non-existence, since the change between existence and non-existence is not a process.

Mendelssohn does not only assert (P) and (W), but the stronger claim (P+) and (W). If one assumes both (P+) and (W), there follows the conclusion that no object ever ceases to be. This is what happens to Mendelssohn (he, however, argues with the concrete example of the soul and, thus, misses the awkward generality of his result). He apparently concludes:

> There must be intermediate states involved in every alteration. Therefore, alterations between existence and non-existence do not occur.

He thus arrives at a false conclusion by arguing from an unsound premiss, namely (P+).

§4 This argument is overlaid by one which is equally bad, and in which dense time is involved:

> Between a last instant of existence and a first instant of non-existence there is another instant at which the object in question neither exists, or does not exist. Therefore changes from existence to non-existence do not take place.

Of course, this is wrong. One can only say (assuming LNC, LEM and dense time):

> If there is a last instant of existence and a first instant of non-existence, then there is at least another instant between them. It must be an instant of either existence or non-existence. If it is an instant of existence, the supposed last instant of existence was not really the last instant of existence. If it is an instant of non-existence, the supposed first instant of non-existence was not really the first instant of non-existence.

But all one may conclude from this is that there cannot be both a last instant of existence and a first instant of non-existence. This argument is (fortunately) no good for proving that there are no changes from existence to non-existence.

§5 Rather than tackling its real problem, i.e. the lack of a distinction between changes and processes in Mendelssohn, Kant, when criticizing Mendelssohn, deals with a further process, the soul's diminuition of intensity. He seems to overlook Mendelssohn's mistaken attempt to construe a process where it is not possible.

This is difficult to explain. My suggestion is that reading Mendelssohn's text with a lot of (conscious or unconscious) charity one might say:

> During a divisible object's phase of dissolution, the object still exists and is far from being in an inconceivable intermediate state between existence and non-existence. Thus, the processes Mendelssohn describes cannot be processes between existence and non-existence as such; he must mean processes between existence *in full size* and non-existence.

Taking this as a starting point, Kant might have reconstructed Mendelssohn's argument like this:

> Towards the end of the existence of every divisible object a process of dissolution into its atomic parts takes place. It is bounded by a last instant at which the object still exists in full size (initial state) and by a first instant at which it has completely dissolved (target state). Yet an atomic object cannot dissolve into parts. Between its existence in full size and its non-existence there could not be a process of diminuition. However one cannot conceive of anything perishing without a process of diminuition. For otherwise the last instant of existence in full size (which always exists) and the first instant of non-existence (which always exists, too) would coincide. Therefore an atomic object is indestructible.

The justification ("for otherwise...") is, again, very dubious. But looking at the text of the first Critique B 413, one sees that Kant does not comment or exploit it at all but just reports it. The gist of his answer to Mendelssohn simply seems to be:

> I agree with you that perishing without a process is inconceivable. But it is quite possible to think of a process of diminuition of an atomic object (personally, I do not think of the soul as such an object anyway, but never mind). Although an atomic object has no parts, it exists with a certain intensity, as you say yourself. But if it does, there can also be a process in the course of which an atomic object may perish: a process of the diminuition of intensity which is bounded by the last instant of full-force intensity and the first instant of zero intensity (= non-existence).

If this is the core of Kant's answer, he emerges as an adherent of the either/or-option for describing the end of a process in the sense of Aristotelian and medieval tradition: there is no last instant at which the intensity of the supposed atomic object would be above zero. So there is a first instant at which zero intensity has been reached. Kant thus describes a process towards the end of existence, but still during the existence of the object in question. He does not describe the alteration between existence and non-existence as a process. He, thus, does not arrive at such bizarre results as Mendelssohn. On the other hand, Kant does not distinguish explicitly between process and change. This, however, he would have to do if he wished to criticize the actual core of Mendelssohn's argument.

4.3. SCHOPENHAUER

In the second edition of his doctoral dissertation[37] Arthur Schopenhauer attempts to interpret Plato's and Aristotle's texts on the moment of change and to correlate them. Although he mainly misinterprets the texts, an examination of his view at this point allows us to look back to antiquity in order to conclude the first part of this book. Schopenhauer is interested in the question of when an alteration ('Veränderung') takes place. He uses this word to translate μεταβολή in Plato as well as in Aristotle:

Plato hat diesen schwierigen Punkt ziemlich cavalièrement abgefertigt, indem er, im Parmenides [...], eben behauptet, die Veränderung geschehe plötzlich und fülle gar keine Zeit; sie sei im εξαιφνης [sic] [...], welches er eine ατοπος φυσις, εν χρονω ουδεν ουσα [sic], also ein wunderliches, zeitloses Wesen (das denn doch in der Zeit eintritt) nennt. Dem Scharfsinn des Aristoteles ist es demnach vorbehalten geblieben, diese schwierige Sache ins Reine zu bringen;[...][38]

Plato did away with this difficult point rather cavalierly by claiming, in the 'Parmenides', [...] that an alteration ('Veränderung') happens suddenly and fills no time whatsoever, being in the εξαιφνης [...] which he calls an ατοπος φυσις, εν χρονω ουδεν ουσα, i.e. a strange timeless object (which, however, does occur in time). It was, thus, left to Aristotle's acumen to clear up this difficult matter.[39]

Schopenhauer thus regards a χρόνος in both Plato and Aristotle as a period: an alteration 'fills' it. Consequently, according to Schopenhauer, Plato does not banish it from time;[40] Schopenhauer's reproach is only that Plato robbed alteration of temporal extension. Although Schopenhauer is not very clear on this, according to his view Plato might well have assigned the taking place of a change to an instant.

Schopenhauer does not realize that Plato and Aristotle, in their use of the word μεταβολή, are referring to something completely different from one another. He finds the Aristotelian meaning of the word (from Physics VI), i.e. 'process', in his reading of Plato. Therefore he arrives at completely the wrong result, that Plato postulated jerks between those states which are typically initial states and the target states of processes. This is the more incomprehensible in view of his reliable summary of Plato's text:

[Die Veränderung] könne nämlich nicht Statt haben, während der frühere Zustand noch dasei, und auch nicht, nachdem der neue schon eingetreten: geben wir ihr aber eine Zeit zwischen beiden; so müßte während dieser [...] z.B. [...] ein Körper weder ruhend noch bewegt seyn; welches absurd wäre.[41]

[An alteration] could not take place while the old state is still there, and neither after the new one has already begun: but if we admit a time between the two [states], then a body would [at that time] have to be neither at rest nor in motion, which would be absurd.

What Schopenhauer, then, reports as Aristotle's argument is the usual mention of the continuitiy of time and process (as we know from ch.I,2., Aristotle had a lot more to say about the moment of change than this):

Wie zwischen zwei Punkten immer noch eine Linie, so ist zwischen zwei Jetzt immer noch eine Zeit. Diese nun ist die Zeit der Veränderung; wenn nämlich im ersten Jetzt ein Zustand und im zweiten ein anderer ist. Sie ist, wie jede Zeit, ins Unendliche theilbar: folglich durchgeht in ihr das sich Verändernde unendlich viele Grade, durch die aus jenem ersten Zustande der zweite allmählig erwächst.[42]

Just as there is always a line between two points, there is always a [period of] time between two nows. This is the time of alteration. If in the first now there is one state and in the second [now] a different state. It is, like every [period of] time, infinitely divisible: consequently in it the changing [object] goes through infinitely many degrees, through which from this first state the second [state] gradually emerges.

In order to make this "comprehensible to the layman as well" ("gemeinverständlich ... zu erläutern"),[43] Schopenhauer puts a rather odd epistemological dressing on top:

Zwischen zwei successiven Zuständen, deren Verschiedenheit in unsere Sinne fällt, liegen immer noch mehrere, deren Verschiedenheit uns nicht wahrnehmbar ist, weil der neu eintretende Zustand einen gewissen Grad, oder Größe, erlangt haben muß, um sinnlich wahrnehmbar zu seyn.[44]

Between two successive states whose being different [from one another] we can perceive, there are always some more whose being different [from one another] is not perceptible for us, because the new state must have reached a certain degree or size in order to be perceptible through the senses.

Thus supposedly, after being pushed a body is in "a certain oscillation" ("in gewisser Schwingung") for a moment which is too minute to be perceived, before it "bursts into outward motion" ("in äußere Bewegung ausbricht").[45] Schopenhauer's result is:

Aristoteles schließt ganz richtig, aus der unendlichen Theilbarkeit der Zeit, daß alles dieses Ausfüllende, folglich auch jede Veränderung, d.i. Übergang aus einem Zustand in einen andern, ebenfalls unendlich theilbar seyn muß, daß also Alles, was entsteht [...] mithin stets allmählig, nie plötzlich wird.[46]

Aristotle is quite right in concluding from the infinite divisibility of time that everything that fills it, consequently every alteration, i.e. transition from one state to another, too, must be infinitely divisible, too, and that therefore everything which comes into being [...] does so gradually, and never suddenly.

So if Schopenhauer's opinion is correct, there must be an infinite number of intermediate states between motion and rest. But what on earth are they? How can one imagine a temporally extended process between being at rest and being in motion, being on and being off, being in the target position and being away from it? Is it really the fault of our limited abilities of perception if we fail to notice any intermediate states here? It seems rather that they cannot exist for 'logical' reasons.

Both Schopenhauer and Mendelssohn teach us what happens if one says "Natura non facit saltus" without thinking about it: both philosophers fail to see that s- and C-changes are something very different from processes. They make us all the more appreciate the, in this respect, unprejudiced reasoning of the late Middle Ages. They also make us see that the clear distinction between processes and their boundaries in Plato and Aristotle was no small analytic achievement.

PART II: THE MOMENT OF CHANGE IN THE 20th CENTURY

CHAPTER 1

THE EITHER/OR-OPTION

1.0. A SURVEY OF PART II AND OF CH.II,1.

In the second part of this book I will present, put into some systematic order and evaluate attempts at a description and classification of the moment of change which have been made in our century. Chronological order is unimportant now. The texts will be classified according to the four systematic options one has for describing the moment of change: the either/or-option (ch.II,1), the either-way-option (ch.II,2), the both-states-option (ch.II,3) and the neither/nor-option (ch.II,4). Since exclusive application of just one option will prove to yield unsatisfactory results, a further chapter (ch.II,5) will present a good compromise: a mixed description using the neither/nor- and the either/or-option, which is known by the somewhat misleading name of 'Neutral Instant Analysis'.

In the present chapter (II,1), the focus is directed towards some contemporary contributions to the problem of the moment of change in which the either/or-option is favoured:

(1) Ch.II,1.1. is concerned with suggestions of how to treat the moment of change made by Richard Sorabji as well as by Frank Jackson and Robert Pargetter.

Sorabji regards the limiting instant at the beginning and at the end of a process as an instant at which either the old state still obtains or at which the new state already obtains. He proposes a *description* of the moment of change without, however, committing himself to a particular *classification* of it. Sorabji's description of the moment of change is an important attempt at a modernization of the Aristotelian and medieval approaches. The concept of momentary velocity plays an important role in enabling Sorabji to assign the limiting instant to either the old or the new state non-arbitrarily. Jackson/Pargetter rely even more strongly on this concept.

When discussing their contribution, I will try to show that it is not attractive to lay so much emphasis on the concept of momentary velocity when describing the moment of change. I would like to point out that even today this concept should not be taken for granted but that it is still quite problematic. However, only the use of the concept of momentary velocity provides us with a plausible reason to assign the limiting instant to the one rather than to the other state. Since it is not advisable to rely on this concept, applying the either/or-option to the s-change between rest and motion turns out to imply a certain arbitrariness. It might, however, very well be a good description for C-changes.

(2) Chapter II,1.2. is about a suggestion of how to treat the moment of change made by Antony Galton in connection with his event logic. Like Sorabji, Galton describes the moment of change by using the either/or-option. He focuses on C-changes; emphasis is on the *classification* of the moment of change (which clearly motivates Galton's description).

Galton rates Plato's premiss very highly. Since he assumes instants to be densely ordered and keeps LNC and LEM, his classification of the moment of change is almost identical with Plato-1: Galton, too, banishes change from time, although he clearly regards it as an event.

Galton's treatment of the moment of change is best understood as part of a tradition in the 20th century starting with Russell's 'Cambridge Criterion for Change' and including v.Wright's T-operator, which exhibits a strong tendency towards viewing the present tense in statements about the moment of change as atemporal. At the end of the chapter, I want to deal with Bertram Kienzle's criticism of Galton's approach and with his alternative proposal.

The discussion of Galton's proposal will show that using the either/or-option for the description of C-changes is very plausible indeed, but that if Plato's premiss is to be kept this enforces the banishment of change from time, which is implausible.

1.1. RICHARD SORABJI, FRANK JACKSON, ROBERT PARGETTER: TYING THE DESCRIPTION OF THE CHANGE BETWEEN REST AND MOTION TO THE CONCEPT OF MOMENTARY VELOCITY

1.1.1. Sorabji's suggestion for a description of the moment of change

Richard Sorabji's treatment of the moment of change coincides in many parts with Aristotelian and medieval tradition. This is no coincidence: Sorabji's systematic suggestion is contained in the last sections of his interpretation of Aristotle's views on the moment of change.[1]

As far as non-comparative properties with respect to the beginnings and ends of processes are concerned, Sorabji's description is identical with the Aristotelian and medieval one. Taking local motion as an example, this means that a last instant of being in the initial position and a first instant of being away from it mutually exclude one another. The same is true for a first instant of being in the target position and a last instant of being away from it. Now since, dense time assumed, there is no first position away from the initial position and no last position away from the target place, the limiting instant at the beginning of the process must be the last instant at which a is still in the initial position; and the limiting instant at the end of a process must be the first instant at which a is in the target place.[2]

Sorabji attempts to construe discontinuous changes (again in perfect agreement with Aristotle and medieval logicians) as depending on processes. He is, however, himself sceptical if this strategy can be successful in all cases.[3]

Sorabji's unprecedented contribution to the discussion of the moment of change is his proposal for describing the s-change between rest and motion. Sorabji's comments on Aristotle show that, like him, he views motion and rest as comparative properties. In contrast to Aristotle (but in agreement with the medieval 'mainstream') he allows talk of motion and rest at instants, in the sense of being in the course of moving or resting at instants.

Sorabji tries to establish an 'asymmetry' which 'recommends'[4] (without being 'mandatory'[5]) the assignation of the limiting instant to the one state rather than to the other. Sorabji believes that even a minor asymmetry should be sufficient to tip the scales in a situation where intuition is so finely balanced. In the second version of his article, Sorabji gives the following two reasons as to why the situation is asymmetrical:

[1] The asymmetry between the position of rest and the positions away from it can provide us with the excuse we want for treating rest differently from motion. It would be perfectly reasonable to mark the asymmetry by saying that just as there is no first or last instant of being away from the position of rest, so equally there is no first or last instant of motion. [...] [2] [...] let us suppose that not only change of place is continuous, but also change of velocity. [...] Now it seems more natural [...] to connect zero velocity with rest, and velocities above zero with motion. If we do, we get the result that there is no first or last instant of motion...[6]

Sorabji does not repeat (1) in the third version, but only (2).[7] I think that he is right in omitting (1), since it is difficult to see why (1) is a reason (in the sense of a justification) for doing one thing and not another. It is not at all clear why, for example, the existence of a last instant at which a is in *the position of* rest should convince us of the existence of a last instant at which a is *at rest*.

Thus only reason (2) remains. The velocities referred to there are 'momentary velocities' of Newtonian Physics.[8] Sorabji restricts himself to cases in which a accelerates and slows down gradually. In these cases a has a 'momentary velocity' at any instant, including the limiting instant. At the limiting instants at the beginning of a motion it equals zero, at any later instant which falls within the period of motion it is greater than zero, and at the limiting instant at the end of the process it is zero again.

It is quite a restriction to exclude abrupt beginnings of a motion. This case should be taken into account in order to assess whether it is recommendable to tie the description of the moment of change between rest and motion to the concept of instantaneous velocity.

Jackson and Pargetter[9] treat this case in detail, but otherwise hold the same opinion as Sorabji. For this reason their suggestion is best discussed as a systematic extension of Sorabji's approach.

1.1.2. Jackson and Pargetter's case: an abrupt beginning of motion

Jackson and Pargetter's suggestion[10] is identical with Sorabji's in all the cases Sorabji deals with (gradual acceleration and slowing down). Unlike Sorabji, Jackson and Pargetter treat the possibility of an abrupt beginning of motion in addition to those cases.

According to Jackson andPargetter (and not implausibly), one should be able to talk about motion and rest by talking about places and times only. The problem of the moment of change does not exist because of any lack of information. Motion and rest are comparative properties (Jackson and Pargetter call them 'relational') such that talk of rest and motion in our context may be reduced to talk about the positions of a at times (i.e. instants):

Full information about position over time, which we have, must be enough because it logically determines motion and rest. [..] ...we cannot excuse our being unable to answer whether X is moving or is at rest at t=0 by pleading ignorance of relevant data.[..] motion is not an intrinsic property of objects at times, it is a relational property.[11]

Just like Sorabji, Jackson and Pargetter associate zero momentary velocity with rest. They do so by saying that t_1 is an instant of rest of a if the differential coefficient of the local funtion of a with respect to t_1 (which is usually interpreted as the 'momentary velocity' of a at t_1) is zero for h tending towards zero. For an instant at which it is not equal to zero, a is in motion:

We define "X is moving at t_1" as "the limit $[F(t_1+h)-F(t_1)]/h$ tends to as h tends to zero, is non-zero".[12]

Thus the problem which Jackson and Pargetter now pose themselves, formulated in the language of physics, is the very problem Sorabji tries to avoid by restricting his cases:

A particle, X, has its position, s, over time, t, relative to some frame of reference fully specified by: s=0 for t<0, s=t for t ≥ 0. Clearly, X is at rest before t=0, and moving after t=0, but what is the correct thing to say about it *at* t=0 ?[13]

Accordingly, we have a section-wise defined local function of an object X, according to which X is at rest up to t=0 (t=0 being excluded) and is in motion from t=0 on (t=0 being excluded) at a constant speed of one distance unit per time unit, e.g. 1mph.[14] The graph of this local function may therefore be represented like in fig.5.

At the decisive instant t=0, no momentary velocity is defined for X, since X's local function cannot be differentiated at this point. It is crucial for Jackson and Pargetter's solution that in this situation they split up momentary velocity into 'left-hand velocity' and 'right-hand velocity'. Instead of admitting positive and negative values for h, they restrict the domain of h to positive values for the following definitions:

X is left-hand moving (with velocity v) at t_1 if and only if the limit of $[F(t_1)\text{-}F(t_1\text{-}h)]/h$ is non-zero (and equals v) as h tends to zero; while X is right-hand moving (with velocity v) if and only if the limit of $[F(t_1+h)\text{ -}F(t_1)]/h$ is non-zero (and equals v).[15]

Fig.5

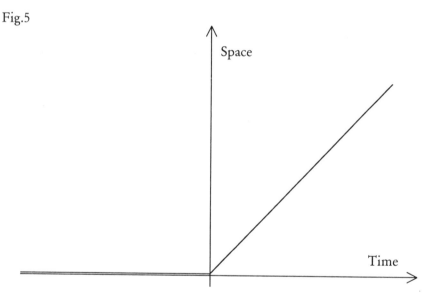

It is true that no momentary velocity of X is defined for t=0; but 'left-hand velocity' is defined for it (it is zero distance units per time unit), and so is 'right-hand velocity' (it is one distance unit per time unit). However, as Jackson and Pargetter notice themselves, they are still one step short of being able to exploit this definition:

...our original question was not about left-hand and right-hand rest, motion and velocity, but about rest, motion and velocity. We need a thesis in semantics how to go from the former to the latter.[...] Statements about velocity, and so about rest and motion, at a time are true (false) if both interpreting them as statements about left-hand velocity and interpreting them as statements about right-hand velocity make them true (false). They are indeterminate otherwise. That is, if switching from interpreting velocity as left-hand velocity to interpreting it as right-hand velocity, or vice versa changes a statement's truth-value, the statement is indeterminate; while if it does not change truth-value, the statement has that unchanging truth-value.[16]

Accordingly, in the situation depicted in fig.5 (abrupt beginning of a motion) the truth-value of the statement "X is moving" with respect to t=0 is 'indeterminate'; and the same is also true for the statement "X is at rest". 'Indeterminate' does not have to be a third truth-value. But obviously Jackson and Pargetter accept that there are statements whose truth-value is not determined as true or false (in view of this, it is quite incomprehensible that they can, then, claim that the statement "X is always moving or at rest" is true).[17]

For the description of their case (abrupt beginning) Jackson and Pargetter use the neither/nor-option. In contrast, for the description of a case as Sorabji permits it, they use the either/or-option.

1.1.3. The concept of momentary velocity
In my opinion tying the description of the s-change between rest and motion to the concept of 'momentary velocity' is not a very attractive option because, among other reasons, this concept itself is not unproblematic. I am aware of the fact that this must today appear to be a rather eccentric opinion, especially to physicists. Physics has been using this concept very successfully since Newton; and if something works, we tend to regard it as completely unproblematic. Nevertheless, I will not conceal my view on this point.

There is no disputing that the limit of the differential coefficient of the local function of a at t is a number which, as soon as it is known, allows · extremely useful predictions as to the future behaviour of a. One may call it the M-value of a at t. What I find problematic is calling the M-value of a at t a *velocity*, no matter what kind of case we are concerned with. In my view, one should distinguish cases in which this is plausible from cases in which it is not.

A velocity is expressed as the proportion of a distance towards the duration of a period. However, if a gets from A to B during a period c, one will not regard the proportion of the distance A-B towards c as a velocity of a during c in every case. One will only do so if a moves in a certain 'uniform' manner throughout c.[18]

An M-value of the local function of a exists for every t which falls within a period during which a is moving uniformly in this sense. It is the same M-value for all those instants. It exists because the series (of velocities) which results if one lets h tend towards zero in the well-known manner is constant, and because a constant series trivially converges towards a limit (which, of course, equals each of its members).

In this case, it is unproblematic to interpret the M-value as a velocity: in c, *a* has the velocity v, and even has the velocity v in any subperiod of c. There can be no objection to assigning to *a* a property with respect to those instants which fall within c if *a* has this property throughout c by saying that *a* is in the course of moving at velocity v then.

One may even regard this as a semantic principle of the phrase 'being in the course of'. This principle already motivated the introduction of the state-prefix in I,3. For the case considered it may be described so: however short the period c may be, throughout which *a* has the velocity v, at t *a* is in the course of moving at v, because t falls within c and *a* is moving at v throughout c.

Nothing of the sort applies if c is a phase of acceleration or of slowing down of *a*.[19] It is true that in this case, too, if *a*'s acceleration or its slowing down is continuous, there is an M-value of the local function of *a* for every t from the interval during which this takes place (a different one for each t). But it does not exist as the limit of a constant series. In this case, t does not fall within a period throughout which *a* is moving at v.

Therefore in the second case there is no justification for saying that *a* is in the course of moving at velocity v at t. It should suffice to say that *a* has the M-value v at t. Saying so removes the concept of momentary velocity where it is problematic, but keeps it where it is plausible.

1.1.4. Evaluation of the momentary velocity approach

Even someone who thinks that the concept of momentary velocity is wholly unproblematic should, in my opinion, seriously consider whether or not to tie the description of the moment of change to this concept. Jackson and Pargetter's case of an abrupt transition can be imagined (although it is a rather bold claim that it is "physically realizable"[20]).

Yet this case shows that the s-change between rest and motion has to be dealt with by using two different options, according to the case in question,[21] if the concepts of motion and rest are tied to momentary velocity in this way. Furthermore, one has to accept statements with an indeterminate truth-value. This should be avoided wherever possible. And we shall see in ch.II,5 that it is possible: Bertrand Russell's and Norman Kretzmann's proposals for defining rest and motion at instants are independent of the concept of momentary velocity. They do not need statements with an indeterminate truth-value and they do not have to use several options in order to describe one kind of change. These suggestions will show themselves to be superior to Jackson/Pargetter's one as regards both economy and simplicity.

If one refrains from tying the definitions of rest and motion at instants to the concept of momentary velocity, there is no more justification for assigning the limiting instant to rest rather than motion. Accordingly, Sorabji's second argument in favour of an asymmetry must be rejected. No possible reason has appeared for assigning the limiting instant to motion rather than to rest. Therefore, using the either/or-option for the description of the moment of change between rest and motion must appear to involve an arbitrary decision of assigning the limiting instant rather to one state than to the other.

However, Sorabji's and Jackson and Pargetter's approaches are elaborate and, to a great extent, plausible. Their logic is not extravagant, and they will look especially intuitive to those who work with M-values in natural science. I prefer the Neutral Instant Analysis, which will be presented in ch.II,5, but on this point, I expect many readers to disagree with me and to favour Sorabji. I have therefore tried to present my own systematic suggestion in part III in such a way that its basic idea may be appreciated independently of the Neutral Instant Analysis and might be accepted by an adherent of Sorabji's position as well.

1.2. ANTONY GALTON'S 'LOGIC OF ASPECT'

1.2.1. Introduction

Antony Galton makes an attempt to describe and to classify the moment of change within the framework of his event logic. It largely corresponds to Plato-1 as presented in ch.I,1.3.2. It is true that Galton does without a paradoxical extratemporal item such as Plato-1's 'sudden', but he, too, is compelled to say that changes take place at no time. Galton's starting point is Priorian tense logic. The basic idea of his event logic is, however, that the applicability of tense logic is more limited than it was thought to be, since it cannot satisfactorily render statements about events, but only statements about states. Galton's analysis of 'begin' and 'stop' is strongly inflenced by v.Wright's T-operator and Russell's 'Cambridge criterion for change'.

Like Plato, Galton does not distinguish between comparative and non-comparative states. The starting of a car, an s-change between rest and motion, is treated on a par with C-changes, on which Galton's analysis is based. Galton's main interest is in the classification of the moment of change, not its description. For the description, he clearly uses the either/or-option. But he does not try to motivate which state the limiting instant should be assigned to, as Sorabji does.

1.2.2.Cambridge-changes and v.Wright's T-Operator
1.2.2.1. Russell's Cambridge-change-definiens
§1 Galton's way of treating change is part of a tradition which starts with Russell and v.Wright. It is true that Galton's opinion that changes take place at no time is not entailed by Russell's and v.Wright's ideas of an atemporal use of the present tense. However it is not only compatible with these ideas, but also very close to them.

Bertrand Russell attempted to find a general definition of change, in §442 of his 'Principles of Mathematics' of 1903. This attempt has become famous, and Geach later baptized it the 'Cambridge Conception of Change'.[22] Russell's definition works with 'classical', i.e. temporally definite propositions which have exactly one truth-value which does not vary with time:

Change is the difference, in respect of truth or falsehood between a proposition concerning an entity and a time T and a proposition concerning the same entity and another time T', provided that the two propositions differ only by the fact that T occurs in the one where T' occurs in the other.[23]

The *definiens* can be easily identified and be rendered in the notation used in this book (taking 'times' to be instants):

$$... \exists t_1, t_2 [(P_a(t_1) \land \neg P_a(t_2)) \lor (\neg P_a(t_1) \land P_a(t_2))].$$

Unfortunately, a barrage of nouns ("Change... difference... truth... falsehood") makes it rather hard to arrive at the *definiendum*. Russell means to specify, as the sentences following the quotation show, under which conditions the classical proposition is true that *a* changes in the course of its history ('changes' being an atemporal present tense).

§2 Russell's attempt fails because of two problems. Russell himself notices the first only a few lines further down in the text (however, as far as I can see, it was rarely noticed that it he had noticed it):

Mere existence at some but not at all moments constitutes change on this definition. [...] This shows that the definition requires emendation if it is to accord with usage.[24]

Hence, in a world in which *a* never changes during its existence, but simply comes to be and perishes, the definiens would be true. But this does not fit the *definiendum* to which Russell holds. One might hope that the Cambridge-definiens (since that is all we have) fits another definiendum better, which is close enough to the original one: the Cambridge-definiens might define under which conditions the proposition is true that *a* changes during its existence *or* comes to be/perishes.

A difficulty here is that there are a lot of propositions which do not only 'concern' one entity but more than one. This is the second problem. Geach's example of this is that, at first, Socrates does not matter at all to a boy called Gary, but that later on, he does. Russell is, of course, looking for a criterion which yields that during this development it is Gary who changes and not Socrates. But the proposition that Gary admires Socrates in 1968 (false) and the proposition that Gary admires Socrates in 1969 (true) are propositions which concern Socrates just as much as Gary.[25]

Furthermore, there is the question of how far Russell would require us to expand our ontology in order to be within reach of an 'entity' which changes whenever Russell's definiens is true: do we have to introduce an entity called 'rain' just because the proposition that it is raining in Münster on the 12th of February, 1996, at 4 o'clock p.m. is false and the proposition that it is raining in Münster on the 12th of February, 1996, at 5 o'clock p.m. is true? What is the subject of change if the proposition that the 6 o'clock train from Münster to Osnabrück on a certain day is in the station at 6 o'clock but the proposition that it is still there at ten past 6 is false? Do we have to introduce an entity called 'the distance between the station and the train'? Is the last example really, according to its logical form (which is concealed by natural language expression), about a thing called 'distance'? Does every change need a clear-cut object as its ὑποκείμενον? If so, what kind of object?

Russell has no answer to these questions. The end of §442 and the following paragraphs up to §445 are a desperate attempt at solving the problems he is faced with by resorting to his early Platonism. There is talk of 'terms' which sometimes exist but, apart from that, extratemporally 'have being' and are related to one another in certain respects. There is nothing to be added to Ayer's criticism of this:

...even if we accept the very dubious assumption that a proper name like 'Socrates' can have an immutable and indestructible sense, it is unhappily just false to speak of Socrates as being either immutable nor indestructible.[26]

§3 In spite of all that, Geach is right in calling Russell's *definiens* the "only clear, sharp conception of change we have".[27] For if we delete the problematic reference to the subject of change, what the *definiendum* can plausibly be becomes clear: the classical proposition that in the course of the history of the world something changes (atemporal present tense). We need to lower our expectations concerning the definiendum a little. But if we do so, it can hardly be disputed that Russell's definition is very intuitive indeed.

§4 It is, however, important to note that the Cambridge definition of change (at which we have now arrived) tells us nothing about the moment of change. It is not at all concerned with the question of *when* something changes (temporal present tense). It does not tell us anything about possible first and last instants of states. It does not tell us anything about when an event of changing might take place. It leaves open the possibility that it takes place at no time. The reason for this is that the *definiendum* is a classical proposition such that if it is expressed in English the verb's present tense is to be considered as atemporal. This makes a great difference in comparison with the medieval approach according to which the present tense of 'incipit' and 'desinit' in the definienda is always a temporal present tense.

1.2.2.2. v. Wright's 'T-Operator'

§1 While Russell had formulated his criterion in terms of classical propositions, the first formal tool for rendering it comes from tense logic: Georg Henrik v. Wright's 'T-operator'.[28] It takes two temporally indefinite propositions (and might therefore also be called T-junctor) and yields another temporally indefinite proposition.[29] On the basis of dense time, it may be interpreted as meaning 'and then':

pTq is true at time t iff
p is true at time t and
q is true at some time t' later than t.

p and q may be compatible (it is even possible to render the continuance of a state by pTp). However they may also be contraries or contradictories. When working with temporally indefinite propositions the Cambridge-definiens will be rendered as

¬pTp ∨ pT¬p.

The T-operator allows to differentiate Russell's idea a little further by saying that the state that p begins if ¬pTp is true and ends if pT¬p is true. However, while doing this one should be aware of the fact that the present tense of 'begins' and 'ends' (again in contrast to 'incipit' and 'desinit') is atemporal. One should be aware of the fact that, as with Russell, several questions are left open: if ¬pTp is true, this, once again, does not tell us anything about *when* the state that p begins, about whether there is a first instant at which the state that p obtains rather than a last instant at which it does not. And this does not tell us anything about *how often* the state that p begins: if there is an instant at which it does not obtain and then, later on, an instant at which it does, there are, in dense time, infinitely many instants between those two at which it may obtain or not obtain, there possibly being some very quick 'oscillation' between its obtaining and its not obtaining.

1.2.3. Events and event radicals in Galton's event logic; event-logical operators

§1 According to Galton, logical relations between statements about events cannot be rendered adequately in Priorian tense logic or in any other logic which works exclusively with propositions. So in addition to propositions, Galton assumes there to be what he calls 'event radicals'. It is these event radicals on which operators of event logic are effective. Galton tries to give an impression of what an event radical (notated: E) is, by saying that it is that which the following two sentences have in common:

I wrote a book.
I shall write a book.[30]

Thus, the event radical involved here roughly corresponds to the phrase 'my writing a book'. As well as distinguishing between propositions and event radicals, Galton distuinguishes between states and events. According to his view, states are 'inherently imperfective' and events are 'inherently perfective'. Temporally indefinite propositions are about states, event radicals about events.[31] Galtonian events are types, not tokens. The token of an event Galton calls an 'occurrence'.

§2 The operators P, F, G and H of Priorian tense logic (as familiar from ch.I,3) take temporally indefinite propositions and yield temporally indefinite propositions. In Galton's event logic there are some operators which take temporally indefinite propositions and yield event radicals, and other operators which take event radicals and yield temporally indefinite propositions.Galton's first examples are the 'progressive' operator (Prog) and the 'ingressive' operator (Ingr).[32] 'Prog' takes, for example, the event radical expressed by 'my writing a book' and yields the temporally indefinite proposition expressed by "I am writing a book". Thus, "I am writing a book" is analyzed as 'Prog E', which is to say: "The event of my writing a book is just taking place".[33] 'Ingr', the operator crucial for Galton's treatment of the moment of change, takes propositions and yields event radicals: the expression 'Ingr p' corresponds to an event radical E which refers to the beginning of a state (conceived of as an event). 'p' might, for example, stand for the proposition that it is raining and E for the beginning of rain. Of course, on this event radical, other operators may be effective, e.g. 'Prog'. An expression such as

¬ Prog Ingr p

might therefore be a formal rendering of the temporally indefinite proposition which is expressed by the following sentence:

It is not the case that it is just starting to rain.

1.2.4. Events take time - do they not?

Most events Galton deals with are temporally extended and have their
definite position in time. The reason for this is that Galton was, as he writes,
motivated to build his event logic by a linguistic phenomenon which might
be called the 'present tense gap'.[34] Galton explains this, using three examples
which contain the simple form of the verb in the present tense:

Sentence (4) [I wrote a book] says that my writing of a book as a whole is past; (6) [I
shall write a book] says it is future; but there is no way that my writing of a book, as
a whole, can be present, since it takes time to write a book.[35]

And he remarks:

...to explain why only states, and not events, can be attributed to the present, we may
remark that since an event in general takes time, it cannot ever wholly be present at
one time; while a state, although it may endure over a stretch of time, does not
change during such a stretch and so is present at each moment of the stretch.[36]

While the question whether a certain state obtains may be answered with
reference to an instant, this is, of course not possible when temporally
extended events are concerned.[37] The time reference for an event is, thus,
typically an interval.[38]

1.2.5. An exception to the rule: 'Instantaneous Events'

§1 Although what was said in the last section, according to Galton, applies
to most events, there are also events which are not extended in time. Galton
calls them 'instantaneous events'. It is precisely for some of these
instantaneous events that 'Ingr' must be introduced.[39]

'Instantaneous events' are, according to Galton's terminology, events
which take no time. So an 'instantaneous event' may be expected to take
place, not throughout an interval, but at a single instant (of course, this
instant falls within some interval, but that is irrelevant here). An
'instantaneous event' may be expected to differ from, for example, the
writing of a book, by wholly taking place in the present, the present being
an instant without any duration. It might be expected to have a definite
beginning and ending. It might end at the same instant at which it begins,
which is the only instant of its taking place (this is exactly what medieval
logicians had to say about instantaneous 'res permanentes' (cf.ch.I,3)).

§2 Surprisingly, Galton maintains that all this is only true for some, but not
for all, 'instantaneous events'. He calls them 'momentary events'. An
example of a 'momentary event', according to his terminology, is what
happens to a ball thrown into the air at the highest point of its trajectory.
The reversing of its direction takes place at just one instant, for at any instant
before it is moving upward, and at any later instant it is falling down.[40]

But there is, for Galton, also another sort of 'instantaneous events'. They are called 'punctual events' and their peculiar property is that, although they are instantaneous events, they do not take place at any instant. 'Punctual events' are just such changes of state as Plato-1 transfers to the somewhat mysterious extratemporal 'sudden'.

Galton introduces 'punctual events' in connection with his Ingr-operator which, 'satisfied' with a proposition which describes a certain state, yields the event radical of the beginning of exactly this state.

1.2.6. Galton's analysis of 'begin'

§1 When introducing the Ingr-operator, Galton analyses the statements (1) "It will start raining" and (2) "It started raining". He begins by using the T-operator together with Priorian tense operators in order to render (1):

(1) $(\neg pTp) \vee F(\neg pTp)$.

Since pTq, as Prior has shown, is equivalent with $p \wedge Fq$, Galton obtains:

(1) $(\neg p \wedge Fp) \vee F(\neg p \wedge Fp)$
(2) $(P\neg p \wedge p) \vee P(P\neg p \wedge p)$

or, in an abbreviated version, writing P* for "It is the case or it was the case" and F* for "It is the case or it will be the case":[41]

(1) $F^*(\neg p \wedge Fp)$.
(2) $P^*(P\neg p \wedge p)$.

§2 Why does Galton not try to formalize the statement (3) "It is just starting to rain" in the same manner? There are two reasons for this. One is that this would be against his basic idea that an event logic is suggested by the existence of the present tense gap: it is his very starting point that not for all *grammatical* past or future tense statements there is a present tense statement such that the grammatical past or future tense statement may also be declared to be its *logical* past or future version. The other reason is that Galton is convinced that there is no instant anyway with respect to which (3) could ever be true. This is because he views the beginning of a state as a 'punctual event'. There is no time at which it is present. At every time it either still lies a bit ahead or it is already over.

§3 This opinion is mirrored in the semantics of the Ingr-operator. Galton does not define it within Priorian tense logic (this is impossible, since event logic is not just an abbreviated version of tense logic but something quite different from it), but he establishes certain equivalences between tense-logical and event-logical expressions which characterize the event-logical operators Perf (to be read: 'is over') and Pros (to be read: 'lies ahead'):[42]

(Def. Perf Ingr) Perf Ingr p = P*(P¬p ∧ p)
(Def. Pros Ingr) Pros Ingr p = F*(¬p ∧ Fp)

§4 Galton's justification for the beginning of a state's never being present is that changes of state are 'instantaneous'. It is also an explicit commitment to using the either/or-option for the description of C-changes:

At any moment just one of p and ¬p must be true, and therefore any change from ¬p's being true to p's being true must be instantaneous.[43]

'Instantaneous' simply means that the change takes no time, not that it takes place at an instant; some instantaneous events, the 'momentary' ones, do take place at instants. On the other hand, it is characteristic of punctual events that the following is true for them:

¬Prog E[44] (to be read as: "E is just taking place at no time").

So a change's being instantaneous does not yet demonstrate it is 'punctual' in Galton's sense. It is true that the instant at which a change of state between contradictories might be taking place cannot be an instant of neither state (assuming LEM, as Galton does). However, this does not rule out the possibility that the instant at which a change of state between contradictories might be taking place and be present could be the first or last instant of one of the states (which must, at least in continuous time, exist). There was a strong tendency to argue this in the Middle Ages (cf.ch.I,3.).

As can be seen, there is something of a gap in Galton's justification at this point. However, one can easily bridge this gap, because exactly the right material for a bridge is easy enough to find in Plato's premiss. Obviously, Galton's view is that an event of 'beginning' of a new state can neither be taking place while the old state still obtains nor be taking place when the new state already obtains. If one, then, (LEM and dense or continuous time assumed) both asserts Plato's premiss and views the change between contradictories as an event, one has no choice but to banish it from time. The formula '¬Prog E' is the shortest possible way of pronouncing this judgement.

1.2.7. Problems of Galton's analysis of 'begin'
§5 Plato-1 introduces the sudden as the 'in which' of change (ἐν ᾧ of μεταβολή) about which a when-question is possible. He thus attempts to save some reference point for the change of state, esoteric though it may be. In determining its logical status he obtains an entity for which the LEM does not hold (at least, fortunately, it is no time).[45]

Galton differs from Plato-1 insofar as he does not introduce an entity as problematic as the 'sudden'. He thus avoids any violation of the LEM. But even without the 'sudden' there remains the problem which we already encountered in connection with Plato-1: how do we distinguish the starting of a car on Monday morning from the starting of the same car from the same place on Tuesday morning? There also remains the problem: how shall we distinguish between a change which takes place but does not take place at any time and a change which never takes place at all?

In his 'Logic of Aspect' Galton's attempt at tackling these problems seems to consist of the following claim: a change neither takes place (1) at an instant nor (2) at (=throughout) an interval, but nevertheless (3) within an interval.[46] This is not really very helpful. Unless something more is added, it remains utterly unclear what kind of time reference 'within an interval' might be. For obviously the interval in question is, in Galton's opinion, not an interval during which the change is ever present; he does not think that there is any time at which a change is present.

§6 Fortunately, Galton has something more to say about this in his article 'The Logic of Occurence'.[47] He there identifies the occurrence of an event, not with the set of times at which it is present, but with what might be called its 'complement': he identifies it with two sets of times, V and N. V is the set of times before the event takes place, and N is the set of times after its taking place.[48] According to this, the occurrence of a punctual event has the peculiar property of every time whatsoever being an element of either its V-set or of its N-set.[49]

This leads to the following solutions to the two problems stated above:

(1) It is clearly well possible to distinguish between an event which takes place at least once, even though it might never be present, and an event which never takes place at all. For any event which does take place, there is a non-empty set of occurrences which are described by non-empty V- and N-sets. In this respect punctual events are no exception. However the set of occurences of an event which never takes place at all (a non-realized event-type) will be empty.[50]

(2) Different occurences of the same event may be distinguished by means of their V- and N-sets. In this respect punctual events are no exception. Let t_1 be the last instant at which a certain car (let us say Jean-Claude, my old Renault 4) is in its usual parking place in Jüdefelderstr. on a certain Monday morning; let t_2 be the last instant at which Jean-Claude is there on the Tuesday morning after. Now the event of Jean-Claude's starting on Monday morning can be distinguished from Jean-Claude's starting on Tuesday morning by their different V- and N-sets: The V-set of Jean-Claude's starting on Monday morning contains all instants up to and including t_1, and its N-set contains all instants after t_1; the V-set of Jean-Claude's starting on

Tuesday morning contains all instants up to and including t_2, and its N-set contains all instants after t_2.[51]

§7 Formally, this is a satisfactory solution. However there remains the question of whether it is intuitively satisfactory. We might still be strongly inclined to consider every event as datable in time, changes of state being no exception. As long as we interpret times, in Galton's formalism, as instants which are densely or continuously ordered, this is impossible. It is, as Galton himself remarks, only possible if they are interpreted within the framework of a discrete time order. In this case, changes of state would take place between times which are interpreted as time atoms.[52] This would exactly correspond to Colin Strang's interpretation of Plato's text on the sudden, the problem which we have already encountered in ch.I, 1.3.3.(b). It is in any case not desirable to have to switch over to a different time-order in order to be able to keep changes datable, let alone to switch over to something as counter-intuitive as discrete time. If the choice is between doing this and abandoning Plato's premiss, one might begin to consider abandoning Plato's premiss instead.

1.2.7. Kienzle's answer to Galton
1.2.7.1. Criticism of Galton: can anyone be present at a punctual event?
A direct answer to Galton (and, thus, indirectly to Plato-1) is found in Bertram Kienzle's article 'Cambridge-Wechsel'. Kienzle objects that Galton makes it impossible for conceptual reasons to be present at ('miterleben') someone's wedding if one takes this to be the change from being unmarried to being married. Galton regards such a change as a punctual event which does not take place at any instant. Therefore he could hardly defend himself by saying that there is no problem because in attending the church service one is present at every instant of an interval within which this change takes place. Kienzle would certainly not deny that. Apparently, his criticism is rather:

> Whatever I can be present at must be something which has some time in common with my existence; for whenever I am present at an event, I must be present at it at a certain time. A punctual event does not take place at any time. Therefore I cannot be present at it.

This criticism clearly shows how problematic Galton's approach remains for intuitive reasons, even though it may be formally satisfactory.

1.2.7.2. 'Cambridge-changes' according to Kienzle
(a) Changes and transitions
Kienzle defines a particular C-change as a repeatable event ("wiederholbares Ereignis"[53]), namely as the set of all its occurences ("Vorkommnisse"); like

Galton, he treats C-changes as types. He identifies an occurence with exactly one non-empty, uninterrupted ("lückenlos"[54]) set of times (instants). This is exactly the mirror-image of Galton's procedure of identifying an occurrence by a V- and an N-set.

An α/β-transition is defined by Kienzle as an occurrence which begins in a state that α and ends in a state that β. In principle, between the state that α and the state that β there could be another state. But in the interesting case of changes between contradictories, in which $\beta = \neg\alpha$, this is not possible, due to the LEM.

(b) The problem of oscillation
Kienzle deliberately defines an oscillation-free α/β-transition. In connection with Russell and v.Wright we have already seen that oscillation is an important but hitherto neglected problem in formally describing changes. We do not want to connect just any obtaining of the state that α with just any other obtaining of the state that β; we want to connect a particular state that α with the state that β as abutting it. Kienzle achieves this by making the following requirement:

Any two proper subsets of an α/β-transition which are themselves α/β-transitions must have a non-empty section.[55]

The following reflection may show that this requirement is appropriate: if we are concerned with an oscillating occurrence v, it may be that v' and v" are subsets of v and are themselves α/β-transitions but do not have a common non-empty section. If we are concerned with an oscillation-free α/β-transition any two v' and v", which are proper subsets of v and also α/β-transitions, must certainly 'overlap'. For since there is no more than one change taking place in v, any v' and v" will have to share it.

(c) Kienzle's definition of a Cambridge-change
A Cambridge transition ('Cambridge-Übergang'), an occurrence of a Cambridge-change, is defined by Kienzle as an oscillation-free $\neg\alpha/\alpha$-transition. A Cambridge-change from the state that $\neg\alpha$ to the state that α is the set of all oscillation-free $\neg\alpha/\alpha$-transitions with respect to a chosen time-order.[56]

According to these definitions, Kienzle claims, a Cambridge-change may (in contrast to Galton's opinion) very well be conceived as 'something occurring in time'. The reason Kienzle gives for this is that "the Cambridge-transitions of which such a change consists are temporally extended processes" so that the intervals in which they are contained may be chosen arbitrarily short.[57]

However, this claim leaves two questions open: in exactly which way are Cambridge-changes something occurring in time? And what exactly is the status of the Cambridge-transitions, the elements of a Cambridge-change? An attempt to answer these questions, in my view, shows that Kienzle has the right approach for convincingly refuting Galton convincingly with a solution of his own, but that unfortunately he does not quite succeed. His definitions provide the logical foundations for a constructive refutation of Galton, but they do not yet provide the refutation itself.

1.2.7.3. Criticism and a proposed amendment of Kienzle's approach

§1 A Cambridge-transition, although called 'occurence' in a formal sense, is not to be identified with an individual change. It is a mere formal construct.[58] A C(ambridge)-transition is not an event-token to be intuitively regardeded as an individual change[59] (a taking place of a change). This can be seen from the following differences between C-transitions and individual changes:

(1) A C-transition may have a duration of many years. One should assume that the duration of a temporally extended event is the extension of the very time throughout which this event is taking place. An individual C-change, however, can hardly be said to be taking place throughout an extended period of time, let alone a period of many years. If, for example, Eva was not married to Heiner, oscillation-free and without any interruption, for the first 25 years of her life, and will be married to him in the same way for (at least) 25 years, then there is a C-transition from Eva's not being married to Heiner to Eva's being married to Heiner which extends across half a century. But it is counter-intuitive to suggest that the change from her not being married to her being married is taking place throughout the whole half a century.

(2) Many changes are assumed to take place a finite number of times only. For example, the same two people generally get married only once. A C-transition, however, never comes alone: in dense time, the existence of one C-transition of a certain type entails the existence of infinitely many C-changes of the same type. For every C-change there is a whole filter-base of C-transitions; and in dense time, such a filter-base consists of infinitely many C-transitions contained within one another.[60] Returning to our example, the wedding of Eva to Heiner takes place only once. Nevertheless, there is an infinite number of C-transitions which are 'occurrences' (in Kienzle's technical sense) of the Cambridge-change from Eva's not being married to Heiner to Eva's being married to Heiner.

§2 It is not to be disputed that a Cambridge-change which is conceived as an event-type may be described by a set of C-transitions. And of course, Kienzle may call a Cambridge-change in this sense something occurring in time, as long as by this he means no more than that this Cambridge-change is a set of entities called occurrences each of which has a certain duration and position in time. However, an 'occurrence' in this sense is not what would be intuitively regarded as an individual event. If so, the question arises as to how Kienzle's criticism of Galton is actually reflected in his formalism. It is the individual event of change to which Galton assigns no time. Galton wants to interpret his logic in such a manner that an 'occurrence' in *his* sense (an ordered pair of a V- and an N-set) is indeed identified with an individual Cambridge-change. Kienzle is right in commenting that noone could ever be present at a Galtonian change. He should therefore make it clear how he, in contrast to Galton, assigns a time to the individual change. Only in this way, by stating at which time the change is taking place, can the possibility of my being present at it be secured, and thus Galton be refuted. However, nothing in Kienzle's explanation could be identified with an individual change. Since there is nothing of the sort, no time can be marked off as the time of the individual change.

Furthermore, Kienzle could not restrain Galton from saying that there is no time at which the change is taking place. Galton might simply interpret the 'occurrences' in Kienzle's sense as intervals within which a change takes place. Galton never denies the existence of such intervals; he only denies that a change takes place *at* (i.e. throughout) an interval.[61]

§3 The situation would be different if, proceding from Kienzle's approach, one could plausibly connect a certain C-transition with the individual C-change that one is looking for. One might declare the duration and position of this C-transition to be the duration and position of an individual C-change during which it is taking place. This would indeed amount to saying that, in contrast to Galton, a C-change takes place *at* a certain interval.

But which C-transition of a filter-base could we choose for this task? Shall we pick out an especially long one? That would hardly be plausible: Caesar is not traversing the Rubicon any more, but would have to be, if we took this line. A very short transition looks better already. However, the problem then emerges that in dense time, for every C-transition however short, there is a shorter one which is contained in it and which already contains what we intuitively regard as an individual C-change.[62] Thus the search for a C-transition whose duration appears plausible as the time throughout which a change is exactly taking place does not yield a satisfactory result. One might therefore say that the controversy Galton vs. Kienzle results in a draw: Kienzle's criticism of Galton is convincing, but his own suggestion cannot be held to be quite convincing either, at least not without some amendment.

Clearly, the discussion of the Galton/Kienzle controversy has shown once again that it is not plausible to view a change as something extended in time and having a certain duration. This confirms the idea that what distinguishes changes from processes is the *lack* of any duration.

§4 However, I think that Kienzle stops only one step short of providing a very plausible solution for C-changes. The necessity of defining individual event-tokens of a C-change-type has become apparent. C-transitions have emerged as the wrong candidates for them. But why should it not be possible to identify an individual C-change with the filter-base of all the C-transitions in which, intuitively, it and no other individual C-change is 'caught'?

A clear objection to this seems to be that we can never hope to assign any clear position in time to a filter-base of C-transitions while what we want is an exact time at which the individual change is taking place. A particular C-transition has a definite position in time; a filter-base of C-transitions has not. But why should we try to do this anyway? We can keep two questions apart:

(1) What entity is to be identified with an individual C-change?
(2) When is the individual C-change taking place?

We can answer the first question independently of the second. Identifying a C-change with a filter-base is, then, a proposed answer to the first question. If we want no more than a uniquely identifying formal description we could simply use Galton's ordered pair of a V- and an N-set for the task instead. What reasons do we have for preferring the filter-base-approach to Galton's? In my view, there are two good reasons:

(a) There is a very intuitive explanation of what the filter-base of an individual C-change is: it is the set of those intervals which describe all the periods during which this individual event of changing (and no other of the same kind) may be *experienced*. One may, thus, call it the set of all possible *aspects* of an individual change.[63] It is certainly more plausible to identify an event with the set of its possible aspects than to identify it with a division of the history of the whole world, with the very event in question as a blind spot (as Galton does). The idea of taking C-transitions to be, not individual C-changes, but aspects of them matches the idea that the only way to witness changes is to experience aspects of them: an aspect of a change is the way in which a change is given to us.[64] We cannot experience a change in isolation, since it takes no time. I will argue for this idea throughout part III of the present book and especially in the last section of part III. We will encounter aspects there once more. I think using them to identify an individual C-change is a very good way to stress their important role.

(b) If we identify individual C-changes with sets of aspects of them it is easy to give an interesting answer, in terms of this identification, to the second question, the question of at which time an individual C-change is taking place. One might say that the time at which it is taking place is the time which all its aspects have in common. This is the intersection of all C-transitions of the filter-base of its aspects, which is the limiting instant. However, this answer conflicts with Plato's premiss if, as is plausible, LNC and LEM are assumed and, therefore, C-changes are described by using the either/or-option which assigns the limiting instant either to the old or to the new state. So once more we are faced with the real dilemma of the classification of the moment of change. I will argue in the last section of part III that the proposed answer should indeed be given and that the dilemma should be removed by abandoning Plato's premiss.

1.3. ADVANTAGES, DISADAVANTAGES AND A DILEMMA OF USING THE EITHER/OR OPTION

The attempt to describe the s-change between rest and motion like a C-change by using the either/or-option has shown itself as not to be recommended (as a result of the discussion of Sorabji's and Jackson and Pargetter's approach). The description of the moment of change between rest and motion should not be tied to the concept of momentary velocity. Only the application of this concept could provide us with a reason for assigning the limiting instant rather to the one than to the other state.

We are now also able to see clearly the real dilemma of the classification of the moment of change. Dense time, LNC and LEM should be assumed. If they are, it is extremely plausible to describe C-changes by using the either/or-option. However in doing so, one must, for the classification of the moment of change, either banish change from time or abandon Plato's premiss. It is certainly implausible to banish change from time. But so far, abandoning Plato's premiss does not seem plausible, either.

CHAPTER 2

THE EITHER-WAY-OPTION

The following statement is characteristic of the application of the either-way-option to describe the moment of change:

> It is correct to say that the old as well as the new state obtains at the limiting instant, although only in a certain sense, so that no contradiction results.

The two articles which advocate this opinion most clearly are among the most frequently mentioned contemporary texts on the moment of change: Roderick Chisholm's 'Beginnings and Endings'[1] and Brian Medlin's 'The Origin of Motion'.[2] Both of them deserve close and critical examination.

In discussing these articles I will attempt to show that it is impossible to apply the either-way-option to C-changes (since a contradiction cannot be avoided in that case) and that its possible application to the s-change between rest and motion has to work with definitions of motion and rest at an instant whose requirements are too weak to be intuitive.

2.1. RODERICK CHISHOLM AND FRANZ BRENTANO

2.1.1. Brentano's doctrine of the 'plerosis' of a boundary

In his 'Beginnings and Endings', Roderick Chisholm takes a concept developed by Franz Brentano as his starting point: the concept of the 'plerosis' ('plenitude') of a boundary. It is mentioned in his 'Philosophische Untersuchungen zu Raum, Zeit und Kontinuum'. The most important remarks on 'plerosis' are contained in an unpublished manuscript in Brentano's bequest (one has to rely on a summary of it in Chisholm's article).[3]

The 'plerosis' of a boundary depends on the number of directions in which it functions as a boundary.[4] A temporal boundary, an instant, can be directed to the past, as an end; or towards the future, as a beginning. If the boundary exists as an end only, but not as a beginning, or if it exists as a beginning only, but not as an end, then the boundary exists, in Brentano's terminology, merely 'in half plerosis'.[5]

An instant which in one respect is the end of a period can at the same time have the property of being the beginning of an abutting period. It is a two-fold boundary which exists 'in full plerosis'. Chisholm explains:

Brentano believes that by means of the concept of plerosis he can speak in a certain sense of the 'parts' of a boundary even though the boundary may have no dimensions. It is one thing to speak of the present as being the end of the past and another thing to speak of it as the beginning of the future.[6]

2.1.2. 'Plerosis' and intervals; 'plerosis' and Aristotle's distinction of the roles of the limiting instant

§1 Brentano's concept of 'plerosis' is reminiscent of the distinction made in mathematics between open and closed intervals. One could describe the last instant of an interval which is closed towards the future as a boundary which is an end but not a beginning. This instant is still an element of the interval, but there is no later instant to have this property. This instant is not also the first instant of an immediately abutting interval, which does not overlap the first one. The abutting interval (in dense time) has no first instant.

Analogously, the first instant of an interval which is closed at least towards the past may be regarded as boundary which is a beginning, but not an end.

§2 Brentano's concept of 'plerosis' is strongly reminiscent of the passage in Aristotle's Physics VIII in which 'a border mark which separates the earlier from the later' is characterized on the one hand as 'numerically one' and on the other as 'conceptually *not* one', but as 'the end of the earlier and the beginning of the later state.'[7]

Aristotle recognized the necessity of assigning the limiting instant uniquely to one of the states 'as far as the thing is concerned' (τῷ πράγματι) in order to avoid contradiction.[8] Aristotle's distinction is more strongly differentiated than Brentano's. To express it in Aristotelian terminology, the core of Brentano's approach is the idea that that which is numerically one can serve a double function. In contrast Aristotle had distinguished between a double function on the 'theoretical' level (numerically vs. conceptually) and a necessarily unambiguous factual assignment of the limiting instant.

Chisholm generally interprets Brentano's concept of 'plerosis' in such a way that it is supposed to allow the assignment of the limiting instant to the one and to the other state without a contradiction. Thus the concept of 'plerosis' emerges as very different to Aristotle's distinction in spite of what one might think at first sight.

2.1.3. Chisholm's application of the concept of 'plerosis' to the s-change between rest and motion

Chisholm begins by considering the example of the s-change between rest and motion.[9] According to his elaboration of Brentano's idea, there is an instant of change between these two states which bounds the state of rest in half plerosis and bounds the state of motion in half plerosis. Chisholm attributes to Brentano the opinion that the last instant of rest and the first instant of motion are 'coincident points' and paraphrases Brentano's approach as follows:

If a thing begins to move is there a last moment of its being at rest or a first moment of its being in motion? [...] Brentano's solution is to say that at one and the same moment the thing ceases to be at rest and begins to be in motion. The temporal boundary of the thing's beings at rest (the end of its being at rest) is the same as the temporal boundary of the thing's being in motion (the beginning of its being in motion), but the boundary is twofold (zweiteilig) with respect to its plerosis. The boundary is in half-plerosis (in halber Plerose) at rest and in half-plerosis in motion.[10]

The meaning of the statement that a temporal boundary (i.e. an instant) is at rest or in motion is not entirely clear. Presumably, Chisholm means that it is an instant of motion as well as an instant of rest.

Moreover, what Chisholm takes to be Brentano's 'solution' is an answer to a different question from the one it was supposed to answer: the original question had been whether there was a last instant at which a was at rest or a first one at which a was in motion. Chisholm tells us that Brentano's answer to this question is that there is an instant at which a begins to move as well as an instant at which it ceases to rest, this being one and the same instant. Surely, however, the question to which this is an answer would be: "Is there an instant at which a begins to move as well as an instant at which it ceases to rest?".

The two questions are not identical in content and quite independent of one another. The instant at which a ceases to rest and starts to move may be regarded as one at which a neither rests nor moves. It may also be regarded as one at which a rests or one at which a moves etc. In short: the question posed is the question of how to *describe* the moment of change. The answer offered, though, provides us with a *classification*.

2.1.3.1. Chisholm's classification of the moment of change

To elaborate his solution of Brentano's ideas, Chisholm consequently starts with a classification of the moment of change. He defines what the statement that t bounds a prior motion of an object A is to mean:

t bounds a prior motion of A = df There is a time t' prior to t which is such that, for any two periods of time between t and t', there is a place which is such that A is at that place within one of those periods of time and is not at that place within the other.[11]

The definition of "t bounds a subsequent motion of A" is analogous, substituting 'subsequent' for 'prior'.

This definition is not quite clear on several points. It provides us with a first impression of how difficult it is to state precisely what makes a period a period of motion of an object. The analysis of Russell's attempt to do this (ch. II,5) will corroborate this impression.

2.1.3.2. *A precise version of Chisholm's definitions*

(1) It is not absolutely clear what Chisholm means by 'periods'. Presumably they are not intervals (as sets of instants) but entities in their own right: Chisholm never mentions instants as elements of what he calls a period, but only as its boundaries.

(2) It is not totally clear what Chisholm means by saying that a period is 'between' two instants. Is it bounded by these instants? Hardly. Many different periods are supposed to be able to be 'between' two instants: according to the definition, something is to be true for any two periods between t and t'. So let us suppose that Chisholm means something similar to the following definition of a three-place predicate to be read as 'lies between' which takes a period in the first argument-place, and an instant in the second and third one and is abbreviated as 'B'[etween]:

$$B(c,t,t_1) \text{ iff } \exists t_2,t_3 [c:[t_2,t_3] \wedge t \leq t_2 < t_3 \leq t_1].$$

(3) It is not clear if the two arbitrarily chosen periods in Chisholm's definition may be identical, may overlap, may contain one another or may abut. I assume that the only restraint here should be that they may not be identical (otherwise the definition could hardly ever be fulfilled).

(4) It is unclear what it is to mean to say that an object A is at a place within a period. It is hardly to be assumed that A, while moving, remains in the same place throughout a period. One should rather assume that A is in only one place per instant. But Chisholm does not say anything about A at instants here. As a result only this much can be said with certainty: for every period c there is a set of places which are positions of A during c. Let us call this set $\mathbf{M}_c$.

According to what may be assumed from (1) to (4), Chisholm's definitions may be rendered as follows (t_1 corrsponds to t' in Chisholm's text and x ranges over positions of A):

t bounds a prior motion of A iff
$$\exists t_1 [t_1 < t \wedge \forall c,c_1 [c \neq c_1 \wedge B(c,t,t_1) \wedge B(c_1,t,t_1) \rightarrow \exists x [x \in \mathbf{M}_c \wedge x \notin \mathbf{M}_{c1}]]].$$
t bounds a subsequent motion of A iff
$$\exists t_1 [t < t_1 \wedge \forall c,c_1 [c \neq c_1 \wedge B(c,t,t_1) \wedge B(c_1,t,t_1) \rightarrow \exists x [x \in \mathbf{M}_c \wedge x \notin \mathbf{M}_{c1}]]].$$

Although they appear somewhat complicated at first sight, these definitions do not seem to imply any counter-intuitive consequences.

2.1.3.3. The beginning and ending of a motion

§1 Chisholm goes on to define what it means that A begins to move at an instant t or ceases to do so:

A begins to move at t = df. t bounds a subsequent but not a prior motion of A.
A ceases to move at t = df. t bounds a prior but not a subsequent motion of A.

He then claims:

Our definitions enable us to say that the time at which a thing begins to move is the same as the time at which it ceases to rest, and that the time at which a thing begins to rest is the same as that at which it ceases to move. And these statements are not contradictory.[12]

§2 The result is not implausible, although it might require a little further explanation. It is, for example, the typical classification of the moment of change which may be attributed to most logicians of the late Middle Ages.[13] It is, however, hard to see why just these of all definitions are to lead to this result, and why Chisholm has not just added a claim to his definitions. In order to justify the identity claim here, one needs at least a definition of what it means that an object begins or ceases to rest. What beginning or ceasing to move means for A has, after all, turned out to be quite a complicated matter. Why should things be easier with rest? In order to do this in analogy to motion, Chisholm would first have to define what it means for an instant t to bound a period of A's rest.

2.1.4. Chisholm's description of the moment of change

Surprisingly, Chisholm's rather sketchy classification of the moment of change is followed by a description of the moment of change, in which Chisholm declares the two questions to be independent of one another although he did not keep them apart in his paraphrase of Brentano.[14] It is even more suprising to see that for the description of the s-change between rest and motion he seems to suggest using the either/or-option.[15] It is very hard to fit this in with the way Chisholm exploited the concept of plerosis before.

2.1.4.1. Chisholm's definition of motion at an instant

Whether an object at an instant t is to be called 'in motion' depends, according to Chisholm, on whether it is in motion during a period *within which t falls*.[16] Thus, Chisholm commits himself to regarding motion as something which can be said to be 'directly' taking place only in periods, and can only 'indirectly', *via* motion in periods, be said to be taking place at instants.[17]

This is not implausible. However, in my view, Chisholm holds an unusual opinion concerning what 'falls within' means. What he means cannot be rendered by the 'falls-within' relation known from the introduction. It rather corresponds to Aristotle's εἶναι ἐν,[18] for, according to Chisholm, such instants as bound a period are to be regarded as falling within the period, too. Chisholm's definition of motion at an instant is:

A is in motion at an instant t =df. Either t bounds a subsequent motion of A, or t bounds a prior motion of A.[19]

Thus Chisholm has a concept of motion at an instant with only a very weak requirement: although a limiting instant bounds a period of motion on only one side, it would, according to this definition, already be an instant of motion of A. In my view, this is a counter-intuitively weak requirement. I think it is more plausible to allow as instants of motion of A only such instants as fall within a period of motion in the strong sense of 'falling within' which is principally used in this book.

No matter how much or how little it has to say for itself intuitively, there can be no doubt that on the basis of these definitions (and assuming his classification) Chisholm may indeed claim:

The answer to our question now becomes: at the instant at which the thing begins to move and also ceases to rest, the thing is in motion. And at the instant at which it ceases to move and begins to rest it is also in motion.[20]

2.1.4.2. A chance missed by Chisholm: the use of the either-way-option for comparative properties

Chisholm's weak concept of motion at an instant does have an advantage for him. It enables him to describe at least the s-change between rest and motion using the either-way -option, as Brentano's concept of plerosis suggests. It only requires an equally weak concept of *rest* at an instant to enable one to consider *a* at the limiting instant to be both at rest and in motion without a contradiction (as would be typical of the either-way-option). This solution cannot reasonably be applied to C-changes (either *a* is white at t or it is not); yet Chisholm makes it clear enough that he regards motion as a comparative property, and it may be presumed that he considers rest, too, as a comparative property. This would make a mixed description of the instant of change possible: it would consist in using the either-way-option for s-changes between comparative properties and using the either/or-option for C-changes. This description would have sufficient motivation for someone who, for the sake of 'plerosis', accepts Chisholm's weak concept of motion at an instant.

In order to arrive at a description of this kind, Chisholm would have to define rest at an instant as follows (and in analogy to the definition proposed above of "t bounds a prior/subsequent motion of A"):

A is at rest at an instant t =df. Either t bounds a subsequent period of rest of A, or t bounds a prior period of rest.

According to this definition, he could also maintain that at the limiting instant *a* is both in motion and at rest without a contradiction: it is in motion on the one hand, and at rest on the other.

2.1.4.3. Instead: an about-turn towards the either/or-option?

Very surprisingly, Chisholm does nothing of the kind. He simply states that *a* is in motion at the limiting instant. There is no mention of *a* possibly also being at rest then. Is there an about-turn in favour of the either/or-option in the middle of the text? If there is, some justification is required why the limiting instant should be assigned to motion and not to rest. It would be no problem to first define rest at an instant such that the limiting instant is an instant of rest and then define those instants at which *a* exists but is not at rest as instants of motion, thereby assigning the limiting instant to rest.

Sorabji (as can be seen in ch.II,1.1.) proposes exactly the latter approach. He gives reasons for doing so, although one might not agree with them. Chisholm does not give reasons here. Thus his description of the moment of change appears not only to be inconsistent in having started with the concept of 'plerosis' and then having abandoned it; it also appears arbitrary.

2.1.5. Chisholm's attempt to use the either-way-option to describe C-changes

However, Chisholm does not merely digress from the either-way-option at a relatively promising point, i.e. the description of the s-change between comparative properties. He also seems to return to it where it makes the least sense: in the description of C-changes.[21] His example is the classic change which happens to Socrates when he is first alive and then no more. Chisholm's opinion is:

Brentano is able to say that there is both a last moment of existence and a first moment of nonexistence; they are one and the same.[22]

In analogy to his classification of the moment of change between rest and motion, Chisholm states that *a* ceases to exist at t iff t bounds a prior but not a subsequent period of existence of *a*.[23] It should be clearly apparent that this definition is equally insufficient to account for the identity claim made as the corresponding one in the case of rest and motion.

2.1.5.1. Avoiding a contradiction?

One wonders how Chisholm is to avoid a contradiction here: is not the last instant of *a*'s existence an instant for which it is true to say that *a* exists? And is not the first instant of nonexistence of *a* an instant for which it is not true that *a* exists? Chisholm offers two different and incompatible answers, one immediately after the other, as to how to avoid a contradiction here.

(1) Chisholm's first answer consists in defining, in analogy with the example of motion and rest, what it means for *a* to exist at t: *a* is supposed to exist at t if t bounds a period of prior *or* of subsequent existence of *a*. Thus, *a* already exists at the limiting instants of its existence.[24] At this point Chisholm does not add an extra definition of *a*'s nonexistence at t. In contrast to a definition of rest at an instant, in this case such a definition is in fact not required. Of course, *a* does not exist at t if and only if t does not fulfil the definition for being an instant of *a*'s existence. However, this compels the use of the either/or-option. As the limiting instant, according to Chisholm, already fulfils the definition for being an instant of *a*'s existence, he cannot call the limiting instant the first instant of nonexistence. I thus find it utterly incomprehensible that he nevertheless does so.[25]

(2) Chisholm's second explanation as to why his description does not result in contradiction is a very unusual interpretation of the use of the phonetic chain 'n-o-t' in certain English utterances:

...'a moment at which Socrates was alive' only *appears* to be incompatible with 'a moment at which Socrates was not alive'. [...] Hence the two phrases are not contraries.[26]

It is possible for Chisholm to arrive at this conclusion because, at his second attempt, he explicitly (and unnecessarily) defines what he considers an instant of *a*'s nonexistence to be: an instant which bounds a prior or a subsequent period of *a*'s nonexistence.[27]

This would mean that in an utterance of the sentence "*a* does not exist throughout *period* c" the phonetic chain 'n-o-t' is somehow concerned with a certain logical constant. In an utterance of the sentence "*a* does not exist at *instant* t", however, the phonetic chain 'n-o-t' means something completely different.

2.1.5.2. A Quinean defence?

I must admit to finding the view rendered in 2.1.5.1. (2) rather bizarre. The only justification for it I can envisage is a sort of Quinean move: As radical translation begins at home and does not stop at logical constants, anybody could try to interpret English utterances as he pleases. If he succeeds, he might write a new dictionary totally deviating from all the usual dictionaries, but one which is, nonetheless, constantly confirmed by the speech behaviour of the speakers of English.[28] However, such an approach is only possible if the dictionary entry does not contradict common speech behaviour. Now in my opinion a Chisholmian dictionary entry for the sentence "*a* does not exist at instant t" does contradict common speech behaviour in at least two respects:

(1) The rule of double negation could not be accepted in statements concerning instants if Chisholm's interpretation were true. For, according to Chisholm, "*a* exists at t" does not imply "It is not the case that *a* does not exist at t", because in his opinion it is possible for someone to speak the truth in referring to one instant and both saying "*a* exists at t" and "*a* does not exist at t", if t is a limiting instant of *a*'s existence.

(2) Imagine a clock with continuously advancing clockhands (my travel alarmclock, for example). If the Chisholmian dictionary were correct a speaker of English could not, looking at this clock, be correct in saying: "At 12:00, a clockhand points to the 12 o'clock mark". For t = 12:00 bounds a prior period throughout which the hand did not point at the 12 o'clock mark and also bounds a subsequent period throughout which it does not point at the 12 o'clock mark. So one would have to say, with Chisholm: "At noon, the clockhand of a (correctly set) clock does not point to the 12 o'clock mark". This is hardly the way we talk.

Thus, no Quinean move is possible to justify Chisholm's view of the word 'not', and it appears that Chisholm's article is best evaluated by saying that it reveals deep problems in the either-way option.

2.2. BRIAN MEDLIN: 'THE ORIGIN OF MOTION'

The s-change between rest and motion is the main subject of Brian Medlin's article on the moment of change.[29] Judging by the frequency with which it is mentioned by other authors, it may be regarded as a classic in the treatment of the moment of change. Medlin clearly distinguishes the strong and the weak concept of motion at an instant. For the most part his suggestion is based on the weak concept of motion at an instant (like Chisholm's), allowing Medlin to call the limiting instant between rest and motion an instant of both rest and motion without contradiction. Thus Medlin is clearly an advocate of the either-way-option.

Since Medlin regards the limiting instant as the instant at which *a* begins to move,[30] there is little doubt that he assumes an instantaneous event to take place there. He obviously denies Plato's premiss since, according to his approach, both the old and the new state obtain at the limiting instant.

Medlin supposes that his approach can be extended to other kinds of changes but that this task would not be trivial.[31] Caution is indeed advisable here; it has already become apparent that the application of the either-way-option is not possible for C-changes.

Medlin charges descriptions of the s-change between rest and motion using the either/or-option with arbitrariness,[32] in that they assign the limiting instant to one of the two states without a better reason for this than for assigning it to the other state. Such a solution he calls, not unsuitably, 'Dedekind's solution'.[33] The criticism of Sorabji's argument in favour of the limiting instant being an instant of rest of a (ch.II,1.1.) may have shown that there is indeed something to this objection.

2.2.1. 'motion$_1$' and 'motion$_2$': the strong and the weak concept of motion at an instant

Medlin calls the strong concept of motion 'motion$_1$' and the weak one 'motion$_2$' and defines them, as can be deduced from his examples, as follows:[34]

> (a) *a* is in motion$_1$ at t iff There is a period before and after t during which *a* is in motion
> (b) *a* is in motion$_2$ at t iff There is a period either immediately before or immediately after t during which *a* is in motion.[35]

Analogously he defines rest at an instant (which Chisholm failed to do):

> (c) *a* is in rest$_1$ at t iff There is a period before and after t during which *a* is at rest
> (d) *a* is at rest$_2$ at t iff There is a period either immediately before or immediately after t during which *a* is at rest.

2.2.2. The weak concept of motion at an instant as the 'true' concept of motion at an instant?

For his description of the s-change between rest and motion, however, Medlin exclusively uses the weak concept of motion ('motion$_2$').[36] The text shows that he also does this with rest. He comments on this:

...while we have indeed solved the paradox, we have not done so by uncovering hidden ambiguities. I do not think that for our purposes, we have the right to talk of different expressions 'in motion' and 'at rest'.[37]

Medlin frankly admits that the weak concepts of rest and motion at an instant he uses are counter-intuitive:

Doubtless this analysis is counter-intuitive. Nonetheless, I claim it [the definition of motion$_2$] to be an account of what we mean when we say in a quite ordinary way that a body was in motion at a certain time. If the analysis were not counter-intuitive, then presumably there would have been no problem to start with.[38]

So the strong concept of motion at an instant is said to be more intuitive than the weak one, but although the weak concept is seen as counter-intuitive it is judged as rendering what has always been our intuition of what motion at an instant is. It is difficult to see whether there is any fundamental difference between this statement and the statement *credo quia absurdum* apart from the latter's being suitably employed only for greater metaphysical problems than the one discussed here.

At least Medlin offers an explanation as to why 'motion$_1$' has hitherto happened to be taken as the correct definition of motion at an instant. In the vast majority of cases in which the definition of 'motion$_2$' ('true' motion) is fulfilled, the definition of 'motion$_1$' is fulfilled as well. For, so Medlin reasons, there are only a finite number of limiting instants, and limiting instants are the only instants for which the definition of 'motion$_2$' is fulfilled but the definition of 'motion$_1$' is not. But between any two limiting instants there are an infinite number of other instants for which both definitions are fulfilled at once.[39] Rather confusingly, Medlin's way of stating this is that 'motion$_1$' at an instant *implies* 'motion$_2$' at the same instant but does not *entail* it. So 'implies' in Medlin means as much as 'statistically suggests that'.[40]

According to the weak concept of motion at an instant, *a* is in motion at t already if t bounds a period of motion of *a*, but does not necessarily fall within it. Analogously, *a* is already at rest at t if t only bounds a period of rest of *a*. The result is indeed a limiting instant at which *a* is both at rest and in motion without any contradiction.[41] One might, once again ask, as in Chisholm's case, whether this is not a point *against* using the weak concepts of motion and rest at an instant in the first place. Certainly, however, Medlin would deny this.

2.2.3. Medlin's keyword: 'predicate negation'
Medlin goes even further. He claims that, in addition to *a* being both in motion and at rest at the limiting instant, *a* is, in a certain sense, also neither in motion nor at rest at the limiting instant:

If 12:00 is the moment of change then
(1) The body was in motion at 12:00
(2) The body was at rest at 12:00
(1+) The body was not in motion at 12:00
(2+) The body was not at rest at 12:00
are all true.[42]

It would be possible to follow this line if Medlin permitted the strong concepts of motion and rest at an instant as an alternative on a par with the weak ones.[43] For according to the strong concept of motion and rest at an instant, *a* is indeed neither in motion nor at rest at the limiting instant (as a discussion of the 'Neutral Instant Analysis' in ch. II,5 will show in detail). However, Medlin explicitly rejects using the strong concepts (although, in my view, without any convincing reason). Rather, he retains the weak concepts and begins, like Chisholm, experimenting with the meaning of the word 'not':

The point does not concern the meaning of the expression 'in motion'. It is rather a general point concerning negation.[44]

So he thinks that the following is true if '12:00' is a limiting instant:

¬(1) [=] ¬(the body was in motion at 12:00) is false.[45]

Presumably, ¬(2) must then be false. Medlin's explanation for this is that (1+) is not identical with ¬(1), since (1+) is not the propositional negation of (1) but the predicate negation of (1).[46] Medlin also says that (2) is the predicate negation of (1).[47] If therefore (1+) and (2), as well as, presumably, in analogy to this (2+) and (1), are equivalent, it is trivial to say that (1+) and (2) on the one hand and (2+) and (1) on the other hand can be true together.

2.2.3.1. What kind of predicate negation?

It is certainly not trivial to claim that all four statements can be true together. This would mean that in two cases a proposition and its 'predicate negation' would be true together. It is true that this is not straightforwardly impossible: There are Brazilian football-players as well as non-Brazilian football players. It is, however, difficult to see how this could be applied in Medlin's case, since there does not seem to be any *existence claim* involved here.

As long as no existence claim is involved, it is very difficult to see how the predicate negation should fail to imply the propositional negation:[48] if Peter is unfriendly it is certainly not the case that Peter is friendly (in some cases, it might be easier to argue the case the other way around,[49] but this depends on a clear concept of predicate negation in the first place). However, if the predicate negation implied the propositional negation, there would be the very contradiction Medlin wants to avoid: if under this assumption both (1) and (1+) are true, then, since (1+) is true, ¬(1) is true as well, so that both (1) and ¬(1) would be true.

Or *is* there an existence claim involved here, after all, and is it of the harmless kind, such as the one mentioned above concerning the football-players? To see whether that might be so one could rephrase Medlin's statements as "There is a t such that..." etc. But after doing so one sees that the resulting conjunct of existence claims would not be harmless after all: Medlin is talking about the *same* instant all the time. On the other hand, the statements "There are Brazilian football-players" and "There are non-Brazilian football-players" are compatible *only because* some football-players are Brazilian and some *others* are not. We would never be able to say of the *same* football-player, for example Socrates, that he is both Brazilian and non-Brazilian.

Thus Medlin would have quite a lot to do to make his claim plausible (which he does not). For example, he would first have to show that (2) is in fact the 'predicate negation' of (1). One wonders in any case what, after all, a predicate negation is exactly supposed to be, and how one is to understand the word 'not' in (1+) and (2+). The logical structure of (1+) and (2+) is anything but clear, if no further explanation is offered. Medlin's explanation does not exactly add to clarity in this matter:

> That two predicates are incompatible means roughly that they cannot be true of the same thing at the same time. But it only 'means' this because *at the same time* implies *during the same time*. Predicate negation, unlike propositional negation, vanishes at the moment of change. [...] it has been pointed out to me [...though] that this is not a general point about predicate negation. It does not hold for predicates like *began to move*.[50]

So much can however be said: a predicate negation is concerned with statements in which we naturally use negative adjectives, i.e. adjectives beginning with the prefixes 'un-', 'non-', 'not-', 'im-', 'in-' etc. This gives us a starting point for considering whether this intuitive understanding provides us with a better understanding of Medlin's idea.

2.2.3.2. Predicate negation with periods?
Medlin's talk of the predicate negation's 'disappearing' at the limiting instant supposedly having something to do with the difference between 'at' and 'during' suggests that predicate negation in his sense might be connected with what I tried to render by introducing the *-prefix. By saying that *a* is non-white in c (c being a period) one might want to express that it fails to be white in at least one part of c. This is indeed compatible with *a*'s being white in another part of c. That it is not the case that *a* is white in c is, however, incompatible with *a*'s being white for a part of c. So if one, plausibly, regards "*a* is non-white in c" in the proposed sense as the predicate negation of "*a* is white in c" and "It is not the case that *a* is white in c" as the propositional negation of it, then in this case, indeed, the propositional negation implies the predicate negation, but the predicate negation fails to imply the propositional negation - as Medlin would require.

Using the *-prefix one may render this as: $\neg P(c)$ is the propositional negation of $P(c)$, $\neg^*\text{-}P(c)$ the predicate negation. $\neg P(c)$ implies $\neg^*\text{-}P(c)$, but $\neg^*\text{-}P(c)$ does not imply $\neg P(c)$. It is also correct that this difference disappears once instants are concerned instead of periods: $\neg^*\text{-}P(t)$ and $\neg P(t)$ (t being an instant) are equivalent. According to this, however, Medlin's claim that (1+) is, like (2), the predicate negation of (1) and is compatible with (1) remains incomprehensible. For in (1), (1+) and (2) only *instants* (of motion and rest) are concerned, never *periods*. No difference between the predicate negation and the propositional negation in the proposed sense exists with respect to instants. Hence nothing prevents a contradiction between (1) and its predicate negation.

The most one might get out of this would be a claim to some structural similarity between *a* not being white throughout c (and therefore being non-white) and t bounding a period of motion of *a* on only one side. This would be reminiscent of Brentano's 'existence of t as a boundary of a white-phase of *a* in half-plerosis'. However it is very unclear what the structural similarity might consist of here, and it is also unapparent what this might have to do with different kinds of negation.

2.2.3.3. Not white vs. non-white?

In a last attempt, one could try to interpret Medlin's mention of 'predicate negation' so:

> It is not true that something is white at the limiting instant. Neither is it true that it is non-white. For being non-white is being a colour different from white, and such a thing does not exist at a limiting instant. 'Non-white' is the disjunction of all colours except white. "*a* is not white at t" is the propositional negation, "*a* is non-white at t" is the predicate negation of "a is white at t".

A possible justification why something cannot be non-white at the limiting instant would be: in order for *a* to be non-white at the limiting instant, this instant would have to bound periods of *a*'s being non-white on both sides. This, however, it cannot, because it is a *limiting* instant which marks off white on one side from non-white on the other. The problem is that this justification presupposes a strong concept of being non-white, which would have to correspond to a strong concept of rest opposed by Medlin.

But also for a second reason the above suggestion is incompatible with what Medlin writes: even if one supposes that at an instant of change from white to another colour an object is no colour at all, being neither white nor non-white, the claim that *a* is non-white at t implies the claim that *a* is not white at t: the predicate negation implies the propositional negation. Medlin, however, would like the predicate negation to be true while the propositional negation is false. In this way, too, it remains incomprehensible what use Medlin's version of the term 'predicate negation' could be for describing the moment of change.

2.2.3.4. Sorabji's criticism of Medlin

In addition to all that has been said, there is a criticism by Sorabji which makes clear that even extremely sophisticated definitions of rest and motion at instants cannot help Medlin's approach with respect to C-changes:

Medlin is free to define motion at an instant and rest at an instant in such a way that they are not contradictories or contraries of each other. But he cannot, and does not, deny that there is a contradictory of the claim that something is in motion at an instant. [...] Once we have found a formula for picking out the contradictory, we can pose our original problem all over again in terms of the new formula. [...] When the problem is posed this way, we see that we shall have to fall back on a different solution from Medlin's...[51]

Thus although Medlin is more stringent in his definitions than Chisholm, his version of the either-way option does not emerge as any more promising than Chisholm's.

2.3. EVALUATION

The attempt to apply the either-way option to the description of the moment of change yields disappointing results. It does not make any sense for C-changes. In the area where the use of this option makes any sense at all (s-changes between rest and motion) it relies upon a weak concept of rest and motion at an instant, in comparison to which the strong one must appear intuitively far more plausible.

CHAPTER 3

THE BOTH-STATES-OPTION

3.1. OBJECTIVE CONTRADICTIONS

3.1.1. Preliminary remarks

The procedure for treating the problems of the moment of change seems, in a way, predetermined. First and foremost one attempts to avoid a result in which an object is simultaneously in two contradictory (or even just contrary) states. As we have seen, there are various ways to achieve this. One should hardly think that it could seriously occur to anyone that accepting a contradiction should be accepted as the solution to the problem, i.e. the best description of what is the case at the limiting instant.

It is, however, part of the charm of the problem of the moment of change that apparently all conceivable solutions have been advocated in literature (this makes telling a systematic history of it possible). So the idea that at the limiting instant between two contradictory states we are faced with an objective contradiction, which need not be avoided but just honestly and appropriately described, does actually occur.

One must take this opinion seriously if a sophisticated and professionally devised formal logic, tailor-made for rendering it, exists which allows contradiction within well-defined limits. Since the late 1970s, the Australian logician Graham Priest has been developing a so-called 'paraconsistent logic', in his view the 'logic of paradox'. It is a kind of propositional calculus, whose tense-logical version he introduces for the very task of applying it to the problem of the moment of change.[1] In order to prevent contradictions from getting out of hand it is crucial that in paraconsistent logic the *ex falso quodlibet* does not hold.[2] It is impossible as well as unnecessary to render in detail here the formal aspects of Priest's work. At this point the reader is requested to just accept that it is possible to construct a system which deserves to be called a formal logic, although the LNC does not hold in it. Priest's philosophical motivation can be satisfactorily examined without entering into his complex formalism.

Within the framework of his paraconsistent logic, Priest describes the moment of change according to the both-states-option. In his opinion the old as well as the new state obtains at the limiting instant. As Priest largely concerns himself with C-changes this means that, at the limiting instant, an objective contradiction is realized.

3.1.2. Some motivation for paraconsistent logic: Hegel's concept of motion

Priest derives the motivation for his paraconsistent logic from Hegel, especially from his famous *dictum* of motion being 'contradiction itself in existence' ('der daseiende Widerspruch selbst').[3] A short look at this concept of motion is therefore appropriate, although Priest does not comment on the s-change between rest and motion but is exclusively occupied with C-changes such that his Hegelian concept plays no role in his description of the moment of change.[4]

Priest's Hegelian concept of motion is opposed to the distinction between comparative and non-comparative properties: according to Hegel's conception of motion as Priest understands it, motion is not a comparative property but an intrinsic property of an object at every instant of its motion, motion consisting in the object's being in several contradictory states at the same time.[5] He refers[6] to the following passage in Hegel:

Es bewegt sich etwas nur, nicht indem es in diesem Jetzt hier ist und in einem andern Jetzt dort, sondern indem es in einem und demselben Jetzt hier und nicht hier, indem es in diesem Hier zugleich ist und nicht ist.[7]

[The] only [way in which] something moves [is] not by being here in this Now and there in another Now, but by being, in one and the same Now, here and not here, simultaneously both being and not being in this Here.

It would be inappropriate to discuss Hegel in detail here, but in this context it should be noted that there seem to be two possible interpretations of this passage: (1) a radical one and (2) a less radical one.

(1) Even at each single instant of a period of motion an object is in several different places. Motion is a contradictory state with respect to each single instant of a period of motion.

(2) An object in motion is never in just one place during a period of motion however short, but in many different places. It is not at several places at a single instant. However we do not observe it at single instants anyway, but always during periods. So, metaphorically speaking, what we observe is always a 'contradictory' state (no photograph of an object in motion is ever completely sharp, since there must always be a period of exposure; the object must always appear a little blurred on the photo).

Priest interprets the passage according to (1) (and seems to subscribe to it).[8] This interpretation suggests itself if the 'now' ('das Jetzt') was meant to be an instant by Hegel. Thus, motion according to Priest is a contradictory state, for if an object *a* is in motion at t_0 the following is true: *a* is at t_0 in position x and also in position y; and x and y are not identical. This does not mean that *a* is everywhere at t_0, but nevertheless it is simultaneously at x and not at x.

In order for (2) to be correct, the 'now' would have to be a short, but extended, period present to consciousness. I admit that (1) is more probable as an interpretation of Hegel's opinion. However, (2) might be an example of what one could develop from Hegel; and (2) is an opinion on which much of part III of this book will be based.

Of course, (1) is not unproblematic: one should assume that the position of an object in space at an instant is the part of space it occupies due to its size. So, even according to Hegel and Priest, a cube the size of one cubic metre occupies one cubic metre of space as long as it is at rest. Once it is in motion, however, it is 'spread'[9] across more space than that. But, presumably, it has not grown, therefore its size should still be 1 cubic metre. If one absolutely had to, one could perhaps imagine this when contemplating one single object moving through empty space. But as soon as two objects are involved, the imagination fails: the locomotive and the first waggon of a train, for example, would blend into one another without physically hampering one another in any way. Perhaps they only blend a little, so that we do not notice. Priest is in any case not interested in what the degree of this spreading might depend on; his concern is to render formally this possibility in principle.[10]

3.2. THE MOMENT OF CHANGE IN PARACONSISTENT LOGIC

3.2.1. Three kinds of change: α-, β-, und γ-changes

When Priest describes the moment of change by means of paraconsistent logic, he focusses his attention on C-changes. He distinguishes three possible kinds of change between two states S_1 and S_2 (and in this is very close to the systematic framework of options in this book):

α-changes: either S_1 or S_2 obtains at the limiting instant.
β-changes: neither S_1 nor S_2 obtains at the limiting instant.
γ-changes: both S_1 and S_2 obtain at the limiting instant.

Priest wants to show that it is plausible to assume the occurrence of γ-changes:

It is argued that some changes are such that at the instant of change the system is both in the prior and in the posterior state. In particular there are some changes from p being true to ¬p being true where a contradiction is realized.[11]

3.2.1.1. Do β-changes imply γ-changes?

Priest's first example in order to demonstrate that there are γ-changes begins with the assumption that there are β-changes.[12] It has nothing to do with C-changes, but is concerned with an s-change between contrary, not contradictory, states. Concerning the function of instantaneous velocities of an object a which 'smoothly' starts moving, there is an s-change with respect to the following states:

S_1: 'instantaneous velocity' of $a = 0$.
S_2: 'instantaneous velocity' of $a > 0$.

At each instant, the object is either in S_1 or in S_2. Up to and at the limiting instant the 'instantaneous velocity' is zero; at any later instant it is greater than zero. Things are, however, different with the following states:

S_3: acceleration of $a = 0$.
S_4: acceleration of $a > 0$.

This is because the acceleration is not defined for the limiting instant here. So there is a β-change with respect to S_3 and S_4: at the limiting instant between the two states neither state obtains. This is, however, unsurprising as we are not faced with a change between contradictories, such that we may say: *tertium datur*, i.e. the state 'acceleration not defined'. Thus, the claim that we are confronted with a β-change here is no more exciting than the claim:

When something is green, it is neither yellow nor blue.

The only difference is that the *tertium quod datur* in Priest's example is present only for a single instant.

In Priest's opinion the existence of γ-changes follows from the existence of β-changes: a γ-change in Priest's example would occur between the states of $S_5 = \neg S_3$ and $S_6 = \neg S_4$.

Now it is true to say that at the limiting instant (t_0) it is not the case that S_3 obtains and neither that S_4 obtains and that, therefore, at t_0 both S_5 and S_6 obtain. This is once again rather unremarkable, since S_5 and S_6 are neither contraries nor contradictories (as Priest himself mentions), but subcontraries (because S_3 and S_4 are only contraries and not contradictories). Thus the claim that both S_5 and S_6 obtain at the limiting instant is as trivial as the claim:

When something is green it is both not yellow and not blue.

Therefore γ-changes of this kind do not compel us to admit to the existence of objective contradictions. One wonders whether Priest, by treating this example in so much detail, wishes to convince the reader by impressing him rather than by giving him good reasons.

3.2.2. C-changes as γ-changes
3.2.2.1. The motivation for treating C-changes as γ-changes

In a second attempt, Priest tries to demonstrate that γ-changes occur between contradictories, too, which is indeed a much more interesting claim.[13] If one uses a classical two-valued logic with LNC, Priest says in agreement with Galton, there can only be α-changes between contradictories: all times are then distributed exhaustively to either p or ¬p. Priest objects that,

> [h]owever, classical logic is built on the unargued assumption that truth and falsity are exclusive and exhaustive, and it is exactly this point which is now at issue.[14]

Priest objects to this that in typical situations of moments of change its description as an α-change would enforce an arbitrary decision of answering the following questions:

> As I write I come to the end of a word and my pen leaves the paper. The instant it leaves the paper is it on or not on [...] the paper? [...] at the instant a solution [to a problem] strikes me, do I or do I not know the answer? [...] As I walk through the door, am I in the room or not in [...] it?[15]

In these examples, Priest has certainly found the weakest point of an advocation of the either/or-option: discontinuous changes which are nothing to do with the beginnings or endings of processes. Up to this point, a satisfactory justification for assigning the limiting instant rather to one than to the other state could only be obtained for changes at the beginning and the end of a process. This seems to compel an advocate of the either/or-option to construe discontinuous changes as at least dependent on processes (this happens in Aristotle, in the Middle Ages and in Sorabji). Only so can he avoid the charge of arbitrariness. But it is doubtful whether this strategy always succeeds. An advocate of the either/or-option would certainly say that, in Priest's first example, the limiting instant is the last instant at which the pen is still on the paper. But the other examples are problematic for him: does he have to hold that an idea occurs at the end of some subconscious process of arriving at it? Does he have to maintain that, in order to have left the room, one has to have cleared the threshold? Or is one already out of the room being on it? The list of these examples could be lengthened. Instances of this kind have indeed been neglected so far. Priest regards them as a strong hint towards the existence of β- or γ-changes between contradictories. I hope to be able to suggest a description of such changes in part III which does not lead to this conclusion.

3.2.2.2 Are β- and γ-changes identical?

Whether a discontinuous change is a β- or rather a γ-change makes little difference to Priest. When dealing with changes between contradictories, he simply identifies β- and γ-changes:

In the case we are considering the duality is, in fact, an identity: to be neither true nor false is to be both true and false.[16]

The reason Priest gives for this opinion is that, in classical as well as intuitionistic propositional calculus, the following formula is generally valid:[17]

$$\neg(p \vee \neg p) \equiv \neg p \wedge \neg\neg p.$$

This is not to be disputed. However, the way Priest interprets this fact is; for his interpretation is:

The lefthand side appears to correctly describe the situation at the instant of a type-β change from p to ¬p. The righthand side describes the situation at the instant of a type-g change from ¬p to ¬¬p.[18]

According to any usual interpretation of classical propositional calculus and also Priorian tense logic, a statement which may be analyzed as the lefthand side of this equivalence as well as a statement which may be analyzed as the righthand side of this equivalence does not describe any situation whatsoever. All that this tautology informs us about is that LEM and LNC are equivalent and cannot be denied independently of one another.

Furthermore, the identification of β-changes and γ-changes is futile for demonstrating the existence of γ-changes between contraries or contradictories unless Priest shows that there are β-changes between contradictories. He has not done so yet, for his only example for the existence of β-changes is a trivial one between contraries. Thus all Priest has put forward in favour of the existence of either β- or γ-changes between contradictories is his personal impression that discontinuous changes cannot be α-changes because one cannot non-arbitrarily decide in which way they are α-changes.

3.2.3. Priest's 'Leibnizian principle of continuity'

Priest's third attempt to demonstrate the existence of γ-changes is based on a postulate he calls 'Leibniz' principle of continuity':

[G]iven any limiting process [...] whatever holds up to the limit holds at the limit.[19]

In this formulation, the principle is not intuitive in every case.[20] So Priest limits himself to applying it in the following shape:

...any physical state of affairs which holds arbitrarily close to a given time holds at that time.[21]

At first sight, this application seems to involve a confusion between different meanings of the word 'limit', i.e. 'limiting instant' on the one hand and 'mathematical limit' on the other. Interestingly, Priest refers to passages in Leibniz where this principle is in fact stated in a very broad sense which comprises both meanings.[22]

If this principle is to be applied to the moment of change, the existence of C-changes in the shape of γ-changes is finally safe. For according to Priest, every state has two limiting instants at which it obtains, the state that the pen is on the paper, just as the state that the pen is not on the paper; the last instant at which the pen is on the paper being identical with the first instant at which it is not:

Suppose that prior to t_0 system S is in state S_0, whilst after it, it is in state S_1. Since S_0 occurs arbitrarily close to t_0, it occurs at t_0. Thus both S_0 and S_1 are realized at t_0, i.e. this is a type-g change. Of course if S_0 is p's being true and S_1 is ¬p's being true, t_0 realizes a contradiction.[23]

3.3. THE MOTIVATION FOR APPLYING THE LEIBNIZIAN PRINCIPLE

The question remains: *is* Priest's 'Leibnizian principle' to be applied to the moment of change? Priest admits that there is no compulsory reason to do so. But, he reasons, it should be applied since otherwise there would be a counter-intuitive jerk at the limiting instant:

A change that violates this principle would have to take place in no time [...] Surely, if something happens, it must take some time, even if just an instant.[24]

It is difficult to see why this must be so; in fact there will hardly be general agreement on this matter. Nevertheless we are at least here at the core of Priest's motivation for describing C-changes by using the both-states option: it is motivated by the (tacit) classification that there is an event of changing at the limiting instant.

That may be surprising, for this classification seems to be rather typically correlated with Plato's premiss. The 'task' of Plato's premiss is marking out the limiting instant by keeping it clear from both states. So Priest violates Plato's premiss not just once (as an advocate of the either/or-option does), but twice: he maintains that both states obtain at the limiting instant. However, Priest, too, wants to mark out the limiting instant. Except that his tool for doing this is not Plato's premiss but his Leibnizian principle, and the result is a rather different one. Interestingly, both results differ from the either/or-option in being symmetrical.

Thus, two opinions as extreme and as acutely opposed as Plato-2 and Priest's have one feature in common: according to both of them, the limiting instant is not marked out sufficiently by being the first or last instant of one of the states (as medieval logicians and Sorabji would say) if it is to be considered as an instant at which an event of changing takes place. In their opinion one would have to consider the event of changing as having either not yet or as having already occurred if either only the old or the new state obtained at the limiting instant. Both extreme opinions agree in that the classification of the change as an instantaneous event at the limiting instant excludes a description of it which uses the either/or-option. This would, for example, mean that during the Middle Ages a theory of the moment of change prevailed in which classification and description are incompatible. Advocates of both opinions may be expected to agree on the point that using the either/or-option forces one to deny an event of changing at the limiting instant (the alternatives are that it might not exist at all or happen beyond time). So both would agree on the following 'symmetry claim':[25]

> An event of changing does not take place when only one state (either the old or the new state) obtains.

They would also agree that a change is a datable, instantaneous event so that (assuming what has been said before) the either/or-option must be rejected.

Taking this into account, I think it is possible to see why Priest needs his 'Leibnizian principle'. In my view, he wants the limiting instant as a sort of weld. In his view the limiting instant is exceptional because there and only there do both (contradictory) states obtain at once. Nowhere else do the ends of the two states overlap one another. It is there that by way of contradiction the two states cling together. It is the metaphor of reaching into one another which motivates this opinion. In Priest's own words:

Contradictions are the *nodal points* of type-γ-changes...[26]

3.4. CRITICISM OF PRIEST'S APPROACH

3.4.1. Chris Mortensen and Joseph Wayne Smith

It has now been explained from a more or less psychological point of view why Priest makes use of the 'Leibnizian principle'. However, this does not mean that its application to the moment of change is to be recommended from a logical point of view.

The application of this principle to the moment of change, brings contradictions. This could already be viewed as a reason against applying it. There are grounds for rejecting the idea of 'objective contradictions' *tout court* (see below: 3.4.2.). But even authors who obviously do not want to reject this idea in general have criticized Priest's particular application of paraconsistent logic to the moment of change. Chris Mortensen has provided the formula (which may, thus, perhaps be called 'Mortensen's shaver'):

[D]o not multiply contradictions beyond necessity.[27]

Joseph Wayne Smith[28] applies 'Mortensen's shaver' to Priest by pointing out that Priest's Leibnizian principle is less plausible than the LNC:

There is an inherent weakness in any argument for real or objective contradictions that rests on a principle that is less plausible than the principle of non-contradiction itself.[29]

One might, so Smith argues, simply stipulate that at the limiting instant an object is always in one certain state;[30] one might even assume an object to be in one or the other state merely by chance.[31] In short: as long as arbitrariness saves the LNC one should choose arbitrarily or presume that nature is arbitrary rather than postulate an objective contradiction.[32]

In summary, one may say that Priest does not seem to have offered any reasons for the existence of objective contradictions beyond his belief in their existence.

3.4.2. What is it exactly that meets the eye?

It is true that Priest declares the limiting instant to be empirically inaccessible:

As if we could see whether it [the pen] was on or not on [the paper] at the instant of change![33]

Nevertheless he is convinced that we are faced with objective contradictions all the time. It seems that it must be mere obstinacy, psychologically explicable narrow-mindedness, if not all of us are reformed into Hegelians on this point:

What would it be like for a light to be both on and off? This description seems to paralyse the imagination. However, *the mental block is removed* once we realize that a light's being both on and off is a situation with which we are very familiar. [...] we literally witness a true contradiction whenever we turn the light on and off! It is just how things are at the point of change. [...] A cup is both a cup and not a cup the instant it fractures into smithereens. Someone is both in the room and not in the room the instant he leaves.[34]

It can surely be accepted that we see something happen when we watch a change. It need, however, not be accepted that what we see are objective contradictions.[35] Firstly, it may well be disputed that the noun 'contradiction' is used as referring to an entity or an event in the world. Possibly "This is a contradiction" is no more than my comment on two statements whose contents stand in a certain relation to one another. There would be no entity there then, to which the word 'contradiction' refers, but rather a relation of contradictoriness between propositions.

An adherent of using the both-states-option might accept this but still claim that a contradictory, paraconsistent description of a situation may be the best description available. However one has to be extremely fond of contradictions to hold this. In spite of his impressive formal work, I do not see that Priest presents any convincing intuitive arguments as to why one must resort to objective contradictions if one happens not to like them.

Yet is it possible to form an objection to Priest (and Hegel) which goes beyond mere matters of taste? When such fundamental assumptions as the LNC are disputed, this is not so easy. The most famous attempt to justify the LNC in the light of these difficulties has been made by Aristotle.[36] One might very approximately say that Aristotle's starting point is that the statements of someone who contradicts himself cannot be in any way informative. Consequently, there could be no paraconsistent description of a situation (the term 'paraconsistent description' would be itself a *contradictio in adiecto*). To me this seems very plausible indeed. But unfortunately, it is very hard to tell what Aristotle's argument exactly is, and a different, clearer one seems to be very difficult to devise.

In addition to the difficulties of fundamentally justifying the LNC, the empirical inaccessibility of instants brings about a certain deadlock: I do not have to accept Priest's idea that I must simply see that things are contradictory at the limiting instant. On the other hand, neither can I justify *on empirical ground* my wish to describe the moment of change without a contradiction. What is the case at an instant is a theoretical question. Our decision as to how to answer it is, just as Quine uses the expression, empirically underdetermined.

Thus it must here suffice to state that Priest has not been able to provide any convincing theoretical reasons as to why one should accept something as problematic as objective contradictions. For this reason, the LNC will be taken for granted again for the rest of this book. Priest's description of the moment of change is unlikely ever to become very popular. It cannot be disputed, though, that he states his case unambiguously, acutely aware of other authors' difficulties, with great clarity and with the courage to do what most people would not even dare to think of.

CHAPTER 4

THE NEITHER/NOR-OPTION

4.1. HAMBLIN'S INTERVAL SEMANTICS

There have been several attempts to define extended periods other than as in terms of sets of instants, regarding periods as either more fundamental than instants or at least introducing them as entities in their own right alongside instants.[1] One of these attempts is C. Hamblin's 'interval semantics'. Its basic ideas have been mentioned in the second part of the introduction, since the notation introduced there as well as the time-ontology containing periods is based to a large extent on a modified version of Hamblin's interval semantics.[2]

So far I have disregarded the fact that Hamblin's first publication on interval semantics topic, his article 'Starting and Stopping', contains an application of interval semantics to the problem of the moment of change.[3] I will now consider this, since the problem of the moment of change seems to have been the very motive for construing an interval semantics.

4.1.1. Hamblin and Plato: an introductory comparison

As will be shown in detail, Hamblin uses the neither/nor-option for his description of the moment of change. This suggests, as an initial approach to Hamblin's ideas, a comparison with Plato, who, according to Plato-2, does the same. There are fundamental and interesting similarities between Hamblin's treatment of the moment of change and Plato-2.

(a) Hamblin agrees with Plato in describing the moment of change as fundamentally neither belonging to the ending nor to the beginning one of the two states it separates. (He differs in that from, for example, Aristotle and philosophers in the Middle Ages who for many cases think that exactly one of the opposite states obtains, from Chisholm and Medlin who do not really have a clear position on which state obtains and from Graham Priest who thinks that, paraconsistently, both states obtain).

(b) While Aristotle treats 'comparative' states such as rest and motion differently from 'non-comparative' states (since they are a kind of second-order state which can be described as depending on positions at instants) Hamblin, like Plato, does not differentiate between comparative and non-comparative states.

(c) Hamblin's so-called 'elementary intervals' are more or less (if not exactly) the same as the chronoi according to Plato-2 (I shall elaborate on that).

However, there are also differences:

(a) Hamblin is clearly concerned with 'Cambridge-Changes' (something not so clear in Plato (cf. I,1.2.3.)): whenever *a* can be said to be in motion it is not at rest and vice versa.[4] So to Hamblin, the change between rest and motion is a C-change.

(b) Furthermore, there are, it seems, somewhat different motives for Plato and for Hamblin using the 'neither-nor'-option in describing the moment of change. One can distinguish *different reasons* for saying that it is both false that *a* is F and that *a* is not F at the limit between an F-phase and a no-F-phase:

(1) The limiting instant between the phases is a quite extraordinary 'time' of which it is neither true that *a* is F at it nor true that *a* is not F at it. However, there are statements which are true concerning this instant, for example that at it, a change between two states is taking place.

(2) There are no instants, let alone limiting instants. Thus, nothing can be true of an instant.[5]

(3) There are instants, namely limiting instants between phases; but nothing can be true of an instant.

According to Plato-2, Plato takes the first alternative: his sudden is the extraordinary limiting instant; and it is true to say that *a* is switching at it (μεταβάλλει). Hamblin, however, takes either the second or the third alternative: in 'Starting and Stopping' he builds an interval semantics without any instants whatsoever, which suggests alternative (2).[6] In 'Instants and Intervals', a later article on interval semantics, he permits the existence of instants, but still denies that any statement could be satisfied by an instant, which corresponds to (3).

Whether one adopts (1), (2) or (3) matters a lot with respect to the classification of the moment of change: (2) and (3) may ultimately lead to the banishing of change from time, since one can no longer say that a change is taking place at the limiting instant if nothing can ever be true of it. Accordingly not only using the either/or-option, but also using the neither/nor-option may result in the banishment of change from time. Hamblin has been rightly criticized for this by Priest and Mortensen.[7] Plato (if Plato-2 is correct), advocating (1), cannot be criticized on these terms.

Nonetheless Hamblin, in informal passages, does not show the least inclination towards banishing change from time. As I will show, what he says informally sounds rather like position (1). Consequently there is some tension between the logic Hamblin uses and the intuition he formulates.

4.1.2. Hamblin's way of posing the problem of the moment of change
Hamblin's formulation of the problem of the moment of change is:

...what was the state of the car *at* 8:00 a.m., as I was starting it? It would be inaccurate to say that it was in motion but it would be inaccurate, also, to say that it was at rest: it was 'just starting'. But, if whenever a thing is not in motion it is at rest, the state of 'just starting' [...] must be either a state of motion or a state of rest.[8]

One may ask what the time-reference '8 a.m.' actually means here. Does it somehow refer to the boundary between the two phases? If so, how? What is the status of this boundary?

4.2. TIME WITHOUT INSTANTS

4.2.1. Relations between periods
It initially seems that Hamblin wants to abolish instants altogether, such that the boundary cannot be regarded as an instant. The only times he admits in the interval semantics of 'Starting and Stopping' are periods as irreducible entities which can be divided ad infinitum and which can abut, overlap or be contained in one another. As stated in the introduction, he begins from a primitive relation between periods, read 'wholly precedes' (and notated: '<'), and uses it to define other relations between periods [9], among others 'abutment' (without thereby assuming the existence of instants as 'points of abutment').[10] The only predicates Hamblin is prepared to allow are 'durable predicates'[11] which can only be satisfied by periods (Hamblin's 'intervals') but not by instants (which do not exist anyway). Other examples for statements involving durable predicates, beside rest and motion are being red and being green.[12]

4.2.2. 'Elementary intervals'
4.2.2.1. Bye-bye bivalence?
The most interesting feature of periods is that something can be true for a part of a period while being false for another part of it. This seems to lead to three-valuedness (a state obtains throughout a period, or partly, or fails to obtain during it). In fact it does not: it has been mentioned in the introduction that the expressions 'throughout', 'throughout not', 'partly' and 'partly not' form a classical 'square of logic'. But Hamblin seems to have been unaware of this while writing 'Starting and Stopping'. So he notates:[13]

> p+a: p is true throughout a.
>
> p-a: p is false throughout a.
>
> p*a: p is true for a part of a and false for another.

But he is dissatisfied with this:

A three-valued logic is in fact an embarrassment, and we would well do something to get rid of it.[14]

In 'Instants and Intervals', his later contribution to interval semantics, Hamblin clearly recognizes the square-of-logic structure of states in periods. In contrast to the notation used in this book, however, Hamblin's primitive case of a state obtaining in a period is obtaining throughout it; obtaining for only part of it is a derived case.

4.2.2.2. Hamblin's two-valued solution

In 'Starting and Stopping', Hamblin has already found an elegant way back to two-valuedness. His solution is especially interesting in connection with the moment of change because it demonstrates how close Hamblin and Plato-2 are to one another:

If we could subdivide intervals in some way which would eventually lead us to 'atoms', within any one of which no change takes place, we would have solved the problem...[15]

Thus, somehow one has to define 'maximally changeless periods'. In order to do this, Hamblin takes a set of elementary statements $(P_1, P_2, P_3...)$ and describes the 'universe' as a sequence of 'conjunction chains' of Ps or their negations.[16] In such a way he can characterize 'elementary intervals' which however, unlike Strang's time-atoms,[17] are neither indivisible nor all of the same duration:

An elementary interval is an interval within which no change of truth-value of any of the Ps occurs, and such that it cannot be enlarged without including such a change. That is to say, intervals which overlap it contain a truth-value change if and only if they are not contained in it.[18]

The way back to two-valuedness is clear:

If, instead of introducing elementarity by definition, we treat it as a new primitive, the logic of intervals becomes fully two-valued and we have a complete basis for a logic of time without instants.[19]

Hamblin's 'elementary intervals', then, are an elegant way of working with periods within the framework of a two-valued logic without having to assume time-atoms and discrete time.

4.2.2.3. Hamblin and Plato in detail: 'chronoi' and 'elementary intervals'

Hamblin's elementary intervals show how near he is to Plato-2: they are at least very similar to if not identical with Plato-2's chronoi. As we may recall, according to one version of Plato-2 the chronoi were F- and not-F-periods of a (periods throughout which a was F or was not); according to a second version they were F- or not-F-phases of a (i.e. F- or not-F-periods of a of maximum length).

(a) If chronoi are F-phases and no-F-phases, then they are a kind of elementary interval with respect to a single property and a single object *a* (not with respect to *all* properties and objects, as Hamblin's). In this reading Hamblin's elementary intervals could be identified with chronoi for the (however extremely unlikely) case that changes with respect to F are the only changes happening during *a*'s existence.

(b) If chronoi are F-*periods*, every Hamblinian elementary interval is a chronos, but not every chronos is an elementary interval. For if nothing at all changes during an elementary interval, then *a fortiori* nothing changes during it with respect to *a* and F. All elementary intervals are F- or no-F-periods. They are simply a special sort of period during which not only no change takes place with respect to *a* and F, but even no change at all.

(c) Hamblin could even go so far as to identify Plato's chronoi and his elementary intervals completely: since an elementary interval has all the properties a 'chronos' is supposed to have, too, this yields a perfectly consistent reading of Plato's text. We achieve this reading by adding to the second alternative of Plato-2 ('F-periods') the assumption that there are no other chronoi than the elementary intervals. We do not find this assumption in Plato's text, however, (he is concentrating on one state and its opposite). For this reason I would regard this idea as an over-interpretation; however, it is an interesting one which does not much harm the text.

4.3. HAMBLIN'S SUGGESTION FOR DESCRIBING THE MOMENT OF CHANGE

4.3.1. Hamblin's solution

Hamblin's explicit suggestion how to treat the moment of change consists of a single sentence which, however, presupposes his whole theory of interval semantics:

If we want to model, in this logic, some statement about an instant of truth-value change of a durable predicate [...] it will be as a statement about the respective values of that predicate in a pair of abutting elementary intervals.[20]

What Hamblin is calling 'truth-value-change of a durable predicate' is, of course, a Cambridge-Change (a predicate does not have any truth-value!). Hamblin is not discussing a limiting *instant*; in the framework of 'Starting and Stopping', such a thing does not exist. Thus, Hamblin holds, it is not possible either to ask whether *a* is F or is not F at it.

4.3.2. Criticism of Hamblin's solution

Once again considering the starting of a car as paradigm case, one can see that Hamblin's idea does have an amazing consequence: the time-reference 'at 8 a.m.' which Hamblin uses when formulating his problem[21], does not refer to anything existent.

A minor problem is that Hamblin provides a definiens in which no instant occurs, but the definiendum is 'a statement about an instant'. This is not entirely stringent: If Hamblin takes himself seriously he can only be talking of "a statement containing the word 'instant'". Being stringent here, one would have to say that before interval semantics was invented philosophers were under the illusion that one could make a statement about an instant. However, it is clear what Hamblin means at this point.

What is more important are the consequences of making instants victims of Ockham's razor. This is exactly what Hamblin does. There is in principle no objection to applying Ockham's razor. It was quite a relief not to have to look for the present King of France and for Pegasus after Russell's 'On Denoting' and Quine's 'On what there is': it can be a real progress in philosophy to notice that one noun (-phrase) or another does not 'label' any entity. One might wonder, however, whether this strategy leads to intuitive results in our special case of the time-reference '8 a.m.'.

Since in 'Starting and Stopping' Hamblin banishes change from those times that he acknowledges (the 'intervals', i.e. periods), one may ask what the statement 'The car was just starting at 8 a.m.' (which he himself uses) might mean. So much is clear: according to Hamblin's conception, it is impossible to isolate any reference of the phrase '8 a.m.' (just as it is impossible to do so for the phrase 'the present king of France'). In fact, one cannot analyse the definiendum at all; one can only say:

> The statement "The-car-was-just-starting-at-8-a.m." is true iff the car was at rest during (at least) a subperiod of the eighth hour before noon abutting the ninth hour before noon and was in motion during (at least) a subperiod of the ninth hour before noon abutting the eighth hour before noon.

Critiscism of this is found, for example, in Mortensen:

[Hamblin's] solution is to sidestep the problem by appeal to time structured only as a collection of temporal intervals rather than instants. [...] because instants are not allowed, the problem of discontinuous change at those instants does not arise. The extent to which it does not arise, however, is the extent to which physics and common sense, which agree that change can take place *at* 12 noon, are rejected.[22]

And Priest adds:

...[Hamblin's] interval thesis may well solve the problem of the instant of change. However, it does so only by producing a curious account of change. [...] given that there is no instant dividing [two elementary intervals] a and b we can not ask whether [a system] S is in [state] S_1 or in [state] S_2 at it. However, because there is no such instant, there is no time at which the situation *is changing*: [interval] a is before the change, [interval] b is after it. Thus, in a sense, there is no change in the world at all, just a series of different states patched together !²³

Thus it can be seen that if this is what Hamblin wants to say, no change is actually taking place; he banishes change from any time he permits.

4.4. INSTANTS AS ASSISTANTS TO INTERVALS

Caution should be urged: Hamblin is not quite as stringent as his critics think. There are many places even in 'Starting and Stopping' at which it becomes clear that he is not intending to abolish instants altogether. Rather, he comments on the idea so:

[This] course is the more heroic, but caution should be urged: [...] for there must surely be time *intervals*, and intervals appear to require instants as their ends even if they are not, in fact, actually made up of continuous assemblages of them.²⁴

In another, very important passage for motivating intervals semantics, in which Hamblin is considering whether one should allow the existence of instants, he can imagine them as 'assistants to intervals'.²⁵ Furthermore, Hamblin cautiously takes only 'most everyday predicates' to be 'durable predicates', so it is possible that not all predicates are durable.²⁶

This very much suggests the idea that there might somehow also be non-durable predicates. A good candidate would, of course, be "*a* is just starting" which would play the same role as Plato's μεταβάλλει. Unfortunately, in Hamblin's formal system of 'Starting and Stopping' there is no room for such a predicate. To allow it would reintroduce talk of truth and falsity at an instant which is to be avoided.

One might wonder if the situation looks different once one allows instants as boundaries of periods. Hamblin has done so in his later (and obviously widely unknown) article 'Instants and Intervals'; there he still takes periods as primitive and elegantly identifies instants with pairs of periods, thereby obtaining a dense, linear order of instants.

4.5. THE MOMENT OF CHANGE IN MODIFIED
INTERVAL SEMANTICS (WITH INSTANTS)

Unfortunately, Hamblin does not reconsider the moment of change in the light of this amendment. And unfortunately, although he has admittted the existence of instants, he still does not allow anything to be true at them. So the only progress we make for analyzing our statement is:

The statement "The-car-was-just-starting-at-8-a.m." is true iff the car was at rest throughout a period which is bound by the instant called '8 a.m' at its end and was in motion throughout a period which is bound by the instant called '8 a.m.' at its beginning.

So we can isolate a meaning of the phrase '8 a.m.': it refers to an instant. But we still cannot say that 'was-just-starting' refers to an event happening or a state obtaining at this instant.

4.6. NONSENSE AS THE REASON FOR APPLYING INTERVAL SEMANTICS TO THE MOMENT OF CHANGE

4.6.1. An inexpressible question?

Why would Hamblin think this an attractive idea? Why is he proud to have made the question of whether the car is at rest or in motion at 8 a.m an "inexpressible question"[27] for interval semantics? When reading Hamblin's informal description of the moment of change one can only wonder whether he has not construed a logic which is totally inadequate for his own intuition. Not only does he pose the question of what might be the case at the moment of change; in 'Instants and Intervals' he even answers the question with a decisive 'neither-nor':[28]

Before 10p.m. it was light; after 10 p.m. it is non-light; but which is it at 10 p.m.? *Of course*, it is neither light nor non-light. [[29]...] and if I destroy a letter by throwing it in the fire the moment at which I do so is a moment of its history at which it is neither in existence nor out of existence but *in limbo*.

Does this not contradict both the radical programme of 'Starting and Stopping' ("abolish all instants!") and also the more moderate programme of "Instants and Intervals" ("no states for instants!")? What might the talk of 'neither..nor' or 'in limbo' mean in the framework of interval semantics? Is not the ultimate consequence a violation of the LEM?

One might think so. But I think it is possible to defend Hamblin in this case and that only by doing so do we reach the centre of his suggestion. He gives a hint how he should be read by using the word 'change' only as a part of the phrase 'instant of truth-value change'. Hamblin is not in fact talking about an instant of a change actually taking place, but about truth-values; he is talking in meta-language about his object-language 'interval semantics', while using the object-language to say what actually happens. Unfortunately, he does not tell us so. However there can be no doubt that the best way of defending him from the basic idea of interval semantics is by claiming:

Hamblin's 'neither...nor' or 'in limbo' are part of a meta-language statement, not part of a description of an actual situation. They simply mean that in the framework of the interval semantics of 'Instants and Intervals' an instant neither satisfies a predicate nor does not, because there are no predicates taking instants.

This idea relies on the assumption that not false but meaningless statements result if one fills in the argument-place of a predicate with the name of an object which does not belong to the domain of this predicate. In my view this assumption is not very plausible, but let us nevertheless consider it. I think that Hamblin basically holds that sentences such as "The car is in motion at 8 a.m." or "*a* is red at instant t" are nonsensical in the same way that the sentence "Cesar is a prime number" is nonsense. Hamblin's position would then be:

A sentence like "*a* is red at t" is just as nonsensical as "Cesar is a prime number". It does not state a proposition and is, thus, neither true nor false. To state *this* does not violate the LEM, though, in our object-language. It is a meta-language statement. It involves no claim that in reality (which is described by the object-language) anything neither is nor is not the case.

This is a thorough suggestion of how to treat the moment of change. It combines the 'neither/nor'-option with the LEM even for Cambridge-changes (which is not easy to achieve). It is a pity that Hamblin is not himself explicit about how he manages to avoid a violation of the LEM, but I think, what I have sketched above reflects his idea.

4.6.2. Should one introduce μ-predicates?

The idea so sketched is interesting for a further reason: it can still be partly applied if one does not want to declare all predicates to be durable predicates (as Hamblin does), but if one allows a certain kind of instantaneous predicates as an exception to the rule.

How intuitively weak Hamblin's radical idea is can be seen when he himself calls the state of the car at 8 a.m. 'just starting' while denying the predicate "*a* is starting". Indeed, Hamblin has no plausible reason not to allow at least one kind of instantaneous predicate. It contains predicates like "*a* is starting", "*a* is stopping", "*a* is changing" etc. which we shall call μ-predicates (from μεταβάλλει).

In this way we can mitigate Hamblin's idea without violating its basic tenet, by distinguishing between durable predicates and μ-predicates. We might hold that such sentences are nonsense in which the argument-place of a durable predicate is filled in with a reference to an instant. One could put this into the slogan: "durable predicate + instant = nonsense". In doing so we need not abolish μ-predicates altogether, since they are not durable but instantaneous predicates.

There is now nothing to be said against the view that instants do not belong to the domain of a durable predicate but do belong to the domain of a μ-predicate.[30] This modification has an enormous advantage: in this way we can obviously avoid banishing change from time. So Hamblin banishes change from time without any real need to do so.

4.7. EVALUATION

4.7.1. Hamblin's solution: an elaborate but unattractive proposal

We have to ask ourselves how plausible this modified Hamblin-approach is. Someone who holds it must accept that it is nonsense to talk of being green or being in motion at an instant. Firstly one might remark that this does not reduce the number of instants there are. It does indeed look like this when Hamblin writes about the "instants of truth-value change":

> ...there is no other kind of instant that we need to make room for...[31]

However an example makes clear: as long as there is a process going on in the world, Hamblin has to assume the existence of all the same instants of a dense time-order as we usually do:

> Imagine a clockhand which is proceeding continuously (i.e. without stopping every second, such as my travel alarm already familiar from ch.II,3). Think of the durable predicate '...is a period throughout which the second hand has an angle of less than 90° to the hour hand'. Some periods satisfy this predicate, some do not. The truth-value changes with respect to this predicate thus force us to admit the existence of *some* instants. By taking any other angle we can thus force Hamblin to admit the existence of any instant we want as long as the clock works.

But the example still displays a much worse consequence of Hamblin's idea: interval semantics implies exactly the same 'staircase theory of motion' which Strang attributes to Plato.[32] Interval semantics does not imply time-atomism, to be sure. But, according to it, any state has to obtain for at least a short while. This contradicts the idea of continuous motion. For this idea entails that an object in motion never stays in a position but only holds it instantaneously: if we want to save the idea of continuous motion, then we must credit predicates which can work as durable predicates as well as as non-durable predicates. A position predicate like "*a* is at place *s*" is an example. In a description of a continuous process 'position-predicates' it obviously works as a non-durable predicate. So there are good reasons for not only admitting μ-predicates as instantaneous predicates but also position-predicates, colour-predicates etc. But while the introduction of μ-predicates does not touch Hamblin's basic idea the introduction of such predicates does: they are supposed to be the classical durable predicates, such that filling in their argument-place with instants would, in Hamblin's view, lead to nonsense.

It is, however, intuitively attractive to talk of colours or positions at instants. Hamblin's suggestion excludes this in principle even if it is modified by the introduction of μ-predicates. So Hamblin's suggestion cannot count as an attractive solution for the problem of the moment of change.[33]

A last example may show that Hamblin's fixation on durable predicates is hardly comprehensible. It is, in Hamblin's theory, even impossible to conclude from (1) "the traffic light is showing red from 9:59 to 10:01" to (2) "The traffic light is showing red at 10:00". If the instant called '10:00' exists (because there is a change taking place at it) one can still only say that "The traffic light is showing red from 9:59 to 10:00 and also from 10:00 to 10:01" (since "The traffic light is showing red" is a durable predicate which cannot be satisfied by the instant 10:00).[34]

4.7.2. The empirical inaccessibility of instants: a logical or rather an epistemological issue?
What can be learnt from both Plato-2's and Hamblin's extremely sceptical stance towards instants? There are, I think, no convincing logical reasons for accepting it. There are, however, epistemological ones: it is true that I cannot observe the position of the clockhand at an instant without observing it for a period of time. I cannot open my eyes for an instant nor take a photograph by exposing the film to light for zero seconds. But this does not mean that it is nonsense to ascribe a distinct position to the clockhand for every instant.[35]

Hamblin and Plato-2 take seriously the difference between periods which are empirically accessible and instants which are empirically inaccessible. Hamblin tries to account for this by degrading instants with what can only be called a certain stubborness. However, building a logic can be the wrong way to cope with an epistemological insight.

Both Plato and Hamblin demonstrate that talking of states at instants means going beyond immediate sense experience. This is not very shocking (except, perhaps to an early Vienna Circle hard-core empiricist): we also do so when talking about causation, about dispositions or about a house having a wall facing the backyard while looking at its front. But it is important to keep in mind that we have no idea what something, be it in motion or at rest, looks like at an instant. We only know what the clockhand looks like at rest when the clock has stopped, and may confuse this with its supposed appearance at an instant. This point will be dealt with in detail in part III. There however, the conclusion will not be that instants should be abolished or degraded, but that we cannot do without them as theoretical entities.

Thus, the conditions which must be fulfilled for a predicate to be satisfied by an instant have to be justified carefully if we want to secure some empirical content for statements about instantaneous states. However we can already see that it is exaggerated to insist on this being impossible.

CHAPTER 5

THE 'NEUTRAL INSTANT ANALYSIS' (NIA)

5.1. A GOOD COMPROMISE

5.1.1. Why use a mixed description?

None of the four options for describing the moment of change has revealed itself as satisfactory in all cases:

(a) Application of the either/or-option suggests itself for C-changes (as one naturally wants to keep LNC and LEM). It also suggests itself for the beginnings and ends of processes, because if only one state may obtain at the limiting instant there are, in this case, good reasons as to which state it is. However, such reasons could not be found for s-changes between comparative properties, and so the impression that applying the either/or-option to them would involve an arbitrary decision prevails. Discontinuous changes remain unexplained. (Cf. ch.II,1)

(b) Application of the either-way-option has proved incomprehensible for C-changes. For s-changes between rest and motion the adherents of this option have to rely on concepts of motion and rest at an instant which are counter-intuitively weak. (Cf.ch.II,2)

(c) Application of the both-states-option necessitates the postulation of objective contradiction in nature and, thus, the denial of the LNC. (Cf.ch.II,3)

(d) If one permits states at instants (for which there is ample reason), then the use of the neither/nor-option for C-changes inescapably violates the LEM. (Cf. ch.II,4)

That the exclusive use of none of the options leads to satisfactory results suggests looking for a mixed description of the moment of change. Such a description should be a good compromise in applying, with good reason, various options, depending on the case involved. Use of the either-way-option at all for this task is not attractive; the same is true for the both-states-option. A good compromise can only be expected between the either/or- and the neither/nor-option. In this chapter I am going to argue that there *is* such a good compromise for describing the moment of change, known as the 'Neutral Instant Analysis'[1] (NIA).

5.1.2. The NIA as a mixed description which keeps the LEM

The term 'Neutral Instant Analysis' is misleading. It suggests that the NIA can only be a description of the moment of change which declares the limiting instant to be neutral with respect to the old and the new states in *all* cases, i.e. that 'NIA' stands for using the neither/nor-option come what may. We have already seen, however, that using the neither/nor-option is inappropriate in the case of C-changes. If the NIA implied this, it could not be a compromise, let alone a good one.

In fact, the name 'Neutral Instant Analysis' alludes only to the most striking feature of this approach; it is in no way a complete characterization. Its striking feature is the application of the neither/nor-option for describing the s-change between rest and motion (but not for describing C-changes). In the context of the NIA, motion and rest are regarded as comparative properties.

As the advocates of the NIA that I am aware of have dealt explicitly only with the s-change between rest and motion, another important component of their approach has so far hardly been noticed:

It is true that the NIA entails that there is neither a first nor a last instant of rest or motion of *a*. But this follows from there being first and last instants at which *a* ist not in motion / at rest. For according to the NIA, the following is true:

> A first instant at which *a* is not at rest any more is identical with a last instant at which *a* is not yet in motion: it is the limiting instant at the beginning of a motion. A last instant at which *a* is not yet at rest is identical with a first instant at which *a* is not in motion any more: it is a limiting instant at the end of a motion.

If one wants to infer from this that there is neither a first nor a last instant of motion or rest of *a* one must presuppose what was already clearly conceived in the Middle Ages:

> If LNC, LEM, dense time and the existence of limiting instants are assumed, the following is true: there is a last instant at which something is the case iff there is no first instant at which something is not the case.

The truth of this principle has to be presupposed in order to see how one can describe the s-change between rest and motion by using the neither/nor-option: Using it is possible only because LNC and LEM necessitate describing the C-change between rest and non-rest and the C-change between motion and non-motion by using the either/or-option. So one might say that in the context of the NIA the use of the neither/nor-option for the s-change between rest and motion is parasitic of the use of the either/or-option for C-changes. The s-change between rest and motion turns out to be a combination of two C-changes which coincide in such a way that *a* is to be regarded as being neither at rest nor in motion (however not for a period, but only for an instant). Not only does such a description leave LNC and LEM untouched; it is based on both.

5.1.3. *The strong concepts of rest and motion at an instant*

During the discussion of the either-way-option (ch.II,3) it emerged that a distinction between a strong and a weak concept of motion at an instant is both possible and useful. The weak concept of motion and rest at an instant permits the application of the either-way-option: according to these concepts, rest and motion at an instant are (with respect to instants at which *a* exists) neither contraries nor contradictories but only subcontraries. It is for exactly this reason that these weak concepts are counter-intuitive. Everyday usage assumes that *a* is never simultaneously at rest and in motion, at the limiting instant as anywhere else. It assumes the two states to be contraries or contradictories.

The application of the neither/nor-option in the context of the NIA is based on the strong concept of rest and motion at an instant which is rejected by the advocates of the either-way-option, although it is intuitively a lot more plausible than the weak concept used by them:

> An instant t is not an instant of motion of *a* if it merely bounds a prior period of motion of *a* or a subsequent period of motion of *a*. Instead, for t to be an instant of motion of *a*, it is required that t bounds both a prior period of motion of *a* and a subsequent period of motion of *a*.

And:

> An instant t is not an instant of rest of *a* if it merely bounds a prior period of rest of *a* or a subsequent period of rest of *a*. Instead, for t to be an instant of rest of *a*, it is required that t bounds both a prior period of rest of *a* and a subsequent period of rest of *a*.

This means that t is an instant of motion of *a* iff t falls within a period of motion of *a*, but not if t merely bounds such a period. The same is true for rest.

According to these strong concepts of motion and rest at an instant, rest and motion are neither subcontraries (as they are according to the weak concept) nor contradictories (as they are, for example, according to Hamblin and Galton); they are contraries. There is no instant at which *a* is both in motion and at rest. But there are instants at which *a* is neither in motion nor at rest, i.e., the limiting instants between motion and rest. So in the context of the NIA it is assumed that there are a few instants for which it is intuitive to have a 'neither/nor' status. This is, however, not true for periods: it cannot be accepted that *a* is neither at rest nor in motion throughout any period, however short, of *a*'s existence; and, indeed, this would contradict the NIA.[2]

5.2. THE ADHERENTS OF THE NIA AND THEIR MOTIVATION

In this chapter a detailed account of the NIA is to be given by discussing the opinions of three 20th century authors who either explicitly, or in all likelyhood, advocate the NIA: Norman Kretzmann, David Bostock and Bertrand Russell. But even though only texts from the 20th century are considered in this chapter, it is very well possible that the NIA is itself much older: we have seen in ch.I,3 that the typical medieval description of C-changes implies the NIA: both rest and motion are 'res successivae'. A 'res successiva' has neither a first nor a last instant. So the s-change between rest and motion, being a combination of two C-changes with respect to 'res successivae', implies that the limiting instant is an instant of neither rest nor motion. However, no medieval logician seems to have drawn this conclusion consciously; or, if he did, did not write it down.[3]

In view of this it is unsurprising that the clearest formulation of the NIA is found in the most important article on the instant of change in the Middle Ages: Norman Kretzmann's 'Incipit/Desinit'.[4]

Another formulation of the NIA is found in David Bostock's discussion of Plato.[5] This is not surprising either: Bostock and Kretzmann approach the NIA from the two possible starting points, Kretzmann from the either/or-option (the option usually chosen in the Middle Ages) and Bostock under the influence of Plato's 'neither/nor'.[6]

5.2.1. David Bostock

In Bostock's formulation of the NIA, it becomes especially clear that he uses the strong concepts of motion and rest at an instant (which exclude the either/or-option in this case):

A very natural view would be that the change occurs at the instant dividing all the instants when the thing is in motion from all the instants when the thing is at rest [...]. And it is quite possible that at that instant the thing is neither in motion nor at rest. For [...] if a thing is to be in motion at a certain instant then that instant must fall within a period such that the thing is moving throughout the period, *and we do not count the endpoints of a period (if any) as falling within it.* Similarly we may say that to be at rest at an instant is to be at rest throughout some period within which that instant falls. Hence the instant dividing a period of motion from one of rest will be an instant at which the thing is neither in motion nor at rest.[7]

Bostock does not try to define exactly what a period of motion or of rest of an object is. He realizes very clearly, though, that the s-change between rest and motion is a combination of two C-changes:

...consider the change from being in motion to not being in motion. This must surely occur at the [...] instant dividing the two periods [...]. So at the time when the thing is changing from being in motion to not being in motion, at that time the thing (already) is not in motion [...]. By a parallel argument, at the time when the thing is changing from not being at rest to being at rest, at that time it (still) is not at rest [.][8]

There can be no doubt, as is seen here, that Bostock *classifies* the change as a datable event: even the C-changes which constitute the s-change are dated to the limiting instant. One may presume that Bostock views the s-change itself in the same way (although he does not say so explicitly). Consequently, Plato's premiss cannot be upheld for C-changes.[9]

5.2.2. Bertrand Russell

Bertrand Russell's description of the moment of change is, in a way, the mirror-image to Bostock's: while Bostock describes the instant of change explicitly, but does not comment on the definition of rest and motion at an instant, the opposite is true for Russell: his description of the moment of change must be inferred from the way in which he attempts to define rest and motion at an instant. He does this only a few pages after proposing his Cambridge-change criterion (but without any material relation to it) in §446 of the chapter on motion in the 'Principles'.

5.2.2.1. The text: 'Principles of Mathematics' §446

§446 of the 'Principles' may be analysed as consisting of the following steps:
(1) Clarification of intuition
(2) Definition of rest at an instant
(3) Definition of motion at an instant
(4) Definition of the limiting instant (called 'term of transition')
(5) Summary characterization of rest and motion
(6) Definition of 'momentary rest'
(7) The postulate that there are no abrupt changes of velocity (continuity postulate)

The extraordinary complexity and density of Russell's text justifies the unusual procedure of quoting almost the entire text of §446 with marks of orientation added:

[1] A simple unit of matter [...] can only occupy one place at one time. Thus if A be a material point, "A is here now" excludes "A is there now", but not "A is here then". Thus any moment has a unique relation, not direct, but via A, to a single place whose occupation by A is at the given moment. But there need not be a unique relation of a given place to a given time, since the occupation of the place may fill several times.

[2] (b) A moment such that
    an interval containing the given moment
    otherwise than as an end-point
    can be assigned
    (c) at any moment within which interval
    A is in the same place
    (a) is a moment when A is at rest.

[3] (b) A moment when this cannot be done
    (a) is a moment when A is in motion,
    (c) provided A occupies *some* place at neighbouring moments on either side.

[4] (b) A moment when there are such intervals
    (c) but all have the said moment as an end-term
    (a) is one of transition from rest to motion or vice versa. [...]

[5] (a) when different times, throughout any period however short, are correlated with different places, there is motion;
(b) when different times, throughout some period however short, are all correlated with the same place, there is rest. [...]
(c) Motion consists broadly in the correlation of different terms of [a one-dimensional series] t with different terms of [a three-dimensional series] s. [...]
(d) A relation R which correlates all the terms of t in a certain interval with a single term of s corresponds to a material particle which is at rest throughout the interval with the possible exclusion of its end-terms (if any) which may be terms of transition between rest and motion.

[6] A time of momentary rest is given by any term for which the differential coefficient of the motion is zero. [...]

[7] It is to be taken as part of the definition of motion that it is continuous and that it has first and second differential coefficients. This is an entirely new assumption, having no kind of necessity...

5.2.2.2. Interpretation: 'Principles of Mathematics' §446 as an NIA
§1 A formal reconstruction of the text

Ad (1): Let us take A to be the centre of mass of an object a.[10] In order to render Russell's intuition about motion as a relation between places, times and objects (which he expresses very distinctly in (1)[11]) let us furthermore introduce a two-place function IS-AT. This function is to be the set of ordered pairs whose first component is an ordered pair of a physical object and an instant and whose second component is a point in space: the 'position' of the object in question at the instant in question (points in space are notated as x, x_1, x_2 ...). The expression 'IS-AT(a,t)' thus denotes the value of the IS-AT-function for *a* at t: the position of *a* at t.

Ad (2): (a) is the *definiendum*, (b) and (c) are two parts of the *definiens*. The task set is to define under which conditions an instant t satisfies the statement 'R_a', which is to be read as "*a* is at rest". So we have:

    (a) $R_a(t)$ iff...

Phrase (b) is concerned with an interval, which has, of course, two bounding instants, which may be called t_1 and t_2. The instant t is supposed to fall within this interval, but not to be one of the boundary instants. A way of rendering this is to stipulate that the interval is open, so that the bounding instants are not elements of it. We then have:

(b) $...\exists t_1,t_2 \,\exists I \,[\, I =]t_1,t_2[\,\wedge\, t \in I...$

The rendering of (c) which comes closest to the text would be:

(c') $...\wedge \exists x \,\forall t_3 \in I \,[\text{IS-AT}(a,t_3) = x]].$

However, for what follows it will be better to work with an equivalent but slightly more complicated rendering of (c):

(c") $...\wedge \forall t_3,t_4 \in I \,[t_3 \neq t_4 \to \text{IS-AT}(a,t_3) = \text{IS-AT}(a,t_4)]].$[12]

We thus obtain as Russell's definition of rest at an instant:

$R_a(t)$ iff $\exists t_1,t_2 \,\exists I \,[\, I =]t_1,t_2[\,\wedge\, t \in I \wedge \forall t_3,t_4 \in I \,[t_3 \neq t_4 \to \text{IS-AT}(a,t_3) = \text{IS-AT}(a,t_4)]].$

Ad (3): In (3), Russell characterizes motion at an instant by negating the definition of rest plus a plausible additional requirement. This requirement ("provided that...") obviously has the purpose of avoiding possible first or last instants of the existence of *a* counting as instants of motion of *a*. Again, (a) is the *definiendum*, while (b) and (c) are the parts of the *definiens*. In order to render this, let B_a be a statement taking instants and to be read "*a* is in motion". We then get:

$B_a(t)$ iff
While   (i) $\neg R_a(t)$
Nevertheless (ii) $\exists t_1,t_2[t_1 < t < t_2 \wedge \exists x_1,x_2[\text{IS-AT}(a,t_1) = x_1 \wedge \text{IS-AT}(a,t_2) = x_2].$[13]

Ad (4): Again, (a) is the *definiendum*, (b) and (c) are meant to be the parts of the *definiens*. But the 'all' in (c) is not at all plausible. Such intervals as are contained in a phase of motion of *a* though being shorter than it do not have a limiting instant between rest and motion as an 'end-term'. Still, it is easy enough to see what Russell must have meant here: if t is a 'term of transition', then t bounds not just one but many intervals of rest while, however, not falling within any such interval. So t is a 'term of transition' iff the following is true:

There is an *open* interval I such that:
$t \in I \wedge \forall t_1,t_2 \in I \,[t_1 \neq t_2 \to \text{IS-AT}(a,t_1) = \text{IS-AT}(a,t_2)],$
but there is no such *closed* interval.

Ad(5): On the one hand, (5b), just as (5d), are mere repetitions of (2), the definition of rest at an instant. On the other hand, (5a) and (5c), like (3) characterizations of motion at an instant, deviate from (3) in content: in (3) motion is defined by using the definition of rest from (2); in (5a) and (5c) we have a definition of motion symmetrical and on a par with the definition of rest which is not presupposed: being in motion is being at different places at different times throughout an interval, being at rest is being in the same place throughout an interval.

In order to render this symmetry, (5a) and (5c) closely suggest a definition of motion at an instant which results from replacing the ' = ' in the definition of rest in (2) by a '≠':

$$B_a(t) \text{ iff } \exists t_1,t_2 \, \exists I \, [\, I = \,]t_1,t_2[\, \wedge \, t \in I \, \wedge \, \forall t_3,t_4 \in I \, [t_3 \neq t_4 \rightarrow \text{IS-AT}(a,t_3) \neq \text{IS-AT}(a,t_4)]].$$

Ad (6) and (7): Russell postulates in (7) that there are no abrupt beginnings of motion, for example of the kind that *a* has, in a certain environment of instants bounded by the limiting instant, a constant 'instantaneous velocity' of $v = 1$. Thus, just as Sorabji does, he excludes one case *a priori* which Jackson/Pargetter have discerned as the really problematic one.[14] Doubtless, Russell was aware that he was here merely stating a postulate.

This postulate has an interesting consequence: according to it, at all limiting instants the 'instantaneous velocity' of *a* is well-defined (this would not be so in the abrupt case), and it is always zero. From this, it follows with (6) that every limiting instant is an instant of 'momentary rest'.

§2 Some embarrassing consequences

i.   From the definition of the limiting instant in (4) it follows that the limiting instant cannot be an instant of rest according to (2) because (4b) is contradictorily opposed to (2b).

ii. From the definition of the limiting instant in (4) it follows that the limiting instant is an instant of motion according to the definition of motion in (3).

iii. From the definition of the limiting instant in (4) it follows that the limiting instant is no instant of motion according to the definition of motion in (5a)/(5c).

iv. The definition of motion in (3) is therefore incompatible with the definition of motion suggested by (5a)/(5c).[15]

v.   From (3) it follows that the limiting instant is an instant of motion. From (6) and (7) it follows that the limiting instant is an instant of momentary rest. The definition of motion in (3) therefore contradicts (6) and (7).[16]

vi. (5) does not contradict (6) and (7). According to (2) and (5), the limiting instant is neutral: it is an instant of neither rest nor motion.

Since it was left neutral, it can, in an additional step (i.e. (7)), be declared to be an instant of momentary rest.

The question is whether the inconsistencies in Russell's text can be removed by an interpretation *ad meliorem partem*. I think this is possible by proceding in two steps:

§3 Interpretation ad meliorem partem, step 1

If the definiens of (3) were degraded from being a sufficient to being merely a necessary condition for motion at an instant (making (3) a one-sided implication), (3) would become compatible with the definition of motion in (5) as well as with (6) and (7).

By this modification of (3) the text can be made consistent. How the limiting instants can *post festum* be declared to be instants of 'momentary rest' then becomes comprehensible. This does, however, not mean that one has to accept (6) and (7); these steps reveal themselves as independent of the rest of the text.

So the first step of the interpretation *ad meliorem partem* of §446 which I propose consists in degrading (3) by tearing off one 'f' from the 'iff' contained in it.

§4 Interpretation ad meliorem partem, step 2

In addition to the first step, I think that there are two good reasons for abandoning (6) and (7).

(i) One reason is that it seems unnecessary to exclude abrupt beginnings of motion *a priori* here. The definitions also work for abrupt beginnings yielding a neutral limiting instant. (7) is a mere postulate and (6) is motivated by no more than the concept of 'instantaneous velocity'. I hope to have shown in ch.II,1. that this concept is not very reliable. Interestingly, this opinion is backed by Russell in §447: he is rather skeptical about the idea of instantaneous velocity, too, and insists on calling the M-value[17] that which it actually is: "no [...] thing [...] except a real number which is the limit of a certain set of quotients". This does not quite fit with rating it so highly in (6)/(7).

(ii) The other reason concerns turning-point instants. By a turning-point instant I mean a limiting instant between the way there and the way back of an object in motion *via* the same places. For example, the instant at which a ball vertically thrown into the air is at the highest point of its trajectory is a turning-point instant. The ball does not stay at the turning point for any time. This speaks against its being at rest. However, the ball has no direction at the turning point, which speaks against its being in motion. This balance of conflicting intuition is motivation for regarding turning-point instants as neutral, i.e. as instants of neither motion nor rest, as with the limiting

instants between phases of motion and phases of rest. Interestingly, the
definitions of (2) and (5) yield just this result: since the ball passes through
the same positions twice, no interval into which the turning-point instant
falls can fulfil the requirements of the interval referred to in the *definiens* of
the definition of motion according to (5). But clearly, the turning-point
instant is no instant of rest according to (2) either. Unfortunately, this result
is destroyed by declaring every instant of zero 'instantaneous velocity' an
instant of (momentary) rest instead of leaving it neutral, as (6) does. For this
reason the second step of the interpretation *ad meliorem partem* of §446
which I propose consists in forgetting about (6) and (7).

5.2.3. Norman Kretzmann

Just like Russell, Kretzmann starts out from a definition of rest and motion
at an instant. However, Kretzmann's text is considerably clearer and does
not ask for extensive interpretation. There is no doubt that Kretzmann
advocates an NIA; he himself coined the term 'Neutral Instant Analysis' and
has characterized it by his description. Kretzmann starts out from defining
motion at an instant with a concrete example (a ball):

If we rule out the possibility of teleportation, then it is true to say of the ball at a
given instant t_n that it is motion if and only if it is at t_n in a position different from
its position at any arbitrarily near preceding or succeeding instant.[18]

Obviously, the 'or' in this sentence is to be read as neither inclusive nor
exclusive but as 'adjunctive'. In that case, Kretzmann's definition of motion
at an instant (with 't' instead of Kretzmann's 't_n') may be rendered as:

$$B_a(t) \text{ iff } (B1) \; \exists t_1 \forall t_2 \, [t_1 < t_2 < t \to \text{IS-AT}(a,t_2) \neq \text{IS-AT}(a,t)] \land$$
$$(B2) \; \exists t_3 \forall t_4 \, [t < t_4 < t_3 \to \text{IS-AT}(a,t_4) \neq \text{IS-AT}(a,t)].$$

Kretzmann's definition of rest at an instant differs from his definition of
motion at an instant only by the replacement of the ' = ' by a ' ≠ ' (this is not
so clear in Russell, although, in the end, I have interpreted his text in this
way). Kretzmann describes a neutral limiting instant t_C at the beginning of
the ball's motion as a last instant at which the ball is not in motion and as a
first instant at which it is not at rest,[19] and comments upon this description
as follows:

The ball [...] is correctly described as being at A at the instant t_C. There is no
difficulty in describing a subject as being at a position at an instant, but that
description applies to [...the ball] equally correctly at any instant in the interval
(t_B, t_C) [which is an interval of uninterrupted rest]. What distinguishes t_C from any
such instant? For any instant t_R during the interval, the positions of the ball at any
arbitrarily near preceding or succeeding instant will be the same as its position at t_R.
For any instant t_M during the interval (t_C, t_D) [which is an interval of uninterrupted
motion], the positions of the ball at any arbitrarily near preceding or succeeeding

instant will be different from each other and from the ball's position at t_M. For t_C however, the position of the ball at any arbitrarily near preceding instant will be the same as its position, A, at t_C, and its position at any arbitrarily near succeeding instant will be different from A. The neutral instant, t_C, is therefore uniquely determinable.

Accordingly, his definition of rest of a at an instant is:

$$R_a(t) \text{ iff } (R1) \; \exists t_1 \forall t_2 \, [t_1 < t_2 < t \rightarrow \text{IS-AT}(a,t_2) = \text{IS-AT}(a,t)] \wedge$$
$$(R2) \; \exists t_3 \forall t_4 \, [t < t_4 < t_3 \rightarrow \text{IS-AT}(a,t_2) = \text{IS-AT}(a,t)].$$

It is easy to show that a is neither at rest nor in motion at the limiting instant if Kretzmann's definition is accepted. In order to see this, one merely has to follow Kretzmann's informal description: if t is a limiting instant at the beginning of a motion, then t is not an instant of motion. For although (B2) is true, (B1) is false because (R1) is true. But t is no instant of rest either. For although (R1) is true, (R2) is not but, instead, (B2) is. Something analogous is true if t is the limiting instant at the end of a phase of motion: t is not an instant of rest; for, although (R2) is true, (R1) is not but (B1) is. But t is not an instant of motion either; for, although (B1) is true, (B2) is not but (R2) is.[20]

5.2.4. A minor difference between Kretzmann's and the Russellian definitions

Kretzmann's NIA and the Russellian one (as reconstructed) differ only very slightly, i.e. on one point which is nothing to do with the limiting instant between rest and motion: according to Kretzmann's definitions, turning-point instants are not neutral; according to the Russellian definition they are.

The reason for this is that the Russellian definitions work with only one interval within which the instant t referred to in the *definiendum* falls. This leads to some positions being alotted to more than one, namely two, instants if t is a turning-point instant, so that the Russellian definition of motion at an instant, i.e. (2), is not fulfilled. On the other hand, Kretzmann's definitions work with two intervals each, which are bounded by t (one towards the future and one towards the past). If t is a turning-point instant, then no position is alotted twice within a single interval. If this is the case, then, according to Kretzmann's definitions, a is in motion at t.

5.3. A TRANSFORMATION OF KRETZMANN'S AND OF THE RUSSELLIAN DEFINITIONS

§1 Although Kretzmann's as well as the Russellian definitions are appropriate for expressing the NIA, neither renders the intuition behind it as clearly as is desirable. This intuition is that an instant t is an instant of motion of a iff t falls within a period throughout which a is in motion; and that an instant t is an instant of rest of a iff t falls within a period throughout which a is at rest. In order to render this, it seems appropriate first to define what makes a period a period of motion resp. rest of a, and to define only then as an instant of motion resp. rest of a such an instant as falls within a period thus characterized.

It is possible to refer to such a period by means of an interval of instants. Let us follow Kretzmann and Russell in this for the moment. The task is to characterize a period of uninterrupted motion regardless of its duration, instead of just defining an environment of motion around an instant t, as has been done so far. A point to be observed in facing this task is that a motion does not have to be at an end when it returns to its starting point. If a is in circular motion it permanently returns to places where it has been before. If a definition of a period of motion were referring to only two instants (positions of a which would be compared with one another), it would yield that a period of circular motion is no period of motion at all. This necessitates referring to a third instant: An object a is in motion throughout an interval I iff between any two different instants from I there is a third instant such that a's position at this third instant is different from its position at the first instant as well as from its position at the second instant. This definition 'reacts' to circular motion because it does not rule out that the positions at the first and the second instant may be equal.

For greater precision let us introduce two two-place predicates, which take a physical object in the first place and an interval in the second:

'B(a,I)' is to be read: I is an interval of uninterrupted motion of a.
'R(a,I)' is to be read: I is an interval of uninterrupted rest of a.

They are defined as follows:

B(a,I) iff
(i) I is an open interval.
(ii) $\forall t_1,t_2 \in I \; \exists t_3 [t_1 < t_3 < t_2 \rightarrow \text{IS-AT}(a,t_3) \neq \text{IS-AT}(a,t_1) \wedge \text{IS-AT}(a,t_3) \neq \text{IS-AT}(a,t_2)]$.[21]

R(I,a) iff
(i) I is an open interval.
(ii) $\forall t_1,t_2 \in I \; \exists t_3 [t_1 < t_3 < t_2 \rightarrow \text{IS-AT}(a,t_3) = \text{IS-AT}(a,t_1) \wedge \text{IS-AT}(a,t_3) = \text{IS-AT}(a,t_2)]$.

Now t may be defined as an instant of motion resp. rest as follows, if $B_a(t)$ is to be read as "t is an instant of motion of a" and if $R_a(t)$ is to be read as "t is an instant of rest of a":

$B_a(t)$ iff $\exists I [B(I,a) \wedge t \in I]$.
$R_a(t)$ iff $\exists I [R(I,a) \wedge t \in I]$.[22]

According to these definitions, the limiting instant is trivially neutral: it can neither be an element of an interval of motion nor of an interval of rest, since both kinds of intervals are open intervals *per definitionem*.

§2 As NIA-definitions of rest and motion, which will be referred to again in part III, the definitions just stated are possible, but still not clear enough on one important issue. They do not refer to periods directly, but only indirectly *via* intervals of instants (to which periods should not be reduced).[23] But it is easy enough to rewrite the definitions in terms of periods, since an open interval $I =]t_1,t_2[$ is simply the set of instants which fall within the period c such that $c:[t_1,t_2]$. So we only have to introduce two more predicates closely related to the ones above (their names only differ by an index '1'):

'$B_1(a,c)$' is to be read as: c is a period of uninterrupted motion of a.
'$R_1(a,c)$' is to be read as: c is a period of uninterrupted rest of a.

They are defined as follows:

$B_1(a,c)$ iff $\forall t_1,t_2[t_1$ falls-within $c \wedge t_2$ falls-within $c \rightarrow$ ...
...$\exists t_3[t_1 < t_3 < t_2 \rightarrow$ IS-AT$(a,t_3) \neq$ IS-AT$(a,t_1) \wedge$ IS-AT$(a,t_3) \neq$ IS-AT$(a,t_2)]$.

$R_1(a,c)$ iff $\forall t_1,t_2 [t_1$ falls-within $c \wedge t_2$ falls-within $c \rightarrow$ ...
...$\exists t_3[t_1 < t_3 < t_2 \rightarrow$ IS-AT$(a,t_3) =$ IS-AT$(a,t_1) \wedge$ IS-AT$(a,t_3) =$ IS-AT$(a,t_2)]$.

Using these predicates, instants of motion or rest may be defined in Kretzmann's manner:

$B_{a1}(t)$ iff   (i) $\exists c_1,t_1 [B_1(a,c_1) \wedge c_1:[t,t_1]]$.
          (ii) $\exists c_2,t_2 [B_1(a,c_2) \wedge c_2:[t_2,t]]$.
$R_{a1}(t)$ iff   (i) $\exists c_1,t_1 [R_1(a,c_1) \wedge c_1:[t,t_1]]$.
          (ii) $\exists c_2,t_2 [R_1(a,c_2) \wedge c_2:[t_2,t]]$.

According to these definitions, limiting instants are clearly neutral because for t to be a limiting instant between rest and motion of a it is required that the following is true:

$\exists c_1,c_2 [B_1(c_1,a) \wedge R_1(c_2,a) \wedge (t$ bounds $c_1 \equiv t$ bounds $c_2)]$.

5.4. MORE WORK TO DO

5.4.1. Summary: The advantages of the NIA

The NIA has all the qualities of a good compromise for a description of the moment of change between rest and motion. It uses the neither/nor-option where this is plausible and meets the intuition that motion and rest are incompatible states. The NIA also uses the either/or-option where this is plausible. According to it, at any instant of its existence, an object is either in motion or not in motion, either at rest or not at rest, as the LEM requires. So, although the limiting instant between rest and motion is neutral with respect to rest and motion, the LEM is untouched. The limiting instant at the beginning of a process is a last instant of non-motion as well as a first instant of non-rest. This is compatible with its being the last instant at which a is still in the initial position. The limiting instant at the end of a process is a last instant of non-rest as well as a first instant of non-motion. This is compatible with its being the first instant at which a is in the target position. The NIA is independent of the problematic concept of 'instanteaneous velocity' and of any continuity postulates (so an abrupt beginning of motion is not ruled out *a priori*).

All these advantages make the NIA, as a mixed description, superior to the exclusive application of just one option for describing the moment of change. We will therefore meet it again in my systematic suggestion in part III, when rest and motion are discussed once more.

5.4.2. Open questions

Even in the version stated above in 5.3. §2, the NIA leaves a number of questions concerning the moment of change open. We could say that as a result of its application, one corner of the picture has been largely worked out in detail, but the rest remains rather sketchy.

(1) The NIA focusses on the s-change between rest and motion. But the s-change between rest and motion is only the paradigm for all sorts of processes' beginnings and endings, and it has remained unclear how exactly the NIA can be transferred to other kinds of processes. In order to clarify this, one must be able to say what local motion has in common with all the other kinds of processes. An answer to this will be given in part III by way of the notions of determinables and determinates.

(2) There remains one detail with respect to rest and motion has not yet been carried out satisfactorily: one would like to regard the 'position' of a (macro-size) physical object as something extended in space: an object occupies a part of space. So taking the centre of mass of an object as its position can be no more than a provisional solution. In part III, extended positions will be taken into consideration.

(3) The NIA as rendered so far makes no statement on discontinuous changes (like the change between 'on' and 'off' or between two immediately succeding notes of different pitch). In part III, a treatment of discontinuous changes will result trivially from a theory of instantaneous states which is developed there.

(4) The NIA is a possible description of the moment of change. It does not commit us to a certain classification. So the question of whether s-changes between rest and motion and C-changes (for example between motion and non-motion or rest and non-rest) on the other should be regarded as events taking place at the limiting instant remains open. In the last chapter of the third part of this book, I will attempt to give reasons why they should be so regarded.

5.4.3. Phenomenological unease

The four points stated above are, in one way or another, related to the most difficult problem of the moment of change, which has until now not been touched upon, but which is philosophically the most interesting. It has nothing to do with a satisfactory description which tries to preserve certain laws of logic; rather, it makes itself felt in some phenomenological unease, which exceeds logic but which should be taken very seriously. When dealing with the NIA, the phenomenological unease occurs in two places. Someone might express it by commenting upon the NIA like this:

> A neutral instant may be conceptually possible. But one thing is that I simply cannnot imagine what a thing which is neither at rest nor in motion is supposed to look like. I have never seen a thing being neither at rest nor in motion. And the other thing is that the NIA seems to be based on a concept of rest and motion which chops up motion into a sequence of photographic stills and declares its characteristic flux to be a mere illusion.

A satisfactory picture of the instant of change must be able to remove this unease. It will become apparent that its two expressions cannot be separated: the solution which will be proposed in order to remove the unease about a neutral limiting instant will be the same as will be proposed to cure the unease with respect to the nature of motion. This solution will be a theory of instantaneous states, which, by chance provides us with a satisfactory description of the moment of change. Thus, a reasonable theory of motion and a satisfactory picture of the moment of change will result from the same theory. It is based on a single epistemological assumption which is simple enough: in contrast to periods, instants are empirically inaccessible. Hardly anyone will doubt this. However, as will be seen, it requires perseverance to unravel the consequences of this assumption.

PART III: A SYSTEMATIC SUGGESTION

INTRODUCTION

1.1. A blueprint of part III

The third part of this book is based on the idea that *instants are empirically inaccessible.* It consists of three sections:

Section 1 aims to introduce the thesis of the inaccessibility of instants by pointing out that this thesis is incompatible with the old project of *reducing* motion to being at different places at different instants (as found in Zeno, Reid, Bergson and Russell). This shows that this 'reductionist' idea is untenable. The criticism of the reductionist project makes clear that theoretical justification is needed in order to secure some empirical content for talk of instantaneous states.

The second section results in a plausible *description* of the moment of change. The content of the description I propose will be no surprise: it is a version of the NIA, and I have argued at length my reasons for favouring this approach. What is new is how this description is reached: it is attained by applying a *theory of instantaneous states,* the need for which was shown in section 1. This theory of instantaneous states is established in the first part of section 2. It is based on the thesis of the empirical inaccessibility of instants. Its main features consist of transferring the concept of *'limes'* from mathematics to epistemology, assuming qualitative *spans* as a new kind of *irreducible entity* and working with the distinction between *determinables* and *determinates.*

In the second part of section 2, the theory of instantaneous states is applied to *s-changes.* It trivially yields a plausible description of s-changes between *non-comparative* properties, i.e. for *beginnings* and *ends* of *processes* as well as for *discontinuous s-changes.* A side-effect of applying the theory of instantaneous states to discontinuous s-changes is an explanation as to why the principle *natura non facit saltus* is so attractive. Furthermore, a plausible description of the *s-change between rest and motion* (and of *process* in general) is achieved through *comparative* definitions of rest and motion, in which the theory of instantaneous states is incorporated and, thus, the empirical inaccessibility of instants is accounted for.

It will be pointed out that by accounting for the empirical inaccessibilty of instants the *phenomenological unease* is removed. Comparative definitions of rest and motion are thus reconciled with the idea of motion as a genuine flux. A side-effect of this is that *Zeno's paradox of the flying arrow* is solved at its very core.

My proposal with regard to *C-changes* involves never treating them in isolation but always as parts of the s-changes they constitute. I also propose to treat the *coming-to-be* and *perishing* of objects in analogy to property-changes.

Section 3 yields a plausible *classification* of the moment of change. Again, the result will be no surprise: I want to avoid banishing change from time and keep all *changes as datable, instantaneous events in time*. In order to be able to do so, I argue for *abandoning Plato's premiss*. In this context, the inaccessibility thesis is once more important: it is easily taken to support Plato's premiss. However, this is not the case, since the inaccessibility thesis is an epistemological claim, wheras Plato's premiss is a stronger ontological claim. Furthermore, the thesis of the empirical inaccessibility of instants serves to explain an important difference between *being present* at an event and *observing* it. Finally, the idea that we *witness* changes not by instantaneously observing them to presently be taking place, but by observing *aspects* of them in time is derived from the inaccessibility thesis.

1.2. The framework of part III
The following statements provide the framework of part III for terminology and assumptions:
1. A time T is empirically accessible iff what is the case at T can be observed.
2. Whatever can be observed takes time.
3. Only periods can contain what takes time.
4. Only periods can contain what can be observed.
5. Of all times, periods alone are empirically accessible.
6. *Instants are empirically inaccessible.*
7. (being mere boundaries, best represented by bar-lines in musical notation, instants cannot 'contain' anything).
8. Machines or measuring devices as well as conscious beings can observe what happens.
9. Machines or measuring devices as well as conscious beings can be present at what happens.
10. 'Inner' states cannot be observed at instants any more than 'outward' states. There is no priviliged access to instants from 'inside'. There is no consciousness at instants.

I will not elaborate on what consciousness is. Somehow, we know. Of course, it exists. As I will use the term, an object *observes* a happening iff it is physically connected with the happening in such a way that what happens is, in some way, represented in the object. A motion may, for example, be represented in a measuring device by bringing about a physical 'trace' on a sheet of paper; in a human being, it may be represented by shifting patterns on a retina (there may, but need not, exist mental representations).

THE SNAPSHOT MYTH

1. THE INCOMPATIBILITY OF A REDUCTIONIST CONCEPT OF REST AND MOTION WITH THE INACCESSIBILITY THESIS

The empirical inaccessibility of instants is incompatible with the idea that motion can be *reduced* to being at different places at different times and rest be *reduced* to being at the same place at different times. If instants are empirically inaccessible, and rest and motion are nothing but a sequence of instantaneous states, rest or motion could not ever be seen or measured. Processes could not be observed any more because they would be nothing but states which could each only be exposed to us or our measuring device at a single instant. But it cannot be doubted that we can observe rest and motion. So if instants are empiricallly inaccessible, which they are, there must be more to motion and rest than the reductionist allows.

2. REDUCTION VS. DEFINITION

Reduction is not the same as definition. Saying that it is impossible to *reduce* motion to being in different places or rest to being in the same place at different instants does not rule out *defining* rest and motion as being in different places or being in the same place at instants. This is what every comparative definition of motion and rest consists in. We require of a definition that the *definiendum* is true whenever the *definiens* is true and vice versa. This might very well be the case if, for example, "*a* is in motion" is the *definiendum* and "*a* is (in a certain way) at different places at different times" is the *definiens*; and motion might still be more than that.[1]

The difference can be seen very clearly in Aristotle's Physics VI, where comparative definitions of rest and motion peacefully and consistently coexist with criticism of the reductionist approach: Aristotle stresses that a process takes time, and therefore takes place in a period;[2] one of his objections against Zeno is that a period does not consist of instants.[3] This rules out the possibility that Aristotle favoured a *reduction* of motion to being at different places at different times. His opinion is clearly very much opposed to the reductionist project: he views positions at times as nothing but 'results of motion'; and he explicitly objects to time-atomism that a motion cannot consist merely of results of motion.[4] But all this does not and need not keep Aristotle from stating comparative *definitions* of rest and motion in the same text.[5]

The reductionist project might seem attractive because, when recalling a motion, it is quite natural to describe it by saying "*a* was first in this place and then in that place etc." (of course, it is impossible to state *all* the positions, since there is an infinite number of them involved). However, every comparative definition of motion accounts for this, and it is thus insufficient for pursuing the reductionist project.

3. THE SNAPSHOT MYTH FROM ZENO TO RUSSELL

The first and perhaps most impressive formulation of the reductionist project is Zeno's paradox of the flying arrow:[6]

> An arrow occupies a particular part of space which is exactly its own size at each instant of its flight. It cannot move forward in any one such part of space, because this part exactly fits its size and there is no room to move forward in it. So when can it move forward? It seems as if it cannot do this at all: it is merely first in one place and then another and then yet another; motion as a flux is therefore just an illusion which we are under when observing the sequence of the 'snapshots' of instantaneous states.

One might call this the snapshot myth. Told in this way, it clearly supports the opinion of Zeno's teacher Parmenides that all process is just illusion. What is worse is that, so portrayed, the story of the flying arrow is immune against Aristotle's 'official' refutation in Phys.VI,9: this refutation extends only to the claim that the arrow is at rest at every instant of its flight, since it is not in motion at any of them. In order to refute this claim one has only to argue that rest and motion are comparative properties, and this is exactly what Aristotle does. However, the disquieting effect of Zeno's flying arrow does not depend on this claim: this assertion does not appear at all if the paradox is rendered as above.[7]

It seems to me that the most influential version of the snapshot myth was the one which is implicitly contained in St. Augustine's subjectivist analysis of time in Confessiones XI, where the present is clearly regarded both as extensionless[8] and as a time at which perception is possible.[9] In the 18th century, the snapshot myth is clearly retold by Thomas Reid.[10] In the 20th century, Bergson[11] as well as Russell favour it. Russell's attempt at defining rest and motion (which was discussed at length in ch.II,5) has, like the Cambridge criterion for change, gained a certain notoriety. This can hardly be due to the fact that, according to the definition of §442 of the 'Principles', Russell considers rest and motion to be comparative properties and assumes time to be dense or even continuous.[12] Aristotle had done just the same and had as a reason for there being no motion or rest at instants explicitly stated that there is only 'being-there' at instants (εἶναι κατά τι), so that positions of an object at at least two times must be *compared* in order to tell if it is in motion (Cf.ch.I,2.2.). What was provocative in the 'Principles of Mathematics' (and what far exceeded Aristotle) was Russell's harshly worded view that talk of rest and motion could be *completely reduced* to talk of places at times:

[...W]e must entirely reject the notion of a state of motion. ... Motion consists *merely* in the occupation of different places at different times, subject to continuity...[13]

Russell has attracted a lot of criticism for this reductionist view. Perhaps the clearest expression of it was formulated by Graham Priest:

On this account ... motion is rather like a sequence of photographic stills ... shown so fast that the body appears to move. But this conception of motion jars against our intuitive notion of motion as a genuine flux. A journey is not a sequence of states ... even a lot of them close together. If God were to take temporal slices of an object at rest in different places, and string them together in a continuous fashion, he would not have made the object move. ... [A]t each instant of the motion the arrow does make no advance on its journey. ... [However,] in the sum of all instants it does. The whole is greater than the sum of its parts. ... [But] can going somewhere be composed of an aggregate of going nowheres?[14]

Priest admits that this is a diagnosis of unease rather than a knock-out argument. However, one can at least demonstrate that the snapshot myth is incompatible with the thesis of the empirical inaccessibility of instants. So if we assume this thesis, we may regard the snapshot myth as untenable.

4. ZERO SECONDS EXPOSURE TIME?

I think that the best way to show why the snapshot myth is not compatible with empirical inaccessibility of instants is indeed illustrating it with the way in which a camera functions. This example makes clear that it is impossible to observe a state of an object at one and only one instant.[15]

Let us stipulate that it is technically possible to expose the film to light for an arbitrarily short time and still get a good picture.[16] We may now ask ourselves: what would a camera have to look like to produce perfectly sharp stills of an object in motion, on each of which the object is represented as being in exactly one position only? If we consider this question we will notice that any definite exposure time greater than zero is a certain period of time. During this period, the object is moving forward; therefore we will never obtain a sharp photograph by choosing a definite exposure time greater than zero. We might think that the problem lies in having a *definite* exposure time, and that we should allow the film to be exposed to light for only an infinitely short time instead. But even if we had the most fantastic technical abilities, we would have no idea how to manipulate the camera in order to do this. So only the possibility of exposing the film to light for zero seconds remains. Technically, this is easy enough to achieve: we simply leave the light stop shut. But, alas, in this way we do not get any picture.

The attempt to expose a film to light for zero seconds is an attempt to measure something at a single, isolated instant. It fails, and no adherent of the snapshot myth will reasonably be able to deny this. He may, however, try to defend his view like this:

> Your thought experiment does not prove that instants are empirically inaccessible in general, but only that they are empirically inaccessible in isolation. Instants are empirically accessible as long as they come in great numbers and are densely ordered.[17]

However, this actually illustrates just how indefensible the adherent of the snapshot myth's position really is. It makes apparent that he cannot even explain how one can take a picture by exposing it for a time *longer than* zero seconds: according to his account of motion, manipulation of the camera is not responsible for the object's being exposed to the film in a single position for not more than an instant. Rather, this lies in the nature of things, even if we do not try to isolate an instant in any way by actively trying to reduce exposure time to zero. Still, the camera does not register an infinite set of instantaneously realized positions, for the registering of a position cannot be conceived in any other way than as its being registered as a single position. But any single position is, according to the snapshot myth, exposed to the film for no time at all. Since this applies to any position, there is no reason for anything to be visible on the photograph at all if we try to take a picture of an object in motion.

Upon a little further reflection one notices that the difficulties with the snapshot myth are not restricted to periods of *motion* but also to periods of *rest*. It is true that we can take a perfectly sharp picture of an object at rest. It is true that in this case, according to the snapshot myth too, a position is exposed to the camera for more than only one instant. However, according to the snapshot myth, if an object is in the same position at several instants, each position has to be registered per instant. This is impossible if instants are empirically inaccessible. Since every object during its existence is always at rest or in motion, we should then wonder how we can ever take any pictures.

It is an important observation that the empirical inaccessibility of instants is not restricted to times of *motion*. While one easily doubts that an object which is in a certain position at one single instant may be observed in this position, at first sight the idea of being able to observe an object at instants if it is in the same position at these instants seems less problematic. This is the reason why one is tempted to *imagine* an object at an instant to look like an object at rest. However, if we take the inaccessibility thesis seriously, there is nothing to imagine at instants.

A defendant of the snapshot myth might still object that an epistemological argument cannot be applied as an objection to an ontological thesis. I would reply that while agreeing that I have given an epistemological argument, in this case it is legitimate to exploit it ontologically. Someone who claims that something is the case should be able to explain how it is possible to know. So an epistemological objection to an ontological claim is justified if, as here, it has the form:

> If the criticized claim were true, we should not be able to know what is claimed to be known to be the case.[18]

5. EVALUATION

The snapshot myth amounts to the claim that putting together an infinite number of stills each produced with zero seconds exposure time creates the illusion of motion as a flux. This should only be accepted by people who think that combining two absurdities yields a deep philosophical insight. Both the idea of actually putting together an infinite number of single items and the idea of a 'picture' taken with a zero seconds exposure time are absurd. The attempt to reduce the history of the world to a sequence of instantaneous states leads, if combined with the thesis of the empirical inaccessibility of instants, to the thesis of the empirical inaccessibility of reality. This may not render the attempt inconsistent. But if one can show that a theory entails the empirical inaccessibility of the world it has been reduced *ad absurdum* so clearly that consistency does not matter.

A PATH TO A PLAUSIBLE DESCRIPTION
OF THE MOMENT OF CHANGE

1. THE NEED FOR A THEORY OF INSTANTANEOUS STATES

Instants are empirically inaccessible. They are like bar-lines in musical notation.[1] At an instant, we cannot hear, see or measure anything. Whatever we hear, see, or measure etc., i.e. whatever we observe, we observe in periods. Nevertheless we talk about positions, pitches or temperatures *at instants*. We want and we need to be able to say that a continuously moving clockhand points towards the 12 o'clock mark at noon and at midnight. However, we have to justify this. We have to secure some empirical content for statements about instantaneous states by relating them to possible observations. This is a theoretical task. Instantaneous states are not observed but construed. Already, the following theory of instantaneous states has proved to be too simple:

> The state that α obtains at instant t iff t both bounds an α-phase towards the past and an α-phase towards the future.

This is too simple because the instant '12:00' bounds, towards both sides, periods throughout which the clockhand does not point towards the 12 o'clock mark.[2] This rules out any equivalence. It may, however, be true and it is plausible that if t both bounds an α-phase towards the past and an α-phase towards the future, then the state that α cannot fail to obtain at t. So in a good theory of instantaneous states, the following implication holds:

> If t both bounds an α-phase towards the past and an α-phase towards the future, then the state that α obtains at instant t.

What else do we intuitively require of a theory of instantaneous states?

1) We certainly require that the clockhand points towards the 12 o'clock mark at noon and at midnight if the clock is working correctly.

2) After what has been said about C-changes at the beginning and end of processes, we would be content to obtain the following results:
a) At the limiting instant at the *beginning of a process* of a, a is still in the initial position. We can apply this to our example if we imagine that the clock has stopped from 3:00 to 5:00 and then moves on: in this case the clockhand should still point towards the 3 o'clock mark at 5:00.

b) At the limiting instant at the *end of a process* of *a*, *a* is still in the initial position. We can apply this to our example if we imagine that the clock *has stopped* in the 4 o'clock position from 4:00 to 6:00 but was working adequately before: in that case the clockhand should have been in the 4 o'clock position at 4:00.

3) We would accept not obtaining an instantaneous position for the limiting instant at all in the case of a *discontinuous change*. If we try to imagine that the clockhand, having stopped at the 2 o'clock position for 5 hours from 2:00 on, suddenly jerks into the 8 o'clock position, we have no intuition whatsoever where it is at 7:00. So if the result of our theory of instantaneous states is that it is not in a position then, this does not conflict with our intuition. It is, however, a strong argument in favour of the idea that such things do not happen.

2. SPANS AND INSTANTANEOUS STATES

2.1. *Spans in general and during periods*

In order to formulate a theory of instaneous states which secures some empirical content for statements about instantaneous states and fulfils the requirements stated, it is necessary to introduce a new technical term: *span*. An initial characterization of it may be:

> A span is, for example, what we can observe as a quality during a period. Since we have meanwhile completely abandoned the idea that what we observe during a period is an accumulation of instantaneous states, it is clear that a span is an entity which is irreducible to such an accumulation. It is, rather, vice versa: we abstract instantaneous states from spans we observe during periods.

Admittedly, this characterization does not give us a satisfactory idea yet of what spans are. However there is no way of introducing them by referring to concepts already introduced. It is rather appropriate at this point to introduce the new term by means of examples to supply some sort of context definition. Let us return to the clock. A typical answer to the question, "What do we see when we observe the clockhand in motion between 11:55 and 12:05?" will be:

> Somehow, we see the clockhand in an infinite number of places where it could be between the 5-to-12 position and the 5-past-12-position. We see a continuum of positions. At every instant we see a different position. And in our consciousness these positions are blended into a process.

Of course there is an infinite number of different angles (relative to some straight line from the centre of the dial to its edge) between the '5-to-12 angle' and the '5-past-12 angle'. But otherwise this answer is again the snapshot myth in disguise and is therefore untenable. Here is a suggestion of what to say instead:

(1) The (two-dimensional) *position-span*: what we see during the ten minutes from 11:55 to 12:05 is the position-span of the clockhand between the 5-to-12 position and the 5-past-12 position. It is here passed through in the usual direction (i.e. clockwise).[3] This span is not a set of positions. It is one individual object, although not in the way a set is an individual object, but as an irreducible whole.[4]

(2) A position-span may be *contained* within another position-span. For example, the position span of the clockhand between 11:00 and 1:00 is contained in the position-span of the clockhand between 10:00 and 2:00.

(3) There may be *discontinuous position-spans*. If, for example, the clockhand performed a jerk in no time the 2-D-span of it during a period within which the jerk falls would be discontinuous.

The essential points of this answer are not restricted to (two-dimensional) positions of clockhands. We can extrapolate from this example and talk in the same way when pitches or temperatures are concerned (one-dimensional cases) or when the position of an object in space is concerned (three-dimensional case). We may thus make the following specifications for spans in general:

(1) $s, s_1, s_2...$ represent spans.

(2) Spans lie within one or several 'boundaries'. The boundaries of the position-span in the clockhand-example were the two lines from the centre to the edge of the dial at the 5-to-12 angle and the 5-past-12 angle as well the edge of this section itself. There are one-dimensional spans with just one boundary, for example specific temperature values, pitches or straight lines. The boundary of a three-dimensional span is a surface. Two spans s_1 and s_2 are identical iff they share all their boundaries.

(3) Two spans may stand in a (primitive) containmemt relation. If s_1 is contained in s_2 let us notate this as $s_1 C s_2$.

(4) Spans may be discontinuous.

In order to facilitate formulating the next section let us add the following definition:

Let S be a set of spans and s be a span. Then s is the overlap of S (sØS) iff
(i) s is contained in all members of S.
(ii) There is no s' which is contained in all members of S such that sCs'.

The 'overlap' of S is thus the maximum 'area' which all members of S have in common.

2.2. Instantaneous spans

So far, all examples have been spans in periods. However, nothing which has been said so far rules out the existence of instantaneous spans. Of course, we do not observe them. But we may find a rule for construing them. The intuitive requirements we make for such a rule have been stated above.

I will now propose such a rule. It cannot be deduced; it can simply be corroborated by plausible results. I hope it seems convincing. In order to arrive at it, let us return to two simple cases which have nothing to do with the moment of change: (A) the simple process of the correctly working clock between 10:00 and 2:00 and (B) the case of its being faulty and having stopped for this time with the clockhand pointing towards the 11 o'clock mark.

(A): The result should be that the instantaneous position-span is the straight line between the centre of the dial and the 12 o'clock mark. We do not see this. But this is where we are convinced that we *would* see the clockhand for a while if it stopped at 12:00, providing it was working correctly previously. Interestingly, this result is achieved by applying a procedure which is very similar to determining a 'limes' in differential calculus:

Let us look at the 'lefthand side' first: consider the position-spans of the clockhand in periods which are bounded by $t = 12:00$ towards the future, for example the period from 10:00 to 12:00, from 11:00 to 12:00, from 11:55 to 12:00 from 11:59 to 12:00 etc. They are all surfaces which are passed through by the clockhand in the respective time. Spans of shorter periods of this kind are contained in spans of longer periods. The surfaces are smaller the shorter the periods are, approaching the straight line between the centre of the dial and the 12 o'clock mark without ever reaching it. Now there is one span which is contained in all these surfaces. It is the overlap of the set of all position-spans of the clockhand in periods which are bounded by $t = 12:00$ towards the future. And this is the straight line between the centre of the dial and the 12 o'clock mark. Now let us turn to the 'righthand side': consider the position-spans of the clockhand in periods which are bounded by $t = 12:00$ towards the past, for example the period from 12:00 to 12:01, from 12:00 to 12:05, from 12:00 to 1:00 from etc. You will notice exactly the same.

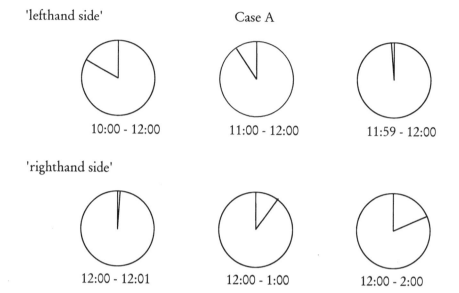

'lefthand side'   Case A

10:00 - 12:00   11:00 - 12:00   11:59 - 12:00

'righthand side'

12:00 - 12:01   12:00 - 1:00   12:00 - 2:00

The identification of the instantaneous position-span of the clockhand at 12:00 with exactly that span which is the straight line between the centre of the dial and the 12 o'clock mark suggests itself in this case.

How did we arrive at this? We took the overlap of all position-spans of the clockhand in all periods which are bounded by $t = 12:00$ towards the future. And we took the overlap of all position-spans of the clockhand in all periods which are bounded by $t = 12:00$ towards the past. We saw that they were identical. We have the first case in which it is plausible that the span which is identical with both these overlaps is the instantaneous position-span of the clockhand at 12:00.

The procedure applied agrees with the intuition that the more briefly we look, the more 'exactly' we see the clockhand. The shorter we make the time during which we take a picturte, the sharper the photo is.[5] The only thing we cannot do is look at it or take a picture of it *at* 12:00.

(B): We apply the procedure we tried in case (A) to case (B), the case of the clock being out of order and the clockhand not moving at all between (at least) 11:00 and 1:00 while pointing towards the 11 o'clock mark.

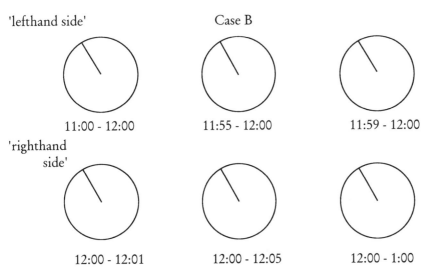

The result is clearly that the instantaneous position-span of the clockhand at 11 o'clock is the straight line between the centre of the dial and the 11 o'clock mark. Again, the result is highly plausible. We might try to generalize our procedure. In order to do this we should be a little more precise concerning what we are talking about.

2.3. Determinable and determinate qualities

The similarity of two-dimensional position-spans (as in the case of the clockhand), temperature-spans, pitch-spans or three-dimensional position-spans is obvious. Clearly, there are more cases similar to these. The similarity stems from the fact that they all have something to do with a distinction made in medieval logic which was rediscovered in 1921 by W.E. Johnson:[6] the distinction between determinates and determinables.[7]

We know brightness, smoothness, speed or tension in several *degrees*. We group 'red', 'green' and 'blue' etc. as colours, 'c', 'd', 'e' etc. as pitches in a scale, '1 cm', '2 cm' etc. as distances, '1 m³', '2 m³' as sizes, '5°', '10°' etc. as temperatures. In all these cases an object's having one property excludes its having the other properties from the same group at the same time in the same respect (for example 'partly', 'all over'):[8] an object which is red all over from 12:00 to 12:05 cannot be blue, green or yellow then. However, its being red does not in any way restrict its weight or shape.

Being red, green or yellow are *determinates,* as are being 5ft6 or 6ft tall. But both groups of examples belong to different *determinables*: the first to colour, the second to height. Being red, being green, being yellow etc. make up a characteristic set, the set of all colours They make up the determinable quality of being some colour. They mutually exclude one another as described. Other determinables are 'being of a certain height', 'being of a certain size' etc. For some determinables it is *indispensable* that they have a determinate 'value' at every time of an object's existence. For example, every physical object must be somewhere in space the whole time it exists. However, a musical instrument does not have to produce a sound of a certain pitch all the time; nevertheless 'producing a sound of a certain pitch' is a determinable quality.

2.4. Determinable functions; the Inst-prefix
It is clearly useful to work with the distinction of determinables and determinates when trying to state the method of empirical limes from 2.2. more generally. It would be rather complicated to introduce a separate predicate for every determinate quality (although it would, of course, be possible). It is more practical to work with determinable functions instead. A determinable p(eriod)-function is to be a two-place function which takes a physical object and a period and yields a span; this span is, then, the determinate 'value' of the determinable quality referred to by the function with respect to an object and a period. In the clockhand-example, we would, for example work with a determinable function called '2DPOS', such that the expression "2DPOS(a,c)=s" is to be read as "s is the (two-dimensional) position-span of the clockhand a which may be observed during c". Or we might have a determinable function TEMP, such that "TEMP(a,c)=s" is to be read as "s is the temperature-span of a which may be observed during c".

The introduction of the method of empirical limes above acquainted us with instantaneous spans. It now seems sensible also to introduce such determinable functions as take physical objects plus instants and yield instantaneous spans: determinable i(nstant)-functions. They will not, however, have simple names of their own. Instead their names will always be a combination of a new prefix 'Inst' and the corresponding p-function. For example, the function which takes physical objects plus instants in order to yield instantaneous 2DPOS-spans is called 'Inst-2DPOS'. As might be expected, the semantics of Inst presupposes the method of empirical limes in a formal version.[9] In order to avoid a very complicated naming rule, let us introduce the following abbreviations:

(i) $S_V^{(D,a,t0)} = \{ s \mid \forall c, t [D(a,c) \wedge c[t,t_0] \}$
(ii) $S_N^{(D,a,t0)} = \{ s \mid \forall c, t [D(a,c) \wedge c[t_0,t] \}$.

I.e., $S_V^{(D,a,t0)}$ is the set of all D-spans of a from all periods which are bounded by t_0 towards the future. And $S_N^{(D,a,t0)}$ is the set of all D-spans of a from all periods which are bounded by t_0 towards the past. We can now introduce Inst with the following naming rule:

NR8) (1) Combination rule: the prefix Inst may be combined with the name of a determinable p-function D in order to yield the name of a determinable i-function.

(2) Semantical rule: Inst-$D(a,t_0) = s_0$ iff (i) $s_0 \varnothing S_V^{(D,a,t0)}$ and (ii) $s_0 \varnothing S_N^{(D,a,t0)}$

So s_0 is the instantaneous D-span of a at t_0 iff s_0 is the overlap of both the set of all D-spans of a from all periods which are bounded by t_0 towards the future and the set of all D-spans of a from all periods which are bounded by t_0 towards the past.

The Inst-prefix thus incorporates the theory of instantaneous states suggested above. Of course, in order for s_0 to be both the overlap of $S_V^{(D,a,t0)}$ and $S_N^{(D,a,t0)}$, $S_V^{(D,a,t0)}$ and $S_N^{(D,a,t0)}$ must be identical.

3. AN APPLICATION OF THE INST-PREFIX TO A DESCRIPTION OF THE MOMENT OF CHANGE

3.1. s-changes
3.1.1. s-changes at the beginnings and ends of processes

§1 One of our intuitive requirements for a good theory of intantaneous states was that it should entail a plausible description of the moment of change for the beginning of a process: if our clock has stopped from 3:00 to 5:00 and then moves on, the clockhand should still be pointing towards the 3 o'clock mark at the limiting instant t = 5:00. It does:

Let us say that s is the straight line from the centre of the dial to the 3 o'clock mark. We will expect s to be the instantaneous position-span of the clockhand a at t. Now the 'lefthand part' of the task of showing this is analogous to the 'lefthand side' of case (B) above: $S_V^{(a,2DPOS,t)}$ turns out to be s. The 'righthand part' of the task is exactly analogous to the righthand part of case (A) above. As a result $S_N^{(a,2DPOS,t)}$ turns out to be s. So $S_V^{(a,2DPOS,t)}$ and $S_N^{(a,2DPOS,t)}$ are identical with s. So the instantaneous position-span of the clockhand at 5:00 is the straight line from the centre of the dial to the 3 o'clock mark, just as we required:

'lefthand side'

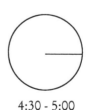

3:00 - 5:00   4:00 - 5:00   4:30 - 5:00

'righthand side'

5:00 - 5:05   5:00 - 6:00   5:00 - 7:00

§2 Another one of our intuitive requirements for a satisfactory theory of
instantaneous states was that it should entail a plausible description of the
moment of change for the end of a process: If our clock has stopped in the 4
o'clock position from 4:00 to 6:00 but was working adequately before, the
clockhand should have been in the 4 o'clock position at the limiting instant
t=4:00. It is: this case is a mirror-image of the one described in §1. The
lefthand part is analogous to the lefthand part of case (A) above, and the
righthand part is analogous to the righthand part of case (B) above. So the
instantaneous position-span of the clockhand when the clock stopped at 4:00
is the straight line from the centre of the dial to the 4 o'clock mark, just as
we required.

'lefthand
side'

'righthand side'

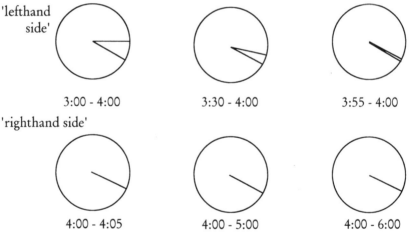

3:00 - 4:00   3:30 - 4:00   3:55 - 4:00

4:00 - 4:05   4:00 - 5:00   4:00 - 6:00

§3 Our theory of instantaneous states thus trivially yields the Aristotelian
result for non-comparative properties that, at the limiting instant at the
beginning of a process, an object is still in the initial state, and that at the
limiting instant at the end of a process, it is in the target state. Since in this
case there is no first instant of having left the initial state or of not yet

having reached the target state[10], we are compelled to use the *either/or-option* for a description of these situations.

3.1.2. Discontinuous s-changes

3.1.2.1. The result: no instantaneous span

The 'weird' clock: let us try to imagine the case that the clockhand, having stopped at the 2 o'clock position from 2:00 for 5 hours suddenly jerks into the 8 o'clock position and remains there. What instantaneous position-span of the clockhand a do we obtain for $t=7:00$? Let us call the straight line from the centre of the dial to the 2 o'clock position s^2. Let us call the straight line from the centre of the dial to the 8 o'clock position s^8. In this case $S_V^{(a,2DPOS,t)}$ is s^2 and $S_N^{(a,2DPOS,t)}$ is s^8. s^2 and s^8 are anything but identical. So in this case no span fulfils the requirement for being the value of Inst-2D-POS for the argument-pair $<$the clockhand, 7:00$>$. Therefore no span can be said to be the instantaneous position-span of the clockhand at 7:00.

'lefthand side'

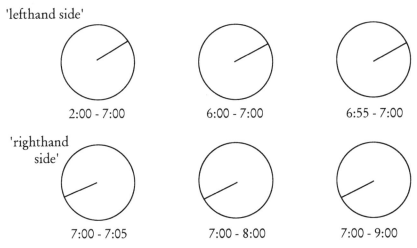

2:00 - 7:00   6:00 - 7:00   6:55 - 7:00

'righthand side'

7:00 - 7:05   7:00 - 8:00   7:00 - 9:00

3.1.2.2. Natura non facit saltus

The theory of instantaneous states is based on what we can imagine and especially on what we cannot: it is based on the thesis of empirical inaccessibility of instants. This thesis was the reason for its being developed in the first place. This theory yields the result that an object cannot be assigned an instantaneous position at the instant of a discontinuous jerk. We intuitively hold that an object must be somewhere at any instant of its existence. We can retain both this intuition and the theory of instantaneous states only if we deny that such jerks take place. If both the intuition and the theory are plausible we should. And I think they are plausible. Thus we have a strong argument in favour of the thesis that nature does not jump. It is based on the idea that we abstract instantaneous states from what we see (I really think that the theory of instantaneous states is applied quite naturally without our ever being aware of it). Jerks conflict with our way of arriving at instantaneous states. For this reason we exclude them.[11]

We should, however, not go so far as to exclude discontinuous changes altogether. The exclusion in the case of positions does not only depend on the theory of instantaneous states, but also on instantaneous positions being indispensable. There are other determinable states which are dispensable even throughout periods, so *a fortiori* at instants: pitch, e.g., is a determinable quality of musical instruments. Nevertheless, as we have said, a musical instrument need not sound a pitch all the time. It does not when it is not being played. That being the case, it is unproblematic if there are some instants to which we cannot assign any pitch. In fact we cannot do this for any change between discrete pitches with no time in between (notated as different notes following one another immediately, without any rest inserted, in a melody).[12] So there are discontinuous changes which we can accept as taking place and which we should be content to describe by assigning no state to the limiting instant. In that case, of course, we have an application of the *neither/nor-option*.

If we restrict ourselves to such cases in which the principle "natura non facit saltus" can be plausibly assumed, we can simplify the semantics of the Inst-prefix in such a manner that it renders the intuitive idea even more clearly: "The shorter the exposure time, the clearer the picture". For, in this case, we might simply define:

$$S^{(D,a,t0)} = \{ s \mid \forall c\, [D(a,c) \land t_0 \text{ falls-within c}]\}.$$
$$\text{Inst-}D(a,t_0) = s_0 \text{ iff } s_0\ \varnothing\ S^{(D,a,t0)}.$$

I.e., if we assume that nature does not jump we can simply define the instantaneous D-span of a at t_0 as the overlap of all D-spans of a from all periods within which t_0 falls.

3.1.3. The s-change between rest and motion
3.1.3.1. The determinable function 3DPOS
Let us first elucidate some presuppositions concerning the position of an object in space which were already implicitly contained in our two-dimensional example of the clockhand, and transfer them to three-dimensional space by introducing a new determinable function 3DPOS:

When discussing Russell's definitions of rest and motion I had provisionally followed Sorabji's suggestion[13] to regard a space-point (the centre of mass of an object) as the position of an object in space. But this is unsatisfactory.[14] First of all, there is the intuition that a physical object is extended and a wish to account for this fact. Secondly, there are the following objections:

(1) The centre of mass of a may shift without a moving. An example would be a sand-clock whose centre of mass is shifting all the time as sand trickles from the upper half down to the lower half of it while the clock stays on the table where it was.[15]

(2) The centre of mass of an object may stay the same, and, nevertheless, the object be moving. An example would be a rotating sphere.[16]

Rotating spheres have always been recognized as being very tricky examples; I will only be able to discuss them in appendix D. Be that as it may both objections add to the motivation for describing the position of an object as something extended in space:

The position of an object is a part of space. Just as periods are not sets of instants, parts of space are not sets of space-points. They are irreducible and continuous. The position of an object at a time is the part of space it occupies at that time. Just as a period can be described by a one-dimensional interval, a part of space can be described as a three-dimensional interval: the set of all space-points which fall within (or bound) this part of space.[17] This suggests regarding parts of space which are occupied by an object as three-dimensional spans. We can therefore without any difficulties introduce a new determinable function 3DPOS which takes a physical object and a period and yields a position-span during a period. Of course, it is possible to combine Inst and 3DPOS. The two-place determinable i-function Inst-3DPOS takes a physical object and an instant and yields an instantaneous position-span. Thus,

"3DPOS$(a,c) = s$" is to be read as
"s is the (three-dimensional) position-span of a in c".

And "Inst-3DPOS$(a,t) = s$" is to be read as
"s is the (three-dimensional) position-span of a at t".

3.1.3.2. Comparative definition for process (motion) and remaining the same (rest)

Due to the theory of instantaneous states, there is now a justification for assigning a position in space to an object at an instant, although instants are empirically inaccessible. We have construed this instantaneous state as a kind of limes of empirical states. We have, thus, obtained a concept of instantaneous position which does not force us to accept the snapshot myth. The concept of span is not only compatible, but actually derived from the idea of processes as irreducible wholes in periods. So if we can tie comparative definitions of rest and motion to the theory of instantaneous states we may use them without being further troubled by any phenomenological unease about chopping up motion: these definitions are far from expressing any reductionist aim.

After what has been said so far, it is easy enough to link comparative definitions of rest and motion to the theory of instantaneous states: the definitions only have to contain the Inst-prefix as an integral part. Apart from that, they may look very similar to what we already know from ch.II,5.[18]

We should, however, not restrict our definitions to POS: it is quite natural to think that there is something common to all continuous processes and to all remaining in a state, and that local rest and local motion are just special cases of this (we saw in ch.I,1 and ch.I,2 that for the Greek words κίνησις and ἠρεμία there is not even any clear borderline as to whether they apply to the general or to the particular case). The concept of a determinable function allows us to give general comparative definitions of process and remaining with respect to a determinable quality. Definitions for rest and motion trivially result by substituting 3DPOS for 'D': local motion is being in process with respect to the determinable quality of position in space; and rest is remaining the same with respect to the determinable quality of position in space.

The general comparative definitions for process and remaining will be formulated by means of four more prefixes: κ, η, κ° and η°. The κ stands for κίνησις, the η for ἠρεμία. κ and η may be combined with the name of a determinable p-function in order to yield the name of a two-place predicate which takes a physical object plus a *period*. κ° and η° may be combined with the name of a determinable p-function in order to yield the name of a two-place predicate which takes a physical object plus an *instant*. This makes the four prefixes different from the prefixes introduced in part I and II which always took a predicate and not a function. It also makes them different from Inst, which yields a function and not a predicate.

"κ-D(a,c)" is to be read as "Object a is in process with respect to the determinable function D throughout period c" or as "c is a period of uninterrupted process of a with respect to D".

"η-D(a,c)" is to be read as "Object a remains the same with respect to the determinable function D throughout period c" or as "c is a period of uninterrupted remaining the same of a with respect to D".

"κ-D(a,c)" is to be read as "Object a is in the course of being in process with respect to the determinable function D at instant t" or as "t is an instant of process of a with respect to D".

"$\eta°$-D(a,c)" is to be read as "Object a is in the course of remaining the same with respect to the determinable function D at instant t" or as "t is an instant of remaining the same of a with respect to D".

κ and η acquire a 'meaning' through the following naming rule:

NR9): (1) Combination rule: The prefixes κ and η may be combined with the name of a determinable function D in order to yield the name of a two-place predicate.

(2) Semantical rule:

(a) κ-D(a,c) iff ...

$\forall t_1, t_2 [t_1$ falls-within $c \wedge t_2$ falls-within $c \wedge t_1 < t_2 \rightarrow ...$

...$\exists t_3 [t_1 < t_3 < t_2 \wedge$ Inst-D(a,t_1) $\neq$Inst-D(a,t_3) $\neq$Inst-D(a,t_2)].[19]

(b) η-D(a,c) iff ...

$\forall t_1, t_2 [t_1$ falls-within $c \wedge t_2$ falls-within $c \wedge t_1 < t_2 \rightarrow ...$

...$\exists t_3 [t_1 < t_3 < t_2 \wedge$ Inst-D(a,t_1) $=$ Inst-D(a,t_3) $=$ Inst-D(a,t_2)].[20]

Thus, applied to the example of rest and motion we get: c is a period of uninterrupted motion of a iff for any two instants which fall within c there is another instant between them such that a's instantaneous position at this third instant is different from a's instantaneous position both at the first and at the second instant. Analogously c is a period of uninterrupted rest of a iff for any two instants which fall within c there is another instant between them such that a's instantaneous position at this third instant is the same as a's instantaneous position at both the first and at the second instant.

In order to fix a naming rule for $\kappa°$ and $\eta°$, it is necessary to decide how to describe the limiting instant between process (resp. motion) and remaining the same (resp. rest). Using the neither/nor-option and, thus, making our description of the moment of change an NIA is achieved with the following naming rule which, again, recalls ch.II,5:

NR10) (1) Combination rule: the prefixes $\kappa°$ and $\eta°$ may be combined with the name of a determinable function D in order to yield the name of a two-place predicate.

(2) Semantical rule:

(c) $\kappa°$-D(a,t) iff (i) $\exists$ c_1,t_1 [κ-D(a,c_1) $\wedge$ c_1:[t,t_1]]

(ii) $\exists c_2$,t_2 [κ-D(a,c_2) $\wedge$ c_2:[t_2,t]].

(d) $\eta°$-D(a,t) iff (i) $\exists c_1$,t_1 [η-D(a,c_1) $\wedge$ c_1:[t,t_1]].

(ii) $\exists c_2$,t_2 [η-D(a,c_2) $\wedge$ c_2:[t_2,t]].

So, applied to the case of motion and rest, a is in motion at instant t iff t bounds a prior and a subsequent period of motion of a; and a is at rest at t iff t bounds a prior and a subsequent period of rest of a. If t is the limiting instant between rest and motion, neither definition is fulfilled. So the limiting instant is neutral according to NR10). However it would be very easy to modify it in line with Sorabji's either/or-suggestion without doing any harm to the theory of instantaneous states.[21]

3.4. The phenomenological unease removed

There have been two reasons for phenomenological unease: one was the general worry that any comparative definition of rest and motion might result in chopping up motion; the other one was a particular worry with regard to the NIA, namely that it introduces a state of neither rest nor motion which noone can imagine and which noone has ever observed, despite the numerous opportunities to watch startings and stoppings every day during rushhour.

3.4.1. A solution to the paradox of the flying arrow

The first worry was removed by incorporating a theory of instantaneous states into comparative definitions of rest and motion which takes motion to be a genuine flux. A side-effect of this is a solution to the very core of Zeno's flying arrow paradox. Zeno (and Reid and Bergson and perhaps even Russell) had argued:

> All that is actually given are instantaneous positions of the flying arrow. It is impossible to compose a process as a genuine flux from them. Therefore the process as a genuine flux is an illusion created by the observer.

However, if instants are empirically inaccessible and the principle of empirical limes is correct, then this is incorrect from the very first sentence: instantaneous positions are not given. We abstract them from the process. What is given *is* the process as a genuine flux: at any time in the process during which we can possibly observe the arrow in motion it occupies a part of space which is larger than the arrow itself, for the only times at which we can observe it are periods.

Zeno made the epistemological mistake of believing that the instantaneous positions of the arrow are given and are prior to the process, and that the process is secondary. Zeno failed to see the abstractive work which has to be done in order to assign instantaneous positions to an object. This assignment goes beyond what we empirically observe, beyond the 'given': it is everyday metaphysics. So the answer to Zeno is:

> All that is actually given is a flying arrow in motion as a genuine flux. From this we abstract its instantaneous positions. It is true that we cannot reconstruct a flux from those. But not only is the flux no illusion; it is even prior to the instantaneous positions: it is the raw material for arriving at them.

3.4.2. The neutral instant

The second worry, concerning the appearance of the neutral instant, is removed even more easily by directly repeating the thesis of the empirical inaccessibility of instants: it is true that we have no idea what anything which is neither at rest nor in motion might look like. But objects have no appearance at instants in any case. We cannot observe anything at the limiting instant because we cannot observe anything at any instant. It should therefore pose no problem if, at instants alone, a state is postulated to obtain which we have never observed and which we therefore cannot imagine. There would only be reason for concern if NR10) entailed neutral *periods*. However, the definitions of NR10) do not entail any neutral period, i.e. a period of a's existence throughout which a is neither at rest nor in motion (this would be very odd indeed). NR10) only entails neutral instants.

Any phenomenological unease in connection with the moment of change, which now remains, cannot be the result of the definition of motion or the concept of a neutral instant. Possibly it stems from our always noticing change a little late, or of never really facing it or of there always being some conjecture involved when we apply the word 'now' to changes. This sort of unease will be considered seriously in the last section of part III and will, hopefully, be cured there. Some problems with defining motion and rest which touch the moment of change at the periphery only are discussed in appendix D at the end of the book.

3.5. C-changes

So far, we have concentrated on s-changes and ignored C-changes yet. The reason for this is that C-changes should be treated as parts of s-changes, which makes it necessary to treat s-changes first. Every s-change consists of two C-changes. Every C-change is the beginning or the ending of a state.[22] However whether the state of which a C-change is a beginning or an ending has a first or a last instant or not depends entirely on which kind of s-change it belongs to. C-changes should always be regarded as components of s-changes. If we look at a C-change without considering to which kind of s-change it belongs, we will never know whether it is a C-change in which the beginning or ending state has a first or last instant or does not have any first or last instant. We cannot say anything about C-changes in isolation.

In order to see how to treat C-changes as components of s-changes, let us look in detail at the three main sorts of s-changes which we have been considering:

1) If, for example, we use the neither/nor-option for describing the s-change from rest to motion, the limiting instant is an instant of neither rest nor motion. The s-change in question consists of two C-changes: an ending

of rest, the change from rest to non-rest; and a beginning of motion, the change from non-motion to motion. There is a first or last instant of non-motion and of non-rest (the limiting instant). There is no first or last instant of rest or motion.

2) If we describe a possible discontinuous s-change, for example between G flat and E sharp on the bar-line, according to the theory of instantaneous states proposed above, then we have to use the neither/nor-option for this s-change, too: neither G flat nor E sharp can be assigned to the instant denoted by the barline as its instantaneous pitch-span. The s-change in question consists of two C-changes: an ending of G flat, the change from G flat being played to G flat not being played; and a beginning of E sharp, the change from E sharp not being played to E sharp being played. In relation to these C-changes, the bar-line denotes a first instant at which G flat is not being played any more and a last instant at which E sharp is not being played yet. There is no last instant at which G flat is being played and no first instant at which E sharp is being played.[23]

3) If we describe an s-change between being in the initial position and having left the initial position at the beginning of a process, we use the either/or-option; there is a last instant of being in the initial position and no first instant of having left it. The s-change in question consists of two C-changes: an ending of being in the initial position, the change from being in the initial position to not being in it; and a beginning of having left the initial position, the change from not having left the initial position to having left the initial position. In relation to these C-changes, there is a last instant of being in the initial position and no first instant of not being in it. There is also no first instant of having left the initial position but a last instant of not having left it. At the end of a process, we have a mirror-image of this situation for the change between being away from the target position and having reached the target position.

One may say that in those cases in which an s-change is described using the neither/nor-option the C-changes which constitute the s-change do not *coincide*, while in those cases in which an s-change is described using the either/or-option they do. Of course, there is no phenomenological difference, since the cases differ with regard to the limiting instant only, which is, like any instant, empirically inaccessible.

As is easily seen, if C-changes are treated as proposed, they are, without exception, described by using the either/or-option. If C-changes are described in this way, the LNC and the LEM are not threatened in any way whatsoever.

3.6. The coming-to-be and perishing of objects

To introduce the principle of empirical limes, I have used only examples of the properties of objects in existence, making use of the notion of a determinable quality. We cannot apply this principle to the coming-to-be and perishing of objects without modification. But we can think about applying it analogously.

The first problem of its application is that existence is not a property of the object which comes into or passes out of existence. A way of avoiding this problem would be to say that an instant at which a exists is an instant at which a has properties, since one cannot imagine that a exists but does not have any properties whatsoever. We can then take some indispensable determinable property of an object, for example, being somewhere, and define that the statement "a exists at t" is true iff a can be assigned a position-span at t. If we do this, we will obtain the result that there are no first and last instants of existence of any object but only first and last instants of non-existence: since, for example, a is nowhere before it exists, the overlap of all position-spans of a in all periods which bound t towards the past is empty if t is the limiting instant between its non-existence and its existence; thus no instantaneous position of a can be assigned to t, and so a, by definition, does not exist at t.

It is questionable whether this is an intuitive result. It might be more convincing to treat the coming to be and perishing of objects in rather closer analogy to the acquisition or loss of properties: if an object comes to be in the course of a process, the limiting instant is the first instant of being in the target state, existence (so there is no last instant of non-existence); and if it perishes in the course of a process the limiting instant is the first instant of being in the target state, non-existence (so there is no last instant of existence). If an object simply materializes without any process, we might be inclined not to assign a first instant of existence to it (if this ever happens). In order to obtain these results as applications of the principle of empirical limes it is necessary to require that, in the case of coming to be and perishing, the position of the parts of matter from which the object in question emerges or into which it dissolves, the position of its future or past parts, must be taken into account.[24]

4. SUMMARY OF THE RESULTS OF SECTION 2 CONCERNING THE MOMENT OF CHANGE

By insisting on the empirical inaccessibility of instants and by means of a theory of instantaneous states which was developed from this insight, it has been possible to propose a plausible description of the moment of change. It is a kind of NIA.

According to it the either/or-option is used for describing
- s-changes at the beginning and end of processes
- C-changes.

And the neither/nor-option is used for describing
- s-changes between process and remaining the same
 (which are conceived as comparative properties)
- discontinuous s-changes (where they are possible).

The LNC and the LEM hold. The phenomenlogical unease about the neutral instant and about the danger of chopping up motion has been removed.

THE CLASSIFICATION OF THE MOMENT OF CHANGE

1. THE NEED TO ABANDON PLATO'S PREMISS

The description of the moment of change proposed in section 2 yields the conclusion that there are changes which should be described using the neither/nor-option and other changes which should be described using the either/or-option. The existence of changes which have to be described using the either/or-option causes a problem for the classification of the moment of change: if LNC, LEM and dense time are assumed, changes can only be kept as datable events in time if Plato's premiss is abandoned. To recapitulate, Plato's premiss is that:

> An event of changing cannot be taking place when the old state is still obtaining or when the new state is already obtaining.

But if the either/or-option is used for describing a moment of change, then the limiting instant is an instant of either the old or the new state. So describing changes by using the either/or-option *while holding that they are events which take place at limiting instants* entails a violation of Plato's premiss (which, alas, looks rather plausible). Galton's banishment of change from time[1] is a symptom of this problem, but not a solution. Neither is Aristotle's denial of instantaneous events.[2] However, it is intuitively attractive to say:

> A change takes place at the limiting instant, the instant which bounds a phase of two different states, one on each side: the instant up to which or until immediately before which the old state obtains and from which on or immediately after which the new state obtains.

In order to be able to say so, I propose to classify changes as events which take place in time but to abandon Plato's premiss, although it looks reasonable.[3] In order to do so I must say why it is not as plausible as it looks.

2. THE PLAUSIBILITY OF PLATO'S PREMISS

Let us consider from where Plato's premiss possibly derives its credibility.

§1 (a) Initially, one might think that Plato's premiss is entailed by the following (true) statement:

> (P) A process between an initial state and a target state cannot be taking place while the initial state still obtains or while the target state already obtains.

However, it has already been made abundantly clear that changes and processes must not be confused. (P) has, thus, nothing to do with Plato's premiss, and Plato's premiss may very well be false while (P) is true.

(b) One might also think that Plato's premiss is entailed by the following statement:

> (T) An event of changing cannot be taking place at an instant t if the old state prevails until *after* t or if the new state has already begun *before* t.

While this is very trivially true, Plato's premiss may clearly be, once again, false although (T) is true. So neither (P) nor (T) can be the reason for the plausibility of Plato's premiss.

§2 Perhaps there is a direct justification for Plato's premiss. One might try to support Plato's premiss by saying:

> If the event of changing were taking place while the old state still obtains, it would be taking place too early; if it were taking place while the new state already obtains, it would be taking place too late.

If asked why this is so, the reply would probably be:

> In the first case the change would already be taking place before the old state has been left. In the second case it would be taking place when the new state has already been reached.

However this means no more than:

> In the first case the change would be taking place when the old state still obtains; in the second case it would be taking place when the new state already obtains. And both is impossible.

This is just a reformulation of Plato's premiss. So we have not arrived at a justification but have merely repeated the claim in slightly different words. There must be something else which makes Plato's premiss plausible.

§3 In my view, the best justification possible for Plato's premiss is as follows:

(Premiss 1)
(a) At no instant at which I am still *in the course of observing* that the old state obtains does a change (between the old and the new state) take place.[4]
(b) At no instant at which I am already in the course of observing that the new state obtains does a change take place.
(In the first case it would be too early, in the second case too late.)

(Premiss 2)
(a) At every instant at which the old state obtains I am in the course of observing that the old state obtains.
(b) At every instant at which the new state obtains I am in the course of observing that the new state obtains.
(I am attentively watching the whole situation)

(Conclusion)
(a) Therefore there is no instant at which the old state obtains and at which a change takes place.
(b) And there is no instant at which the new state obtains and at which a change takes place.

Clearly, the conclusion is simply a precise version of Plato's premiss. And the inference is valid; it is a twofold version of Celarent, a syllogism from the first figure:

$$\text{No G is H}$$
$$\text{All F are G}$$
$$\text{No F is H.}$$

G stands for "is an instant at which I am still/already in the course of observing that the old/new state obtains". H stands for "is an instant at which a change between the old and the new state takes place". And F stands for "is an instant at which the old/new state obtains".

§4 The question is whether the inference is sound. It is not if at least one of the premisses is false. I think that the answer depends on what exactly "an instant at which I am still in the course of observing that the state that α obtains" is, as this is the crucial phrase of the terminus medius. Interestingly the answer to this questions depends in turn on whether one takes instants to be empirically accessible or not. Someone who thinks that instants are empirically accessible will take the crucial phrase simply as meaning that if he attentively watches the whole situation, he will at any single instant be in the course of observing what is the case at this instant. If this were so he would be in the course of observing at the limiting instant that it is, for example, the first instant at which the clockhand is pointing upwards. So someone who thinks that instants are empirically accessible will have no reservations about accepting premiss 2. In fact he will think that it is true. Neither will he find anything problematic about premiss 1 in his interpretation of the terminus medius. He will thus accept the inference as not only valid but sound.

However, if instants are empirically inaccessible, we cannot be as naive as this in dealing with the phrase "is an instant at which I am still in the course of observing that the state that α obtains". The only plausible way in which we could then use the phrase would be, in my view, according to the following convention:

(C) An observer O is *in the course of observing* the obtaining of the state that α at t iff there is a period c such that O observes the state that α to be obtaining throughout c and t falls within c.

If we remain with this convention then premiss 2 is anything but plausible. According to this convention, the limiting instant which separates a phase of the old state from a phase of the new state is neither an instant at which I am in the course of observing the old state nor is it an instant at which I am in the course of observing the new state. The limiting instant neither falls within a phase of the old state nor within a phase of the new state. So if instants are empirically inaccessible and if we use the phrase 'in the course of' according to (C), we should reject premiss 2 as false. Premiss 1 is unproblematic with regard to (C). But premiss 1 alone is well compatible with, for example, the statement:

The instant at which the change takes place is the first instant of the new state.

So without premiss 2 we do not arrive at the conclusion, i.e. Plato's premiss. We should therefore abandon it.

3. BEYOND PLATO'S PREMISS

§1 It is important to notice that abandoning Plato's premiss does not amount to denying that changes take place suddenly. With the preceding section in mind it is easy to define precisely what is meant by saying that a change takes place suddenly:

A change takes place suddenly iff for any observer O it is true that O can neither be in the course of observing the old state nor be in the course of observing the new state when the change is taking place.

Let us call the following statement the thesis of the sudden occurrence of changes:

(SOC) All changes take place suddenly.[5]

This means that no observer can be neither in the course of observing the old state nor the new when the change is taking place. SOC is evidently true. SOC is even *compatible* with the idea that changes take place beyond time; surely no observer can ever be in the course of observing them if they do. However, SOC *does not entail* that changes take place beyond time.

SOC is entailed by Plato's premiss, but does not entail it. An important difference between the two statements is that Plato's premiss is an ontological claim while SOC is a (weaker) epistemological claim. They are easy to confuse, however: SOC states that when an event of changing takes place one can neither still be in the course of observing the old state nor already be in the course of observing the new state. This is easily taken to be equivalent or to entail that when an event of changing takes place neither the old state still obtains nor the new state already obtains. But this would be wrong.

In order to appreciate that SOC does not entail Plato's premiss (and is therefore certainly not equivalent with it), let us consider the beginning of a state that α, where the state that α (due to the structure of the s-change to which it belongs) has a first instant. The limiting instant between the non-α-phase and the α-phase we are considering is, thus, already an instant at which the state that α obtains. Let us imagine that this situation is observed by an observer O. Let us stipulate that this limiting instant is the instant at which the event of changing takes place, the instant at which the old state (the state that non-α) ends and the new state (the state that α) begins.[6] This amounts to stipulating that Plato's premiss is not true.

The result is that this does not in any way conflict with SOC: it is true that at any instant which falls within the non-α-phase, O is in the course of observing the state that non-α; and that at any instant which falls within the α-phase, O is in the course of observing the state that α.[7] However, the limiting instant which bounds both phases falls neither within the non-α-phase nor within the α-phase. Therefore, O can neither be said to be in the course of observing the state that non-α nor be said to be in the course of observing the state that α at the limiting instant.[8] So SOC may be true even if Plato's premiss were not; SOC does not entail Plato's premiss.

§2 The denial of Plato's premiss allows us to regard all changes as datable, instantaneous events,[9] i.e. as events of changing which do not *take* time but which, nevertheless, *take place* in time.

We can now also say for a change which is described using the either/or-option that an event of changing takes place at the limiting instant; for:

> The limiting instant is the instant at which the old state ends and the new state begins, even though it may be the last instant of the old state or the first instant of the new state.

We may also assert:

> A state begins to obtain at t iff it has not obtained immediately before t, but obtains at t or immediately after t. A state ceases to obtain at t iff it has obtained immediately before t, but does not obtain at t or immediately after t.[10]

And we may add:

> An event of changing takes place at the instant up to which we can experience the old state to be obtaining and from which we can experience the new state to be obtaining, at the instant which we know to be the boundary between the old and the new state.

In my view, we should say so.

4. THE PHENOMENOLOGY OF THE MOMENT OF CHANGE

4.1. Observing, being present and witnessing

After abandoning Plato's premiss, we can say that a change, being an instantaneous event, is taking place at the limiting instant; and I think we should do so. The banishment of change from time is, thus, avoided. Nonetheless phenomenologically, the situation of watching a change is still amazing, as two examples remind us:

a) In a psychological experiment, I am to press a button, which causes some sound, while watching a particular change. My task is to make the beginning of the sound coincide with the occurrence of the change as I watch it. If the objects of the change are physically completely unknown to me, I am very often late in pressing the button; if the beginning of the sound and the change coincide, it was merely due to a lucky guess. Only if I can predict the behaviour of the objects because I know them do I have a fair chance of succeding. But it is still true that, if I want to be absolutely sure and, therefore, wait until I have seen that the change has happened, I will be late.

b) If an orchestra has a *tutti* entry at the beginning of a piece of music or after a general pause, it requires practice by the players to ensure that all their actions coincide. What do we hear when we listen to such an entry? We experience a period throughout which noone is playing, and then a period throughout which everyone is playing. As soon as a player can hear the others playing, he has already missed the entry. We do not hear anything at the instant which is denoted by the bar-line of the first bar of the entry. Nevertheless, we know exactly what it means if the entry goes wrong: there is, then, a period throughout which we can already experience some players playing, but not some other players.

A plausible description of the moment of change and a plausible classification of it based on the denial of Plato's premiss has not changed this peculiar impression that changes make on us. It should not in any case. Logic can only teach us how to cope with the moment of change, without giving up fundamental principles of thought such as the LNC and the LEM. It may prepare the ground for attempts to describe the phenomenological situation without being imprecise but it does not change the phenomena. It does not change our life. We must do justice to change as such a peculiar phenomenon. So we need to clarify in what sense changes are given to us and how we experience them. From the phenomenological point of view the following questions are still open:

> How do I experience a change if it is, as proposed, an event which takes place at an instant but if instants are empirically inaccessible? How am I going to witness a change at all if instants are empirically inaccessible? How am I ever present at it? How do I observe a change?

I would like to answer these questions by giving some of the expressions used in it differentiated meanings which they do not usually have.

1) 'being present at'. It is already rather clear that, since the banishment of change from time is avoided, we should be able to be present when it takes place. One necessary condition for O being present at a change is, intuitively, that the time at which E takes place is also a time of O's existence (i.e. a period which is contained in or, respectively, an instant which falls within O's existence). Another is that O is in some spatial proximity to E or some physical representation of E (for example on a TV screen). If we take these conditions as jointly sufficient, the result is that we can be present at a change just as we can be present at a temporally extended event.

When, for example I watch an extended process, such as a sunset on the Isle of Juist, which takes half an hour, and the half-hour during which it is taking place is a subperiod of my existence (for example, Sept 2nd, 1995, 7:30 p.m. to 8:00 p.m.), I am present at this temporaly extended event during this half-hour. When I am standing in front of a traffic-light and the traffic-light begins to be green at a particular instant t on a certain day, and if t falls within the period of my existence (is an instant of it), I am present at an instantaneous event: the traffic-light's beginning to be green. There is no logical obstacle to this if the banishment of change from time is avoided.[11]

The term 'observation', on the other hand, I propose to use in a more restricted sense:[12]

> 2) Let us say that an observer O *observes* an event E iff (i) E is a temporally extended event and (ii) O is present at E. Thus, football-matches, sunsets, TV-shows or lectures can be observed, but *changes cannot be observed*.

According to 1), we are present at both kinds of events, instantaneous as well as temporally extended ones. However, we do not stand in the same relation to them in all respects: we can observe only temporally extended events.

I think that all this does not in the least diminish my ability to *witness* a change. This can be best explained by introducing the notion of 'an *aspect* of a change' as I propose to use it:

> 3) An *aspect* of a (particular) change's taking place between a certain old state and a certain new state is to be a period of which division into two (abutting) subperiods exists such that the old state obtains throughout the first subperiod and the new state obtains throughout the second subperiod.

Aspects, as defined, are periods and are, thus, empirically accessible. They can be observed. So although we cannot observe instantaneous events, nevertheless, we can *witness* both extended and instantaneous events. This may be taken quite literally: in court, it may be just as important to find out whether the traffic-light had switched to green (an instantaneous event) as to find out how long it took the driver of a car to brake (a temporally extended event). How we witness temporally extended events is clear: we witness them by simply attending their taking place, by observing them while conscious. The difficulty lies in how we witness changes as instantaneous events: since instants are empirically inaccessible we cannot witness them by simply observing their occurrence. But as a result of the teminology introduced, this is not a great problem any more:

> We witness changes not by observing their taking place, but by observing *aspects* of them.

Indeed, the observation of an aspect of a change is required in order to witness it: in order to be able to tell if the traffic-light had switched to green, I must have observed at least a very short green-phase of the traffic-light after the change. If I had been miraculously blindfolded at the very instant at which it switched, I would not be of any value as a witness. This is also the reason why we wait a moment to be sure on New Year's Eve.

This agrees with what has been said above about being in the course of observing something: at any instant which falls within an aspect of change I am *in the course of* observing this *aspect* of the change. But I am *not* in the course of observing the change to be tak*ing* place at any such instant, not even at the limiting instant, because the change happens suddenly.

4.2. 'present': a last objection

"But", someone might object, "do we not experience changes in the present, as presently taking place? Is a change not the paradigm of a happening in the present moment of which we are immediately aware? Does not the thesis of the empirical inaccessibilty of instants entail that the present itself is not empirically accessible? And for this reason is the whole suggestion you have made not based on an absurd thesis?"[13]

This objection is worth considering, because I hold it to be very important to recognize that the view expressed by it is fundamentally wrong. Recalling the criticism of the snapshot myth, it is certainly no surprise that I think so. My answer to the objection is that one should be very careful about using the word 'present' as a noun.

We use the word 'now' for referring to quite different entities (according to the ontology chosen for this book): often, we use it in order to refer to a *period* which is *present* in the sense that it has begun and has not yet ended, be it a phase, an hour or a century. This does not exclude, however, that on other occasions we may be referring to a present *instant* when using the word 'now' (or a gesture which plays the role of the word 'now'; the downbeat of the conductor at an entry during a piece of music would be such a gesture). It seems quite possible to say that the instant called '12:00' is the present instant at twelve o'clock, and that a present instant is the non-extended boundary between past and future.[14] However, there seems to be no real need to look for an entity called 'the present'. 'Present' is primarily an adjective, and wherever it occurs as a noun it should be regarded as simply an abbreviation for a phrase in which it occurs as an adjective. Not on every noun an object should be foisted to which it is supposed to refer. Certainly, 'present', if it appears as a noun, is a noun which does much better without a reference.[15]

I can observe a process happening during the present hour by following it with my eyes and this is my way of witnessing it. This is how I experience a process. I can observe an aspect of a change which is part of the present hour, and this is my way of witnessing a change. This is how I experience a change. So the closest one comes to characterizing 'experience' might be to say that experiencing an event is consciously witnessing it. With this characterization in mind I maintain that, in contrast to the objection stated above, I do not experience a change *at* any instant, even though I can refer to the instant as a 'present' instant (by performing a procedure similar to that of the conductor). I do not experience changes as presently taking place, because they take no time. I experience changes by consciously witnessing them, i.e. by consciously observing aspects of them. And this takes time. So a change is not the paradigm of a something happening at some obscure instantaneous present of immediate awareness. I do not think that such a thing exists. Leaving plans and expectations aside, the paradigm of experience might rather be a sleigh-ride with one's back turned to the airstream, against the direction of travel. If I were to shut my eyes and try to open them during the ride for zero seconds, I would see *nothing*. But if I had not thought about it I would have expected to see a lot. So work on the moment of change has confirmed a typical experience of philosophy:

> Was ist das Schwerste von allem? Was Dir das Leichteste dünket.
> Mit den Augen zu sehen, was vor den Augen Dir liegt.[16]
>
> The hardest task of all? What seems the easiest one:
> Just seeing with the eyes what lies in front of them.

5. CONCLUDING REMARK

The preceding section may have shown that the thesis of the empirical inaccessibility of instants on which part III is based is, contrary perhaps to one's first impression, not metaphysically harmless. I hope that also those who disagree with me on my decision to hold it true will at least be able to profit from the historical parts of this book.

APPENDICES

APPENDIX A

A formal characterization of s-changes and C-changes (cp. Introduction 2.4.)
For a formal characterization of s-changes and C-changes it is useful to distinguish between predicates which take instants and predicates which take periods. This means that we will have to characterize changes with regard to the different kinds of predicates independently. Let us call them i-predicates and p-predicates.

1. p(eriod)-predicates
§1 Let P and Q be p-predicates; an s-change between the state that P as the old (ending) state and the state that Q as the new (beginning) state then takes place iff

(1) $\forall c[(*\text{-}P(c) \to \neg Q(c)) \wedge (*\text{-}Q(c) \to \neg P(c))]$
(2) $\exists c_1, c_2[*\text{-}P(c_1) \wedge *\text{-}Q(c_2) \wedge c_1 A c_2].$

I.e. an s-change according to this definition presupposes two contrary (though not necessarily contradictory) temporally extended states which abut in such a way that there is no period between them during which any other state obtains.

The ending of the state that P takes place iff
   $\exists c_1, c_2[*\text{-}P(c_1) \wedge \neg P(c_2) \wedge c_1 A c_2].$
The beginning of the state that P takes place iff
   $\exists c_1, c_2[\neg P(c_1) \wedge *\text{-}P(c_2) \wedge c_1 A c_2].$

A C-change with regard to the state that P takes place iff
an ending or a beginning of the state that P takes place.

§2 "Every s-change with regard to p-predicates consists of two C-changes":

(A) An s-change between the state that Q as the old state and the state that P as the new state contains a C-change with regard to the state that Q, namely an ending of the state that Q. For if an s-change of this kind takes place, it is trivially true by definition from what was to be an s-change:

   $\exists c_1, c_2[*\text{-}Q(c_1) \wedge \neg Q(c_2) \wedge c_1 A c_2].$

(B) An s-change between the state that Q as the old state and the state that P as the new state contains a C-change with regard to the state that P, namely a beginning of the state that P. For if an s-change of this kind takes place, it is trivially true by definition from what was to be an s-change:

   $\exists c_1, c_2[\neg P(c_1) \wedge *\text{-}P(c_2) \wedge c_1 A c_2].$

235

2. i(nstant)-predicates

§1 Let P' and Q' be i-predicates, then: An s-change between the state that P' as the old state and the state that Q' as the new state with t as the limiting instant takes place iff

(1) $\neg\exists t[\, P'(t) \wedge Q'(t)]$

(2) (a) or (b) is true:

(a) (i) $\exists t_1[t_1 < t \wedge \forall t_2[t_1 < t_2 < t \to P'(t_2)]]$
    (ii) $Q'(t) \vee \exists t_3[t < t_3 \wedge \forall t_4[t < t_4 < t_3 \to Q'(t_4)]]$

(b) (i) $P'(t) \vee \exists t_1[t_1 < t \wedge \forall t_2[t_1 < t_2 < t \to P'(t_2)]]$.
    (ii) $\exists t_3[t < t_3 \wedge \forall t_4[t < t_4 < t_3 \to Q'(t_4)]]$.

I.e. an s-change between the state that P' as the old state and the state that Q' as the new state with t as the limiting instant takes place iff the two states are contraries and (a) or (b) is true:

(a)(i) The state that P' obtains for a while (immediately) before t, and (ii) the state that Q' obtains at t or for a while (immediatey) after t.

(b) (i) The state that P' obtains at t or for a while before t and (ii) the state that Q' obtains for a while after t.

An ending of the state that P' with t as the limiting instant takes place iff (a) or (b) is true:

(a) (i) $\exists t_1[t_1 < t \wedge \forall t_2[t_1 < t_2 < t \to P'(t_2)]]$
    (ii) $\neg P'(t) \vee \exists t_3[t < t_3 \wedge \forall t_4[t < t_4 < t_3 \to \neg P'(t_4)]]$.

(b) (i) $P'(t) \vee \exists t_1[t_1 < t \wedge \forall t_2[t_1 < t_2 < t \to P'(t_2)]]$
    (ii) $\exists t_3[t < t_3 \wedge \forall t_4[t < t_4 < t_3 \to \neg P'(t_4)]]$.

Thus, an ending of the state that P' with t as the limiting instant takes places iff either

(a) the state that P' obtains for a while before t; and at t or for a while after t the state that P' does not obtain.

(b) the state that P' obtains at t or for a while before t; and for a while after t the state that P' does not obtain.

A beginning of the state that Q' with t as the limiting instant takes place iff (a) or (b) is true:

(a) (i) $\exists t_1[t_1 < t \wedge \forall t_2[t_1 < t_2 < t \to \neg Q'(t_2)]]$
    (ii) $Q'(t) \vee \exists t_3[t < t_3 \wedge \forall t_4[t < t_4 < t_3 \to Q'(t_4)]]$.

(b) (i) $\neg Q'(t) \vee \exists t_1[t_1 < t \wedge \forall t_2[t_1 < t_2 < t \to \neg Q'(t_2)]]$
    (ii) $\exists t_3[t < t_3 \wedge \forall t_4[t < t_4 < t_3 \to Q'(t_4)]]$.

Thus, a beginning of the state that Q' with t as the limiting instant takes places iff either

(a) the state that Q' does not obtain for a while before t; and at t or for a while after t the state that Q' obtains.

(b) the state that Q' does not obtain at t or for a while before t; and for a while after t the state that Q' obtains.

A C-change with regard to the state that P' with t as the limiting instant takes place iff an ending or a beginning of the state that P' with t as the limiting instant takes place.

§2 "Every s-change with regard to i-predicates consists of two C-changes":

(A) An s-change between the state that P' as the old state and the state that Q' as the new state contains a C-change with regard to the state that P', namely an ending of the state that P'. This follows from the fact that the state that P' and the state that Q' are contraries if an s-change is to take place between them. For from this follows that all Q'-instants are also ¬P'-instants. If this is true, then the definition for the taking place of an ending of the state that P' is fulfilled whenever an s-change with the state that P' as the old state takes place.

(B) An s-change between the state that P' as the old state and the state that Q' as the new state contains a C-change with regard to the state that Q', namely a beginning of the state that Q'. This follows from the fact that the state that P' and the state that Q' are contraries if an s-change is to take place between them. For from this follows that all P'-instants are also ¬Q'-instants. If this is true, then the definition for the taking place of a beginning of the state that Q' is fulfilled whenever an s-change with the state that Q' as the new state takes place.

3. s- and C-changes at the limiting instant

The definitions stated may look very complicated indeed for an everyday phenomenon as (prima facie) simple as a change. They have turned out so complicated for several reasons: one should not presuppose that both of the two states between which an s-change takes place (or the beginning or ending state in a C-change) obtain for a while. It is possible that a state obtains at the limiting instant only in such a way that its beginning and ending takes place at the same time. Such cases were discussed in detail during the Middle Ages (cf. ch. I,3). But one should neither presuppose that any of the states between which a change takes place obtains at the limiting instant. The limiting instant might be 'neutral'. The definitions allow this, too. Neither has any decision been made in the definitions as to whether the state that ends still obtains at the limiting instant or whether the state that begins already obtains in a C-change.

The idea might arise that these definitions already provide a description of the moment of change by precisely defining what it means to say that a change takes place with t as the limiting instant without any commitment to one of the four options presented in the introduction. One might regard this as a fifth option of describing the moment of change which has not been mentioned so far. Since it eliminates the question of how to correctly describe the moment of change rather than answers it, it might be called the 'eliminative option'.[1] I think, however, that the very eliminative character of this idea should prevent us from ranking it option among the options for describing the moment of change. Intuitively, we want an answer to a clear-cut and answerable question. The definitions given look extremely artificial, in fact much too artificial in order to count as an intuitively satisfactory answer to the question of description. They do so because they are designed in such a way as to leave this question open. Their sole purpose is to be precise, not to solve the problem. This is left to the application of one or several of the real options.

APPENDIX B

A formal version of Aristotle's proof in 235b26ff. for: "At the limiting instant at the end of a process, a is already in the target state" (cp. ch.I,2.2.)
The informal reconstruction of Aristotle's argument cannot make clear how density of time influences the result or demonstrate that the argument is up to the logical rigour of our time. Both can be shown by formally reconstructing the proof. Here is an attempt to do so:

Proof for: "At the limiting instant at the end of a process, the target state has been reached already" taking positions in space as the states concerned.

Definitions
An i(nstant)-predicate, R, is defined as follows:

R(t,x) iff a is at t in position x. (x,y... range over positions, t's over instants of a's existence).
Be Z (from German = Ziel) the target position of a's motion. We define using R:

Q(t) iff R(t,Z).
P(t) iff $\exists x[x \neq Z \land R(t,x)]$.
G(t) iff (i) $\exists t'[t' < t \land \forall t'' [t' < t'' < t \rightarrow P(t)]]$
        (ii) $\exists t''[t < t''' \land \forall t''' [t < t''' < t''' \rightarrow Q(t)]]$.[2]
Q(t) is to be read: "t is an instant at which a is in the target position".

P(t) is to be read: "t is an instant at which a is away from the target position".[3]

G(t) is to be read: "t is a limiting instant at the end of a process".

⊠ is to be used as an exclusive disjunction sign, i.e.

φ ⊠ χ iff $(\varphi \vee \chi) \wedge (\varphi \rightarrow \neg\chi) \wedge (\chi \rightarrow \neg\varphi)$.

Presuppositions

(*P1*) Object a is in some position at any instant: $\forall t \exists x [R(t,x)]$.

(*P2*) *natura non facit saltus.*

(*P3*) Instants are densely ordered: $\forall t_1 < t_2 [t_1 < t_2 \rightarrow \exists t_3 [t_1 < t_3 < t_2]$.

Lemmas

1. No-last-position lemma (NLP): There is no last position before Z

(P2) implies at least:[4]

(A) $\forall t_1, t_2, x, y [t_1 < t_2 \wedge R(t_1,x) \wedge R(t_2,y) \wedge x \neq y \rightarrow$...

$...\exists t_3, z [R(t_3,z) \wedge t_1 < t_3 < t_2 \wedge x \neq z \neq y]]$.

Between any two different instants at which a is at different places there is another instant at which a is at a third place: a jerk from one place to another is impossible. This already implies that there is no last position before Z. For B would be the last position before Z iff:

$B \neq Z \wedge \exists t_1, t_2 [t_1 < t_2 \wedge R(t_1,B) \wedge R(t_2,Z) \wedge$...

$...\neg \exists t_3, x [R(t_3,x) \wedge t_1 < t_3 < t_2 \wedge B \neq x \neq Z]]$.

This obviously contradicts (A), since it simply means: although A and Z are different, such that there is a distance between them, there is no further place for a to traverse in order to get from A to Z.

2. Contradiction-lemma (K) for P and Q

Since due to the definitions of P and Q we have:

$Q(t) \rightarrow \neg P(t)$ and $P(t) \rightarrow \neg Q(t)$,

we may state the following 'contradiction-lemma' (K): $\forall t[Q(t)$ ⊠ $P(t)]$.

3. Implication-lemma (I) for P

P(t) implies: $\exists t_1 [t < t_1 \wedge \forall t_2 [t < t_2 < t_1 \rightarrow P(t_2)]$,

i.e. every P-instant is followed by an environment of other P-instants. Reason: the contrary of this statement may, due to the definition of P, be rendered as:

$\exists x [x \neq Z \wedge R(t,x)] \wedge \neg \exists t_1 [t < t_1 \wedge \forall t_2 [t < t_2 < t_1 \rightarrow \exists x [x \neq Z \wedge R(t_2,x)]]$.

Let B be the place at which a is at t; then we get: B is a's last position before reaching Z. Such a last position does not exist due to (NLP).

Aristotle's argument
(Parts of the proof which correspond to explicit statements in the text are given in boldface)
(i) aim of the proof: $G(t_0) \rightarrow P(t_0)$.
(ii) We may presuppose:
      (iib) $\forall t\, \exists x\, [R(t,x)]$, **i.e. at any instant, a is somewhere** (*P1*)
      (iic) $G(t_0) \rightarrow (P(t_0) \boxtimes Q(t_0))$ (this follows a fortiori from (K)).
(iii/iv) assumption: $P(t_0) \wedge G(t_0)$.
$P(t_0)$ implies $\exists t_1[t_0 < t_1 \wedge \forall t_2[t_0 < t_2 < t_1 \rightarrow P(t_2)]$, due to (*P2*) *via* (I).
However, $G(t_0)$ implies $\exists t_3[t_0 < t_3 \wedge \forall t_4[t_0 < t_4 < t_3 \rightarrow Q(t_4)]]$.
(due to clause (ii) of the definition of G).
This is, due to (K), equivalent with:
$\exists t_3[t_0 < t_3 \wedge \forall t_4[t_0 < t_4 < t_3 \rightarrow \neg P(t_4)]]$.
As both $P(t_0)$ and $G(t_0)$ are true by assumption, the following must be true:
$\exists t_5[t_0 < t_5 \wedge \forall t_6[t_0 < t_6 < t_5 \rightarrow \neg P(t_6) \wedge P(t_6)]]$.
Since time is dense (*P3*), we have: $t_0 < t_5 \rightarrow \exists t_6[t_0 < t_5 < t_6]$...
(v/vi)...so we get a contradiction: $\exists t_6[\neg P(t_6) \wedge P(t_6)]$.
(vii) Therefore: $G(t_0) \rightarrow \neg P(t_0)$, from which follows with (iic): $G(t_0) \rightarrow Q(t_0)$
QED.

APPENDIX C

Informal proofs for some important statements concerning first and last instants of states in dense time
(cp. ch. I,2)
(a) If there is a first instant for which something is true (a first instant of the existence of a 'res'), then there is no last instant for which it is not true.
(b) If there is a last instant for which something is not true, then there is no first instant for which it is true.
(c) If there is a first instant for which something is not true, then there is no last instant for which this is true.
(d) If there is a last instant for which something is true, then there is no first instant for which it is not true.

Firstly, one has to consider what exactly is meant by the claims (a) to (d). (a), for example, does not mean: "if there ever is a last ¬P-instant, then there never is a first P-instant". Rather, (a) means: "in dense time, there is no first P-instant if there is, in the environment of the same change from ¬P to P, a last ¬P-instant". So we shall first define what it means for an interval of instants I to be an environment of a ¬P/P-change.

I is an environment of a ¬P/P-change iff
  (i) I is a closed interval
  (ii) There is a non-empty interval of instants I_1
    and there is a non-empty interval of instants I_2, such that:
      (a) $I_1 \cup I_2 = I$
      (b) For all $t_1 \in I_1$ holds: $P(t_1)$
      (c) For all $t_2 \in I_2$ holds: $\neg P(t_2)$.

Now we can prove (a) and (b) informally:

(a) Let t be a first P-instant in the environment of a ¬P/P-change; then there is no t_1, such that t_1 is a last ¬P-instant in I. For, for any $t_1 \in I$ the following is true: if t_1 is the last ¬P-instant in I, then t_1 can either be t, earlier than t or later than t. Instant t_1 cannot be t, if it is to be the last ¬P-instant in I. For t is a first P-instant and, thus, a fortiori, a P-instant. Neither can t_1 be later than t, if it is to be the last ¬P-instant in I. For if t is a first P-instant in I, then there are no ¬P-instants after t in I. Instant t_1 must therefore be earlier than t, if it is to be the last ¬P-instant in I. However, due to dense time, there is always an instant t_2 between t_1 and t. Instant t_2 cannot be a P-instant, since only t is the first P-instant, so it must be a ¬P-instant. But if this is so, t_1 is not the last ¬P-instant in I. Therefore: if there is a first P-instant in I, there is no last ¬P-instant in I.

(b) Let t be a last P-instant in the environment of a ¬P/P-change; then there is no t_1, such that t_1 is a first ¬P-instant in I. For, for any $t_1 \in I$ the following is true: if t_1 is the first ¬P-instant in I, then t_1 can either be t, earlier than t or later than t. Instant t_1 cannot be t, if it is to be the first ¬P-instant in I. For t is a last P-instant and, thus, a fortiori, a P-instant. Neither can t_1 be earlier than t, if it is to be the first ¬P-instant in I. For if t is a last P-instant in I, then there are no ¬P-instants before t in I. Instant t_1 must therefore be later than t, if it is to be the first ¬P-instant in I. However, due to dense time, there is always an instant t_2 between t_1 and t. Instant t_2 cannot be a P-instant, since t already is the last P-instant, so it must be a ¬P-instant. But if this is so, t_1 is not the first ¬P-instant in I. Therefore: if there is a last P-instant in I, there is no first ¬P-instant in I.

Proofs for (c) and (d) are analogous.

§2 There remains the question, of how far from the non-existence of, for example, a last ¬P-instant one could conclude the existence of a first P-instant (this would be especially interesting for the end of a process of a with respect to a's being in the target position). If this were so, implications (a) to (d) would become implications in both directions, i.e. equivalents. The following argument might be used to establish this result:

Definition: t is the limiting instant in the environment I of an ending of the state that P iff   (i) There is no t with $t_1 < t$ in I, such that: $\neg P(t_1)$.

(ii) There is no t with $t < t_2$ in I, such that: $P(t_2)$.

Let t be a limiting instant of this sort. Clearly, if t is a $\neg P$-instant, then it is a first $\neg P$-instant; and if it is a P-instant, it is a last P-instant. If in I, which contains t, there were to be neither a last $\neg P$-instant nor a first P-instant, t could neither be a P-instant nor a $\neg P$-instant. But this would violate the law of excluded middle. Therefore: if there is no last $\neg P$-instant and if we assume that a limiting instant exists, there is a first P-instant.

Analogously, it can be shown, if we assume the existence of a limiting instant, that there is a first $\neg P$-instant if there is no last P-instant; that there is a last P-instant if there is no first $\neg P$-instant (this would be especially interesting for the beginning of a process of *a* with respect to *a*'s being in the initial position); and that there is a last $\neg P$-instant if there is no first P-instant. The assumption that there is a limiting instant involved in a change has been made throughout this book (cf. introduction 1.2. §2 and 2.4.), and I think plausibly so. There can be hardly any doubt that it was made in the Middle Ages, too. However, it is important to realize that the existence of a limiting instant is not a feature of dense time, as one might think, but has to be made in addition to assuming dense time in order to establish the above conclusions.[5]

APPENDIX D

Paraphernalia about rest and motion
1. Different stages of rest and motion

The definition of motion given in section 2 of part III has been elaborated on in the main text only in so far as it had a direct connection with the theory of instantaneous states and the moment of change. However, since motion is a very complicated everyday concept, what is said there is still oversimplification and does not satisfy intuition in all cases.

One problem with the definitions in II,5 and III,2 has been recognized since Aristotle: rotating spheres.[6] In order to clarify this case (it is not actually the kind of problem which requires a *solution*, once it has been clarified) I propose to introduce a concept of motion which is weaker than the one defined above and a concept of rest which is stronger than the one above. According to these concepts, a rotating sphere is in weak motion although it is in rest in the 'standard' sense of II,5 and III,2. Only a non-rotating sphere can be in strong rest and not in even weak motion. Standard motion implies weak motion.

Another problem of the definitions in II,5 and III,2 is met if, besides rigid objects, one tries to account for elastic objects too. The standard definition is appropriate for the locomotion of rigid objects. And this is certainly the example which everyone usually has in mind when considering a definition of motion. However, there is the problem of how to assess the locomotion of an (imaginary) amoeba which gets from one place to another by simply growing and contracting. In order to clarify this case I propose to introduce a concept of motion which is stronger than the standard one and a concept of rest which is weaker than the standard one. The amoeba will prove to be in standard motion but not in strong motion. It is not at standard rest but at weak rest. Standard rest implies weak rest (but not vice versa), and strong motion implies standard motion (but not vice versa).

When introducing these elaborated stages of motion and rest, I will always regard motion and rest 'geometrically' and without regard to any physical forces. It would not be helpful to rely on forces here, because they are also measured in a reference frame with respect to which a sphere, which is rotating from our point of view, is at complete rest.[7]

The problem of the rotating sphere: weak motion and strong rest.
Intuitively, a rotating sphere is in some kind of motion. However, according to the standard definition it is at rest: it occupies the same part of space the whole time. So if it is in motion it is in motion in a weaker sense of the word than has been defined. Aristotle is quite right in saying that in one respect it is at rest and in another respect it is not; for he already indicates in what sense it is not at rest: as a whole, 'itself' (αὐτὸ) it stays in the same place, but its parts (τα μέρη) do not (cf. Phys. 239a27). So if one wishes to speak of a rotating sphere's kind of motion one needs a concept of motion which requires less than the standard concept: a concept of weak motion.

If one grasps motion metaphorically as leaving a part of space and conquering another part of space then one might say: the rotating sphere is constantly reconquering the same part of space which it is at the same time leaving. This is clearly different from not leaving or conquering any space whatsoever. If one arbitrarily divides up the sphere into two halves (which one might paint in different colours) then it is clear that each half, taken for itself, both leaves and conquers a part of space. It is only that one half simply conquers exactly that part of space which the other half leaves. (One does not notice anything of the sort when, for example, regarding a sandclock: as long as only the inner parts of an object are in motion, but nothing of this has any effect on the surface, one would not say that the object is in motion at all.

The idea of considering different parts of the sphere already gives a hint as to how precisely to define a concept of weak motion which applies to the rotating sphere. It should simply be:

a is in weak motion iff there is a division of a into two halves such that both halves are in standard motion.

A concept of strong rest corresponds to the concept of weak motion: the rotating sphere is at standard rest because it is not in standard motion. But a sphere at a complete standstill is at rest in a still stronger sense because it is not even in weak motion. Standard rest and weak motion are compatible but strong rest is incompatible with standard motion. a is to be at rest in the strong sense iff for any division of a into two halves it is true that both halves are at rest in the standard sense. This definition cannot be fulfilled even if a is in no more than weak motion; in this case there is at least one division of a according to which one half of a is in standard motion.

The amoeba: weak rest and strong motion
A rigid object cannot get from one place to another without being in motion with respect to all its parts. However, for example, a person (which is an elastic object) can raise her arm while staying seated on the same chair. Even by only raising an arm, the whole person fulfills the definition of standard motion. This causes no real problem: not every kind of motion has to result in getting from one one place to another. If this is required, the word motion is used in a very strong sense, which will not be touched upon in the definitions given here.

But it seems amazing that mere growing and shrinking is already motion according to the standard definition. Nonetheless, this must be so if motion is to be regarded as a necessary condition for getting from one place to another, if nothing can change location without having been in motion in any sense. Now an object may in fact get from one place to another by simply growing and shrinking, for example our amoeba which first grows and then contracts into a different place. In this case, the leaving of one part of space and conquering of another is not exactly simultaneous, which is unconceivable for rigid objects. However one wishes to have a concept of motion which is so strong that growing and shrinking is excluded. It would have to require that leaving a part of space and conquering another have to happen simultaneously. Whatever is in strong motion should be in standard motion, but not everything which is in standard motion must also be in strong motion (our amoeba is not). A concept of weak rest corresponds to the concept of strong motion: standard motion is to be compatible with weak rest (e.g. in the case of our amoeba); but weak rest should be incompatible with strong motion. Standard rest (and *a fortiori* strong rest) should imply weak rest. The amoeba is at weak rest but not at standard rest because it is in standard motion.

In order to state things precisely, let us introduce a modified indentity sign between sets ($=°$): $M_1 =° M_2$ iff $M_1 \subset M_2 \vee M_2 \subset M_1$. Let us call the relation which is expressed by this sign weak identity, because for $M_1 =° M_2$ less is required than for $M_1 = M_2$ to be true: The latter can only be true if $M_1 \subset M_2 \wedge M_2 \subset M_1$ is true. Standard identity between sets implies weak identity. The absence of weak identity can be rendered by a modified non-identity sign between sets: $M_1 \neq° M_2$ iff $\neg (M_1 =° M_2)$. The expression "$M_1 \neq° M_2$" is to be read as "M_1 strongly differs from M_2"; for in order that $M_1 \neq° M_2$ be true, more is required than for $M_1 \neq M_2$ to be true. M_1 can strongly differ from M_2 only if neither M_1 is contained in M_2 nor M_2 in M_1. So strong non-identity implies standard inequality for which it would be enough if one of these conditions were fulfilled. Proceding from these definition we can also define a strong non-identity and a weak identity between spans. As mentioned, a certain set can be to describe a span, just as an interval in the technical sense describes a period. Hence let M_{s1} be the set which can be said to describe the span s_1, and let M_{s2} be the set which can be said to describe the span s_2:

$$s_1 =° s_2 \text{ iff } M_{s1} =° M_{s2}.$$
$$s_1 \neq° s_2 \text{ iff } M_{s1} \neq° M_{s2}.$$

A precise definition of strong motion is now obtained by simply substituting the non-identity sign in the definition of motion in III,2 with a strong non-identity sign. A precise definition of weak rest is now obtained by simply substituting the identity sign in the definition of motion in III,2 with a weak identity sign. Strong motion thus defined implies standard motion. Standard motion thus defined implies weak rest. Our amoeba, while getting from here to there by growing and shrinking, is never in strong motion but only in standard motion. Between any two position-spans of its growth- phase or between any two position-spans of its contraction-phase the relation of standard non-identity holds but never the relation of strong non-identity. The concept of motion introduced in III,2 thus emerges as a concept of 'medium strong' motion; where it is counterintuitive, other degrees of motion apply. As has been shown, they can easily be precisely defined.

2. Is motion more than a 'change of location'? - Peter Forrest's 'Achilles-weed'
Another possible problem for the kind of definition of motion proposed in II,5 and III,2 is highlighted by Peter Forrest.[8] He argues that motion must be more than a change of location and illustrates this by describing a widely unknown vegetable, which is delicious not only for tortoises, but also for philosophers. This vegetable is called 'Achilles weed':

Achilles weed grows 'forward' in long stripes. Now the particular stripe of Achilles weed which Forrest describes has a very special fate: At exactly the same speed at which it is growing forward at its foremost edge, a tortoise is eating the rear edge of the stripe. This seems as though, within a day or so, a patch of Achilles weed moves through the garden. But it seems rather inappropriate to call this motion. Thus, the patch of Achilles weed would be a case of getting from here to there without motion: not every change of location presupposes motion.

What can be said about this example? The patch of Achilles weed might be a pseudo-object, an intentional object such as a 'light cone' which is 'following' an actor on stage or a 'person' who is 'running' across the cinema screen, whose motion is just as unreal as itself.[9] One might say that continuously new patches of Achilles weed are emerging while the tortoise is completely eating up old ones (there only seems to be one patch at each time; actually, two half-patches of different generations exist). But if the tortoise had spared the Achilles weed no one would have thought about a patch multiplying: everyone would have merely considered it to be one patch growing into a long stripe. Do we have to take into account what would have happened counterfactually if the tortoise had spared the patch? Or do we have to take into account what is the nature of the Achilles weed (or even its Aristotelian soul?) in order to state what happened to it? I do not want to propose any solution to these quite fascinating problems. This is not necessary here. It is already clear that the problem which is really highlighted by Forrest's story has nothing to do with how to define motion; it is the problem of identity over time. The definitions of rest and motion proposed already presuppose identity over time: they contain a comparison of the states of one and the same object a at different times. What criterion we have for identity over time is unimportant with regard to them.

3. Heraclitus' objections

A further difficulty for the definition of motion proposed can perhaps be seen in the following two objections which might well be called Heracleitean: (a) There are no absolutely rigid objects. (b) All objects are to some extent in motion all the time (just take a close enough look at a metal cube and you will notice that it only gradually differs from a jellyfish). I think that the best one can do concerning these objections is to admit them. They are not objections against the definition proposed: in order to be able to say that nothing is ever at complete rest one needs a definition of rest. So if someone claims that no object ever fulfills the definition of rest this is an implicit recognition of the definition.[10]

NOTES

INTRODUCTION 1 (CONTENT)

[1]Graham Priest: Inconsistencies in Motion, American Philosophical Quarterly Vol. 22, No.4, October 1985, p.339.

[2]Roderick Chisholm: Beginnings and Endings, in: Peter van Inwagen (ed.): Time and Cause, Dordrecht 1980, p.17.

[3]David Bostock: Plato on Change and Time in the 'Parmenides', Phronesis 1978, p.238.

[4]Brian Medlin: The Origin of Motion, Mind April 1963, p.155.

[5]All talk of rest and motion in what follows is talk about rest and motion with respect to some freely chosen reference frame. With this in mind we can forget about Special and General Relativity for the rest of the book. As will be seen, the prominence of the change between rest and motion is a bit of a problem, since here the question of how to define rest and motion is involved and makes this change an exceptionally complicated example.

[6]The 'C' stands for 'Cambridge', because this type of change is called 'Cambridge change', since Bertrand Russell first drew attention to it. Cf. Bertrand Russell: The Principles of Mathematics, London 1964 [first edition 1903], §442.

[7]Richard Sorabji: Aristotle on the Instant of Change, Proceedings of the Aristotelian Society, Suppl. Vol. 50 (1976) [first version], p.69.

[8]Even the mere existence of instants is extraordinary for some authors, though (probably, e.g., for Plato, cf. ch. I,1.). Extreme opinions on this point are that talk of instants is reducible to talk of periods (Hamblin) or even to talk of simultaneity of events (William Charlton). Cf. C. Hamblin: Instants and Intervals, in: Studium Generale 24 (1971), pp.127-134; W. Charlton: The Analytic Ambition, Oxford 1991, pp.83-87.

[9]Strangely enough, it has sometimes been thought that the existence of such changes can be excluded *a priori* by uttering the words "natura non facit saltus".

[10]A useful summary of this debate is, e.g., found in Ralf Stoecker: Was sind Ereignisse?

[11]Cf. L. Lombard: Relational Change and Relational Changes, in: Philosophical Studies 34 (1978); a similar opinion is found in Carol Cleland: The Individuation of Events.

[12]Galton: The Logic of Aspect, Introduction.

[13]The situation for temporally extended events apart from instantaneous ones: temporally extended events are typically heterogeneous (a property which can be characterized rather precisely, cf. introduction 2 and Galton loc.cit.). The difficulties are in the realm of events which do not take time. Unfortunately, if changes are events, they are events which take no time.

[14]That both Plato and Aristotle had something to say about the moment of change has always been clear. However, so far only G.E.L. Owen has paid any attention to the fact that the relevant texts are very closely related. Cf. G.E.L. Owen: Tithenai ta Phainomena, in: J.Barnes/M.Schofield/R.Sorabji (eds.): Articles on Aristotle, vol.1, London 1975.

[15]To my knowledge, the term 'Neutral Instant Analysis' was introduced by Norman Kretzmann in: Incipit/Desinit, in: Machamer/Turmbull (eds.): Motion and Time, Space and Matter, Columbus (Ohio) 1976, p.114.

INTRODUCTION 2 (FORM)

[16]About the possibility of regarding tense logic as a logic of predicates, cf.Bertram Kienzle: Zustand und Ereignis, Frankfurt 1994, p.10 and the translation of Prior's 'Tense Logic and the Logic of Earlier and Later', p.103 (original in A.N. Prior: Papers on Time and Tense, Oxford 1968). The 'classic' text of tense logic is Prior's 'Past, Present and Future', Oxford 1967.

[17]Prior's (loc.cit.) "time a is p-ing" expresses this intuition especially clearly.

[18]In my view, it would be wrong to think that they have 'indefinitely short' (or, worse, 'infinitesimal') duration. I cannot make any sense of that, since I think that whatever has an extension has a definite extension. My view has not been altered by learning about so-called non-standard analysis. It may be a formally satisfactory theory. The problem is in the realm of interpretation: only in interpreting the formal system does one commit oneself to talk about something which has an extension but no definite extension. Cf. about non-standard analysis: William Mc Laughlin and Sylvia L. Miller: An Epistemological Use of Nonstandard Analysis to Answer Zeno's Objections against Motion, in: Synthese, vol. 92, pp.371-384; Edward Nelson: Internal Set Theory - A New Approach to Nonstandard Analysis, in: Bulletin of the American Mathematical Society, vol. 83 (Nov. 1977), pp.1165-1198; Alain Robert:, Nonstandard Analysis, New York 1988. I am grateful to Eva Maria Krause for telling me about non-standard analysis and for (controversial) discussions about it.

[19]These expressions should be taken *cum grano salis*. There are good reasons for claiming that duration in the strict sense is peculiar to events, e.g. William Charlton's idea that, since events have a duration in time, periods of time, if they had duration would have to have it in some kind of Super-Time. So in order to be very precise one should perhaps rather talk of the ability of a period to contain an event of a certain duration than of the duration of a period. Cf. William Charlton: The Analytic Ambition, pp.83-86.

[20]Cf. C. Hamblin: Starting and Stopping, in: The Monist 53 (1969), pp.410-425 and C. Humberstone: Interval Semantics for Tense Logic, in: Journal of Philosophical Logic 8 (1979), pp.171-196. A sceptical evaluation of the project of Interval Semantics is found in Pavel Tichy: 'Do we need Interval Semantics?' (in: Lingusitics and Philosophy 8 (1985), pp.263-282) and in Antony Galton: 'The Logic of Aspect', Oxford 1984, ch.1.

[21]loc.cit.

[22]Cf. Hamblin: Instants and Intervals, pp.127f.

[23]Ibid., p.131.

[24]Ibid., p.130.

[25]Cf. Hamblin: Starting and Stopping, p.130.

[26]I here follow a suggestion for which I am grateful to Eva Maria Krause. Hamblin's definition of containment is a little more complicated in using an 'O(verlap)' relation between periods. A C-relation as defined above intuitively represents containment in most imaginable kinds of branching time (an exception would be a rather odd time in which time branches can reunite after splitting up). Hamblin's C-relation does not, because his 'O'-relation does not intuitively represent overlap for branching time. I am grateful to Bertram Kienzle for pointing this out to me.

[27]Hamblin: Instants and Intervals, p.132. Another approach working with both instants and periods is found in Alexander Bochmann: Concerted Instant Interval Semantics I + II, Notre Dame Journal of Formal Logic Summer/Fall 1990, pp.404-414/580-601. An informal plea for this kind of time ontology is found in Richard Swinburne's 'God and Time', and apparently also in Chisholm's 'Beginnings and Endings' as well as in his 'On Metaphysics' (compare the chapter on 'Boundaries').

[28]This distinction may look strange to the mathematician or logician. However, I really think that an instant is no more a pair of periods than a single child is a pair of parents, although in both cases a mention of the pair can be used for uniquely identifying the entity. Mentioning an entity A in order to uniquely identify an entity B is not the same as identifying A with B.

[29]Cf. Hamblin: Instants and Intervals, p.132: "The double use of '=' and '<' causes no ambiguity since we use [different...] letters for instants and for intervals".

[30]This convention is the exact opposite of a convention stated by Hamblin in 'Instants and Intervals'. According to Hamblin, a temporal predicate satisfies a period only if what it is about is the case throughout the period. This convention is reflected in axioms 9 and 10 of his interval semantics in 'Instants and Intervals'. Both conventions are formally possible. So one can decide which to use for practical reasons. It will be seen that, especially for reconstructing arguments of Aristotle in ch.I,2.,the opposite convention to Hamblin's will be more practical in the context of this book.

[31]Galton maintains that this is even characteristic of all events, and marks them off from states. It is, however, difficult to see how instantaneous events can be heterogeneously structured.

[32]One should note, however, that $*-\sim-P(c)$ does not hold ('$\sim$' being a negation prefix equivalent to '$\neg$'). There is, of course, a period contained in c which satisfies P, i.e. c itself.

PART I
CHAPTER 1 - PLATO

[1]Alfred North Whitehead: Process and Reality, p.63: "The safest general characterization of the European philosophical tradition is that it consists of a series of footnotes to Plato."

[2]Translation: H.N. Fowler (Loeb edition of Plato's works vol. vi), my changes in $<...>$ brackets. Why I leave χρόνος untranslated here should become clear further down.

[3]Probably to Plato τὸ ἐξαίφνης is both. However, I here limit myself to treating Plato as if he were an analytic philosopher. The text shows that he is. But he is more than that and I am aware of the limitations of acting as if he were nothing but that.

[4]Cf. e.g. W. Beierwaltes: Ἐξαίφνης oder die Paradoxie des Augenblicks, in: Philosophisches Jahrbuch LXXIV (1966/67), pp.271-283.

[5]Cf. e.g. Symposium 210d/e and 7th letter 341c/d.

[6]I think that a misunderstanding (however fruitful) exists concerning the sudden, taking it as if it were a short, perceivable duration which stands out in the usual experience of time, for example when there is mention of 'evidence', 'happiness' or 'beauty' in the sudden (im Augenblick). Duration is certainly a feature Plato's exaiphnes lacks.

[7] Owen: Tithenai ta Phainomena, p.123.

[8]Strang: Plato and the Instant, Proceedings of the Aristotelian Society Suppl. Volume 48 (1974), p.73.

[9] Bostock: Plato on Change..., p.236. In the preceding three quotations: my italics.

[10]Where the Greek word is used as a technical term, I transliterate, when commenting on particular passages in the text, I do not.

[11]In 151e-153b 'was', 'is' and 'will be' are defined as partaking respectively in past, present or future time. Of course, this again points towards the theory of forms, but this allusion is once more of little help. Cf. also David Bostock: Plato on Change..., p.229: "The passages I wish to discuss [including 155e/157b, N.St.] are all of a quite general nature, and nothing to do with 'the One'. Indeed we may go further and say that they have no very noticeable relevance to any feature of the theory of forms."; Colin Strang: Plato and the Instant, p.73: "Both passages [including 155e/157b] are offered by Plato as serious analyses. Neither has any proprietary connection with Unity or the One, the nominal topic of the dialogue; all that is said applies indifferently to anything capable of change."

[12]This becomes clear in 156e 3-7, cf. § 9.

[13]Cf. Strang: Plato and the Instant, pp.71f.

[14]157a2. Concerning the difficulty of how broad or narrow the meanings of κίνησις and στάσις are to be taken here, cf. David Bostock: Plato on Change..., pp.235f. I agree with his evaluation that this is only a 'minor interpretative problem' (ibid.).

[15]This becomes clear in the formulation of 156c4/6 and in the distinction of cases in 156e1/3 or 156c1/4: case 1 - κινούμενον τε ἵσταται, κινούμενον ὕστερον ἑστάναι; case 2 - ἑστός ἐπι το κινεῖσθαι μεταβάλλει, ἑστός τε πρότερον, ὕστερον κινεῖσθαι. (Note how, during this complicated argument, Plato still pays attention to employing the stylistic device of chiasm.)

[16]Strang:Plato and the Instant, p.71:"[The] topic [of 155e-157b5] is instantaneous change, for which Plato here reserves the term metabole, and which I shall call 'switching'. A switch is what occurs between a state (stasis) and a process (kinesis)."

[17]Cf. 1.4. § 3.

[18]Strang : Plato and the Instant, p.72.

[19]156d6/7 ...ἡ ἐξαίφνης αὕτη φύσις ἀτοπός τις ἐγκάθηται μεταξὺ τῆς κινησεώς τε καὶ στάσεως, ἐν χρόνῳ οὐδενὶ οὖσα.

[20]εἰς ταύτην δὴ καὶ ἐκ ταύτης 156e1.

[21]156e3-7.

[22]156e8-157a3. Plato is here occupied with a μεταβολή ἐκ τοῦ εἶναι εἰς το ἀπόλλύσθαι and a μεταβολὴ ἐκ τοῦ μὴ εἶναι εἰς το γίγνεσθαι, i.e. the change from κίνησις to στάσις and vice versa.

[23]This is, more or less, the conclusion drawn by Bostock in 'Plato on Change...'.

[24]This thesis is rather convincingly argued by Constance Meinwald in her book 'Plato's Parmenides' (Oxford 1991), as far as the general idea of the matrix of demonstrations in the second part is concerned. However, Meinwald does not have much to say about the digression.

[25]The preposition by which something's being the case can be related to a 'then-object' is to be 'at'.

[26]A statement 'about a' attributes to a then-object the property that a is F at it.

[27]This is very close to the demonstration of a real paradox. However, it is no such demonstration in the strict sense, because in such a demonstration one would have to use a presupposition in order to show that it does not hold. However, Plato simply states the LNC as a presupposition in section (a) without using it in section (c).

[28]In 'First Principles, Substance and Action - Studies in Aristotle and Aristotelianism' (unpublished) Fernando Inciarte mentions that some authors see a possibly close connection between ancient and intuitionist logic. A good introduction to intuitionism from a philosophical point of view is Michael Dummett's 'Elements of Intuitionism', Oxford 1977.

[29]Principles of non-contradiction exist in many-valued logics, too. They are of the form: "A proposition may not bear more than one of the following n statement-values...". It is only in classical logic that n equals 2 and all the statement values that exist are 'true' and 'false'.

[30]This principle is independent of the principle 'no multiple statement values'. It would always take the form: "A proposition always has at least one of the following n statement values:..." . Only in two-valued logic is this a principle of excluded third. More generally, one would have to call it 'principle of excluded n + 1st '.

[31]When defending the LNC, cf. Met.IV 1008b11.

[32]It would not be easy to incorporate 'non' in a predicate logic, since it involves the use of modal concepts. It would, however, be a very interesting and rewarding task, since I think a lot more can be done with this prefix than that which has been done above.

[33]It does not matter here why we do not want to admit this. Pressed for an answer, one might say: We simply do not know what this neither-nor should look like; and if this state

obtained for a period of time, we should know, since we witness changes all the time. But there might also be different justifications for this.

[34]K.W. Mills: Plato and the Instant (Reply to Colin Strang), in: Proceedings of the Aristotelian Society Suppl. Vol. 48 (1971), p.88; in the same sense Owen: Tithenai ta Phainomena, p.123.

[35]Owen: Tithenai ta Phainomena, p.123.

[36] Bostock: Plato on Change..., p.237.

[37]Ibd. p.236.

[38]Colin Strang: Plato and the Instant, in: Proceedings of the Aristotelian Society, Suppl. Vol. 48 (1974), pp.63-79.

[39]Strang: Plato and the Instant, p.68.

[40]Ibd. pp.70f.

[41]Cf. ch. I,2.1.

[42]In the Meno (86d12) Plato even uses νῦν as an adjective when he is talking about a person being in the νῦν βίῳ (present life) in contrast to other lives which are assumed in the myth of anamnesis. However, this contradicts Strang's additional idea that a 'now-item' in Plato must be indivisible and not contain any change, since this is clearly not true of a lifetime.

[43]Strang: Plato and the Instant, pp.70f.

[44]Ibd. p.73.

[45]Ibd. pp.74f.

[46]K.W.Mills, Plato and the Instant (reply to Colin Strang), in: Proceedings of the Aristotelian Society, Suppl. Vol. 48 (1974), pp.81-96.

[47]Ibd. p.83.

[48]Ibd. pp.85-87.

[49]In Mills's text: 'O'.

[50]The existence of a is to be the period throughout which a exists and which is not contained in any other period throught which a exists.

[51]Strang: Plato and the Instant, p.71.

[52]The following quotations from Gellius are all from: Auli Gelli Noctes Atticae, L VI,13 in: The Attic Nights of Aulus Gellius, translated by J.C. Rolfe, London 1961 (Loeb Classical Library).

[53]Taurus, the philosopher, has to inform the party guests that this is a serious question and not just a game for after-dinner conversation: Gravissimi philosophorum super hac re serio quaesiverunt.

[54]Gellius seems to be uncertain whether he is writing about a problematic instant (as the examples suggest) or about a problematic period, for he reports one opinion so: "alii nihil in eo tempore vitae reliquerunt; totumque illud, quod mori dicitur, morti vindicaverunt." Thus the whole process of dying (totum, quod mori dicitur) is here attributed to death already. This might indicate that Gellius did not think at length about the puzzle he reports.

[55]Sextus Empiricus: Adversus Mathematicos I §269 (pp.132/133 in the volume 'Against the Physicists' of the Loeb complete edition, engl./gr., London 1953).

[56]Translation: R.G. Bury. He correctly recognizes the χρόνοι as 'periods'. The very weak spot of the 'proof' is, of course, "wherefore he must necessarily die in one or other of these periods": Sextus does not seem to notice Plato's idea that Socrates may die at the boundary between the periods at all. A short version of the same example is found in 'Outlines of Pyrrhonism' III, ch. 16, §111. The passage quoted is an example of the sceptical use of ἄτοπον.

[57]Knuuttila: Remarks..., p.247.

[58]The following quotations are all from De Civitate Dei, book 13 ch.11.

[59]According to Galton's view, it is just this assumption which Priorian tense logic cannot overcome and the reason why it cannot cope with the moment of change. This, again, motivated Galton to develop his event logic. Cf. Antony Galton: The Logic of Aspect, Oxford 1984, Introduction and ch.1. as well as ch. II,1 of the present book.

[60]It is worth comparing this passage with Sextus Empiricus: 'Outlines...', I §23.

[61]Knuuttila: Remarks on the Background..., p.247: "...there were theories in ancient philosophy according to which a change between contradictory terms is a positive event taking place between the periods during which the terminus a quo and the terminus ad quem of the change obtain, respectively. We find this theory in Plato's Parmenides (156c - 157a) [...] In these texts it is assumed that there is an instantaneous third state between the two consecutive contradictory states, and the reason for postulating such a special state seems to be that the change between contradictories is understood as an indivisible positive event. [...] the junctions between contradictory states of affairs [...] are presumed to have autonomous ontological status." Knuuttila holds St.Augustine and Plotinus to be other advocates of this position. I do not think that this is very clear in the case of St.Augustine, but it is well possible. (cf.I,1.4.) . The relevant text by Plotinus will be discussed in connection with Aristotle's Physics in ch.I, 2.5.2.

[62]Bostock: Plato on Change..., p.204.

CHAPTER 2 - ARISTOTLE

[1]From a systematic point of view, it does not matter which contribution to the debate is earlier. But it is a fascinating idea indeed that the 'Parmenides' might be the later text, in which Plato defends himself against his former pupil. Cf. for this idea David Bostock: Aristotle on Continuity in Physics VI in: L. Judson (ed.): Aristotle's Physics, Oxford 1991, pp.179-213 (cf. pp.204-208, esp. p.206 footnote 25: 'One might indeed wonder whether my presumed chronology is correct. Perhaps Plato's Parmenides replies to Aristotle's Physics VI, rather than vice versa?'). There are some hints towards this in the context of the 'Parmenides': Plato's defence of the theory of Forms against an oversimplified textbook-version of it (which had to face the problem of the Third Man), as well as the name of the old Parmenides' interlocutor in the second part: Aristotle. This hypothesis would also explain why there is a digression in the second part at all, despite its very systematic structure, and why the topic of this digression comes so near to Physics VI. On the other hand, I show in this chapter that Aristotle differentiates certain things much further than Plato does. This can only be brought to agree with Bostock's conjecture by assuming that Aristotle knew Plato's opinion well before Plato wrote it down as a reaction towards Aristotle's criticism. This is, however, not improbable.

[2]It would be wrong to speak of more than an 'association' here, for Aristotle does not use the word ἐξαίφνης as referring to a period: he does not make a noun out of the adverb, as Plato does in order to gain a name for a new kind of 'Then-object'. The τὸ in front of the word may in Aristotle be regarded as referring to an arbitrary event which happens suddenly; so the adverb remains an adverb; often enough, τὸ in definitions just seems to be a sort of verbalized quotation marks.

[3]E.g. the 1/36 second during which the eye is presented with a single picture of a film (remember the discussion of subliminal perception in psychology).

[4]Unless stated otherwise, I refer to passages in the 'Physics'. The Greek text I used is in: Aristoteles' Physik, übersetzt und mit einer Einleitung und Anmerkungen herausgegeben von Hans Günter Zekl [2 vols.,Gr./Gn.], Hamburg 1988.

[5]My translation. A note on translations of Physics VI: I frequently found that the translation by R.P.Hardie and R.K. Gaye agrees with my interpretation. It is contained in: The complete works of Aristotle - the revised Oxford translation edited by Jonathan Barnes, vol.1,

Princeton 1984 (in what follows: H/G). I will often follow this translation, indicating my changes of it by the following kind of brackets: < ... >. As to the passages I wish to discuss I found that I rarely agree with the translation by Cornford and Wicksteed (Loeb edition). I am less happy with the style of H/G, but using an established translation as a base is the most convenient thing to do. However, I agree with Jonathan Barnes' caveat who writes in the preface to the revised Oxford translation: "[T]he [...] translators [did not] try to mirror in their English style the style of Aristotle's Greek. For the most part, Aristotle is terse, compact, abrupt, his arguments condensed, his thought dense. For the most part, the Translation is flowing and expansive, set out in well-rounded periods [...] and sometimes orotund. [...] the Translation produces a false impression of what it is like to read Aristotle in the original [...] making [Aristotle's philosophizing] seem more polished and finished than it actually is. [...] Aristotle's sinewy Greek is best translated into correspondingly tough English; but to achieve that would demand a new translation."(p.xi). H/G translate 222b14/15 as: " 'Suddenly' refers to what has departed from its former condition in a time imperceptible because of its smallness." Here I disagree: 'suddenly' as an adverb does not refer to anything, let alone to a changing object, and the ἐκστάν is rather inflated by "has departed from its former condition".

[6]This is one of the rare cases in which it would be appropriate to write something such as "cf. Physics VI passim", so numerous are the passages to which I could refer for this; in direct connection with the moment of change cf. e.g. 239a8, 237a25, 227b19/22.

[7]Cf. e.g. the function of the expression πέρας in 236a7/15 (a passage which is central for the moment of change).

[8]Cf. for this use of the preposition ἐν 234a34/b5 and 263b9/264a6.

[9]H/G has 'time' instead of 'a period'.

[10]This comes out very clearly in a digression in Physics VIII, 263b9/264a6 compare also 234a34b5.

[11] 236b19/22, 236b25/32, 236a15/27.

[12]similarly unambiguous: 237a3/9.

[13]Contrast with: [τὸ ἓν] ὅτε μεταβάλλει, [...] οὐδὲ κινοῖτ' ἄν τότε - Parm. 156e5/7.

[14]This is very clear in Physics VI in e.g. 239b1, 234a24/34, 239a20/21.

[15]Cf. Richard Sorabji: Aristotle on the Instant of Change, second version, p.166 (footnote): "Aristotle] seems [..] to deny motion or rest at *any* instant. It might be replied that he only means that an instant has no duration within which a thing could get any distance - and indeed some of his arguments seem to suggest only this. This would leave him free to go on to say (a) that at an instant a thing can nonetheless be *in course of* moving or resting, and (b) that it is so at all instants, except the instant of transition between motion and rest. [...] But [...] I do not find statements (a) and (b) spelled out by Aristotle."

[16]As Sorabji (Aristotle on the Instant of Change, second version, p.159) remarks. Sorabji himself does not agree with this reproach. It is indeed unjustified as I hope to show in ch. I,3, for it presupposes that the medieval philosophers in the Aristotlelian tradition followed the 'philosophus' in this point without considering it for themselves. And this is simply not true.

[17]A terminological exception is Physics V1. Cf. on this matter Knuuttila: Remarks..., p.246 and the section on substantial change in this chapter.

[18]234a31: οὐκ ἄρα ἔστιν κινεῖσθαι ἐν τῷ νῦν. ἀλλὰ μὴν οὐδ' ἠρεμεῖν. (There is no moving in the now, but no resting either). On the other hand, what Aristotle in 239b2 explicitly declares to be possible at an instant (ἐν τῷ νῦν) is the non-comparative 'just being here' (εἶναι κατά τι).

[19]An almost identical description is found in 234a31/34.

[20]Cf. on this meaning (but also on other possible uses of ἐν ᾧ which can sometimes be found) Wagner's commentary in the appendix of his German translation of the 'Physics', p.625.

[21]Frank Jackson/Robert Pargetter: A Question about Rest and Motion. This distinction is not made by them with regard to Aristotle, though. Their approach will be discussed in ch. II,1.

[22]The reason for this is that in chapter II,1, in connection with Russell's Cambridge-Change Criterion, I will use the word 'relational' in a different, well-established sense. Using Jackson/Pargetter's terminology at the same time would lead to confusion.

[23]The distinction between comparative and non-comparative properties is not identical with the distinction between κίνησις and ἐνέργεια (which is dealt with in ch.2.5.). It is true that examples are often similar: motion is a κίνησις, and being in motion is a comparative property. An act of watching something is an ἐνέργεια and watching something is a non-comparative property. However, (1) the distinction between κίνησις and ἐνέργεια is not supposed to classify properties but acts (it might be extended to distinguish states from events, but those are not properties either). (2) Even if, instead of identity, one simply wanted to state a one-to-one correspondence, there would be a problem: rest is neither intuitively, nor according to Aristotle's criterion, a κίνησις; but being at rest is a comparative property.

[24]Bertrand Russell: The Principles of Mathematics, §446/447.

[25]H/G reads: "...it is in just these circumstances that we use the term 'being at rest' - when at one now after another it can be said with truth that a thing ... occupies the same space". Here 'space' is too narrow and, much worse, 'one now after another' suggests a discrete time order, which is alien to Physics VI.

[26]Richard Sorabji: Time, Creation and the Continuum, London 1983, p.413; Aristotle and the Instant of Change, second version, p.171. Sorabji (correctly) refers to the following passages for this: 262a30; b20, 239a35-b3, 263b20-23.

[27]According to Plato-2. Plato-1 makes Plato more modern than Aristotle, since according to Plato-1, Plato allows motion at an instant (this does not exactly help to the plausibility of Plato-1).

[28]Norman Kretzmann: 'Incipit/Desinit', in Machamer/Turnbull (ed.): Motion and Time, Space and Matter, Columbus (Ohio) 1976, p.101-136.

[29]Richard Sorabji: Aristotle on the Instant of Change, Proceedings of the Aristotelian Society, Suppl. Vol. 50 (1976).

[30]Sorabji: Aristotle on the Instant of Change, second version, p.166; Sorabji, Time..., p.408.

[31]Second version = Richard Sorabji: Aristotle on the Instant of Change, in: J.Barnes/ M.Schofield / R.Sorabji: Articles on Aristotle vol. 3, London 1979. Third version = Sorabji: Time... ch. 26.

[32]The problematic passage (236a17ff) reads: ἔτι δ' ε' τῷ ΓΑ χρόνῳ παντὶ ἠρεμεῖ (...) καὶ ἐν τῷ Α ἠρεμεῖ, ὥστ' ε' ἀμερές ἐστι τὸ ΑΔ ἅμα ἠρεμήσει καὶ μεταβεβληκὸς ἔσται. ἐν μὲν γὰρ τῷ Α ἠρεμεῖ, ἐν δὲ τῷ Δ μεταβέβληκεν (If [something] is at rest throughout a period GA, then it is also at rest at A. Therefore, if AD has no parts, it will both be at rest and have changed.: For in A it is at rest, but in D it has [already] changed).

[33]In contrast to the very careful labelling throughout the rest of the 'Physics', we get a Γ here which has not been introduced before, so we do not learn whether it is an instant (which divides the period ΑΔ which has been properly introduced) or something else. This might point towards an error in an ancient edition or towards a marginal note which slipped into the text.

[34]Cf. Aristoteles: Physikvorlesung, übersetzt von [tr. by] Hans Wagner, Berlin 1983 and Aristotle: The Physics II [engl./gr.], translated by Philip H. Wicksteed und Francis M. Cornford, London 1934.

[35]The other one is 263b9ff.

[36]in the same sense Knuuttila: Remarks..., p.246-250, esp. p.249: "There is [according to Aristotle] no rest in an instant and hence no intrinsic limits of the period of rest."; and Sorabji: Time..., p.412: "Aristotle allows that, when something stops moving, there is a single instant which is both the last of the period during which the object is moving, and the first of the period during which it is resting [...]. And something parallel is true when a thing starts moving. But this does not in the least commit him, as he makes very clear, to saying that this an instant at which the object is moving or resting. [...] Aristotle will say, for reasons similar to those already quoted [...] that there is no first or last instant, nor indeed any instant, at which it is changing colour, or remaining the same colour."

[37]Cf. ch. II,3.

[38]Cf. ch. I,3.4.3.

[39]Sorabji comments (Time..., p.413): "...this is one of the passages where he [Aristotle] does not construe the process as one of white spreading part by part over the surface." I do not think this is so clear. I think that the passage allows to imagine an object which is gradually painted black as well. But nothing really depends on this. Passages like 236a27/b18 show that alterations analogous to gradually being painted white are use by Aristotle in Phys. VI. On the other hand, examples can be found in Aristotle for an alteration happening all at once on the entire surface of an object: Sorabji points towards De Sensu 447a1-3, where Aristotle uses the example of a pond where the whole surface is suddenly frozen after a process of cooling down. A short version of this example also appears in Phys. VIII,3, 253b23/28.

[40]Sorabji writes about this passage: "[Aristotle] switches his example in mid-discussion..." Sorabji: Time..., p.413), but it is difficult to see in which way. Hardie and Gaye drop a λευκόν at 263b23, but this does not really seem to help either.

[41]Hamblin, after an obviously rather cursory reading of the text, really thinks that this is Aristotle's opinion (Cf. 'Instants and Intervals', Studium Generale 24 (1971), p.131: "The best anyone seems to be able to do with the problem [of the moment of change] is to solve it by fiat, by specifying a priori that the instant of change shall be considered as the first instant of the subsequent state, or the last instant of the preceding one: the latter is the traditional solution attributed to Aristotle, based on a reading of Physics 236a7-15. The arbitrary and ad hoc nature of this decision makes it... unsatisfactory...". Detailed discussion of the passage Hamblin mentions in this chapter shows that it is far from presenting an ad-hoc solution.

[42]Sorabji (Time...) and Knuuttila (Remarks...) are of the same opinion. By contrast, M.C. Morkowsky seems to miss Aristotle's motivation in her article 'The Elastic Instant of Aristotle's Becoming and Perishing' (The Modern Schoolman XLVI, March 1969, pp.191-217). During the Middle Ages (cf. ch. I,3) Aristotle's motivation seems to have been rather well understood.

[43]Knuuttila: Remarks..., p.248/249.

[44]Sorabji: Time..., p.410: "...in all four kinds of change [Aristotle thinks to be genuine], he thinks that there is a gradual process of transition [...]. Qualitative change, such as change of colour, is said to take time. Change to a new place or size involves passing through intervening points; the creation of something like a house takes time, and occurs part by part, the foundation before the whole."

[45]ibd. p.411: "...colours [...] and other ranges of sensible qualities have a kind of derivative continuity [...] ... in the case of colour, a change to the next discriminable shade in the discontinuous series of discriminable shades, may be produced by a continuous change in the proportions of earth, air, fire and water in a body."

[46]Not the 'freezing over', because this would suggest an instantaneous event. Cf. 2.6.2.

[47]Knuuttila states that Aristotle's account of substantial change has been a problem among commentators for a long time ('Remarks...' footnotes 23 and 61). He refers to commentaries on

the Physics by Averrroes (32 on book VI), Albert the Great (book VI, tract.2 cap.1) and Aquinas (book VI, lect.5, n.796-805 and 839-40) as well as to an anonymous Paris commentary of 1273 on the Physics (ed. by Albert Zimmermann, Berlin 1968) and to the work 'Theorems of Existence and Essence' by Giles of Rome (ed. by W.V. Murray, Milwaukee 1952).

[48]Knuuttila: Remarks..., pp.246ff.

[49]225b1-3; cf. also 225a26/27, 225a29, 225b10-12. The tenet that there are no degrees of substance is quite compatible with the historically influential view that at the times at which a substance exists it might exist to a lower or higher degree.

[50]'Remarks...' p.246. However, as Knuuttila makes clear, Aristotle does not regard this as an instantaneous *event* (pp.246-48). Cf. on this topic ch.2.6.2.

[51]Cf. 201a9-19.

[52]Phys. IV loc.cit and VII, 249b19-23, Gen. et Cor. 331a22-26.

[53]'Remarks...' p.249.

[54]Cf. The Encyclopaedia of Philosophy, ed. by Paul Edwards (New York 1967 ff.), vol. 5, Article 'Logic' 42b-43a.

[55]Already in late antiquity, Simplicius, in his commentary on the Physics, wonders why Aristotle did not do this although the analogy would have been obvious: Cf. Simplicius: On Aristotle Physics 6, transl. by David Konstan, London 1989, 986,1.

[56]Sorabji: Time..., p.414.

[57]The somewhat indirect translation is necessary in order to account for the aspectual character of the perfect tense here. Details about this in ch. 2.4.2.

[58]It is usually assumed that in the 'essay on time' Phys. IV 10-14, χρόνος means 'time' as an abstract noun, and does not mean 'period'. I am not so sure whether this is correct or whether Aristotle rather has a concrete, though arbitrarily chosen, period in mind. Hussey distinguishes a concrete, a semi-abstract and an abstract use of the word and holds that the essay on time progresses to ever higher abstraction (cf. Aristotle's Physics, translated by Edward Hussey, Oxford 1983, introduction section (c) (xli - xlii) and p.145).

[59]237a7, 237a26, 237b21, 238a14/22, 239a8.

[60]For the formal definition of 'division' cf. introduction 2.

[61]Cf. Ross: Aristotle, London 1923, p.92.

[62]Aristoteles: Physikvorlesung, übersetzt von [transl. by] Hans Wagner, Berlin 1983, appendix (in what follows: Wagner commentary), pp.625ff.

[63]τοιοῦτόν functions here as a double reference. The Loeb edition (Aristotle: The Physics, London 1934 [Cornford/Wicksteed]) has a second πρῶτον in this sentence which I cannot make sense of. The Meiner edition does not have it (Aristoteles' Physikvorlesung, Hamburg 1988 [Zekl]). H/G translate "not because of some part of it". I disagree: ἕτερον τι αὐτου is much more general and has nothing to do with parts.

[64]Met. 1012b31, 1070a1, 1070b35, 1012b7, Phys.243a32, 245a8, 245a25, 256a9, 260a25. Met. 1012b7 contains the idea that a prime mover himself is unmoved. In 1072b30 the prime mover is identified with god.

[65]Met. 1073a14-1074a17.

[66]For the πρῶτον κινοῦν the proximity of the temporal and the hierarchic meaning of πρῶτον has always been clear. Lloyd calls it the "...ambiguity of the term πρῶτον in the key passages, where it may mean either 'first' in a series, or 'prime' in the sense of 'ultimate' ". (G.E.R. Lloyd: Aristotle - The Growth and Structure of his Thought, Cambridge 1982, pp.154f. [first edition 1968]).'Prime mover' is a telling translation here, since 'prime' is always meant in a hierarchic sense (cf. 'Prime Minister'). The hierarchic sense is, of course, suggested

by Aristotle's explanation that the prime mover moves like an object of love or desire (Met. 1072b2: κινεῖ δὲ ὡς ἐρωμένον).

[67]This method is applied for precision's sake. The application of it does not involve any claim that Aristotle is actually working on the analysis-of-language level here. I rather think he is not.

[68]My translation. H/G translate: "Now everything that changes changes in time, and that in two senses may be the primary time, or it may be derivative, as e.g. when we say that a thing changes in a particular year because it changes in a particular day. That being so, that which changes must be changing in any part of the primary time in which it changes." The talk about 'two senses' of 'primary time' suggests a διχῶς which is not in the text. The second sentence is not well understood at all.

[69] Cf. 2.1.§4.

[70]As we have seen in introduction 2, the contrary is typical of statements about events.

[71]M.Th. Liske: Kinesis und Energeia bei Aristoteles, in: Phronesis 199, p.161-178 (esp. p.162).

[72]B3: 238b36/239a2 ὥσπερ δὲ τὸ κινούμενον οὐκ ἐστιν ἐν ᾧ πρώτῳ κινεῖται, οὕτως οὐδ'ἐν ᾧ ἵσταται το ἱστάμενον (And just as there is no primary time in which that which is in motion is in motion, so too there is no primary time in which that which is coming to a stand is coming to a stand). B4: 236α27 οὐκ ἐστι ἐν ᾧ πρώτῳ μεταβέβληκεν (It is evident, then, that there is no primary time in which it has changed).

[73]235b32 ἐν ᾧ δὲ πρώτῳ μεταβέβληκεν τὸ μεταβεβληκός, ἀνάγκη ἄτομον εἶναι - The first [time] in which something can be said to be changed is necessarily indivisible. 236a4 ὥστ' οὐκ ἐν εἴη διαιρετόν ἐν ᾧ μεταβέβληκεν (Now the time primarily in which that which has changed has changed must be indivisible).

[74]Cf. ch. I,1.

[75]239a10/22.

[76]My translation. H/G is not widely different, but I disagree with quite a number of details.

[77]Wagner calls this a 'strictly presentic perfect tense' ('streng präsentisch gemeintes Perfekt' Wagner commentary, p.627). Zekl recalls a parallel dinstinction in grammar which is well-known as the distinction between an ingressive and a perfective aorist (Aristoteles'Physik Bd.2, Hamburg 1988, p.272, endnote 44). This parallel is transferred into the two different meanings of μεταβέβληκεν, since one of them is explained by the ingressive aorist ἤρξατο μεταβάλλειν, while the other is explained by the perfective aorist ἐπετελέσθη ἡ μεταβολή. The method of the proofs in 236a15/27 (B3) and 235b32/236a4 (B4) also suggests that the perfect tense cannot be meant historically here: none of the proofs takes into account the case that both subperiods of a period might satisfy μεταβέβληκεν. However, if the perfect tense had a historical meaning here, this case would have to be considered; only if it refers to the completion of a process is Wagner right in saying that this case is impossible ('keine Denkbarkeit' Wagner commentary, p.626).

[78]Of course, Aristotle does not deny that a motion can begin at all, i.e. that there is a transition from perfect rest to motion (cf.in the same sense: Wagner commentary, p.628).

[79]236a15/27. I am ignoring the strange passage about 'rest at A' (cf. ch. I,2.2.1.(e)).

[80]235b32/336a4.

[81]My translation. Wagner's commentary, pp.626f. Similarly Ross loc.cit.: "An event is in a nest of times as a body is in a nest of places; the death of Cesar took place in March B.C. 44, and also in B.C. 44, and also in the first century B.C. The 'first' time of an event is the time it precisely occupies, its exact or commensurate time." The fact that Wagner uses the example of life and death, which we already know from Aulus Gellius (ch.I,1.4.), is due to his conjecture

that it can also be found in some other ancient statements on the moment of change in Simplicius and Themistius (p.627): "Interessant ist hier ein Exzerpt aus Alexandros bei Simpl[ikios] (938a25ff.) [misprint; correctly: 983,1-25]; es spricht von einer Sophistenfrage: 'In welcher Zeit starb Dion?' Eine Andeutung in gleicher Richtung bei Them[istius] (194.12ff.)". Cf. Simplicius: On Aristotle Physics 6, transl. by David Konstan, London 1989 for a translation of the passage to which Konstan draws attention in his introduction (p.8), too.

[82]On this issue cf. e.g. Ackrill: Aristotle's Distinction between Kinesis and Energeia, M.Th. Liske: Kinesis und Energeia bei Aristoteles, Phronesis (1991), pp.161-181 and Ludger Jansen: Aristotle and the Talk about Events, M. Litt. Thesis [unpublished], St.Andrews 1994.

[83]Liske suggests this (loc.cit). Galton identifies ἐνέργειαι with states and κινήσεις with events. He holds that events are characteristically heterogenous, states are homogenous (see Galton: Logic of Aspect, Introduction). For temporally extended states and events I think that this criterion is plausible. Kienzle and Jansen reject Galton's criterion referring to Aristotle's distinction between κίνησις and ἐνέργεια: As both κίνησις and ἐνέργεια are πρᾶξεις, and as every πρᾶξις is an individual event, but as an ἐνέργεια in contrast to a κίνησις is always homogeneous, there must also be homogeneous events. The conclusion is valid, but I deny the premiss that a πρᾶξις is always an event. A πρᾶξις such as 'enjoying the magnificent view' (= ἐνέργεια, in contrast to 'scanning the hills from East to West' = κίνησις) does not seem to me to be an individual event but rather a state. I would answer the counter-objection that a specific action is just the prototype of an event by saying that πρᾶξις should not be translated by 'specific action' then, but just by 'a case of (human) action/acting'. 'Enjoying the magnificent view' may not be a specific *action*, but it certainly is a case of *acting*. Cf.: Ludger Jansen loc.cit. and Bertram Kienzle: Ereignislogik, in: Bertram Kienzle (ed.): Zustand und Ereignis, pp.413-469 (cf. footnote 9, p.417).

[84]Knuuttila refers to this passage in 'Remarks ...'. He interprets it as a passage showing that Plotinus agrees with Plato on assuming the existence of instantaneous events. I do not think that this is very clear in that passage but it is quite possible to read it so. Knuuttila does not elaborate on the connection of the passage with Aristotle's 'Physics' although it contains a literal quotation from the 'Physics'.

[85]Translation: A.H.Armstrong (Loeb edition of Plotinus' works vol. vi).

[86]Following the Loeb edition. Some manuscripts have ἀναλογία, which does not make much sense, since it is difficult to see what is to be compared to what here.

[87] He might just as well have referred to De sensu 446 or to Phys. 253b23, where Aristotle gives the example of the freezing pond.

[88]Cf. Liske loc. cit. and above 2.4.2.

[89]In this sense also Knuuttila: Remarks...p.246.

[90]This is one of the rare passages where ἐν ᾧ is not meant temporally (cf. also Zekl's translation in: Aristoteles' Physik, Hamburg (Meiner) 1988).

[91]This is not quite so clear for Physics VIII. There Aristotle writes about the instantaneous freezing of the pond (253b25). Zekl is right in commenting (Aristoteles'Physik, Hamburg 1988, p.284): "...das will nicht ganz zur Kontinuitätslehre des Z [VI. Buches] passen." ("This does not really fit the doctrine of continuity expressed in Physics VI").

[92]Kretzmann: Incipit/Desinit, p.115.

[93]Ibid., p.102.

CHAPTER 3 - MIDDLE AGES

[1]Curtis Wilson: William Heytesbury, Madison (Wisconsin) 1956. Norman Kretzmann: Incipit/Desinit in : Machamer/Turnbull (eds.): Motion and Time, Space and Matter, Columbus (Ohio) 1976. I have tried to work with the original texts as far as possible. This was

facilitated by a lot of excellent editing work in recent years. Wherever the texts were edited and accessible I found Kretzmann's and especially Wilson's summaries to be reliable. A very helpful article for putting the medieval texts in a broader perspective is Knuuttilas 'Remarks...'. A good short introduction to the medieval treatment of beginnings and endings from a formal point of view is found in Peter Øhrstrøm: Temporal Logic - From Ancient Ideas to Artificial Intelligence, Dordrecht 1995. Another interesting introductory study is J.E. Murdoch's 'Propositional Analysis in Fourteenth Century Natural Philosophy' (Synthese 40, 1979, p.117-146). Knuttila/Lehtinen 'Change and Contradiction: A fourteenth century controversy' (Synthese 40 - 1979 - p.189-207) is occupied with a 'counter-current', not with the 'mainstream' of medieval texts on the moment of change. I refer to it in ch. I, 3.4.

[2]Kretzmann and Wilson differ on this point. Cf. Kretzmann: Incipit/Desinit, p.103-105.

[3]Kretzmann: Incipit/Desinit, p.105.

[4]Averroes' remarks on the moment of change are in his commentary on Aristotle's Physics VI, sections 40-46. A detailed discussion of them is provided by Knuuttila in: Remarks..., pp.254-256. Text: Aristotelis Opera cum Averrois Commentariis, Venetiis apud Junctas 1562-1574, reprint Frankfurt 1962.

[5]Cf. Knuuttila: Remarks..., p.257. The relevant remarks are in: Albertus Magnus [Albert the Great] Physicorum libri VIII (in: Opera omnia, ed. A.Borgnet Vivès., Paris 1890), commentary on book VI, tractatus 2, ch.4.

[6]Ibd. The relevant text is Aquinas' commentary on Physics VI (Torino 1954), lectio 7, 822 and lectio 8, 838.

[7]Cf. Knuuttila/Lehtinen: Change..., pp.191f.

[8]Walter Burleigh [also: Burley]: De primo et ultimo instanti, ed. by Herman and Charlotte Shapiro, Archiv für Geschichte der Philosophie 47 (1966), p.157-173.

[9]Concerning John of Holland and Wiliam Heytesbury cf. Wilson: William Heytesbury, pp.34ff.

[10]William of Ockham: Summa Logicae part I, 75 and especially part II, 19.

[11]Text in Nielsen op. cit.

[12]These two examples are counted as the most frequently treated sophisms containing 'incipit' and desinit' by Andrea Tabarroni. They appear as early as in Peter of Spain or in Matthew of Orléans. Cf. A. Tabarroni: 'incipit' and 'desinit' in a thirteenth century sophismata-collection, Cahiers de l'institut du moyen-âge grec et latin [CIMAGL] 59 (1989), pp.61-111 (p.78). More sophisms on the topic are edited in the same volume of CIMAGL by Alain de Libera (Le sophisma anonyme 'Sor desinit esse non desinendo esse' du Cod. Parisianus 16135, pp.113-120) and by Sten Ebbsen ('Three 13th century sophismata about beginning and ceasing', pp.121-180). Cf. also Alain de Libera: La problematique de l'instant du changement au 13me siècle: contribution à l'histoire des 'sophismata physicalia', in: S.Caroti: Studies in Medieval Natural Philosophy, Firenze 1989. An impressive formal reconstruction of some sophisms of this kind is found in Øhrstrøm, p.52-64.

[13]The Sophismata of Richard Kilvington, Introduction, translation and commentary by Norman and Barbara Kretzmann, Cambridge 1990. Examples for the kind of sophismata in Kilvington are: Socrates is whiter than Plato begins to be white (No 1), Socrates is infinitely whiter than Plato begins to be white (No 2), Socrates begins to be whiter than Plato begins to be white (No 3), Socrates will begin to be as white as he himself will be white. Cf. also Norman Kretzmann: Socrates is whiter than Plato begins to be white, Nous 11 (1977), pp.7-15.

[14]It is important to note in this context that most of the peculiar features of the Greek verb aspect do not translate into Latin.

[15]An important exception is Walter Burleigh's 'De primo et ultimo instanti'. This text is not formulated in terms of the analysis-of-language level about 'incipit' and 'desinit' statements but directly about first and last instants. In this way the motivation is very clear and there is room

for direct proofs with dense time, which are very good. Burleigh gives an account on the analysis-of-language level in his 'De puritate artis Logicae' (ed. by Ph. Boehner, Louvain 1951) in the chapter 'incipit et desinit'. Lauge O. Nielsen correctly recognizes that not only the form but also the contents of the two texts considerably differ in detail (L.O. Nielsen: Thomas Bradwardine's treatise on 'incipit' and 'desinit', edition and introduction, Cahiers de l'institut du Moyen-Age grec et latin 42 (1982) [Copenhague], p.1-83; cf. p.17.)

[16]Knuuttila: Remarks..., p.254; Sorabji: Time..., p.419 and esp. Kretzmann: Incipit/Desinit, pp.133f. (footnote 32). According to Kretzmann the most important passage in Aristotle for this context is Cat.6, 5a15-37.

[17]A tractatus exponibilium, sometimes attributed to Peter of Spain, differs in an interesting respect. Its author characterizes res permanentes as objects "quarum totum esse *acquiritur* simul in instanti", i.e. which acquire their whole being at a single instant. He characterizes res successivae as such objects "quarum esse acquiritur successive et pars post partem", i.e. which acquire their being part by part. His examples are unusual, too: for rather odd reasons 'white' and 'black' are declared to be res successivae. Kretzmann thinks that the attribution to Peter of Spain is incorrect (Kretzmann: Incipit/Desinit, p.133, footnote 26 and p.134, footnote 39). Text: The Summulae Logicales of Peter of Spain, ed. by Joseph P. Mullally, Notre Dame/Indiana 1945, p.114-117.

[18]Wilson: Heytesbury, pp.32f. A revival of this seems to be the classification into 'endurers' and 'non-endurers' as made in Harold W. Noonan: Personal Identity, New York 1991.

[19]In what follows I will use this plural. It seems to me correct because 'res' is feminine. Wilson, during English text, uses 'res permanentia' (cf. e.g. p.34), obviously taking 'res' to be neuter. I think he is wrong there.

[20]Walter Burleigh: De Puritate Artis Logicae (Tractatus Brevior), Section 'De incipit et Desinit' (quoted according to the edition by Ph. Boehner, Franciscan Institute Publications, St. Bonaventure/Louvain 1951, p.59.

[21]This example is found in the Summulae Logicales (p.114/115 Mullally-edition) wrongly attributed to Peter of Spain, in Peter of Spain's 'Syncategoreumata' (ed. by L.M. de Rijk, transl. by J.Spruyt, Leiden 1992, p.250/251; cf. also Kretzmann: Incipit/Desinit, p.122) as well as in Peter of Mantua (Wilson: Heytesbury, p.37).

[22]Cf. ch.I 2.2.1.

[23]William of Sherwood: Tractatus Syncategorematum, transl. by Norman Kretzmann as Treatise on Syncategorematic Words, Minneapolis 1968, p.109. Latin text: William of Sherwood, 'Syncategoremata', ed. by J.R. O'Donnell, in: Medieval Studies vol. 3 (1941), pp.46-93.

[24]E.g. in Walter Burleigh: De Puritate..., p.61; Bradwardine, p.77.

[25]William of Sherwood: Tractatus..., p.109.

[26]Burleigh: De Puritate..., p.61; William of Sherwood: Tractatus..., p.110.

[27]Peter of Spain: Syncategoreumata, p.257/258. Cf. also Kretzmann: Incipit/Desinit, p.124. Summulae Logicales, p.116/117.

[28]William of Sherwood: Tractatus..., p.109.

[29]One wonders whether there might not also be something 'in' which Socrates exists. Spinoza's bold answer a few centuries later was: "Yes. God/the universe/Substance". As is clearly seen, this may be a big leap for a metaphysician but it is only a small step for a logician.

[30]Apart from these rather fundamental problems, there is the rather more theory-immanent problem that it is difficult to see why 'whiteness' or 'being well' should be 'res permanentes'. One can hardly say that 'all their parts exist at the same time'. For it is difficult to see what, for instance, the parts of 'being well' might be. The problem could be alleviated by regarding the definition of 'res successiva' as the crucial one and regarding as 'res permanens' simply

what is not covered by the definition of 'res successiva', no matter if this is the case as its parts exist simultaneously or rather because it lacks parts altogether. This seems to be the line taken by Burleigh in 'De primo et ultimo instanti' where an example for a 'res permanens' is the truth of the statement "Sortes currit" (p.164). Burleigh's reason is that the truth of a statement, unlike the succession of words in it, is a quality which is wholly there at once: "veritas est qualitas propositionis qu[a]e habet esse tota simul". This clearly means no more than that there are no consecutive parts of the truth of a statement, but does not imply that the truth of a statement has any parts.

[31]Doing so amounts to thinking in the manner of predicate logic. However, one should be aware of the fact that this habit is an exact mirror-image of the medieval logicians' habit of thinking. *Cum grano salis* one can say that medieval logic turns everything into nouns (even words for colours); predicate logic turns everything into adjectives (since Quine even proper names).

[32]This is stated in order to facilitate the definition of the State-prefix in what follows. It would be possible, but more complicated, to work with constant target and starting positions.

[33]'Referring to' here indicates the relation which holds, e.g., between the property of being white and the predicate "...is-white". F and P are meta-language variables.

[34]Mind that F might stand for the predicate "...is a time at which Socrates exists". This is, however, no existence-predicate; for it is possible to define it in a Quinean manner by saying that it is satisfied by a time iff there is something at this time which socratizes.

[35]The example is rendered in Wilson: Heytesbury (p.34).

[36]I have taken the expression 'in the course of' in this context from Sorabji: Time...p.408 (footnote 9). A similar view to that of John of Holland seems to be expressed in Burleigh's 'De primo et ultimo instanti' (p.173, point (8)). The point Burleigh makes here is rather complicated, but it is clear enough that Burleigh presupposes that there are instants of motion ("de re successiva bene tenet quod si haberet esse in instanti, habet esse in quolibet instanti ilius temporis in quo est primo [...] si motus, vel quelibet res successiva, habet esse in instanti, instans esset pars temporis.")

[37]Cf. the summaries in Wilson: Heytesbury, p.33-44, esp. his evaluation on p.44 and Kretzmann: Incipit/Desinit, p.111 as well as Sorabji: Time..., p.419.

[38]There are some (as a rule, early) authors who work with discrete time, especially when dealing with sophisms. This becomes clear because they use phrases like 'paenultimum instans' which make sense only for discrete time. For example, this phrase appears in an anonymous English 13th century sophisma edited by Ebbesen (cf. p.123) and in Henry of Ghent (cf.ibid. p.126; text also in M. Braakhuis: 'De 13de Eeuwse Tractaten over Syncategorematische Termen, vols. 1-2, Leiden 1979). The phrase also appears in William of Sherwood (Tractatus, p.114); cf. ibid. Kretzmann's footnote 12. The most detailed reconstruction of treating the moment of change with a discrete model is in Øhrstrøm loc. cit. Øhrstrøm mentions Richard Lavenham as an author in whose work a growing awareness of continuous time can be studied (op.cit. p.56). Dense time is also explicitly argued for in connection with the moment of change in Peter of Auvergne's sophisma VII (edited in Ebbesen loc. cit, cf. pp.168f).

[39]Cf. p.166 of the Shapiro edition. Burleigh gives explicit rules for the assignment of limiting instants since, as mentioned, his treatise is not formulated on the analysis-of-language-level.

[40]Cf. Shapiro edition, p.163.

[41]Cf. Burleigh: De puritate..., p.62 line 8-11.

[42]Kretzmann conjectures that motivation for not allowing last instants of any states whatsoever is that a putative last instant t cannot be identified as a last instant at t already, as one can only say after t that t was in fact the last instant of the state in question. If, however, t is the first instant of a state, it can already be identified as such at t (Kretzmann:

Incipit/Desinit, pp.112f). I agree with Sorabji that this epistemological motivation is rather weak (cf. Sorabji: Time..., p.419). I think much stronger motivation could be inferred from what I take to be Aristotle's view on substantial change: perishing is a process towards the end of existence of an object while this object still exists and of which there is no last instant. It terminates in a first instant of an object's non-existence. Nielsen holds a similar view (cf. Nielsen, p.22). It is a little puzzling that Kretzmann and Sorabji discuss the point by referring to Peter of Spain. According to the critical edition of his 'Syncategoreumata' Peter seems to take the opposite view that there are in fact last instants of 'res permanentes' (cf. 5 on pp.252f).

[43]Sorabji writes that this motivation is made explicit in Walter Burleigh's 'De primo et ultimo instanti', which he takes to be the best medieval text on the moment of change. He is sceptical whether other authors' opinions are as clearly motivated as Walter's or whether they just follow a more or less Aristotelian tradition. Sorabji: Time..., p.419. It is true that it is hard to see what else might have motivated those philosophers who took time to be discrete (for example William of Sherwood) to assign limiting instants in the way they did. Of course there then arises the question (to which I have no answer) of why someone who is acquainted with the 'Physics' would ever take time to be discrete in the first place.

[44]Shapiro edition, p.166.

[45]It is important to notice that i) to iv) are implications and not equivalences. They can be turned into equivalences by asssuming the existence of a limiting instant in dense time, or by assuming that time is continuous (which is a stronger claim than that time is dense). Details in appendix C.

[46]Cf. Wilson: Heytesbury, pp.39f and the Mulally edition of 'Summulae logicales'.

[47]Burleigh: De puritate..., pp.59ff.

[48]Cf. John Le Page: Syncategoremata, partially edited in Braakhuis op. cit., pp.198f. Cf. on this topic Tabarroni op. cit. p.75.

[49]Edited in Ebbesen op. cit. Cf. p.158: "nunc autem tempus vitae Socratis est terminatum ad dua instantia, primum et ultimum; est ergo dare ultimum instans vitae Socratis, et in illo instanti vivit..." (Socrates' lifetime is limited by two instants, a first and a last one; so there is a last instant of Socrates' life, and at it he is still alive).

[50]Peter of Spain: Syncategoreumata, pp.253-55 (cf. also Wilson: Heytesbury, pp.38f). William of Sherwood: Tractatus..., p.110.

[51]Cf. Tabarroni, p.75.

[52]This is also exactly Galton's characterization of a 'momentary event'. Cf. ch.II,1.

[53]Cf.Wilson: Heytesbury, p.33, Burleigh: De primo et ultimo instanti, p.164, 167, 169. Burleigh: De puritate...p.62 (In 'De puritate...' instantaneous 'res permanentes' become an exception to the rule as they have a last instant of existence).

[54]Burleigh: De primo et ultimo instanti, p.165; cf. also Wilson: Heytesbury, pp.33-35. Kilvington must have held a similar view. In sophisma No 1 he plausibly renders a process of becoming white by 'remotio prasenti' plus 'positio futuris' (he does not allow himself to be confused by the fact that white is a 'res permanens').

[55]Cf. Wilson loc. cit.

[56]For the differences between Burleigh I and Burleigh II compare also Nielsen op.cit. pp.17f. By keeping Burleigh I and Burleigh II apart I do not want to claim that 'De puritate...' is the earlier work. In fact, according to Nielsen's view, it must be the later work. However, I would claim that the view of 'De primo et ultimo instanti' is more progessive and more differentiated. Perhaps Burleigh even chose a simpler version for his elementary logic textbook than for his specialists' treatise.

[57]Guillelmi de Ockham Summa Logicae, St.Bonaventure, N.Y. 1974, pp.310f (Pars II,Cap.19).

[58]Sorabji: Time..., p.418/419. Ockham's earlier treatment of 'incipit' and 'desinit' in Summa I,75 is no better than II,19 in this respect, since it is not occupied with assigning limiting instants at all, but with the question to what kind of 'suppositio' incipit- and desinit-statements belong. I shall not consider this point. Details are found in Nielsen's introduction to Bradwardine. Nielsen convincingly argues that Ockham changed his view on the supposition question between writing I,75 and II,19 because of Bradwardine's explicit criticism (found on pp.74f). Interestingly, Ockham's very simple suggestion is the revival of some earlier authors' views, which is called the (outdated) 'expositio communis' by John Le Page (Cf. John Le Page: Syncategoramata in: Braakhuis, pp.198. Cf. also Tabarroni, p.75). The opposite, equally over-simplified view that there are neither first nor last instants whatsoever is found in Matthew of Orléans (cf. Tabarroni, p.77).

[59]For a discussion of this point I am grateful to Simo Knuuttila who, if I remember correctly, agreed that rest was usually regarded as a 'res successiva' as well as motion. Kretzmann thinks so too ('Incipit/Desinit' cf. p.114).

[60]While I think that Kretzmann is wrong in claiming that Aristotle favoured a 'Neutral Instant Analysis' for the s-change between rest and motion, I agree with him that most medieval logicians did (cf. Kretzmann: Incipit/Desinit, p.114).

[61]Phys.VIII 264a27.

[62]Cf. Wilson: Heytesbury, p.34.

[63]E.g. Walter Burleigh in 'De primo et ultimo instanti', cf. esp. p.163. Cf. also Peter of Spain: Tractatus syncategorematum, translated in: Kretzmann: Incipit/Desinit, p.123: "...permanent things are intrinsically limited while successive things are not limited intrinsically but limited by permanent things - for example a change is limited by a quantity or a quality." (res permanentes sunt in se terminate, sed res successive non habent in se terminos ut motus qui terminatur ad res permanentes, ut alteratio ad qualitatem, augmentum ad diminutio ad quantitatem, critical edition, pp.250f). Peter's detailed analysis of 'res permanentes' follows further down in his text; as we have seen, it is a little more complicated than he states in these introductory remarks.

[64]Wilson: Heytesbury, p.38.

[65]Cf. esp. William of Sherwood: Tractatus..., p.110.

[66]As I will show in ch. II,1 Antony Galton is a most radical contemporary advocate of reading the present tense of 'begins' atemporally: he combines the idea that a begins to be F in the course of the history of the world with the idea that it does not do so at any time.

[67]Ockham: Summa..., pars II, Cap. 19 (p.311).

[68]The awareness that sentences are true with respect to times is, incidentally, once again a remarkable anticipation of Prior's ideas.

[69]According to Wilson: Heytesbury, p.42, William Heytesbury is criticised for this by Peter of Mantua and Gaetano de Thiene. The argument in which their criticism consists is also found in a text of Johannes Venator (died c.1427) rendered by Kretzmann in 'Incipit/Desinit' p.128-130 (Logica, Tractatus III, Cap.6). Another indication that 'incipit' should be read temporally is found in Peter of Spain: " 'incipit' et 'desinit' sunt presentis temporis" (Syncategoreumata, p.254/5, cf. also Kretzmann op.cit. p.125). In Walter Burleigh's 'De Puritate Artis Logicae (Tractatus Brevior)' we find the opinion that both analyses are equally correct alongside the opinion that one has to decide on one analysis according to 'res permanens' or 'res successiva': "Sortes incipit esse albus' potest dupliciter exponi...uno modo per negationem praesentis et positionem praeteriti... alio modo per positionem praesentis et negationem futuri" (p.60). "Sed 'incipit' in successivis et permanentibus aliter et aliter debet exponi, secundum quod propositiones sunt verae in permanentibus per positionem praesentis et negationem praeteriti. Sed in successivis debet exponi per negationem praesentis et positionem futuri." (p.61). Since the second opinion is very well motivated in the text, I assume

that the first opnion is just meant as a working hypothesis in the sense of "According to what has been said so far, one might think that...".

[70]Cf. William of Sherwood: Tractatus..., p.109/110 and Wilson: Heytesbury, pp.38f. I do not agree with Kretzmann (footnote 12, p.109 of his translation). It is important to note that the point at stake is not at all influenced by the fact that William works with discrete time while most other logicians later on do not.

[71]Annotation for experts in tense logic: A Priorian notation for (1a') would be 'p ∧ P¬p', for (1a') 'p ∧ ¬Pp' or 'p ∧ H¬p'; for (3b') '¬q ∧ Fq' and for (3b') '¬q ∧ Gq'. A notation for (3b') in the manner of v.Wright would be '¬qTq'. All formulas would have to be interpreted for t while p stands for 'a is white' and q stands for 'a is in the course of moving'. 'pTq' is true at t iff p is true at t and there is a t' > t, such that q is true at t'. This is the semantics of the T-operator as v.Wright introduces it in ch. 2 of 'Norm and Action' and in 'And Then' (p and q are so-called 'generic propositions' which are false and true relative to times).

[72]Ockham: Summa... Pars II, Cap.19 (p.311).

[73]In my view, Ockham is correctly referring to 222a20/21.

[74]Ockham loc. cit.

[75]E.g. Bradwardine's treatise on 'incipit' and 'desinit' and Kilvington's 'sophismata'.

[76]Ockham, Summa... II,19.

[77]Wilson: Heytesbury, p.42.

[78]Kilvington comes very close to it in sophisma 16 at the beginning point (c). In fact he seems to use Paul's definiens. But the connection with the word 'immediate' is not explicit yet.

[79]Paulus Venetus: Logica, p.107. Perreiah translates the sentence (p.203): " 'before A you were and there was no instant before A unless between that and a you were' [...] 'no instant will be after B unless between that and B you will be' ". Wilson, who (p.42) points out Paul's merits for our topic, translates: " 'prior to a you existed and there was no instant prior to a such that between that instant and a you did not exist' [...] 'after instant b you will exist, and there will be no instant after b such that between that and b you will not exist' ".

[80]For this term also cf. the discussion of Kienzle in ch. II,1.

[81]If this were the case, it would be incomprehensible why Paul analyses 'immediate' in this sense directly after having dealt at length with examples involving oscillation on the preceding pages.

[82]It is easy to see that ImmP-P(t) implies P-P(t) and that ImmF-P(t) implies F-P(t).

[83]The following quotations are all from pp.60-62 of Walter Burleigh's 'De puritate...'

[84]On the assumption that a limiting instant exists. This would be entailed by presupposing continuous time.

[85]Explicitly so in William of Sherwood's Tractatus..., p.110. This is especially interesting since William takes time to be discrete, so that one might expect him to prefer a solution similar to Strang instead (cf. ch. I,1.3.2. (b)).

[86]Cf. Simo Knuuttila/Anja Inkeri Lehtinen: Change and Contradiction: A Fourteenth Century Controversy, Synthese 40 (1979), pp.189-207 and Knuuttila: Remarks...

[87]Knuuttila/Lehtinen: p.190. See esp. the quotation from Carracioli in footnote 5, p.200.

[88]Knuuttila/Lehtinen: Change..., pp.195f.

[89]I follow Knuuttila/Lehtinen: Change..., p.194. cf. also the quote from Carracioli at the very beginning of Knuuttila: Remarks..., p.245.

[90]Knuuttila/Lehtinen: Change..., p.194: "In this solution a real contradiction is accepted in nature, because the termini of instantaneous change cannot, according to it, belong to different instants of time."

CHAPTER 4 - KANT, MENDELSSOHN, SCHOPENHAUER

[1]Concerning the history of the 'Phädon' cf. the introduction of vol. III,1 (Schriften zur Philosophie und Ästhetik bearbeitet von Fritz Bamberger und Leo Strauss) in the edition of Gesammelte Schriften [collected writings of] von Moses Mendelssohn, Berlin 1932. The 'Phädon' is contained in this volume on pp.5-129. I have kept to the 18th century spelling of this edition.

[2]Mendelssohn: Phädon, p.62.

[3]Ibid.

[4]Ibid., p.63: "So müssen die stets wirksamen Kräfte der Natur schon vorher an dieser Veränderung gearbeitet, und den vorhergehenden Zustand gleichsam mit dem zukünftigen beschwängert haben."

[5]Die "Augenblicke der Zeit [folgen] in einer stätigen Ordnung aufeinander"(p.65). "Es giebt keine zwey Augenblicke, die sich einander die nächsten sind" (Ibid.).

[6]Cf. esp. p.66 point 4 of Socrates' summary of the first result.

[7]Ibid., p.69.

[8]Ibid.

[9]Ibid., p.68.

[10]Ibid. The simple present tense 'dies' sounds rather odd here. The German 'stirbt' does not sound quite so odd, because German does not distinguish between verb aspects. German grammar does not commit Mendelssohn to any precision here. So I cannot translate the text any more accurately than it was written. One might try 'is dying', 'has (just) died' or 'is (just) dead' instead.

[11]Ibid., p.69.

[12]Cf.ibid.

[13]Ibid., p.67.

[14]Ibid.

[15]Ibid.

[16]Ibid., p.69.

[17]Ibid., p.70.

[18]Ibid.

[19]Ibid., pp.70f.

[20]Ibid., pp.71-73.

[21]Ibid., p.71.

[22]Ibid., p.72.

[23]Ibid., pp.72f.

[24]Ibid., p.73.

[25]Critique of pure reason B 413.

[26]Translation by Norman Kemp Smith, in: Immanuel Kant's Critique of Pure Reason tr. by N. Kemp Smith, London 1929.

[27]Ibid.

[28]Ibid.

[29]Mendelssohn: Phädon, p.71.

[30]Ibid., p.72: "So lange der Körper gesund ist, [...] so besitzt auch die Seele ihre völlige Kraft, empfindet, denkt, liebet, verabscheuet, begreift und will. [...] Der Leib wird krank. [...] Und die Seele? Wie die Erfahrung lehret wird sie indessen schwächer, empfindet

unordentlich, denkt falsch und handelt öfters wider ihren Dank. Der Leib stirbt. [...] aber innerlich mögen wohl noch einige schwache Lebensbewegungen vorgehen, die der Seele noch einige dunkele Vorstellungen verschaffen: Auf diese muß sich also die Kraft der Seele so lange einschränken."

[31]Ibid., p.72.

[32]Ibid., pp.72f.

[33]Ibid., p.73.

[34]Brentano: Kategorienlehre, Hamburg 1976, pp.92f (Text 4: Kants Intensitätslehre, 20. April 1916).

[35]Translation by Roderick Chisholm; cf. his 'Beginnings and Endings', pp.23f.

[36]Cf. also a similar section in the Inaugural-Dissertation of 1770, SectioIII, §14 'De tempore'. Kant is probably following Leibniz' law of continuity (Nouveaux Essais IV,16): "Tout va par degrès dans la nature et rien par saut, et cette règle à l'égard des changements est une partie de ma loi de la continuité."

[37]Arthur Schopenhauer: Über die vierfache Wurzel des Satzes vom zureichenden Grunde, second edition §25: 'Die Zeit der Veränderung' .

[38]Ibid., p.118. The quotation appears without accents in the original.

[39]My translation.

[40]This reproach can only be made if χρόνος is translated by 'instant'.

[41]Ibid., p.118.

[42]Ibid., p.119.

[43]Ibid.

[44]Ibid.

[45]Ibid.

[46]Ibid.

PART II
CHAPTER 1 - EITHER/OR-OPTION

[1]In the first version of his article 'Aristotle on the Instant of Change', Sorabji still views his own suggestion as an interpretation of the relevant passages in Aristotle. The reason for this is that in this version he favours the opinion that Aristotle allowed talk of rest and motion at instants. He abandoned this position in the second and third version (ch.26 of 'Time...').

[2]Sorabji: Time..., p.405.

[3]Ibid., pp.406f.

[4]Sorabji: Aristotle... [second version], p.72.

[5]Ibid.:"We must make a recommendation [...] It would be reasonable but not mandatory. Reasonableness is all we need in order to escape the charge of arbitrariness."

[6]Ibid.

[7]Sorabji: Time..., pp.405f.

[8]Moody shows that the concept of momentary velocity developed gradually in the late Middle Ages and was by no means a sudden revolution brought about by a few Renaissance physicists. Of special importance were the contributions of some logicians of Merton College, Oxford, among them Willam Heytesbury. Cf. Ernest A. Moody: Laws of Motion in Medieval Physics, in: Studies in Medieval Philosophy, Science and Logic, Collected Papers 1933-1969, University of California Press, Berkeley 1975, pp.189-201.

⁹Frank Jackson/Robert Pargetter: A Question about Rest and Motion, in: Philosophical Studies 53 (1988), pp.141-146.

¹⁰Cf. Ibid., p.143, point (vi).

¹¹Ibid., p.142.

¹²Ibid., p.144.

¹³Ibid., p.141.

¹⁴Jackson/Pargetter are right in remarking (p.141): "We might have specified X's position over time by : s=0 for t ≤ 0, s=t for t > 0. This specification and the original one are precisely equivalent. They put X in exactly the same positions at the same times."

¹⁵Ibid., p.144.

¹⁶Ibid.

¹⁷Ibid., p.146.

¹⁸Definition: An object a moves 'uniformly' throughout a period c iff the proportion of the distance covered by a in c to the duration of c equals the proportion of the distance covered by a in any subperiod c_1 of c to the duration of c_1, or (which amounts to the same) the local function of a is linear with respect to the interval of all instants which fall within c.

¹⁹In this case the proportion of the distance covered in c to the duration of c does not equal the proportion of the distance covered in any subperiod c_1 of c to the duration of c_1 and the local function of a is not linear with respect to the interval of all instants which fall within c.

²⁰Jackson/Pargetter, p.141.

²¹The question also arises whether the importance of the difference between abrupt and smooth change of 'momentary velocity' might not be exaggerated if it is assigned such a crucial role for the description of the moment of change. This difference does not seem to have anything to do with the questions from which philosophers started out (Plato and Aristotle had no idea of this difference). That it might be problematic to lay very strong emphasis on this difference can be seen in Chris Mortensen's 'The Limits of Change' (Australasian Journal of Philosophy, March 1985, Vol. 63 No.1, pp.1-10). It contains valuable criticism of other authors on the moment of change; and this initially appears to be the article's intended theme. However unfortunately then Mortensen becomes hopelessly entangled in the question "Is Change Continuous?" without thereby obtaining any result about the moment of change.

²²Peter Thomas Geach: God and the Soul, London 1969, pp.71f.

²³Betrand Russell: The Principles of Mathemathics, London 1964 (first edition 1903), §442.

²⁴Ibid.

²⁵Cf.Geach: God and the Soul, pp.91, 99. This criticism is the core of a debate about how one might amend the Cambridge-Criterion in such a way that the difference between mere 'relational change' on the one hand and 'real change' on the other hand is reflected by it. In my view, all attempts to do so have shown no more than that Russell's original formula is inadequate for this (this is also Geach's opinion in loc.cit.). Cf. for this debate Carol Cleland: The Difference between mere Cambridge Change and Real Change, in: Philosophical Studies 60 (3), Nov. 1990, pp.257ff.; Paul Helm: Are Cambridge Changes Non-Events?, in: Analysis 1975, pp.140-144; and: Zum Problem der Veränderung und ihrer Feststellung, in: Ratio 14 (Nov. 1977), pp.35-39; Frederick Schmitt: Change, in: Philosophical Studies 34 (1978); P.T. Smith: On the applicability of a criterion for change, in: Ratio 15 (1973), pp.312-319.

²⁶A.J. Ayer, Russell and Moore - The Analytical Heritage, London 1971, p.17.

²⁷Peter Thomas Geach: Truth, Love and Immortality, London 1979, p.91.

²⁸V.Wright introduced the T-operator in his article 'And next' for discrete time (Acta Philosophica Fennica Bd. 18, 1965, p.293-304), for continuous time in 'And then' (Commentationes Physico-Mathematicae of the Finnish Society of Sciences, vol. 32, No 7,

1966). The discrete version is of no interest here. A very readable introduction about the T-operator is ch.2 of his 'Norm and Action' (London 1963). The T-operator also plays an important role in 'Time, Change and Contradiction' (Philosophical Papers vol. 2, London 1983).

[29]V.Wright calls the propositions which the T-operator takes 'generic propositions'. They are, as his description makes clear, just what is usually called 'temporally indefinite propositions'. v.Wright has a very complicated classification of propositions according to the kinds of facts they reflect, which I shall neglect here.

[30]According to Galton, both statements have logically nothing in common with the sentence 'I write a book'.

[31]The examples are all taken from the introduction to Galton's 'Logic of Aspect'; for an impression of how event logic works one should read at least the first three chapters of it.

[32]Galton: The Logic of Aspect, pp.5f.

[33]This might mean a lot of things: is it taking place if I do not finish the book? Is it taking place during my coffee break? Galton tries to catch the various possible meanings of 'is just taking place' in the last chapters of 'The Logic of Aspect' by different versions of Prog. We can neglect those (otherwise important) details here.

[34]I am grateful to Bertram Kienzle for suggesting this expression (German: 'Präsenslücke').

[35]Galton: The Logic of Aspect, p.5.

[36]Ibid., p.15. There is obviously some sort of parallel here between 'event' and 'res successiva' as well as between 'state' and 'res permanens'. Galton himself draws a connection between 'event' and κίνησις as well as between 'state' and ενέργεια (which I find less convincing).

[37]Ibid., p.18.

[38]One should note that Galton views the state/event-dichotomy not as an ontological difference but as a difference in describing the world: "The main difference between these two ways of presenting the situation is that in presenting it as an event we regard Jane's swimming as a unitary whole with a definite beginning (when she starts swimming) and a definite end (when she stops), wheras if we present it as a state we do not treat it in this way." (Galton: The Logic of Aspect, p.24).

[39]It is quite surprising that the first operator which Galton introduces deals with a kind of event which is untypical and does not agree with the intuition concerning events from which Galton originally motivated his project.

[40]Ibid., p.61.

[41](Def. P*) P*α = $\alpha \vee$ Pα. (Def F*) F*α = $\alpha \vee$ Fα.

[42]Galton: The Logic of Aspect, p.50.

[43]Ibid., p.33. Galton provides a second argument as to why a '¬p/p-change' must be 'instantaneous': "...although the change can only be located within an interval, and not at a moment, it is still an instantaneous change because there is no lower limit to the length of intervals which contain it." (Logic of Aspect, p.34). This is rather cryptic. Galton's reasoning seems to be: 'Instantaneous' means 'has no duration'. Whatever has a duration must have a definite duration by 'filling' a certain interval. But for any interval in dense time which contains a change there is another interval which is shorter and contains the change, too. So an interval which contains a change may be chosen to be arbitrarily short. An interval which is to contain an event of definite duration cannot be chosen to be arbitrarily short. Therefore a change has no duration, but is instantaneous. This reasoning is definitely weaker than the first one. Kienzle is right in criticizing: "Da er [Galton] die Instantaneität eines Wahrheitswertwechsels [...] damit erläutert, daß die Länge der Intervalle, die ihn enthalten, keine untere Grenze haben [...], sollte man eigentlich annehmen, daß sie von Null verschieden

ist." ("Since Galton explains the instantaneity of a truth-value change [.. by saying that] that there is no limit as to the shortness of intervals which contain it, [...] one should expect it to be greater than zero.) Cf.Bertram Kienzle: Cambridge-Wechsel, Prima Philosophia 1991, p.108).

[44]Ibid., p.100.

[45]It is important to remember that combining version C of the logical reconstruction, which avoids a violation of the LEM, with Plato-1 does not make any sense.

[46]Galton: The Logic of Aspect, p.34. Similar, but also similarly unclear: v.Wright's treatment of change taking place "...at the 'point of division'...during the interval in question" (Time, Change and Contradiction XIV, p.128).

[47]Antony Galton: The Logic of Occurrence in: Antony Galton (ed.) Temporal Logics and their Applications, London 1987, pp.169-196. Page references here refer to the authorized German translation in 'Die Logik des Vorkommens' by Bertram Kienzle in: Bertram Kienzle (ed.): Zustand und Ereignis, Frankfurt am Main 1994, pp.377-412. The Vs and Ns in the names of the sets are taken from the translation, too. They are derived from 'before' (German 'vorher') and 'after' (German 'nachher').

[48]Galton: Die Logik des Vorkommens, p.387f.

[49]Ibid., p.388.

[50]Ibid., p.389.

[51]In 'The Logic of Occurrence' Galton also introduces a simultaneity-operator for events. By means of it, he tries to reduce talk of instants to talk of the simultaneity of events (Cf. a similar project in Charlton's 'Analytic ambition'). The definition of this operator involves some commitment as to how to describe the moment of change. Galton's 'solution' is to assign a first instant and deny a last instant to every event (this is due to a '$\leq$' in the definition on p.406) which can hardly be taken seriously. Galton himself views the part of his article in which this definition occurs rather as the presentation of a project than as its elaboration (cf.p.412).

[52]Galton: Die Logik des Vorkommens, p.406.

[53]Ibid.

[54]This property is also called 'convex'. The following is characteristic of it: if t lies between t' and t'', and t' nd t'' are elements of v, then t is also an element of v.

[55]Cf. Kienzle: Cambridge-Wechsel, definition 5, p.110.

[56]Ibid., p.111.

[57]Ibid., p.112.: "[Ein Cambridge-Wechsel läßt sich]... durchaus als etwas in der Zeit Vorkommendes auffassen. Jedenfalls sind die Cambridge-Übergänge, aus denen ein solcher Wechsel besteht, zeitlich ausgedehnte Prozesse. Und [...es] gibt [...] in einer kontinuierlichen Zeit tatsächlich keine untere Grenze für die Länge der Intervalle, die einen solchen Übergang enthalten."

[58]Kienzle calls Cambridge-transitions 'processes', using the word in a different sense to that in which I use it.

[59]I am grateful to Bertram Kienzle for a very detailed discussion of his approach and my criticism. I could not have formulated it as clearly as this without his support and explicit encouragement.

[60]Kienzle: Cambridge-Wechsel, pp.110f: "Die Menge der Übergänge zwischen zwei Zuständen, die in einen oszillationsfreien Übergang zwischen diesen Zuständen enthalten, bilden eine Filterbasis auf diesem oszillationsfreien Übergang.(Eine Menge F von Teilmengen von M heißt Filterbasis auf M iff (i) $\emptyset \notin$ F, (ii) $\emptyset \neq$ F und (iii) wenn A, B $\in$ F, dann gibt es ein C$\in$F mit: C $\subseteq$ A $\cap$ B.)" ("The set of transitions between two states which contain an oscillation-free transition between these states is a filter-base on this oscillation-free transition. A set F of subsets of M is a filter-base on M iff (i) $\emptyset \notin$ F, (ii) $\emptyset \neq$ F and (iii) if A, B $\in$ F, then there

is a C ∈ F such that: C ⊆ A ∩ B.") It is crucial here that every element of the filter-base is itself a transition which may be proved to be oscillation-free, because there exists a further filter-base of transitions 'upon' it etc. ad inf.

[61]If he wanted to express this in an Aristotelian manner, he might very well say that an 'occurrence' in Kienzle's sense is an ἐν ᾧ of the taking place of a change, but no ἐν ᾧ πρώτῳ, of which he could still claim that it does not exist. Cf.ch. I, 2.4.2.

[62]In Aristotelian terminology: for every C-transition there is another C-transition which is *superior* to the first one with respect to the taking place of the change.

[63]Taking, of course, 'aspect' in its original, concrete sense: the way of looking at something; not 'aspect' as an abstract noun or as a technical term of grammar.

[64]In this sense, aspects correspond to 'Gegebenheitsweisen' in Frege's sense. Cf. about 'Gegebenheitsweisen' (aspects in the concrete sense) Bertram Kienzle: Identität und Erkenntniswert - eine fast fregesche Deutung, in: Allgemeine Zeitschrift für Philosophie 10/1985, pp.27-40.

CHAPTER 2 - EITHER-WAY-OPTION

[1]Roderick Chisholm: Beginnings and Endings, in: Peter van Inwagen (ed.): Time and Cause, Dordrecht 1980, pp.17-25.

[2]Brian Medlin: The Origin of Motion, in: Mind, April 1963, pp.155-175.

[3]Franz Brentano: Philosophische Untersuchungen zu Raum, Zeit und Kontinuum, ed. by Stephan Körner and Roderick Chisholm, Hamburg 1976. Chisholm refers to a short, undated manuscript from the bequest entitled 'Megethologie [Nr.] 15' and to pp.50-52 of an unpublished manuscript (M96) from Brentano's 'Würzburger Metaphysik-Kolleg'.

[4]Chisholm: Beginnings..., p.17.

[5]Ibid., p.18.

[6]Ibid., p.19.

[7]Cf.ch. I,2.3. §1 and Phys. 263b9f.

[8]Cf. ibid.

[9]Chisholm: Beginnings..., pp.18f.

[10]Ibid.

[11]Ibid., p.19.

[12]Chisholm: Beginnings..., p.19.

[13]Cf. ch. I,1.3.4.2.

[14]Chisholm: Beginnings..., p.19: "One may ask: 'If the thing both begins to move and also ceases to rest at t, then is it in motion at t or is it at rest at t?' [...] We find the answer to these questions if we say what it is for a thing to move at instant t."

[15]Ibid., pp.19f.

[16]Ibid., p.18.

[17]Ibid., pp.18f.

[18]Cf. ch. I, 2.1. §3.

[19]The 'either...or' is meant as an inclusive disjunction here. Otherwise one would exclude that *a* has ever been in motion at any instants which are not limiting instants. An inclusive use of 'either...or' appears in Medlin, too. I may remark that if one learns English as a foreign language at school, one will usually learn that 'either...or' is exclusive. The international communication of scientists might be facilitated if some convention - in analogy to 'iff' and

'if' - was accepted, consisting in, say, using 'or' for the inclusive disjunction and 'orr' for the exclusive disjunction.

[20]Chisholm: Beginnings..., p.20.

[21]Ibid., pp.21ff.

[22]Ibid., p.22.

[23]Ibid.

[24]Ibid., pp.22f.

[25]Ibid., p.23:"And so if t is the first moment of the thing's existence and the last moment of its nonexistence, then the thing exists at t. And if t is the last moment of the thing's existence and the first moment of its nonexistence, then the thing also exists at t." (sic!)

[26]Ibid., p.23.

[27]Ibid.: "...the moments at which he was not alive [after he once had been so...] are of two different kinds: [...] the moments such that Socrates failed to exist up to those moments and also failed to exist from those moments on; [...] a moment such that Socrates existed from a certain time up to that moment but did not exist from that moment on."

[28]This is, of course, based on Quine's famous doctrine of indeterminacy of translation as stated in ch.2 of 'Word and Object' and, even more readably, in his article 'Ontological Relativity'.

[29]Brian Medlin: The Origin of Motion, Mind, April 1963, pp.155-175.

[30]Cf. e.g. Medlin, p.165.

[31]Ibid., p.155: "The paradox appears to be quite general. It concerns not only motion but every thing or property that begins or ceases to exist. Here I have found that my remarks are not quite so easily extended. For this reason the task of extending them is left entirely to the reader."

[32]Ibid., p.174.

[33]Ibid.

[34]Medlin, pp.165f. Medlin formulates his definitions using the specific example of a body at 12:00.

[35]This 'either..or' is inclusive again.

[36]I am afraid Medlin does not even notice that his definition of 'motion$_2$' (p.165) is equivalent with his 'motion [at an instant]' (pp.169f.) (at least, he does not mention this important feature). There can be no doubt that it is in fact equivalent. The definition of motion at an instant Medlin gives is: "Either the body was moving throughout a period beginning at 12:00 or the body was moving throughout a period ending at 12:00.", while he explicitly asserts that the 'either...or' is meant as a 'non-exclusive disjunction'(p.170).

[37]Ibid.

[38]Ibid.

[39]Ibid., pp.163f. Medlin says he wants to give a 'more fundamental explanation' for this in part III of his article. I have been unable to find it.

[40]Ibid., p.162 (footnote): "I mean by 'implies' something like 'strongly suggests' rather than 'entails'."

[41]Ibid., p.170: "...'The body was both in motion and at rest at 12:00' is not a contradiction."

[42]Ibid., p.172.

[43]In this case, in (1) and (2) 'motion' and 'rest' would mean 'motion$_2$' and 'rest$_2$', but in (1+) and (2+) 'motion$_1$' and 'rest$_1$'.

[44]Ibid., p.171.

[45]Ibid., p.172.

[46]Ibid., pp.171f.

[47]Ibid., p.171: "The propositions ¬(1) and (1+) differ in that while ¬(1) is the propositional negation of (1), (1+) like (2) is merely the predicate negation."

[48]The same is true for existence claims involving *uniquely* identifying descriptions. This can be seen by, plausibly, identifying the primary negation of Russell's 'On Denoting' with predicate negation for this case and his secondary negation with propositional negation. Russell's analysis of the proposition expressed by this statement can be rendered as follows, in the usual notation of predicate logic and with 'KoF' standing for 'is King of France in 1905' and 'B' for 'is bald':

$$\exists x \, [KoF(x) \, \wedge \, B \, (x) \, \wedge \, \forall y \, [KoF(y) \, \wedge \, x=y]].$$

The 'primary negation' of this is:

$$\exists x \, [KoF(x) \, \wedge \, \neg B \, (x) \, \wedge \, \forall y \, [KoF(y) \, \wedge \, x=y]].$$

And the 'secondary negation' is:

$$\neg \exists x \, [KoF(x) \, \wedge \, B(x) \, \wedge \, \forall y \, [KoF(y) \, \wedge \, x=y]].$$

So here, too, the primary negation implies the secondary negation, but the secondary negation does not imply the primary negation (for it is possible, in fact true, that there is no King of France in 1905). Cf. Bertrand Russell: 'On Denoting', Mind 1905, pp.479-493. The passage important here is pp.488-490 (Russell explicitly distinguishes a 'primary' and a 'secondary occurrence of a denoting phrase', but it is clear that (unlike the example about George IV) there is only *one* analysis of the statement "The King of France in 1905 is bald" and that the distinction actually exists between a 'primary' and a 'secondary occurence' of the negation).

[49]For example the proposition (if it is one) that it is not the case that the Golden Gate Bridge is friendly might fail to imply the proposition that it is unfriendly. Remember in this context the non-prefix as applied in ch. I,1.

[50]Ibid., pp.171f.

[51]Sorabji: Time..., p.408.

CHAPTER 3 - BOTH-STATES-OPTION

[1]Graham Priest: Dialectical Tense Logic [Priest DTL], in: Studia Logica XLI 2/3 (1981), pp.249-268. Cf. also his: Logic of Paradox, in: Journal of Philosophical Logic 8 (1979), pp.219-241, and for an application to Hegel's concept of motion and for the 'spread principle' his: Inconsistencies in Motion, in: American Philosophical Quarterly, vol. 22, Number 4, October 1985, pp.339-346.

[2]Cf. Chris Mortensen: The Limits of Change, in: Australasian Journal of Philosophy vol.63 No.1 March 1985, pp.3f.

[3]G.W.F. Hegel, Logik part 1, book 2, section 1, ch.2., remark 3 ad point C (Werke [collected works] vol.6, p.76).

[4]Hegel's concept of motion is dealt with in Priest's 'Inconsistencies...', the moment of change in DTL.

[5]The same opinion is found in Friedrich Engels. Cf. Anti Düring, Moskow 1947 (first edition 1878), p.139 and Priest: DTL, pp.266f.

[6]Ibid.

[7]Hegel loc.cit.

[8]Cf. Priest: Inconsistencies... , from p.341 passim.

[9]Priest: Inconsistencies..., p.342 and p.344. On p.344 Priest, in a sketch, represents the positions of an object at rest as a mere line, but the position of the same object in motion as a kind of flatworm of considerable breadth.

[10]Priest sees Quantum Mechanics as a possible field of application for paraconsistent logic. Cf. Inconsistencies: p.345. Time will tell whether this is plausible. Anyhow the idea is not far-fetched.

[11]Priest: DTL, p.249.

[12]Cf. about the following Priest: DTL, pp.250f.

[13]Ibid., p.251.

[14]Ibid., p.252.

[15]Ibid.

[16]Ibid., p.253.

[17]Ibid.

[18]Ibid.

[19]Priest: DTL, p.254. I am unable to recognize very much of this in the passage in Leibniz Priest refers to, which is a letter from Leibniz to Bayle, edited in: Die philosophischen Schriften von G.W. Leibniz, hrsg. von C.J. Gerhardt, vol.3 Hildesheim 1965, pp.52ff.

[20]For example Priest himself mentions (loc.cit.) that by applying this principle without any restriction one could prove that every real number is a rational number, since a real number is defined as the limit of a rational number.

[21]Priest DTL: p.262.

[22]Ibid.

[23]Ibid., p.263.

[24]Ibid.

[25]Priest himself holds it to be an important reason for regarding discontinuous changes as either β- or γ-changes that "[t]he situation is symmetrical" (Priest: DTL, p.252).

[26]Priest: DTL, p.266.

[27]Mortensen: The Limits of Change, esp. p.4.

[28]Joseph Wayne Smith: Time, Change and Contradiction, Australasian Journal of Philosophy, vol.68 No.2, June 1990, pp.178-188.

[29]Smith: p.184.

[30]Ibid., p.183.

[31]Ibid., p.184: "[Priest] does not exclude the possibility that nature may be arbitrary so that either s_0 or s_1 may obtain quite randomly at the point of change. This option should be preferred [...] unless demonstrated to be inadequate on an independent basis..."

[32]I am sympathetic to the view which Michael Esfeld expressed to me on this point, that there might be no case in which arbitrariness would not save the LNC; this would probably leave paraconsistent logic without application.

[33]Priest: DTL, p.252.

[34]Ibid., p.266 (my italics).

[35]This is, no doubt, genuine Hegel; cf. again Logik loc.cit. remark 3: "Die gemeine Erfahrung aber spricht es selbst aus, daß es wenigstens eine Menge widersprechender Dinge, widersprechender Einrichtungen usf. gebe, deren Widerspruch nicht bloß in einer äußerlichen Reflexion, sondern in ihnen selbst vorhanden ist." (Common experience itself pronounces that there is a lot of contradictory things, contradictory institutions etc. whose contradiction is not only present in external reflection but in themselves). A clear critical introduction into this concept of contradiction is found in Michael Wolff: Der Begriff des Widerspruchs - eine Studie zur Dialektik Kants und Hegels, Königstein/Taunus 1981 (Philosophie, Analyse und Grundlegung vol.5).

[36]In Met.IV (G), 4-6. Cf. for a very detailed analysis of the text and discussion of the literature on this issue: Burkhard Hafemann: Aristoteles' Transzendentaler Realismus - Zur Rechtfertigung erster Prinzipien in der 'Metaphysik' (Dissertation WWU Münster 1996, forthcoming with De Gruyter), §6.

CHAPTER 4 - NEITHER/NOR-OPTION

[1]Cf. introduction2. As was shown in ch.II,2, Chisholm and Medlin in their articles on the moment of change also seem to be working with periods as entities in their own right.

[2]C. Hamblin: Instants and Intervals, in: Studium Generale 24 (1971), pp.127-134.

[3]C. Hamblin: Starting and Stopping. In: The Monist 1969, pp.411-425.

[4]Hamblin: Starting..., p.410: "When a thing is not in motion, it is at rest, and when it is not at rest, it is in motion."

[5]One might say that (1)corresponds to a Russellian 'primary negation' plus 'secondary negation', but (2) to a 'secondary negation' without 'primary negation' of the statement that a is F or not F at the limiting instant.

[6](1) and (3) obviously result in using the neither/nor-option. This may not be so apparent for (2): at every interval either the old or the new state, or, if it is a 'mixed' interval, both states obtain. At first sight this seems to be the either/or-option: all times (since intervals are the only times allowed) are exhaustively distributed to one or the other state. But although this cannot fail to be so for the either/or-option, it is not characteristic of it. There may be other cases in which the same is true, but which are not instances of the either/or-option. What is characteristic of the either/or-option is rather that the limiting instant is assigned either to the old or to the new state. Of course, this is not possible, if no limiting instant exists. So Hamblin does not use the either/or-option here. On the other hand, certainly neither the old nor the new state obtains at the limiting instant if no limiting instant exists. Thus, although according to Hamblins 'Starting and Stopping', all times are are distributed exhaustively to the two states, he uses the neither/nor-option even in those places where he advotaces (2).

[7]Priest: DTL, p.254. Mortensen, p.3.

[8]Hamblin: Starting..., p.410.

[9]Ibid., pp.415-417.

[10]Hamblin: Starting...p.415: "The basic idea behind the logical system I am about to describe is that intervals may abut one another independently of whether there also exist other entities describable as 'points of abutment' ".

[11]Cf. esp. Ibid., p.414 and p.425.

[12]Ibid. It is clearly seen from the fact that Hamblin treats these examples on a par, that he does not distinguish between comparative and non-comparative poperties.

[13]Cf. Ibid., p.421.

[14]Ibid., p.422.

[15]Ibid., p.423.

[16]Ibid., p.424.

[17]Cf.ch. I,1.3.3. (b).

[18]Hamblin: Starting..., p.424.

[19]Ibid., pp.424f.

[20]Hamblin: Starting...., p.425.

[21]Ibid...., p.410.

[22]Mortensen, p.2.

[23]Priest: DTL, p.254.

[24]Hamblin: Starting..., p.412.

[25]Ibid., p.414: "The red book on my desk could turn green for half a second or half a century but it could not turn green temporarily and durationlessly at the stroke of twelve, remaining red at all times earlier and later. This being so, the time-continuum, modeled on the real numbers, is richer than we need for the modelling of empirical reality. Clicks, jerks, flashes, glimpses [...] - which are our paradigms of 'instantaneous' events - we would well be able to accomodate in a less lavish time-scale containing short but no infinitesimal intervals; and it begins to appear that *changes* of value of a predicate are the only true candidates for instantaneity. But if this is so, why should we ever talk of truth or falsity *at* an instant? If instants exist at all, it is surely in some secondary sense derived from their role as assistants to intervals.".

[26]Ibid.

[27]Hamblin: Instants and Intervals, p.132: "We can suppose that [interval] a abuts [interval] b and that some property f holds throughout a and fails throughout b [...] *without raising the inexpressible question* of whether φ or ¬φ may be predicated of the point of abutment.".

[28]Ibid., p.130.

[29]Compare this to Priest taking it equally as a matter of course that the light is both on and off (ch.II,3.4.2.).

[30]By comparison: The idea that Caesar does not belong to the domain of "...is a prime number" does not imply that he does not belong to the name of any predicate at all: there are a lot of meaningful statements about Caesar; for example Caesar belongs to the domain of the predicate "...was a great writer" (it is quite different matter as to whether he belongs to the *extension* of this predicate).

[31]Hamblin: Starting..., p.425.

[32]Cf.ch.I,1.3.2.(b).

[33]Mortensen is therefore right in criticizing Hamblin (The Limits of Change, p.3) by demanding: "...Hamblin would have to show, what he does not show, how enough of the theory of differential equations to describe such physical systems can be construed within his assumptions. Without this we should wonder how much physics has to be sacrificed in the interest of saving Hamblin's solution."

[34]Chisholm and Medlin from not dissimilar starting points had at least tried to define what 'being in the course of' being F at t (with F='being in motion'/'at rest') may mean (Cf.II,2). Hamblin attempts nothing of the sort. Ch.II,2, while dealing with Chisholm's suggestion, discussed in how far it is useful to say that *a* is in the course of being F iff t falls within a period c such that *a* is F throughout c (it would, of course, be easy to introduce this requirement into a modified version of interval semantics). It was seen that this requirement would not be useful, because it yields the result that the clockhand of a correct clock does not point to '12' at 12 o' clock.

[35]Interestingly, Hamblin himself writes (Starting..., p.412): "....it is not clear whether one is supposed to reason that there is no such thing as an instant of time, or merely that no instant of time is ever observed separately from its fellows."

CHAPTER 5 - NEUTRAL INSTANT ANALYSIS

[1]To my knowledge, the term is from Kretzmann who uses it in 'Incipit/Desinit'. Sorabji uses this name as well when criticizing Kretzmann ('Time...', ch. 26).

[2]The relation of rest and motion in the context of the NIA can, thus, also be described in terms familiar from the chapter on Plato: rest and motion together are incompatible but

dispensable for instants; in relation to periods, however, they are both incompatible and indispensable. Cf.ch. I,1.3. §3f.

[3]Cf. Kretzmann: Incipit/Desinit, p.114.

[4]The fact that Kretzmann not only discovers the NIA as implicitly contained in the medieval approach (which is plausible), but also in Aristotle (which is not plausible at all), does not matter in this chapter, where it is dealt with purely as a contemporary systematic solution.

[5]In Bostock: Plato on Change...

[6]Although, as was shown in ch.I,1.2.1., he does not attribute the use of the neither/nor-option to Plato.

[7]Bostock: Plato on Change..., p.238.

[8]Ibid.

[9]If it sounds implausible that a when changing from being at rest to not being at rest, for example, is already not at rest, this demonstrates some plausibility of Plato's premiss.

[10]So, for the time being I am following a proposal by Sorabji (Time..., p.404). In part III, however, the position of an object is to be defined as an extended part of space.

[11]Perhaps it was conscious Anti-Hegelianism which provoked Russell to state his intuition so very clearly here. Cf.ch.II,3.

[12]The reason for this is that it becomes very easy to obtain a parallel definition of motion. If only rest at an instant were to be defined, it would not be necessary to require the two instants to be different. So in the definition of rest this requirement is, strictly speaking, redundant.

[13]It is assumed here that there are no gaps in the existence of a physical object, and that at any time of its existence it is somewhere. If this is assumed it is true that if there are any positions of a at all both before and after t, then there are positions of a both arbitrarily shortly before t and arbitrarily shortly after t.

[14]Cf.ch.II,1.1.2.

[15]So Sorabji is absolutely right to remark (Time..., p.416): "Bertrand Russell gives a definition of motion at a moment in §446 of the Principles of Mathematics and denies [...] that the instant of motion can be an instant of rest. He does not, however, make it so clear whether or not it can be an instant of motion."

[16]This is clearly noticed by Priest ('Inconsistencies..' p.339): "Russell is actually slightly inconsistent, since after giving his definition he permits that something may be momentarily at rest if its position derivative with respect to time is zero. This is quite compatible with its being in motion in the official sense."

[17]Cf. ch.II,1.1.

[18]Kretzmann: Incipit/Desinit, p.114.

[19]Kretzmann: Incipit/Desinit, p.115:"The instant t_C is the extrinsic limit of the state of rest as well as the extrinsic limit of the state of motion. But how can it be both at once? [...] Considered as belonging to the interval during which the ball is in its initial state of rest, t_C is the t_{NBz} [= last instant of non-being] of the interval during which the ball is in motion; considered as belonging to the interval of motion, t_C is the t_{NBa} [= first instant of non-being] of the interval of rest." Fortunately, the wording is unambiguous, but nevertheless this much has to be said against it: (1) It is not quite clear what 'belonging to' is supposed to mean here. t cannot be an element of an interval all instants of which are instants of rest of a, and at the same time be the first instant at which a is not at rest. Therefore 'belonging to' cannot refer to the relation 'is an element of', as one would expect at first sight;but it means something like 'being an extrinsic boundary of the interval'. (2) Of course, there is no "first/last instant of non-being" of an interval but, at most, of a state obtaining during an interval. An open interval (and this is what Kretzmann is concerned with here) simply has no first or last instant.

Kretzmann originally introduces his index labels 'NBa' and 'NBz' with respect to medieval 'res permanentes' and 'res successivae', which he regards as states. That is where they make sense.

[20]As for the classification of the moment of change, Kretzmann is not quite as clear here as he is in his description of it. On the one hand, he seems to deny an instantaneous event for the s-change between rest and motion.(Kretzmann: Incipit/Desinit, p.115: "There is no change of rest to motion or of motion to rest. [...] The instant t_C is simply the the extrinsic limit of the state of rest as well as the extrinsic limit of the state of motion.") On the other hand, he states that the verbs 'leave', 'arrive' and 'begin' may refer to what occurs at an instant. In connection with this, his opinion is that the last instant at which a is in position A is the very instant for which it is true to say "[a] is leaving from [position] A". (Ibid., p.116.)

[21]Wolfgang Büchner has pointed out to me that the second conjunct is strictly speaking redundant. With his permission I will keep this redundant expression because in this way the intuition behind the definition is easier to recognize.

[22]According to these definitions turning-point instants are not neutral. If they are to be, one has to add the requirement that t is an instant of motion of a only if it falls within a period of uninterrupted motion of a and if its M-value at t differs from zero.

[23]Cf. Introduction2.

PART III
INTRODUCTION AND SECTION 1

[1]In a different terminology one calls what I have called a definition a *criterion*; this is a question of terminological convention which has no impact on the content of my approach.

[2]Cf. I,2.2.1. (b).

[3]Phys. 239b5-9 and 239b30-33.

[4]Phys. 232a8/9: ...εἴη ἂν ἡ κίνησις οὐκ ἐκ κινήσεων ἀλλ᾽ ἐκ κινεμάτων.

[5]Cf.ch. I,2.2.1. (d).

[6]There is abundant literature on the flying arrow paradox. I recommend: Milos Arsenijevic: Eine Aristotelische Logik der Intervalle, die Cantorsche Logik der Punkte und die physikalischen und kinematischen Prädikate, Philosophia Naturalis 29, 1992, Heft2, pp.161-210. Wesley Salmon: Space, Time and Motion, Encino/Calif. 1975 ch.1. G.E.L. Owen: Zeno and the Mathematicians, in: Proceedings of the Aristotelian Society LVIII (1957/58), pp.199-223; Adolf Grünbaum: Zeno's Metrical Paradoxes of Extension, in: Wesley Salmon (Hrsg.): Zeno's Paradoxes, Indianapolis 1970. Gregory Vlastos: A Note on Zeno's Arrow, in: Phronesis 11 (1966), pp.3-18. Jonathan Lear: Aristotle - The Desire to Understand, Cambridge 1988, ch. 3.5. 'Change'.

[7]This is also the only explanation of why the flying arrow has ever worried anyone after Aristotle. We know it from Physics VI,9 together with Aristotle's attempted refutation. If this refutation had been a convincing refutation reaching the crux, the flying arrow would have been an outdated problem from about 400BC on. It has proved not to be so. This does, however, not mean that Aristotle had nothing better to say against Zeno: in my view, Aristotle's idea that a motion could not consist of results of motion undermines Zeno more significantly than the 'official' refutation in Physics VI,9. Unfortunately, Aristotle does not make explicit how to use this opinion as an objection to Zeno. Something like this is done at the end of section2.

[8]Cf. e.g. Conf. XI, 15 l.23.

[9]Conf. XI, ch. 19 and 20. St. Augustine relies on the empirical accessibility of the present to such an extent that in a famous phrase of ch.20 he suggests replacing all talk of past, present and future with talk of a present of past things, of present things and of future things. This does not quite fit the view that times are measured only as they pass by (XI, 16 l.28) and that

the present always tends towards non-being (XI, 14). I take these metaphors to describe a view of time that I am much more sympathetic with.

[10]Thomas Reid: Essays on the Intellectual Powers of Man, Glasgow 1785, III,v. "...though in common language we speak with perfect propriety and truth, when we say that we see a body move, and that motion is an object of sense, yet when as philosophers we distinguish accurately the province of sense from that of memory, we can no more see what is past, though but a moment ago, than we can remember what is present: so that speaking philosophically, it is only by the aid of memory that we discern motion, or any succession whatsoever. We see the present place of the body; we remember the successive advance it made to that place. The first can then only give us a conception of motion, when joined to the last." I have taken the reference to this passage from Michael Inwood: Aristotle on the Reality of Time, in: Lindsay Judson (ed.): Aristotle's Physics - A Collection of Essays, Oxford 1991, pp.151-178.

[11]Henri Bergson: Essai sur les données immédiates de la conscience. In: Œuvres [1 vol.], Paris 1959, pp.72ff.:"En dehors de moi, dans l'espace, il n'y a jamais qu'une position unique... [d'un objet mouvant], car des positions passées il ne reste rien. Au dedans de moi un processus d'organisation ou de pénétration mutuelle des faits de conscience se poursuit, qui constitue la durée vraie... [L]a succession existe seulement pour un spectateur conscient qui se remémore le passé... le mouvement, en tant que passage d'un point à un autre, est une synthèse mentale, un processus psychique et par suite inétendu. ...[E]n quelque point de l'espace que l'on considère le mobile, on n'obtiendra qu'une position. Si la conscience perçoit autre chose que des positions, c'est qu'elle se remémore les positions successives et en fait la synthèse."

[12]PM § 447: There is no transition from place to place, no consecutive moment or consecutive position, no such thing as velocity except in the sense of a real number which is the limit of a certain set of quotients [i.e. not a "property belonging at each instant to a moving point"].

[13]Russell: Principles... §447. The reference of the expression'Russell' here is the person called Bertrand Russell in 1903. This should be noted since it is well known that Russell often changed his opinion on important philosophical matters. A good survey on Russell's changing ideas on instants is found in M. Capek: The Fiction of Instants, The New Aspects of Time, Dordrecht 1991, pp.43-56. It is mainly about the question in how far one might assume some minimal empirical accessibility of instants. As far as I am aware, Russell held on to the reductionist theory of motion for a lifetime.

[14]Priest: Inconsistencies..., p.340. It is interesting to note how close Priest's "aggregate of going nowheres" is to Aristotle's "nothing but results of motion". Cf. above. Of course, Priest tries to use this as an argument against any comparative definition of motion (as we have seen in ch.II,3, in his 'paraconsistent logic' motion is an instrinsic, self-contradictory, property of an object at an instant). This is not convincing, as the independence of comparative definition and reductionism in Aristotle shows.

[15]Those readers who are addicted to some sort of 'subject of experience' may substitute all talk of opening the light stop of a camera in the following by talk of opening an eye and substitute 'exposure time' by 'time of experience'. They will probably notice after a while that the problems are, in our context, just the same with and without substitution. The fact that it does not matter here if we assume a subject of experience, which performs some sort of spontaneous synthesis, might already cause some mistrust of the snapshot myth: actually, the snapshot myth cannot do without such a subject; for an adherent of it must explain, if there is no flux, how and where the illusion of the flux comes about (cf. the quotation from Bergson above for an example how to do this). Of course, there are subjects of experience. But their existence should be mentioned in an argument only when this is really necessary.

[16]This is, of course, not so in reality: even if the light stop could be opened for as short a time as we desired, there are limits to the sensitivity of films.

[17]Unconsciously and in a different context (actually while arguing the opposite) Hamblin expresses this objection by saying that an instant may not be observed "separated from its fellows". Cf. Hamblin: Starting and Stopping, p.412 and ch.II,4.

[18]If one absolutely had to give this form of argument a name, it should, alluding to Kant, be called a *negative transcendental argument*.

SECTION 2

[1]Musical notation agrees with the Aristotelian assumption of instants as mere boundaries. It also agrees very nicely with the Aristotelian assumption of the potentially infinite divisibility of periods: One can notate the same melody in arbitrarily many different ways by inserting as many bar-lines as one wishes without changing its audible form. Of course, one cannot actually insert infinitely many bar-lines. And, of course, no matter how many bar-lines one puts together, one will never create an aural extension (one requires at least to put a rest in between as something that has duration!).

[2]Cf. ch.II,2 and II,4.

[3]Spans have no temporal 'direction'. However, it is not necessary to recur to instantaneous states in order to distinguish the clockhand's passing through a 2-D-span clockwise and its passing through anti-clockwise. They can be distinguished by the different sequences of subprocesses into which they may be divided: If, for example, the clockhand is moving clockwise between 11:55 and 12:05, it passes through the span between the 11:55 and the 12:00 position first and only then through the span between the 12:00 position and the 12:05 position and if it is moving anti-clockwise, vice versa.

[4]The position-span for the ten minutes in question is not identical with the set of all space-points which fall within and bound the surface through which the clockhand passes between 5 to 12 and 5 past 12. However, there is a close relationship between this set and the span: To every position-span exactly one set can be assigned which may be said to 'describe' it. This set describes a span in the same way as an interval may be said to describe a period.

[5]It will be seen below that if the principle "natura non facit saltus" is assumed, this intuition can be expressed even more clearly and the distinction between lefhand side and righthand side may be dropped.

[6]Cf. W.E.Johnson: Logic, Cambridge 1921.

[7]I presume that the distinction has an Aristotelian origin: the idea of grouping incompatible properties into 'points of view' (German: 'Hinsichten', typically by using the preposition κατὰ). After Johnson, Searle has (with little success) tried to revive the distinction by an attempt to formalize it. Cf. J.Searle: Determinables and the Notion of Resemblance, in: Proceedings of the Aristotelian Society Suppl. Vol. 1963, and Searle's excellent introduction 'Determinates and Determinables' in the Encyclopedia of Philosophy (ed.Paul Edwards, New York 1967 ff.). Cf. also Antti Hautamäki: Points of View and their Logical Analysis, Helsinki 1986 (Acta Philosophica Fennica 41), ch.1'Determinables'. Cleland identifies determinables with sets of determinates and takes the view that determinables are the real ὑποκείμενα of every alteration. Cf. Carol Cleland:The Individuation of Events In: Synthese, February 1991.

[8]Cf. Aristotle's cautious additional clause to the classical formulation of the LNC in Met. 1005b20-23.

[9]This definition is, of course, not operational; its function is to clarify the notion of an instantaneous state. For, of course, no actual measurements from all periods which are bounded by t can be performed and compared (there are infinitely many such periods). We are, however, convinced of what these measurements would look like if we could perform them; and any measurement we do indeed perform confirms our expectations.

[10]Details: ch. I,3 and Appendix C.

[11]This might again be called some kind of transcendental argument. Here we would have a typical Kantian case in which we make Nature behave according to our way of describing it, because we cannot imagine it behaving otherwise.

[12]This example is somewhat idealized; but it is nonetheless worth considering.

[13]Russell sidesteps the problem by restricting his definitions to a 'material point' as his object of motion. Cf.ch. II,5 and Principles of Mathematics §442.

[14]Cf. Sorabji: Time..., pp.404f.

[15]I am grateful to Ludger Jansen for this example.

[16]I am grateful to Bertram Kienzle for drawing my attention to this problem.

[17]It will easily be seen at this point that it would be possible to develop a theory of properties of non-extended spatial entities exactly analogous to the theory of instantaneous states. The motivation for doing this would be the empirical inaccessibility of space-points and lines, which is clearly apparent, since those entitites, too, are mere boundaries in a continuum. In order to build such a theory, one needs a spatial version of modified interval semantics based on spatial intervals and with a spatial version of the 'fall-within' relation. A Point-prefix in the spatial version should have practically the same semantics as Inst in the temporal version.

[18]Note that the only difference between the two-place determinable function IS-AT from ch.II,5 and Inst-POS is that IS-AT yields space-points while Inst-POS yields spans.

[19]It may well be the case that Inst-$D(a,t_1)$ = Inst-$D(a,t_2)$. Cf. ch.II,5 on the problem of circular motion.

[20]I strongly suspect that the definiens of (a) is equivalent to the following formula which does not involve the Inst-prefix and in which motion as a genuine flux is very clearly apparent:

$$\forall\ c_1\ [c_1 {}^\circ c \rightarrow \exists\ c_2\ [c_2 {}^\circ c_1 \wedge D(a,c) \neq D(a,c_2)]].$$

Phrase (b) would, of course, have to be analogous. The somewhat indirect procedure of working with two subperiods (c_2!) is necessary because of the usual difficulty concerning circular motion (cf.II,5). So far I have been unable to prove that the equivalence holds.

[21]If $L(t)$ is to be read as "t is a limiting instant between rest and motion", we may say that $L(t)$ is true iff either clause (i) of (c) and clause (ii) of (d) are fulfilled or clause (ii) of (c) and clause (i) of (d) are fulfilled. It is easy then to state a comparative definition of rest and motion at an instant which assigns the limiting instant to rest (with POS for 'D'): t would have to be an instant of rest iff clause (d) of NR10 were fulfilled or $L(t)$ were true, the definition of motion remaining clause (c) of NR10. This definition would agree with Sorabji's proposal (ch.II,1.1).

[22]For formal definitions of 'beginning' and 'ending' and for formal proofs of these claims see AppendixA.

[23]Some changes which one would intuitively consider to be 'discontinuous', such as on/off-changes (cf. ch. II,3) are C-changes which should be described by using the either/or-option: nobody except Hamblin (cf.ch.II,4) and Priest (cf. ch. II,3) would think that there is an instant at which an existing lamp is neither 'on' nor 'off'. To describe such a change using the either/or-option, we should decide first which state is primitive and which is derived. This decision should usually be easy. One will naturally define 'off' as 'not on', and not 'on' as 'not off' (although it is, of course, true that a lamp can be seen to be on whenever it can be seen to be not off; but since instants are empirically inaccessible, this is not the whole story). If a lamp is off whenever it is not on, we simply have to ask ourselves whether it is on at the limiting instant if we want to know whether it is off or on. The limiting instant cannot be assigned the state 'on' (if it could it should bounded by an on-phase on either side). So, by definition, the lamp is off at it.

[24]I am aware of the fact that these remarks are rather sketchy. But not every conceivable case needs to be discussed in detail here, if the general framework within which the discussion

might take place is recognizable. Apart from that, (at least epistemic) vagueness is probably of greater importance here than can be accounted for in the present book. The topic is difficult and has an impact on ethics when abortion or brain death are concerned.

SECTION 3

[1]Galton, Logic of Aspect, ch.1 and 2; ch.I,1.1.

[2]Cf.ch.I,2.

[3]If one is absolutely determined to keep Plato's premiss, it is, in my view, still better to deny that those changes which are described by the either/or-option are events than to say that they are events but take place at no time. The first alternative is the Aristotelian way of sidestepping Plato's premiss. It should be preferred to the second, Galtonian, alternative, if Plato's premiss must be kept. It is not too counterintuitive, and certainly not self-contradictory. Nevertheless, as is clear from the text above, I think that Plato's premiss should rather be given up altogether.

[4]The expression 'in the course of' might initially sound clumsy in this context. The need to use it will become apparent below.

[5]Indeed *all* changes. It does not matter whether they have a neither/nor- or an either/or-structure. For this is the structure of the limiting instant only, which is empirically inaccessible. Changes which are described differently do not have to look different. In fact, they all look the same. It is also important to note that SOC does not, of course, make the existence of events dependent on the presence of an observer. A change has, when observed, a certain appearance, with which we are concerned. But, of course, it also takes place if it is not observed.

[6]Theoretically, it could be denied that an instant at which the change is taking place is identical with the instant at which the old state ceases to be and the new state begins. But this seems quite absurd. I assume this identity to hold.

[7]Of course, O does not make an instantaneous observation; what 'in the course of' means here instead has been defined above.

[8]It should be clear that, since SOC is an epistemological claim, this is far from being a violation of the LEM.

[9]There are authors (e.g. Smart and Chisholm) who hold instantanous events to be the paradigm of events. In my view, this is highly exaggerated. But so would be the opposite view that every event must take time. Cf. J.J.C. Smart: The River of Time, in: Mind LVIII (1949), pp.483-494; Roderick Chisholm: On Metaphysics, Minneapolis 1989 (ch. 'Boundaries').

[10]Rules for using the word 'immediately' are discussed in ch.I,3 in connection with medieval authors.

[11]Remember that this had been Kienzle's very sensible requirement for a good description of C-changes, and that he has shown that Galton does not meet it.Cf. ch.II,1.3.

[12]This precise definition should not contradict any way in which the word was used more loosely previously.

[13]This might plausibly be called an Augustinian objection. Cf. section1.

[14]as introduced by Aristotle (cf., e.g., Phys. 222a20). Remember that Aristotle did allow a νῦν καθ' ἕτερον alongside with the present instant (Phys. 233b33) and that William of Ockham was still aware of this (Cf. ch. I,3).

[15]It seems to me that not even Robert Clay and William James, who have the merit of going beyond instants, really get away from 'the present' as some kind of entity. Only Wittgenstein makes this point convincingly in the Brown Book, p.108; a passage which is rightly assessed by Monk to be of crucial importance for the project of Wittgenstein's late

philosophy. Cf. William James: A pluralistic universe, New York 1909 Lectures VI and VII, David L. Miller: William James and the Specious Present in: Walter Robert Corti (ed.): The philosophy of William James, Hamburg 1976, pp.51-81. Ludwig Wittgenstein: The Brown Book, London 1975, Ray Monk: Ludwig Wittgenstein - The duty of genius, New York 1990, p.346.

[16]Johann Wolfgang Goethe, from: Xenien (No. 155), collected works [Hamburg edition] vol.1, p.230. I am grateful to my mother for drawing my attention to these lines.

APPENDICES

[1]I am grateful to Betram Kienzle for suggesting this idea.

[2]The way in which Q and G are defined here entail the presupposition for my reconstruction of the proof that Aristotle is talking about a limiting instant after which a remains in the target position for a while, such that the limiting instant is a genuine end to a process. One cannot exclude the possibility that Aristotle's proof might in fact be even more general and also takes into account such instants at which only a subprocess is completed and an intermediate target reached. The nerve of the proof would then be basically the same; one would only have to define that t satisfies Q iff a is at or beyond an intermediate target. A formal rendering of what 'or beyond' means here would have made the rconstruction of the proof very complicated, though. I therefore rather make the presupposition mentioned.

[3]$\neg Q(x)$ would not do as the definiens, since it should not be excluded by definition that there might be times of an object's existence where it cannot be assigned a definite position. Limiting instants might be such instants. With regard to them $\neg Q(x)$ would be satisfied without x being in place different to Z.

[4]Wolfgang Büchner has pointed out to me that (A) is actually weaker than our meaning of "natura non facit saltus". It would be more complicated to formally render what "natura non facit saltus" means; this would, for example, require a topology on places. Since "natura non facit saltus" cannot hold if (A) does not hold, it is admissable to use (A) instead of it for the reconstruction.

[5]Only the assumption of continuous time (which is a little more than dense time) entails this presupposition. I am grateful to Wolfgang Büchner for pointing this out to me.

[6]Aristotle treats it extensively in Phys. 240a29/b7 and Phys.265b2/11. At first sight, the solution he proposes looks a little uncertain: on the one hand, the rotating sphere is said to be in motion, on the other hand it is said to be at rest. A rotating sphere certainly does not fulfil Aristotle's own definition of rest in Phys.239a27/29. For in this definition a clause is incorporated which is tailor-made for excluding rotating spheres and the like: rest of a is characterized as *a*'s staying in the same place both with regard to itself (i.e. as a whole) and to all ist parts (καὶ τα μέρη).

[7]They cannot be interpreted as forces due to motion then, but must be regarded as a gravitational field. Details from the horse's mouth in: Albert Einstein: Über die spezielle und die allgemeine Relativitätstheorie, Braunschweig 1917.

[8]Peter Forrest: Is Motion Change of Location?, in: Analysis Oktober 1984, pp.177f.

[9]Some adherents of ontological holism will say that all objects except for the universe as a whole are pseudo-objects. A strong tendency in this direction is found in Jonathan Bennett (cf. A Study in Spinoza's Ethics, Cambridge 1984, pp.89ff.) I am grateful to Michael Esfeld for telling me about Bennett on this point and for many fascinating discussions on holism.

[10]Similar reactions to this objection are found in Hamblin's 'Starting and Stopping' and in Sorabji's 'Aristotle...' (first and second version) as well as in 'Time...' under the nice heading "Does the problem apply to the real world?".

(Medieval authors are listed under their first names)

Ackrill,J.L.: Aristotle's Distinction between Energeia and Kinesis, in: R. Bambrough (ed.): New Essays on Plato and Aristotle, London 1965, pp. 121-141.

Albert the Great: Physicorum libri VIII, in: Opera omnia, Paris 1890, commentary on book VI, tractatus 2, ch.4.

Aristotle: The Physics, in: The complete works of Aristotle (translation: R.P. Hardie/R.K. Gaye), the revised Oxford translation ed. by Jonathan Barnes, Princeton 1984.

The Physics [2 vols., Engl./Gr.], transl. by Philip H. Wicksteed and Francis M. Cornford, London 1934 [Loeb Classical Library].

Aristoteles: Physikvorlesung, übersetzt von Hans Wagner, Berlin 1983 [vol.11 of the complete edition by Akademie-Verlag Berlin].

Aristoteles' Physik übersetzt und mit einer Einleitung und Anmerkungen herausgegeben von [transl. and ed. by] Hans Günter Zekl [2 vols., Gr./Gn.], Hamburg 1988.

Aristotle's Physics 3 + 4, transl. by Edward Hussey, Oxford 1983.

Arsenijevic, Miloš: Eine Aristotelische Logik der Intervalle, die Cantorsche Logik der Punkte und die physikalischen und kinematischen Prädikate, in: Philosophia Naturalis 29 (1992), pp.161-210.

Augustine: De civitate Dei, ed. B. Dombart and A. Kalb (CCSL 47-8), Turnholt 1955.

Bekenntnisse [confessions, Latin and German], translated by Joseph Bernhart, Frankfurt 1987.

The City of God against the Pagans [Lat./Engl.] in seven volumes, English tanslation by George M. Cracken et al. [Loeb], London 1957-72.

Averroes: Aristotelis Opera cum Averrois Commentariis, Venetiis apud Junctas 1562-1574, reprint Frankfurt am Main 1962.

Ayer, A.J.: Russell and Moore - The Analytical Heritage, London 1971.

Beierwaltes,W.: Ἐξαίφνης oder die Paradoxie des Augenblicks, in: Philosophisches Jahrbuch 74 (1966/67), pp.271-283.

Bennett, Jonathan: A Study in Spinoza's Ethics, Cambridge 1984.

Bergson, Henri: Essai sur les données immédiates de la conscience, in: Œuvres [works in 1 vol.], Paris 1959.

Bochmann, Alexander: Concerted Instant Interval Semantics I (Temporal Ontologies) + II (Temporal Valuations and Logics of Change), in: Notre Dame Journal of Formal Logic 31/3 (1990), pp.404-414/580-601.

Bostock, David: Aristotle on Continuity in Physics VI, in: Judson, Lindsay (ed.): Aristotle's Physics - A Collection of Essays, Oxford 1991, pp.179-213.

Plato on Change and Time in the "Parmenides", in: Phronesis 23 (1978), pp.229-242.

Braakhuis, M.: De 13de Eeuwse Tractaten over Syncategorematische Termen, vol.1: Inleidende Studie; vol.2: Uitgave van Nicolaas van Parijs' Sincategoremata, Leiden 1979.

Bradwardine, Bradwardinus: see Thomas Bradwardine

Brentano, Franz: Philosophische Untersuchungen zu Raum, Zeit und Kontinuum, Hamburg 1976.

Kategorienlehre, Hamburg 1974.

Burleigh, Burlaeus: see Walter Burleigh

Čapek, Milič: The Fiction of Instants, in: Čapek, Milič, The New Aspects of Time, Dordrecht 1991, pp.43-56.

Chappell, V.C.: Time and Zeno's Arrow, in: The Journal of Philosophy 59 (1962), pp.197-213.

Charlton, William: The Analytic Ambition, Oxford 1991.

Chisholm, Roderick M.: Beginnings and Endings, in: Peter van Inwagen (ed.): Time and Cause, Dordrecht 1980, pp.17-25.

On Metaphysics, Minneapolis 1989.

Cleland, Carol: On the Individuation of Events, in: Synthese 86 (1991), pp.229-254.

The Difference between Mere Cambridge Change and Real Change, in: Philosophical Studies 60/3 (1990), pp.257-280.

Dummett, Michael: Elements of Intuitionism, Oxford 1977.

Ebbesen, Sten (ed.): Three 13th century sophismata about Beginning and ceasing, Cahiers de l'Institut du Moyen-âge Grec et Latin [CIMAGL], Université de Copenhague 59 (1989), pp.121-180.

Edwards, Paul (ed.): The Encyclopaedia of Philosophy, New York 1967 ff.

Einstein, Albert: Über die spezielle und die allgemeine Relativitätstheorie, Braunschweig 1917.

Engels, Friedrich: Anti-Düring, Moskau 1947 [first edition 1878].

Forrest, Peter: Is Motion Change of Location?, in: Analysis 44 (1984), pp.177f.

Galton, Antony: The Logic of Aspect, Oxford 1984.

The Logic of Occurrence, in: Galton, Antony (ed.):Temporal Logics and their Application, London 1987, pp.169-196 (Gn. transl. by Bertram Kienzle as: Die Logik des Vorkommens, in: Kienzle, Bertram (ed.): Zustand und Ereignis, Frankfurt/Main 1994, pp.377 - 412).

Geach, Peter Thomas: God and the Soul, London 1969.

Truth, Love and Immortality, London 1979.

Aulus Gellius: Noctes Atticae, Rec. brevique adnot. [ed. and annotated by] P.K. Marshall, 2 vols., Oxford 1968.

The Attic Nights of Aulus Gellius [Noctes Atticae, Lat./Engl.], tr. by J.C. Rolfe [Loeb], London 1961.

Giles of Rome: Theorems of Existence and Essence, ed. by W.V. Murray, Milwaukee 1952.

Goethe, Johann Wolfgang: Werke, Hamburger Ausgabe [Hamburg edition] vol.1, ed. by Erich Trunz, Hamburg 1948 ff.

Grünbaum, Adolf: Zeno's Metrical Paradoxes of Extension, in: Salmon, Wesley (ed.): Zeno's Paradoxes, Indianapolis 1970, pp. 176-199.

Hafemann, Burkhard: Aristoteles' Transzendentaler Realismus, PhD thesis, Münster1996, forthcoming with De Gruyter, Berlin 1998.

Hamblin, Charles L.: Instants and Intervals, in: Studium Generale 24 (1971), pp.127-134.

Starting and Stopping, in: The Monist 53 (1969), pp.410-425.

Hautamäki, Antti: Points of View and their Logical Analysis, Acta Philosophica Fennica 41, Helsinki 1986.

Henry of Ghent, partial edition in: Braakhuis, M.: De 13de Eeuwse Tractaten over Syncategorematische Termen, vol. 1, Leiden 1979, pp.340-374.

Hegel, Georg Wilhelm Friedrich: Wissenschaft der Logik, Werke, vols. 5 und 6, Frankfurt/Main 1991.

Helm, Paul: On a criterion for change, in: Ratio 19 (1977), pp.35-39.

Are Cambridge Changes Non-Events?, in: Analysis 35 (1975), pp.140-144.

Humberstone, C.: Interval Semantics for Tense Logic, in: Journal of Philosophical Logic 8 (1979), pp.171-196.

Inciarte, Fernando: First Principles, Substance and Action - Studies in Aristotle and Aristotelianism, unpublished.

Inwood, Michael: Aristotle on the Reality of Time, in: Judson, Lindsay (ed.): Aristotle's Physics - A Collection of Essays, Oxford 1991, pp.151-178.

Jackson, Frank / Pargetter, Robert: A Question about Rest and Motion, in: Philosophical Studies 53 (1988), pp.141-146.

James, William: A Pluralistic Universe, New York 1909.

Jansen, Ludger: Aristotle and the Talk about Events, M. Litt. Thesis (unpublished), St. Andrews University 1994.

John Le Page: Syncategoremata, partial edition in: Braakhuis, M.: De 13de Eeuwse Tractaten over Syncategorematische Termen, vol.1, Leiden 1979, pp.168-246.

Johnson, W.E.: Logic, Cambridge 1921.

Kant, Immanuel: Kritik der reinen Vernunft nach der ersten und zweiten Original-Ausgabe neu herausgegeben von Raymund Schmidt, Hamburg 1956.

Kant's Critique of Pure Reason, transl by Norman Kemp Smith, London 1929.

De mundi sensibilis atque intelligibilis forma et principiis / Über die Formen und Prinzipien der Sinnen- und Geisteswelt, Inaugural-Dissertation von 1770, übersetzt von Klaus Reich, Hamburg 1958.

Kienzle, Bertram: Cambridge-Wechsel, in: Prima Philosophia 4 (1991), pp.107-112.

Ereignislogik, in: Zustand und Ereignis, pp.413-469.

Identität und Erkenntniswert - Eine fast fregesche Deutung, in: Allgemeine Zeitschrift für Philosophie 10 (1985), pp.27-40.

(ed.): Zustand und Ereignis, Frankfurt am Main 1994.

Kilvington: see Richard Kilvington

Knuuttila, Simo: Remarks on the Background of Fourteenth Century Limit Decision Controversies, in: M.Asztalos (ed.): The Editing of Theological and Philosophical Texts from the Middle Ages, Studia Latina Stockholmiensia 30, Stockholm 1986, pp.245-266.

Knuuttila, Simo/ Lehtinen, Anja Inkeri: Change and Contradiction: A Fourteenth Century Controversy, Synthese 40 (1979), pp.189-207.

Kretzmann, Norman: Incipit/Desinit, in: Machamer, J. / Turnbull, P. (eds.): Matter and Time, Space and Motion, Columbus (Ohio) 1976, pp.101-136.

Socrates is whiter than Plato begins to be white, in: Nous 11 (1977) pp. 7-15.

Lear, Jonathan: Aristotle - the Desire to Understand, Cambridge 1988.

Leibniz, Gottfried Wilhelm: Nouveaux Essais sur l'Entendement Humain, Philosophische Schriften [Fr./Gn.] vol. III,1, ed. and tr. by Wolf Engelhardt und Hans Holz, Darmstadt 1959.

Brief an Bayle [letter to Bayle], in: Die philosophischen Schriften von G.W. Leibniz, ed. by C.J.Gerhardt, vol.3, Hildesheim 1965, pp.52ff.

Libera, Alain de: Le sophisma anonyme "Sor desinit esse non desinendo esse" du Cod. Parisinus 16135, Cahiers de l'Institut du Moyen-âge Grec et Latin [CIMAGL], Université de Copenhague 59 (1989), pp.113-120.

La problematique de l'instant du changement au 13me siècle: contribution à l'histoire des "sophismata physicalia" in: S.Caroti: Studies in Medieval Natural Philosophy, Firenze 1989.

Liske, Michael-Thomas: Kinesis und Energeia bei Aristoteles, in: Phronesis 36 (1991), pp.161-178.

Lloyd, G.E.R.: Aristotle - The Growth and Structure of his Thought, Cambridge 1982.

Lombard, Lawrence: Relational Change and Relational Changes, in: Philosophical Studies 34 (1978), pp.63-79.

Mc Laughlin, William / Miller, Sylvia L.: An Epistemological Use of Nonstandard Analysis to Answer Zeno's Objections against Motion, in: Synthese 92 (1992), pp.371-384.

Medlin, Brian: The Origin of Motion, in: Mind 72 (1963), pp.155-175.

Meinwald, Constance: Plato's "Parmenides", Oxford 1991.

Mendelssohn, Moses: Phädon, ed. in: Schriften zur Philosophie und Ästhetik, bearbeitet von Fritz Bamberger und Leo Strauss, Gesammelte Schriften vol. III,1, Berlin 1932.

Miller, David L.: William James and the Specious Present, in: Corti, Walter Robert (ed.): The Philosophy of William James, Hamburg 1976, pp.51-81.

Mills, K.W.: Plato and the Instant (Reply to Colin Strang), in: Proceedings of the Aristotelian Society, Suppl.Vol. 48 (1974), pp.81-96.

Monk, Ray: The Duty of Genius, New York 1990.

Moody, Ernest A.: Laws of Motion in Medieval Physics, in: Studies in Medieval Philosophy, Science and Logic, Collected Papers 1933-1969, Berkeley 1975, pp.189-201.

Morkowsky, M.C.: The Elastic Instant of Aristotle's Becoming and Perishing, in: The Modern Schoolman 46 (1969), pp.191-217.

Mortensen, Chris: The Limits of Change, in: Australasian Journal of Philosophy 63 (1985), pp.1-10.

Murdoch, J.E.: Propositional Analysis in the Fourteenth Century Natural Philosophy, in: Synthese 40 (1979), pp.117-146.

Nelson, Edward: Internal Set Theory - A New Approach to Nonstandard Analysis, in: Bulletin of the American Mathematical Society 83 (1977), pp.1165 - 1198.

Nielsen, Lauge O.: Thomas Bradwardine's treatise on "incipit" and "desinit", edition and introduction, Cahiers de l'Institut du Moyen-âge Grec et Latin [CIMAGL], Université de Copenhague 42 (1982), pp.1-83.

Noonan, Harold W.: Personal Identity, London 1989.

Ockham: see William of Ockham

Øhrstrøm, Peter / Hasle, Per: Temporal Logic - From Ancient Ideas to Artificial Intelligence, Dordrecht 1995.

Owen, G.E.L.: Tithenai ta Phainomena, in: J. Barnes/M.Schofield/R.Sorabji(eds.): Articles on Aristotle vol. 1, London 1975, pp.113-127.

Zeno and the Mathematicians, in: Proceedings of the Aristotelian Society 58 (1957/58), pp.199-223.

Paul of Venice [Paulus Venetus]: Logica Parva. Translation of the 1472 edition by Alan R. Perreiah, München 1974.

Logica [parva], Hildesheim 1970 (reproduction of the 1472 edition).

Peter of Spain: Peter of Spain's "Syncategoreumata", ed. by L.M. de Rijk, transl. by J.Spruyt, Leiden 1992. (Another translation of important passages is contained in the appendix of Kretzmann's "Incipit / Desinit".)

(wrongly attributed): Tractatus Exponibilium, in: The Summulae Logicales of Peter of Spain, ed. von Joseph P. Mullally, Notre Dame, Indiana 1945.

Plato: Parmenides [Gr./Engl.], Loeb-edition of Plato's works, vol. 6, translated by H.N. Fowler, London 1926.

Plotinus: Opera [Gr./Engl.], transl. by A.H. Armstrong [Loeb], London 1966ff.

Priest, Graham: Inconsistencies in Motion, in: American Philosophical Quarterly 22 (1985), pp.339-346.

Dialectal Tense Logic [DTL], in: Studia Logica 41 2/3 (1981), pp.249-268.

Logic of Paradox, in: Journal of Philosophic Logic 8 (1979), pp.219-241.

Prior, Arthur: Tense Logic and the Logic of Earlier and Later, in: Papers on Time And Tense, Oxford 1967, German translation in: B. Kienzle (ed.): Zustand und Ereignis, Frankfurt am Main, 1994, pp.101-124.

Past, Present and Future, Oxford 1967.

Quine, Willard Van Orman: Word and Object, New York 1960.

Ontological Relativity, in: Ontological Relativity and other Essays, New York 1969, pp.26-68.

Reid, Thomas: Essays on the Intellectual Powers of Man, Glasgow 1785.

Richard Kilvington: The Sophismata of Richard Kilvington, Introduction, translation and commentary by Norman and Barbara Kretzmann, Cambridge 1990.

Robert, Alain: Nonstandard Analysis, New York 1988.

Ross, Sir David: Aristotle, London 1923.

Russell, Bertrand: The Principles of Mathematics, London 1964 [first edition 1903].

On Denoting, in: Mind 14 (1905), pp.479-493.

Salmon, Wesley: Zeno's Paradoxes, Indianapolis 1970.

Space, Time and Motion, Encino (Calif.) 1975.

Schmitt, Frederick: Change, in: Philosophical Studies 34 (1978), pp.401-416.

Schopenhauer, Arthur: Über die vierfache Wurzel des Satzes vom zureichenden Grunde, Hamburg 1976.

Searle, John: Determinables and the Notion of Resemblance, in: Proceedings of the Aristotelian Society, Suppl. vol. 37 (1963), pp.48-63.

Determinates and Determinables, in: Paul Edwards (ed.): The Encyclopaedia of Philosophy, vol. 2, pp. 357-9, New York 1967 ff.

Sextus Empiricus: Outlines of Pyrrhonism, vol.1 of: Sextus Empiricus, works in four vols. [Gr./Engl., Loeb Classical Library], transl. by R.G. Bury, London 1953.

Adversus Mathematicos, contained in vol.3 ("Against the Physicists") of: Sextus Empiricus: works in four vols., transl. by R.G. Bury, London 1955.

Simplicius: On Aristotle Physics 6, translated by David Konstan, London 1989.

Smart, J.J.C.: The River of Time, in: Mind 58 (1949), pp.483-494.

Smith, Joseph Wayne: Time, Change and Contradiction, in: Australasian Journal of Philosophy, 68 (1990), pp.178-188.

Smith, P.T.: On the applicability of a criterion for change, in: Ratio 15 (1973), pp.312-319.

Sorabji, Richard: Aristotle on the Instant of Change, in: Proceedings of the Aristotelian Society, Suppl. vol. 50 (1976), pp.69-91 [first version].

Aristotle on the Instant of Change, in: J. Barnes/M.Schofield/R.Sorabji(eds.): Articles on Aristotle vol. 3, London 1979, pp.159-178 [second version].

Time, Creation and the Continuum, London 1983 [ch.26 = third version].

Stoecker, Ralf: Was sind Ereignisse?, Berlin 1992.

Strang, Colin: Plato and the Instant, in: Proceedings of the Aristotelian Society, Suppl.vol. 48 (1974), pp.63-79.

Swinburne, Richard: God and Time, in: Stump, E. (ed.) Reasoned Faith, Ithaca 1993, pp.204-222.

Tabarroni, Andrea: "Incipit" and "desinit" in a thirteenth century sophismata-collection, Cahiers de l'Institut du Moyen-âge Grec et Latin [CIMAGL], Université de Copenhague 59 (1989), pp. 61-111.

Thomas Aquinas: In octos libros Physicorum Aristotelis Expositio, ed. M. Maggiòlo, Turin 1954

Thomas Bradwardine: Thomas Bradwardine's Treatise on 'incipit' and 'desinit', ed. by L.O. Nielsen, in: Cahiers de l'Institut du Moyen-âge Grec et Latin [CIMAGL], Université de Copenhague 42 (1982), pp.1-83.

Tichy, Pavel: Do we need Interval Semantics?, in: Linguistics and Philosophy 8 (1985), pp.263-282.

Vlastos, Gregory: A Note on Zeno's Arrow, in: Phronesis 11 (1966), pp.3-18.

Wagner, Hans (Wagner Commentary): see Aristoteles: Physikvorlesung.

Walter Burleigh: De Puritate Artis Logicae (Tractatus Brevior), ed. Ph. Boehner, The Franciscan Institute Publications, St. Bonaventure/Louvain 1951.

De primo et ultimo instanti, ed. by Hermann and Charlotte Shapiro, in: Archiv für Geschichte der Philosophie 47 (1966), pp.157-173.

Whitehead, A.N.: Process and Reality, New York 1960.

William of Ockham: Summa Logicae, ed. Ph. Boehner, G. Gál, S. Brown, St. Bonaventure, N.Y. 1974.

Ockham's Theory of Propositions, Part II of the Summa Logicae, transl. by A.J. Freddoso and Henry Schuurman, Notre Dame (Indiana) 1980.

William of Sherwood: Syncategoremata, ed. by J.R. O'Donnell, in: Medieval Studies 3 (1941), pp.46-93.

Tractatus Syncategorematum, transl. by Norman Kretzmann, as: Treatise on Syncategorematic Words, Minneapolis 1968.

Wilson, Curtis: William Heytesbury, Madison/Wisconsin 1956.

Wittgenstein, Ludwig: The Brown Book, London 1975.

Wolff, Michael: Der Begriff des Widerspruchs - eine Studie zur Dialektik Kants und Hegels, Königsstein/Taunus, 1981.

Wright, Georg Henrik von: And Next, in: Acta Philosophica Fennica 18 (1965), pp.293-304.

And Then, in: Commentationes Physico-mathematicae of the Finnish Society of Sciences 32, No. 7, 1966.

Norm and Action, London 1963.

Time, Change and Contradiction, in: Philosophical Papers, vol.2, Oxford 1983, pp.115-132.

Zimmermann, Albert (ed.): Ein Kommentar aus dem Jahre 1273 zur Physik des Aristoteles aus der Pariser Artistenfakultät, Berlin 1968.

INDEX OF NAMES

(Medieval authors are listed under their first names)

INDEX OF SUBJECTS

QUICK REFERENCE TO THE MAIN TEXTS
ON THE MOMENT OF CHANGE
DISCUSSED IN PARTS I AND II
(see detailed references above)

Antiquity (ch. I,1 und I,2):

Plato, Parmenides 155e-157b.
Interpretations:
Colin Strang, Plato and the Instant,
David Bostock, Plato on Change and Time in the 'Parmenides'.

Aristotle, Physics VI, Ch. 5, 6 and 8, and Phys.VIII, 263 b9 ff.

Interpretations:
Richard Sorabji, Time, Creation and the Continuum Ch. 26
Hans Wagner, Commentary in 'Aristoteles: Physikvorlesung'
Simo Knuuttila, Remarks on the Background of 14th century
      Limit Decision Controversies.

Sextus Empiricus, Adversus Mathematicos I §269

Aulus Gellius, Noctes Atticae L, VI 13

Plotinus, Enneads VI, 1 §16

St. Augustine, De Civitate Dei XIII, 11.

Middle Ages (ch.I,3):

Texts are very numerous. Valuable summaries are found in:
Curtis Wilson, William Heytesbury, ch.2
Norman Kretzmann, Incipit/Desinit
Simo Knuuttila, Remarks on the Background of 14th century
      Limit Decision Controversies.

For an impression of original texts cf. for example:

William of Sherwood, Syncategoremata, chapter 'De incipit et desinit'

Peter of Spain, Syncategoreumata, chapter 'De incipit et desinit'

William of Ockham, Summa Logica I,75 and II,19

Walter Burleigh, De primo et ultimo instanti,
          De puritate artis logicae (chapter 'incipit et desinit')

Richard Kilvington, Sophismata

18/19th century (Ch. I,4):

Moses Mendelssohn, Phädon, pp.62-72

Immanuel Kant, Critique of pure reason, B395-397 and B253 f.

Arthur Schopenhauer, Über die vierfache Wurzel des Satzes vom zureichenden Grunde, second edition §25: 'Die Zeit der Veränderung'.

20th century:
"either/or-option" (ch.II,1):
Richard Sorabji, Time, Creation and the Continuum, ch.26
Frank Jackson and Robert Pargetter, A Question about Rest and Motion
Antony Galton, The Logic of Aspect ch. 1 and 2; The Logic of Occurrence.

"either-way-option" (ch.II,2):
Roderick Chisholm, Beginnings and Endings
Brian Medlin, The Origin of Motion.

"both-states-option" (ch.II,3):
Graham Priest, Dialectical Tense Logic.

"neither-nor-option" (ch.II,4):
Charles Hamblin, Starting and Stopping.

"Neutral Instant Analysis" (ch.II,5):
David Bostock, Plato on Change and Time in the 'Parmenides'
Norman Kretzmann, Incipit/Desinit
Bertrand Russell, The Principles of Mathematics §446.

Synthese Historical Library

Texts and Studies in the History of Logic and Philosophy

Series Editor: Simo Knuuttila (*University of Helsinki*)

1. M.T. Beonio-Brocchieri Fumagalli: *The Logic of Abelard.* Translated from Italian by S. Pleasance. 1969   ISBN 90-277-0068-0

2. G. W. Leibniz: *Philosophical Papers and Letters.* A Selection, translated and edited, with an Introduction, by L. E. Loemker. 2nd ed., 2nd printing. 1976
                                                     ISBN 90-277-0008-8

3. E. Mally: *Logische Schriften.* Grosses Logikfragment – Grundgesetze des Sollens. Herausgegeben von K. Wolf und P. Weingartner. 1971   ISBN 90-277-0174-1

4. L. W. Beck (ed.): *Proceedings of the Third International Kant Congress.* 1972
                                                     ISBN 90-277-0188-1

5. B. Bolzano: *Theory of Science.* A Selection with an Introduction by J. Berg. Translated from German by B. Terrell. 1973   ISBN 90-277-0248-9

6. J. M. E. Moravcsik (ed.): *Patterns in Plato's Thought.* 1973   ISBN 90-277-0286-1

7. Avicenna: *The Propositional Logic.* A Translation from *Al-Shifā': al-Qiyās*, with Introduction, Commentary and Glossary by N. Shehaby. 1973   ISBN 90-277-0360-4

8. D. P. Henry: *Commentary on* De Grammatico. *The Historical-Logical Dimensions of a Dialogue of St. Anselms's.* 1974   ISBN 90-277-0382-5

9. J. Corcoran (ed.): *Ancient Logic and its Modern Interpretations.* 1974
                                                     ISBN 90-277-0395-7

10. E. M. Barth: *The Logic of the Articles in Traditional Philosophy.* A Contribution to the Study of Conceptual Structures. 1974   ISBN 90-277-0350-7

11. J. Hintikka: *Knowledge and the Known.* Historical Perspectives in Epistemology. 1974
                                                     ISBN 90-277-0455-4

12. E. J. Ashworth: *Language and Logic in the Post-Medieval Period.* 1974
                                                     ISBN 90-277-0464-3

13. Aristotle: *The Nicomachean Ethics.* Translation with Commentaries and Glossary by H. G. Apostle. 1974   ISBN 90-277-0569-0

14. R. M. Dancy: *Sense and Contradiction.* A Study in Aristotle. 1975
                                                     ISBN 90-277-0565-8

15. W. R. Knorr: *The Evolution of the Euclidean Elements.* A Study of the Theory of Incommensurable Magnitudes and its Significance for Early Greek Geometry. 1975
                                                     ISBN 90-277-0509-7

16. Augustine: *De Dialectica.* Translated with Introduction and Notes by B. D. Jackson from the Text newly edited by J. Pinborg. 1975   ISBN 90-277-0538-9

17. Á. Szabó: *The Beginnings of Greek Mathematics.* Translated from German. 1978
                                                     ISBN 90-277-0819-3

18. Juan Luis Vives: *Against the Pseudodialecticians.* A Humanist Attack on Medieval Logic. Texts (in Latin), with Translation, Introduction and Notes by R. Guerlac. 1979
                                                     ISBN 90-277-0900-9

Synthese Historical Library

19. Peter of Ailly: *Concepts and Insolubles*. An Annotated Translation (from Latin) by P. V. Spade. 1980
ISBN 90-277-1079-1

20. S. Knuuttila (ed.): *Reforging the Great Chain of Being*. Studies of the History of Modal Theories. 1981
ISBN 90-277-1125-9

21. J. V. Buroker: *Space and Incongruence*. The Origin of Kant's Idealism. 1981
ISBN 90-277-1203-4

22. Marsilius of Inghen: *Treatises on the Properties of Terms*. A First Critical Edition of the *Suppositiones, Ampliationes, Appellationes, Restrictiones* and *Alienationes* with Introduction, Translation, Notes and Appendices by E. P. Bos. 1983
ISBN 90-277-1343-X

23. W. R. de Jong: *The Semantics of John Stuart Mill*. 1982
ISBN 90-277-1408-8

24. René Descartes: *Principles of Philosophy*. Translation with Explanatory Notes by V. R. Miller and R. P. Miller. 1983
ISBN 90-277-1451-7

25. T. Rudavsky (ed.): *Divine Omniscience and Omnipotence in Medieval Philosophy*. Islamic, Jewish and Christian Perspectives. 1985
ISBN 90-277-1750-8

26. William Heytesbury: *On Maxima and Minima*. Chapter V of *Rules for Solving Sophismata*, with an Anonymous 14th-century Discussion. Translation from Latin with an Introduction and Study by J. Longeway. 1984
ISBN 90-277-1868-7

27. Jean Buridan's *Logic. The Treatise on Supposition. The Treatise on Consequences*. Translation from Latin with a Philosophical Introduction by P. King. 1985
ISBN 90-277-1918-7

28. S. Knuuttila and J. Hintikka (eds.): *The Logic of Being*. Historical Studies. 1986
ISBN 90-277-2019-3

29. E. Sosa (ed.): *Essays on the Philosophy of George Berkeley*. 1987
ISBN 90-277-2405-9

30. B. Brundell: *Pierre Gassendi: From Aristotelianism to a New Natural Philosophy*. 1987
ISBN 90-277-2428-8

31. Adam de Wodeham: *Tractatus de indivisibilibus*. A Critical Edition with Introduction, Translation, and Textual Notes by R. Wood. 1988
ISBN 90-277-2424-5

32. N. Kretzmann (ed.): *Meaning and Inference in Medieval Philosophy*. Studies in Memory of J. Pinborg (1937–1982). 1988
ISBN 90-277-2577-2

33. S. Knuuttila (ed.): *Modern Modalities*. Studies of the History of Modal Theories from Medieval Nominalism to Logical Positivism. 1988
ISBN 90-277-2678-7

34. G. F. Scarre: *Logic and Reality in the Philosophy of John Stuart Mill*. 1988
ISBN 90-277-2739-2

35. J. van Rijen: *Aspects of Aristotle's Logic of Modalities*. 1989
ISBN 0-7923-0048-3

36. L. Baudry: *The Quarrel over Future Contingents (Louvain 1465–1475)*. Unpublished Latin Texts collected and translated in French by L. Baudry. Translated from French by R. Guerlac. 1989
ISBN 0-7923-0454-3

THE NEW SYNTHESE HISTORICAL LIBRARY
Texts and Studies in the History of Philosophy

37. S. Payne: *John of the Cross and the Cognitive Value of Mysticism.* An Analysis of Sanjuanist Teaching and its Philosophical Implications for Contemporary Discussions of Mystical Experience. 1990   ISBN 0-7923-0707-0

38. D.D. Merrill: *Augustus De Morgan and the Logic of Relations.* 1990
ISBN 0-7923-0758-5

39. H. T. Goldstein (ed.): *Averroes' Questions in Physics.* 1991   ISBN 0-7923-0997-9

40. C.H. Manekin: *The Logic of Gersonides.* A Translation of *Sefer ha-Heqqesh ha-Yashar* (The *Book of the Correct Syllogism*) of Rabbi Levi ben Gershom with Introduction, Commentary, and Analytical Glossary. 1992   ISBN 0-7923-1513-8

41. George Berkeley: *De Motu* and *The Analyst.* A Modern Edition with Introductions and Commentary, edited en translated by Douglas M. Jesseph. 1992   ISBN 0-7923-1520-0

42. John Duns Scotus: *Contingency and Freedom.* Lectura I 39. Introduction, Translation and Commentary by A. Vos Jaczn., H. Veldhuis, A.H. Looman-Graaskamp, E. Dekker and N.W. den Bok. 1994   ISBN 0-7923-2707-1

43. Paul Thom: *The Logic of Essentialism.* An Interpretation of Aristotle's Modal Syllogistic. 1996   ISBN 0-7923-3987-8

44. P.M. Matthews: *The Significance of Beauty.* Kant on Feeling and the System of the Mind. 1997   ISBN 0-7923-4764-1

45. N. Strobach: *The Moment of Change.* A Systematic History in the Philosophy of Space and Time. 1998   ISBN 0-7923-5120-7

Kluwer Academic Publishers – Dordrecht / Boston / London